The Right Side of the Sixties

Previous Publications

Laura Jane Gifford
The Center Cannot Hold: The 1960 Presidential Election and the Rise of Modern Conservatism (2009).

Daniel K. Williams
God's Own Party: The Making of the Christian Right (2010).

The Right Side of the Sixties

Reexamining Conservatism's Decade of Transformation

Edited by Laura Jane Gifford
and Daniel K. Williams

THE RIGHT SIDE OF THE SIXTIES
Copyright © Laura Jane Gifford and Daniel K. Williams, 2012

All rights reserved.

First published in 2012 by PALGRAVE MACMILLAN® in the United States—a division of St. Martin's Press LLC, 175 Fifth Avenue, New York, NY 10010

Where this book is distributed in the UK, Europe and the rest of the world, this is by Palgrave Macmillan, a division of Macmillan Publishers Limited, registered in England, company number 785998, of Houndmills, Basingstoke, Hampshire RG21 6XS.

Palgrave Macmillan is the global academic imprint of the above companies and has companies and representatives throughout the world.

Palgrave® and Macmillan® are registered trademarks in the United States, the United Kingdom, Europe and other countries.

ISBN: 978-1-137-01478-8

Library of Congress Cataloging-in-Publication Data
   The right side of the sixties: reexamining conservatism's decade of transformation / edited by Laura Jane Gifford and Daniel K. Williams
      p. cm.
   Includes bibliographical references and index.
   ISBN 978-1-137-01478-8 (hardback)
   1. Conservatism—United States—History—20th century. I. Gifford, Laura Jane. II. Williams, Daniel K.

   JC573.2.U6R538 2012
   320.520973'09046—dc23   2012001876

A catalogue record of the book is available from the British Library.

Design by Scribe Inc.

First edition: August 2012

10 9 8 7 6 5 4 3 2 1

Printed in the United States of America.

Contents

INTRODUCTION

What Happened to Conservatism in the 1960s?

Laura Jane Gifford and Daniel K. Williams

It was December 1961. As the first year of the Kennedy administration came to a close, all seemed from the outside to be well with the liberal consensus. Willem Visser't Hooft, general secretary of the World Council of Churches, posed for *Time* magazine's cover story—a detailed exposition on "The Second Reformation" of liberal, ecumenical world Christianity. Inside *Time*'s pages, however, lurked evidence that society's seemingly solid consensus was riddled with growing cracks. A profile on "The Ultras" spoke of a recent resurgence in ultraconservative anticommunism. Hundreds of anticommunist groups were springing up across the United States, in some cases mushrooming into formidable organizations seemingly overnight. The South and Southwest, in particular, were hotbeds of organization—Dallas alone was home to more than one hundred anticommunist study groups. Despite their prevalence in the South, these groups were a national phenomenon with national political implications. Politicians backed by these groups, which ranged from the John Birch Society to the Christian Anti-Communism Crusade, were planning runs for Congress in 1962.

The overall tenor of *Time*'s article suggested that this phenomenon, while dangerous, was a temporary aberration from "normal channels of political expression." Rather than attacking a population already prone toward conspiracy theories, the best course of action was to "patiently face the task of convincing them that at the present time the real danger to the nation lies from without, and that the way to fight that danger is to encourage unity at home and unflinching policies abroad that reflect the best interests of the U.S."[1]

In its efforts to minimize the influence of the "ultras," however, *Time* neglected to note the implications of some of the very demographic and ideological characteristics it included in its profile. The "ultras" were gaining greatest prominence in high-growth regions of the country like the West, the Southwest, and the South, and they were therefore well positioned for future political influence. Most of the movement's support came from middle- and upper-income professionals who were concerned about the United States' position in the Cold War. Many movement leaders were active or retired members of the American military. Specific groups focused on a wide variety of issues, from segregation and isolationism to higher tariffs and income tax repeal.

Conservatism experienced a few major setbacks over the course of the 1960s, and there were moments, such as Barry Goldwater's landslide loss to President Lyndon Johnson in 1964, when it seemed as though *Time*'s liberal vision of the future had been vindicated. Several of the "ultra" organizations that *Time* profiled faded into oblivion before the end of the decade. Yet in the end, conservatives triumphed. The world that emerged from the 1960s looked almost nothing like the politically, economically, and religiously ecumenical world liberals had envisioned. By the end of the decade, not only was there a Republican in the White House, but the vice president of the United States had positioned himself as a tough-talking conservative populist, and the president was receiving his speech lines from Pat Buchanan, a writer so conservative that some of his views were barely distinguishable from those of the "ultras" that *Time* had profiled. After Ronald Reagan's election in 1980, conservatism's triumph was even more evident, and after the Republican take-over of Congress in the 1990s, more obvious still. By the beginning of the twenty-first century, conservatism had become so entrenched in the political order that Goldwater was now hailed for having waged the nation's most important unsuccessful presidential campaign, a temporary setback that in turn launched a "conservative revolution."[2] The "ultras" proved to be the future of American politics.

Historians' Understanding of 1960s Conservatism

The 1960s were vibrant and transformative years for conservatism. Two or three decades ago that statement might have seemed shocking, but today it surprises few historians of postwar politics. The early histories of the 1960s focused mainly on the conflict between Great Society liberals and New Left activists, confining conservatism to a marginal footnote in the story of a leftward political and cultural turn. By contrast, contemporary scholarship on the 1960s gives central focus to the right wing. Scholars writing in the 1960s and 1970s largely ignored Barry Goldwater's campaign of 1964, dismissing it as a curious misadventure in Republican political history. In contemporary scholarship, Goldwater's status has been transformed, and his presidential campaign, far from being dismissed as an anomaly, has been the subject of several important monographs. Historians have also cited Ronald Reagan's successful gubernatorial campaign of 1966, Richard Nixon's presidential election victory in 1968, and George Wallace's strong working-class appeal as signs of conservatism's emerging strength in the 1960s.[3]

Recent historians have written at length about the "movement conservatism" of the 1960s, as represented by *National Review*, William F. Buckley Jr., and Frank Meyer. The decade also saw the development of an increasingly intransigent "Far Right," as evidenced by the strength of the John Birch Society, the Christian Anti-Communism Crusade, and the various anticommunist radio broadcasts that were a staple of Southern radio. Even college campuses, a supposed bastion of leftist politics in the 1960s, have been recast as vanguards in a conservative movement, with Young Americans for Freedom challenging Students for a Democratic Society in prominence and tactics.[4]

This narrative of conservatism's inexorable rise has become so widespread that many historians now routinely characterize the 1960s as the decade that created the modern conservative movement. A new narrative has emerged to replace the traditional view of the decade as a culturally leftist decade. According to contemporary scholarship, the early 1960s was a time of staunch anticommunism and free-market advocacy among an emerging Republican majority in Southern California and the "Gun Belt" of the South and Southwest, regions where a strong military-industrial complex fused Cold War ideals with a faith in individual enterprise and a strong suspicion of unions and any hint of "socialism." In the Deep South, a backlash against the tepid civil rights measures of the Kennedy administration fueled a rising grassroots conservative movement. In 1964, economic libertarians from the West, segregationists from the South, and anticommunists from throughout the nation united around the presidential candidacy of Barry Goldwater. Although he experienced a resounding defeat, Goldwater's candidacy strengthened the conservative movement, while his failure weeded out fringe elements, facilitating Ronald Reagan's election as governor of California in 1966. At the same time, a grassroots backlash against the civil rights movement throughout the nation that accelerated in the wake of the race riots of the late 1960s contributed to George Wallace's popularity, Richard Nixon's "Southern Strategy," and the movement of Southern conservative Democrats such as Strom Thurmond into the Republican Party. Nixon's election to the presidency in 1968 through a campaign of "law and order" politics signaled the death knell for whatever rights-oriented liberalism had existed in the decade.[5]

Now that historians have begun to accept the idea of the 1960s as a conservative decade, studies of the era have seemingly examined every facet that contributed to conservatism's rise. Is there a need for yet another anthology of scholarship on conservatism in the 1960s? What more can be said about conservatism during this decade? What stones could the numerous monographs, articles, and anthologies on the subject possibly have left unturned?[6]

As historians of modern American conservatism, we welcome the attention that our colleagues in the field have begun to give to the activities of the Right during the 1960s, but we also believe that the conventional narrative of '60s conservatism has devoted too much attention to conservatism's reaction against the liberalism of the decade and too little attention to shifts and transformations within the movement itself. While the leaders of the movement have received extensive analysis, and the pro-Goldwater movement of the early 1960s has received attention, economic, religious, and regional grassroots activists have often been ignored. How did the conservatism of 1960 become the conservatism of 1968—and beyond? What foundations needed to be laid for Goldwater's failure to eventually generate Reagan's success? How did the New Right assemble itself from the congeries of disparate elements that began to assert themselves more stridently as the New Frontier commenced?

Much of the scholarship on conservatism has portrayed it as a more fledgling movement during the decade than it actually was. The 1960s was not the decade that invented conservatism. Perhaps historians' propensity to overlook conservatism in earlier decades has resulted from excessive willingness to give credence to Lionel Trilling's oft-quoted pronouncement on the lack of conservative ideas in the mid-twentieth century. Perhaps it has stemmed from the profession's focus on recognized movement leaders such as Buckley, Goldwater, and Reagan, whose conservative political careers did not begin until after World War II. Historians in the field have generally followed George Nash's lead in locating the birth of the conservative movement in the postwar era, particularly the 1950s and 1960s.[7]

Recent scholarship, however, has located the origins of modern conservatism in an earlier time period, whether among the opponents of the New Deal in the 1930s, the fundamentalists and cultural conservatives of the 1920s, or even the probusiness politicians of the late nineteenth century. According to the new historical narrative that is now emerging, postwar conservatism represented not a new development but merely another manifestation of a long-standing American belief in the importance of free markets, religious institutions, and the family, coupled with a suspicion of the centralized state.[8] In the 1920s Americans may not have used the word *conservative* to describe President Calvin Coolidge's promotion of business interests, Treasury Secretary Andrew Mellon's tax cuts, or fundamentalists' campaigns against the teaching of evolution in public schools, but in some respects these developments bore a striking resemblance to the agenda of the modern Right. This early twentieth-century form of conservatism continued to develop in the 1930s, when business executives organized a coalition against the New Deal, and in the 1940s, when Senator Robert Taft led a successful campaign to limit the bargaining power of unions. In the 1950s conservative intellectuals such as William F. Buckley Jr. melded anticommunism with a defense of religious faith and free enterprise to promote a movement that quickly claimed the *conservative* label and began carving out a place for itself in the Republican Party. Yet if the latest scholarship is correct—and we think it is—in arguing that conservatives had already staked out positions on economics, race, and cultural politics decades before the 1960s, did the events of the '60s play any role in the formation of modern conservatism? Was there anything new about Goldwater's offer of a "choice not an echo"? Was there anything significant about Reagan's gubernatorial election victory in 1966?

Clearly, something significant did happen to conservatism in the 1960s, as the news media's coverage of the movement attested. At the beginning of the decade, news publications still portrayed conservatives as marginal extremists, as evidenced by *Time*'s coverage of the "ultras." By the end of the 1960s, journalists no longer spoke of the Silent Majority as a marginal group.

The increase in conservatism's public visibility during the 1960s reflected even more substantive changes in the movement's ideology and growth. Though the 1960s was not the decade in which conservatism was invented, it was a decade in which it was transformed. Conservatives of the 1960s adopted new ideas that would determine the movement's course for the rest of the century and make conservatism a dominant strand in American politics. During the 1960s, conservatives shifted from a defense of segregation to a "color-blind" ideology; abandoned their defense of the "Far Right"; exchanged their traditional religious factionalism for a new interreligious coalition of Protestants, Catholics, and Jews; and began to acquire control of the Republican Party. As they began to forge an identity beyond the reactionary role of a minority movement, conservatives constructed organizations to formulate and promote public policy and proactively responded to the increasingly complex dynamics of a globalizing world. Conservatives had far more political power at the end of the decade than at its beginning. The dimensions of these transformations remain easily recognizable today.

To understand these transformations, the essays in this volume go beyond the campaigns of Goldwater, Reagan, and Nixon to examine change at the grassroots level. If the first generation of scholarship on 1960s conservatism focused on movement leaders, the emerging scholarship gives more emphasis to local developments that often presaged national trends. Instead of confining our analysis of the emerging language of "freedom of association" and "color-blind" rhetoric to Southern politicians, we have included an essay demonstrating the role college students defending white Southern sororities played in promulgating these ideas. Rather than limiting discussion of Jewish participation in the conservative movement to the nascent neoconservatism of the late 1960s, we have included an essay demonstrating Orthodox Jews' growing opposition to the secular trends of the decade, a transition that helped enable the future development of an ecumenical conservative coalition.

This book also goes beyond previous scholarship in its attention to the international context of conservatism's development. Conservatism was not merely a reaction against the growth of the liberal state but was instead a development that responded to the growth of international Communism, globalization, and the changing dynamics of American influence overseas. The essays in this volume examine international influences on American anticommunist organizations, the role that conservative evangelicals' global vision played in formulating a foreign policy doctrine based on promotion of American power and ideals, and the way in which debates over the Vietnam War influenced conservatives. If all politics is local, as Tip O'Neill famously said, politics in our time is also global, and a full understanding of conservatism in the 1960s examines the movement in the light of both dimensions. Our study provides a local and global thematic reexamination of the major forces driving the conservative movement—race, free-market ideology, religion, and foreign policy.

The Politics of Race

For decades, scholars have recognized the central importance of race in the conservative movement. The Deep South began voting Republican in 1964, when Republican presidential candidate Barry Goldwater won the votes of white segregationists because of his opposition to President Lyndon Johnson's Civil Rights Act. Some of the first Southern Democrats to become Republicans, including Strom Thurmond, did so because of issues of race in the 1960s. A decade later, when conservatives came to power, they attempted to dismantle national affirmative action programs. With only a few exceptions, the mid-twentieth-century conservative movement was entirely white, and many of its leading voices in the 1950s and 1960s evinced little sympathy for civil rights.

It was thus not surprising that early political science studies of the partisan realignment of the South gave primacy to the white backlash theory as an explanation for Southerners' growing disillusionment with the Democratic Party in the postwar era. Recent historical studies of George Wallace, Richard Nixon, the Goldwater presidential campaign, and Southern Republican organizations have traced the connections between race, partisan realignment, and the formation of a national conservative movement. Other recent work has examined the segregationist ideas included in mainstream conservative publications such as *National Review*, connections between white segregationists and conservative ideology, and the role that "white flight" and racially induced suburban growth played in the formation of a conservative coalition.[9]

The articles on race in this volume advance beyond current scholarship by tracing the emergence of conservative ideas on race to some unlikely sources.

Stephanie Rolph's essay examines the Citizens' Council of Mississippi, a white segregationist group that most conservatives today would disavow, and examines the way in which it became a proponent of a "color-blind" ideology nearly identical to that of the Reagan administration. Rolph argues that during the 1960s, Southern segregationists transformed their regional rhetoric of racial separatism into a nationally acceptable, egalitarian-sounding language of opportunity for all regardless of race. Similarly, Margaret Freeman examines the way in which the white sororities of the South reached out to national conservative organizations such as Young Americans for Freedom in their attempt to remain segregated in defiance of civil rights directives. Freeman traces the connections between anticommunism, Protestant Christianity, class-based gentility, and the defense of segregation and examines the process by which white Southern sororities melded those ideas into a coherent conservative ideology that influenced the political choices of a new generation of white, college-educated women in the South.

Joshua Farrington's essay examines the question of race from a very different perspective and suggests a new way to view the use of race in Richard Nixon's conservative coalition. Farrington demonstrates the role played by black Republicans in developing a black capitalist narrative of racial empowerment that challenged some tenets of the liberal civil rights movement, and he explains the appeal of conservative self-help ideology for a significant minority of African American entrepreneurs. Black conservatives were so influential among a contingent of African Americans that the Nixon administration appropriated their policy ideas as a way to attract black votes.

Collectively, these three essays demonstrate a previously unnoticed influence of local grassroots organizations on the formation of the national conservative movement's approach to race in the 1960s. Rolph and Freeman demonstrate that the link between conservatism and Southern segregation was driven from below, with Mississippi radio programs and Southern white sororities forging links with national conservative movement leaders in order to bring respectability to what, by the early 1960s, seemed to be a beleaguered campaign. They point out that Southern segregationists seized on the transition to a "color-blind" rhetoric of anticommunism, property rights, and "freedom of association" in order to bolster their national influence in the face of civil rights changes and that the impetus for conservative leaders to adopt this line of reasoning often came from local groups that had previously had no connection to organized political parties. Similarly, Farrington's essay demonstrates that African Americans' long tradition of self-help ideology influenced the conservative movement's approach to racial issues. His essay presents black conservative entrepreneurs as agents of change, rather than as pawns of the GOP, and shows how they were able to use the language of free enterprise to forge alliances with Republican politicians and gain concessions from the white conservatives in power.

Shaping Conservative Ideology

Although it would be an exaggeration to characterize the American intellectual world of the 1950s and early 1960s with Lionel Trilling's claim that there were "no conservative ideas," it is nevertheless true that nearly all the country's leading public intellectuals during that era subscribed to the liberal consensus. Had Alexis de Tocqueville made his famous survey of the United States in 1960, he would have found a world shaped economically by the Keynesian propositions of the New Deal order and ideologically by the tensions of the Cold War at its height. The "consensus" world of the 1950s legitimated government involvement in the economy and marginalized the efforts of big business to promote unrestrained free enterprise even as it established anticommunism as a central aspect of American identity. Businesses occasionally attempted to promote free market economics in the workplace, as with Ronald Reagan's activities on behalf of General Electric. In the public arena, however, the prosperity of the postwar years enshrined British economist John Maynard Keynes's advocacy of using fiscal policy and regulatory power to promote economic growth as gospel. The leading intellectuals of the early 1960s, such as John Kenneth Galbraith and Arthur Schlesinger Jr., accepted this blend of economic management and Cold War ideology, the two mainstays of the prevailing liberal consensus. There were plenty of conservatives who warned from the fringes about the dangers of "socialism" and "collectivism," but most of the nation's intelligentsia did not consider their arguments worthy of serious attention. At a time when liberals were fully committed to the Cold War, conservative anticommunists who accused liberals of taking the nation down a path toward Communism found it difficult to gain a hearing in the mainstream press.

Conservatives lacked not only a credible message but also the institutions necessary to gain a public hearing for their ideas. No recognizable conservative think tanks yet existed. When readers of mainstream periodicals tried to envision a purveyor of conservative ideas, the image that came to mind was usually Robert Welch, not Robert Bork—as *Time*'s profile on the "ultras" demonstrated. Even William F. Buckley Jr. had not yet attained intellectual respectability in some liberal circles. In the early 1960s his *National Review* was still putting in an occasional good word for the members of the John Birch Society.[10] Yet by the end of the decade, Buckley was a national television host, syndicated columnist, and public intellectual who was well on his way to becoming ambassador to the United Nations. Conservatives had started to form think tanks, and they had found ways to move their ideas beyond the pages of *Human Events* to the public square.

Conservatives who aspired to national influence were helped by the collapse of the Keynesian economic miracle. The United States had entered the 1960s riding a wave of relative prosperity. Union membership was near its all-time high, and the dominant "consensus" mindset of the time favored continuing emphasis on government funding of research and development, high tax rates, and Keynesian manipulation of the economy. By the end of the 1960s, however, the mounting cost of the Vietnam War and increasing economic competition from other countries brought inflation and growing unemployment. Urban renewal programs and other efforts did little to alleviate the intractable poverty of American inner cities. As the ghettos' frustrated and hopeless citizenry erupted in violence, much of the rest of the country recoiled from the idea of further outreach programs, focusing instead on defensive law and order. The declining fortunes of the American economy over the course of the 1960s accelerated the search for alternative economic visions, providing conservatives with an opening to promote the free enterprise theory of economists such as Milton Friedman.[11]

Yet to gain a hearing for their views in this changed political climate, conservatives had to show not only that liberalism had failed but also that conservatism offered a responsible solution. To become respectable, conservatives had to purge their movement of "extremists." As Samuel Brenner's essay argues, at the beginning of the decade, Buckley and his cohort of conservative movement leaders had tolerated—and occasionally even touted—the views of conspiracists who thought the nation's federal bureaucracy was filled with Communists. In a world where even liberals characterized themselves as hawks, the anticommunist organizations that historians have often characterized as "extremist" articulated views nearly indistinguishable from mainstream conservatism on issues ranging from their support for free enterprise to their concerns about growing secularism. Over the course of the early 1960s, however, mainstream conservatives, who were embarrassed by exposés of the John Birch Society's "extremist" ideas, excised the Far Right from their movement and reshaped the nature of their anticommunist campaign.[12] Anticommunism would no longer involve ferreting out subversives in government or uncovering a Communist conspiracy—the favorite activities of the "extremists"—but would instead mean defending the free market as an alternative to both Communism and Keynesianism.

Once conservatives escaped the taint of "extremism" and rebranded themselves as responsible defenders of a free market, business leaders who favored deregulation and government promotion of industry felt free to make alliances with the movement as a way to advance their own agenda. In turn, these business leaders transformed the public's view of economics and encouraged them to think of the free market as an inviolate representation of American values. Jason Stahl uses the example of the American Enterprise Institute (AEI) to trace the development of conservative think tanks from objective, nonpartisan entities outside of the conservative movement into important free-market advocates and an influential component of conservative politics. By the 1970s, AEI had achieved such prominence in political and intellectual circles that even liberal politicians had to pay attention to its ideas; no one could afford to be seen as an opponent of the free market.

Each of these essays demonstrates the ways in which conservatives themselves played key roles in altering the acceptable range of mainstream ideological discourse in the United States. The efforts of Buckley and many others to delineate mainstream conservatism from the "extremists" indicate that beneath the surface there was less difference than ultimately appeared and that the decision of the "mainstream" members of the movement to brand the Birchers as "extremists" was a conscious choice to change how the public perceived conservative ideas. The experiences of William Baroody and AEI demonstrate the agency the early conservative think tanks exercised in breaking the bonds of the Keynesian economic establishment and convincing Americans that the free market was sacrosanct. Aided by a fortuitous turn in the nation's economy, conservatives demonstrated the political savvy to rebrand their ideology, transform the public's political views, and write the future of their movement.

God and Country

The connection between religion and conservatism in the 1960s has received less attention from scholars than it deserves. In part, that may be because the most noticeable religious trends of the 1960s seemed far removed from conservatism. During the 1960s, the National Council of Churches organized mainline Protestant ministers on behalf of civil rights and other liberal causes, while some of the most liberal Protestant theologians pioneered a "Death of God" theology that attempted to discover a system of Christian ethics that did not depend on belief in a deity. Jewish and Christian clergy came together in Selma to march for African American equality. The Catholic Church experienced an internal revolution when Vatican II overturned centuries of tradition by doing away with Latin Mass, nuns' habits, Friday fasts, and previous proscriptions on clerical political activity. Priests such as Daniel and Philip Berrigan invaded draft board offices to destroy draft files, while Msgr. George Higgins aided César Chavez's efforts on behalf of migrant farm workers. A charismatic renewal swept through Protestant and Catholic churches, turning staid Episcopalians and reverent Catholics into Spirit-filled tongues-speakers. At the end of the decade, younger evangelicals launched the Jesus movement, which combined traditional evangelical theology with folk rock, hippie slang, and a left-leaning social consciousness. Many young people left Christianity altogether and experimented with Eastern religions or avant-garde forms of spirituality. Most Jews who remained religiously observant—which was a decreasing number during the 1960s—were loyal Democrats, as were most Catholics and a large number of evangelicals. Few in the 1960s envisioned an alliance between religion and the Republican Party or the conservative movement.[13]

For years, historians generally ignored conservative religion in the 1960s, but a few recent works have begun to trace the origins of the Christian Right of the late 1970s to the religious changes of the preceding decade.[14] The essays in this volume further this scholarship by tracing the way in which representatives of several religious movements—not merely evangelical Protestants—adopted new religious understandings in the 1960s that made them more amenable to politically conservative ideology. Robert Daniel Rubin traces the way in which a contingent of American Orthodox Jews abandoned their traditional belief in church-state separation and began to accept the idea that a state founded on Judeo-Christian principles could become a guardian of public morality in the name of religion. This important but largely unknown shift enabled the formation of an interreligious conservative coalition that was willing to compromise church-state separation in order to protect public morality. Daniel Williams's essay examines the reasons why evangelicals and Catholics abandoned their mutual suspicion of each other and joined a common coalition in support of Richard Nixon, an often-polarizing candidate who ironically may have done more than any other politician in the decade to bring evangelicals and Catholics together.

Although many scholars have focused on the 1970s as the decade that produced the Religious Right, the articles in this volume suggest that it was actually a decade earlier, in the 1960s, when evangelicals, Catholics, and Orthodox Jews began coalescing into a conservative coalition that attempted to fight secularization by promoting a closer relationship between church and state. By placing religion at the center of the conservative coalition's formation in the 1960s, these essays suggest that instead of viewing '60s conservatism as the product solely of secular concerns about Communism, race, and the economy, historians need to examine religious issues as a central force in the Republican Party's ascendancy during this decade.

The International Arena

As scholars are only beginning to discover, the conservative movement of the 1960s was forged in a global context as Americans reacted to perceived foreign policy failures and unexpected international developments. The 1960s were a decade bookmarked by heightened anxieties about the future of a viable national defense, and in the early years of the decade, *hawk* was a term easily applied to both liberal and conservative leaders. When John F. Kennedy squeaked through to electoral victory in 1960, for example, he did so partly by arguing for the presence of an alarming—if utterly fictional—missile gap between the United States and the Soviet Union. Kennedy successfully projected an image of strenuous opposition to Communism that resulted, among other things, in growing US involvement in Southeast Asia. By the end of the decade, of course, the United States was deeply mired in the Vietnam War. Citizens from across the political spectrum loudly and sometimes violently argued their positions for and against this involvement, and *hawk* became increasingly synonymous with *conservative*. Richard Nixon made good use of his foreign policy credentials to simultaneously project strength and a new global vision, winning the election in 1968 with a campaign that promised "peace with honor." The year 1970, however, saw bombing in Cambodia rather than the forging of a peace agreement.[15]

While the growing specter of Vietnam was a central characteristic of the 1960s, a number of factors made the world an increasingly confusing place. Decolonization multiplied the number of countries in the world, bringing with it a whole host of challenges—and opportunities. The Sino-Soviet split fractured the United States' conception of a monolithic Communist threat. The accelerating economic growth of once-decimated economies from Western Europe to Japan resulted in new challenges for American policy makers, emphasizing the United States' need to come to grips with a globalizing economic and national security environment. Conservatives made innovative efforts to come to grips with these massive structural changes.[16]

Much of the existing literature in the field emphasizes national policy debates at the highest levels of power and influence. The pivotal roles played by grassroots conservatives have largely been overlooked. The essays in this volume bring new perspective to the tumultuous foreign policy of the 1960s, restoring the significance and agency of citizen activism and demonstrating the previously unacknowledged diversity of conservative thought—as well as the contentious nature of many of these issues within the conservative movement. Laura Jane Gifford's chapter on the Christian Anti-Communism Crusade demonstrates the organization's uniquely internationalist perspective on the anticommunist fight and shows that the grassroots anticommunist movement of the early 1960s had a global vision that in some ways presaged later conservative foreign policy positions. Michael Brenes's study of the conservative campaign against nuclear détente in the 1960s draws important new links between national policy making and grassroots activism. Brenes explains how grassroots conservatives, and especially defense workers and local conservative activists in the burgeoning, military industry–dependent Sun Belt, mobilized to oppose reductions in military defense spending. Seth Offenbach brings much-needed attention to conservatives' debates over the proper direction of the conflict in Vietnam, demonstrating that prior to 1965, conservatives were far from unified behind this conflict's Cold War importance. Many leading foreign policy experts argued that Cuba, Berlin, and even Africa deserved higher priority, and Vietnam's perceived similarity to Korea was a cause of considerable anxiety. Following Goldwater's overwhelming loss in 1964, however, conservatives turned to support for Vietnam as a way to keep the grass roots engaged with a reeling movement. Andrew Preston reverses common perceptions about the growth of globalism in the late twentieth century by demonstrating the leading role conservative evangelicals played in fashioning a new approach toward American engagement in a newly globalizing international system. Evangelicals were able to blend both nationalism and universalism to forge a global worldview that depended on a leading role for the United States in promoting a just and orderly international society.

Collectively, these essays demonstrate that—far from being reactionary—conservatives were often at the forefront of generating informed and proactive responses to their changing world. Sometimes, as in the case of Vietnam, these patterns were traceable to older patterns, such as a legacy of strident anticommunism; in other cases, new challenges brought new visions for an international society characterized by both American leadership and a global ideal of human rights and opportunities. Early on, some conservatives were able to see the United States in the context of a complex international system, and even rank-and-file members of the military-industrial complex were engaged in influencing the national policy decisions that would impact their own livelihoods—and the future of the Cold War.

The Conservative Triumph in the GOP

This book's primary emphasis is on changes in political culture at the grass roots rather than on the "high politics" of party conventions and national political campaigns, but we conclude this volume with an essay that traces the conservative capture of the GOP. At first glance, the subject may seem familiar. After all, many historians have told the story of conservatism's triumphal takeover of the Republican Party, from the effective grassroots networks forged in 1960 to the refining of the movement in the wake of Goldwater's 1964 defeat, the new hope represented by Reagan's 1966 gubernatorial victory in California, and finally to the growing influence of both neoconservatism and the Religious Right in the 1970s. Emphasis on leading lights such as Goldwater, Nixon, and Reagan, however, has elided the stories of politicians who did not enjoy figurehead status but instead struggled to come to terms with the changes in their political party and continue to enjoy electoral success.[17] For that reason, this book presents the story of party takeover not by focusing on any of the leading characters in the traditional narratives of Republican Party politics in the 1960s but by examining the political career of a national politician who has received little coverage in most histories of the conservative movement.

Spiro Agnew is remembered today mainly for the scandalous end of his vice presidential term, but as Justin Coffey's essay points out, many conservatives considered him a hero in the early 1970s. Yet, as Coffey also argues, Agnew spent the first half of his political career as a moderately liberal Republican. A study of his shift to the right and his success in branding himself as a conservative populist thus offers the opportunity to explore the conservative co-option of GOP moderates. Coffey's essay shows how concerns about race, crime, and social order led moderates such as Agnew to shift to the right of the political spectrum, thus transforming the Republican Party.

The 1960s was a decade in which conservatives found their voice on the issues of race, economics, religion, and foreign policy. It was a period in which conservatives gained control of the Republican Party and formulated a set of objectives that shaped American politics for the next half century. The thousands of activists profiled in *Time* magazine's December 1961 essay—and thousands more of similar mind—were mobilized into political and social forces that significantly shifted and reshaped the agenda of American life. Ideas once considered outside the pale of respectable opinion now occupied an increasingly central role in policy dialogues on Main Street and Capitol Hill alike.

New innovations in economic theory, social movement activism, and political dynamism would come not from the New Frontier but from the ideological descendants of Goldwater and his supporters. With this transition came increasing diversity within the conservative movement itself, as the acquisition of power brought with it opportunities to specialize, from Phyllis Schlafly's anti–Equal Rights Amendment movement to prolife campaigns and supply-side economics. A reexamination of the developments of the 1960s is thus critically important for understanding the political context of our time and the continued vitality of conservative ideas today.

Notes

1. "Organizations: The Ultras," *Time*, December 8, 1961.
2. For an example of this interpretation, see Steven F. Hayward, *The Age of Reagan: The Fall of the Old Liberal Order, 1964–1980* (Roseville, CA: Forum, 2001).
3. For early studies of the 1960s focusing on liberalism and the New Left without extensive treatment of conservatism, see Jim F. Heath, *Decade of Disillusionment: The Kennedy-Johnson Years* (Bloomington: Indiana University Press, 1975); Alan Matusow, *The Unraveling of America: A History of Liberalism in the 1960s* (New York: Harper and Row, 1984); and Todd Gitlin, *The Sixties: Years of Hope, Days of Rage* (New York: Bantam Books, 1987). For an early study of Goldwater's campaign that treated it as an anomaly in presidential politics, see Bernard Cosman, *Five States for Goldwater: Continuity and Change in Southern Presidential Voting Patterns* (Tuscaloosa: University of Alabama Press, 1966). For more recent studies of Goldwater's 1964 campaign and its enduring influence on the conservative movement, see Rick Perlstein, *Before*

the Storm: Barry Goldwater and the Unmaking of the American Consensus (New York: Hill and Wang, 2001); J. William Middendorf II, *A Glorious Disaster: Barry Goldwater's Presidential Campaign and the Origins of the Conservative Movement* (New York: Basic Books, 2006); and Jeffrey J. Volle, *The Political Legacies of Barry Goldwater and George McGovern: Shifting Party Paradigms* (New York: Palgrave Macmillan, 2010). For Reagan's growing connections to the conservative movement, see Lisa McGirr, *Suburban Warriors: The Origins of the New American Right* (Princeton, NJ: Princeton University Press, 2001), 187–216. For a sampling of the extensive scholarship on Richard Nixon's influence on conservatism, see Rick Perlstein, *Nixonland: The Rise of a President and the Fracturing of America* (New York: Scribner, 2008); and Robert Mason, *Richard Nixon and the Quest for a New Majority* (Chapel Hill: University of North Carolina Press, 2003). For more on Wallace's relationship to the conservative movement, see Dan T. Carter, *The Politics of Rage: George Wallace, the Origins of the New Conservatism, and the Transformation of American Politics* (New York: Simon and Schuster, 1995).

4. Jonathan Schoenwald, *A Time for Choosing: The Rise of Modern American Conservatism* (New York: Oxford University Press, 2001), 243–49.

5. See, for example, Schoenwald, *A Time for Choosing*; McGirr, *Suburban Warriors*; Bruce J. Schulman, *From Cotton Belt to Sunbelt: Federal Policy, Economic Development, and the Transformation of the South, 1938–1980* (Durham, NC: Duke University Press, 1994); Ann Markusen et al., *The Rise of the Gunbelt: The Military Remapping of Industrial America* (New York: Oxford University Press, 1991); Mary C. Brennan, *Turning Right in the Sixties: The Conservative Capture of the GOP* (Chapel Hill: University of North Carolina Press, 1995); Donald T. Critchlow, *The Conservative Ascendancy: How the GOP Right Made Political History* (Cambridge, MA: Harvard University Press, 2007); and John A. Andrew III, *The Other Side of the Sixties: Young Americans for Freedom and the Rise of Conservative Politics* (New Brunswick, NJ: Rutgers University Press, 1997).

6. For a collection of recent scholarship on conservatism in the 1960s, see David Farber and Jeff Roche, eds., *The Conservative Sixties* (New York: Peter Lang, 2003).

7. George H. Nash, *The Conservative Intellectual Movement in America Since 1945* (New York: Basic Books, 1976).

8. See, for instance, Kim Phillips-Fein, *Invisible Hands: The Businessmen's Crusade against the New Deal* (New York: W. W. Norton, 2009); Joseph E. Lowndes, *From the New Deal to the New Right: Race and the Southern Origins of Modern Conservatism* (New Haven, CT: Yale University Press, 2009); Matthew Avery Sutton, *Aimee Semple McPherson and the Resurrection of Christian America* (Cambridge, MA: Harvard University Press, 2007); Allan J. Lichtman, *White Protestant Nation: The Rise of the American Conservative Movement* (New York: Atlantic Monthly Press, 2008); Patrick Allitt, *The Conservatives: Ideas and Personalities throughout American History* (New Haven, CT: Yale University Press, 2009); and Gregory L. Schneider, *The Conservative Century: From Reaction to Revolution* (Lanham, MD: Rowman and Littlefield, 2009). Our summary of conservatives' main concerns is partly drawn from David Farber, *The Rise and Fall of Modern American Conservatism: A Short History* (Princeton, NJ: Princeton University Press, 2010), 2–3.

9. Jack Bass and Walter DeVries, *The Transformation of Southern Politics: Social Change and Political Consequence since 1945* (New York: Basic Books, 1976); Earl

Black and Merle Black, *Politics and Society in the South* (Cambridge, MA: Harvard University Press, 1987); Carter, *Politics of Rage*; Perlstein, *Nixonland*; Lowndes, *From the New Deal to the New Right*; Nancy MacLean, *Freedom Is Not Enough: The Opening of the American Workplace* (Cambridge, MA: Harvard University Press, 2006); Nancy MacLean, "Neo-Confederacy versus the New Deal: The Regional Utopia of the Modern American Right," in *The Myth of Southern Exceptionalism*, ed. Matthew D. Lassiter and Joseph Crespino (New York: Oxford University Press, 2010), 308–330; Joseph Crespino, *In Search of another Country: Mississippi and the Conservative Counterrevolution* (Princeton, NJ: Princeton University Press, 2007); Kevin M. Kruse, *White Flight: Atlanta and the Making of Modern Conservatism* (Princeton, NJ: Princeton University Press, 2005); Matthew D. Lassiter, *The Silent Majority: Suburban Politics in the Sunbelt South* (Princeton, NJ: Princeton University Press, 2006).

10. For more on Reagan and General Electric, see Thomas W. Evans, *The Education of Ronald Reagan: The General Electric Years and the Untold Story of His Conversion to Conservatism* (New York: Columbia University Press, 2006). Samuel Brenner's chapter in this volume highlights the early 1960s as representing the height of anticommunist movement activity; movement leaders, too, have made this observation (see, for example, Fred Schwarz, *Beating the Unbeatable Foe: One Man's Victory over Communism, Leviathan, and the Last Enemy* [Washington, DC: Regnery, 1996]). Brenner's chapter also analyzes the relationship between Buckley and the John Birch Society. Some of the leading representations of the ideology of the liberal consensus include Arthur M. Schlesinger Jr., *The Vital Center: The Politics of Freedom* (Boston: Houghton Mifflin, 1949); John Kenneth Galbraith, *The Affluent Society* (Boston: Houghton Mifflin, 1958); and Richard Hofstadter, *The Age of Reform: From Bryan to F.D.R.* (New York: Knopf, 1955). For intellectuals' dismissal of conservative ideas during the years of the liberal consensus, see Daniel Bell, ed., *The New American Right* (New York: Criterion, 1955); and Richard Hofstadter, *Anti-Intellectualism in American Life* (New York: Knopf, 1963).

11. For recent scholarship on the conservative movement and economic issues, see Phillips-Fein, *Invisible Hands*; Schneider, *The Conservative Century*; and Bethany Moreton, *To Serve God and Wal-Mart: The Making of Christian Free Enterprise* (Cambridge, MA: Harvard University Press, 2009). Jennifer Burns has made an excellent contribution to the intellectual history of economic conservatism with *Goddess of the Market: Ayn Rand and the American Right* (New York: Oxford University Press, 2009).

12. See Schoenwald, *A Time for Choosing, 116–17*, for strong coverage of the Kennedy administration's investigation of the radical Right undertaken by Americans for Democratic Action founders Victor and Walter Reuther and Joseph L. Rauh Jr. in 1961. Period exposés of "extremist" organizations include Donald Janson and Bernard Eismann, *The Far Right* (New York: McGraw-Hill, 1963), and Arnold Forster and Benjamin R. Epstein, *Danger on the Right: The Attitudes, Personnel and Influence of the Radical Right and Extreme Conservatives* (New York: Random House, 1964).

13. For histories of liberal and mainline religion in the 1960s, see Ronald B. Flowers, *Religion in Strange Times: The 1960s and 1970s* (Macon, GA: Mercer University

Press, 1984); Robert S. Ellwood, *The Sixties Spiritual Awakening: American Religion Moving from Modern to Postmodern* (New Brunswick, NJ: Rutgers University Press, 1994); and Patrick Allitt, *Religion in America since 1945: A History* (New York: Columbia University Press, 2003), 43–147.

14. For examples of the emerging scholarship in this area, see Patrick Allitt, *Catholic Intellectuals and Conservative Politics in America* (Ithaca, NY: Cornell University Press, 1993); Donald T. Critchlow, *Phyllis Schlafly and Grassroots Conservatism: A Woman's Crusade* (Princeton, NJ: Princeton University Press, 2005); Steven P. Miller, *Billy Graham and the Rise of the Republican South* (Philadelphia: University of Pennsylvania Press, 2009); Daniel K. Williams, *God's Own Party: The Making of the Christian Right* (New York: Oxford University Press, 2010); and Darren Dochuk, *From Bible Belt to Sunbelt: Plain-Folk Religion, Grassroots Politics, and the Rise of Evangelical Conservatism* (New York: W. W. Norton, 2011).

15. For the effects of international developments on American politics in the 1960s, see, for example, Jeremi Suri, *Power and Protest: Global Revolution and the Rise of Détente* (Cambridge, MA: Harvard University Press, 2004); Julian Zelizer, *Arsenal of Democracy: The Politics of National Security from World War II to the War on Terrorism* (New York: Basic Books, 2009); and Campbell Craig and Fredrik Logevall, *America's Cold War: The Politics of Insecurity* (Cambridge, MA: Belknap Press of Harvard University Press, 2009). For more on the 1960 presidential election, see Laura Jane Gifford, *The Center Cannot Hold: The 1960 Presidential Election and the Rise of Modern Conservatism* (DeKalb: Northern Illinois Press, 2009). Christopher A. Preble contributes an excellent study of the missile gap debate in *John F. Kennedy and the Missile Gap* (DeKalb: Northern Illinois University Press, 2004). Few historians have produced book-length studies of the effect of international developments on the conservative movement in the 1960s, but for some examples of important new studies that touch on this subject, see Colin Dueck, *Hard Line: The Republican Party and U.S. Foreign Policy since World War II* (Princeton, NJ: Princeton University Press, 2010); Andrew Preston, *Sword of the Spirit, Shield of Faith: Religion in American War and Diplomacy* (New York: Knopf, 2012); and Ann Ziker, "Race, Conservative Politics, and U.S. Foreign Policy in the Postcolonial World, 1948–1968" (PhD diss., Rice University, 2008).

16. In addition to Suri, *Power and Protest*, see Ronald Findlay and Kevin H. O'Rourke, *Power and Plenty: Trade, War, and the World Economy in the Second Millennium* (Princeton, NJ: Princeton University Press, 2007). John Lewis Gaddis, *The Cold War: A New History* (New York: Penguin, 2005) includes a concise and accessible account of the changing world of the 1960s. Thomas Borstelmann, *The Cold War and the Color Line: American Race Relations in the Global Arena* (Cambridge, MA: Harvard University Press, 2001) provides a useful context for understanding the changing postcolonial world. For more on the impact of Western European and Japanese economic recovery on the United States from the 1960s onward, see Judith Stein, *Pivotal Decade: How the United States Traded Factories for Finance in the 1970s* (New Haven, CT: Yale University Press, 2010).

17. For more on changing political dynamics in the Republican Party, see Gifford, *The Center Cannot Hold*; Brennan, *Turning Right in the Sixties*; Schoenwald, *A Time for Choosing*; Critchlow, *The Conservative Ascendancy*; and Matthew Dallek, *The Right*

Moment: Ronald Reagan's First Victory and the Decisive Turning Point in American Politics (New York: Free Press, 2000). Justin Vaïsse's *Neoconservatism: The Biography of a Movement*, trans. Arthur Goldhammer (Cambridge, MA: Belknap Press of Harvard University Press, 2010) is an excellent resource on the growth of the neo-conservative movement. Williams's *God's Own Party* is the most prominent account of the growing influence of the Religious Right in the GOP during this period.

PART 1

The Politics of Race

CHAPTER 1

Courting Conservatism

White Resistance and the Ideology of Race in the 1960s

Stephanie R. Rolph

In 1959 Howard Zinn described the American South as a region where the worst qualities of American culture flourished. White Southerners were not, he argued, unique in their racial prejudices, and the rest of the nation could not in good conscience describe them as such. National rage about white resistance to racial reform, Zinn continued, was not rooted in ethical incompatibility. Instead, he explained, "Those very qualities long attributed to the South as special possession are, in truth *American* qualities, and the nation reacts emotionally to the South precisely because it subconsciously recognizes itself there."[1]

Zinn's remarks about white Southern resistance articulated the sentiment of white Southerners actively involved in resisting racial change in the 1950s and 1960s. Far from seeing themselves as the exception, proponents of segregation consistently tapped into what they perceived as national agreement about racial difference, unchecked federal power, and the need for a grassroots movement that would challenge the political status quo. It was the cultivation of grassroots opposition that the Citizens' Council sought to mine in the thrust of their efforts. This essay examines the council's public relations campaign and its attempt to sell the message of white resistance to the South and the nation. Proponents of white resistance took pains to establish the principles of resistance within a broader political conversation, one that could be considered at the heart of American values. Doing so meant describing federally mandated racial policies as only the most current example of dangerous political trends. In the midst of this effort, resistance leaders directly referenced conservative ideology as their foundation and eschewed any insinuation of Southern exceptionalism.

White resistance to the civil rights movement appeared in a variety of forms. For the purposes of this examination, the term *white resistance* is used to describe organized attempts to resist racial reform in the South, specifically through the efforts of the Citizens' Council. Organizations like the council appeared throughout the South in the aftermath of *Brown*.[2] Their value as historical sources lies in their deliberately constructed *public* opposition to change. Each of these organizations spoke to audiences in the hopes of unifying opposition as well as broadening support among critics of Southern segregation. It is impossible to determine with any certainty the ideological impact these organizations had upon white Southerners. Their public relations campaigns, newsletters, and other forms of public rhetoric, however, reveal the process of racial reconstruction. The Citizens' Council's public treatment of the evolving civil rights movement suggests that in the midst of its opposition, the organization described race as having meaning only within the landscape of broader, conservative principles. In its cultivation of a grassroots movement against racial change, the council's efforts were instructive to a white Southern audience desperate to justify their racial system to the rest of the nation.

The growth of scholarship on white Southern resistance during the civil rights movement has correctly identified a variety of factors that made the South a conservative stronghold. Historians have debunked regional exceptionalism by explaining the contours of resistance to racial reform outside of Dixie. Equally significant has been the attention scholars have devoted to identifying white Southern moderates (both public figures and private businesspeople) as crucial in the failure of sustained public opposition to civil rights legislation. Topical treatments of the civil rights South have bolstered understandings of anticommunism, longstanding Southern discontent with the national Democratic Party, and Southern suburbanization, each of which was crucial in defining the ways in which white Southerners resisted federal oversight.[3] White resistance as a field of study has benefited from this enrichment. In fact, it is the recognition of simultaneity that has enabled us to reexamine the dynamics of race during a period where it became the most contested.

Southern political leaders had connected existing racial policies with conservative ideology for years prior to the civil rights movement. Splits in the national Democratic Party accelerated during the last years of the New Deal, especially when the party adopted a civil rights plank in 1948. Consequently, some Southern Democrats pursued alliances with Republicans and vice versa. The South's future within the national party structure was at the very least unclear. The failure of the Dixiecrat revolt to produce unified Southern opposition to this inclusion alerted Southern leaders to the fact that leadership among disgruntled party members was no substitute for grassroots rebellion. As early as 1948, these leaders imagined an educational campaign aimed at white Southerners that would create a dynamic partnership between elected officials and their constituents.[4]

Flirtations with the Republican Party and identification with conservative ideology, then, were not new forms of resistance in the 1960s. Southern political leaders had employed them for over two decades before the announcement of *Brown v. Board of Education*. The differences between previous attempts at opposition and those employed through the Citizens' Council in the midst of the civil rights movement, however, are worth noting. While the structure of party politics provided an organized and elite platform to debate racial change, the council movement represented a grassroots approach that sought to arm white Southerners and their Northern sympathizers with an ideological defense of their racial system. The language was not new, but the audience and the political climate had changed. The implementation of this defense toward a broad audience had the same goal that the Dixiecrats and their sympathizers had imagined. Southern party leaders were not just talking to each other or their colleagues in the opposition party. The Citizens' Council deliberately situated its defense of segregation within a hierarchy of conservative values. As events unfolded and opposition to racial change seemed futile, the council's presentation of these events provided a lens of interpretation that became more deeply identified with conservative values. This commitment was especially significant as the civil rights movement drew attention in places outside of the South.

The Citizens' Council as a Channel of White Resistance

The Citizens' Council was born within weeks of the *Brown v. Board of Education* decision in 1954. Its first chapter arose in the fertile soil of the Mississippi Delta, but its influence rapidly spread, making the organization the most recognizable representative of white resistance in the South. The council's ambitions were not limited to its home state or even the South, however. A well-funded, sophisticated public relations campaign carried the Citizens' Council's message beyond its birthplace. The organization produced pamphlets, a monthly newspaper, and a weekly radio and television broadcast, all of which sought to familiarize readers, listeners, or viewers with defenses of the legitimacy of sustained resistance.

The 1960s were a crucial period for the council and its agenda. Although the council was founded explicitly for the purpose of maintaining segregation, the leaders of the organization realized in the immediate years of *Brown*'s aftermath that, nationally speaking, the raw language of white supremacy had a shrinking audience outside of the South. By the 1960s, with civil rights legislation passed and more sweeping legislative changes looming, the council carefully packed away its more abrasive racist tirades in favor of a more adaptive race-neutral strategy. This strategy virtually ignored the civil rights movement, focusing instead upon the intellectual underpinnings of the American system. Citing the founding fathers and borrowing from the language of modern conservative intellectuals, council spokesmen and their sympathizers presented their efforts as part and parcel of an existing legitimate political ideology. In doing so, the council's audience could normalize their views within mainstream ideas while distancing themselves from the issue of race.

The Citizens' Council was born in Indianola, Mississippi, in July 1954. The cover of its first official pamphlet described the organization as "dedicated to the maintenance of peace, good order and domestic tranquility . . . and to the preservation of our States' Rights." While its motto seemed benign, the explanation of the council's function was more explicit. Claiming that the organization was an answer to "mongrelizers," the pamphlet declared unequivocally that members were proud of their white heritage and vowed to "stand fast and preserve an unsullied race."[5]

Less than three months after the first council organized, 21 chapters existed in Mississippi, and in October 1954 they merged into the Mississippi Association of Citizens' Councils (ACC). With headquarters in Winona, approximately sixty miles east of Indianola, the ACC preserved the independence of individual chapters but began a public relations campaign to market the council's message throughout the South and nation. A year later, the organization published the first issue of *The Citizens' Council*, a monthly newsletter. In its maiden edition, the paper described itself as "a means of exchanging information among the responsible movements throughout the South" as well as a mouthpiece to non-Southern audiences who failed to understand the "Southern viewpoint."[6]

From its inception, the Citizens' Council envisioned a two-pronged marketing tactic. In its early years (1954–60) the council's primary objective was to unify white Southern resistance organizations as a means to obstructing federal implementation of *Brown*. Through this unification, council organizers hoped to counteract white apathy about desegregation and voting rights. *The Citizens' Council* newsletter was especially focused on this objective. It carried a number of news items related to the National Association for the Advancement of Colored People (NAACP) as well as international events that almost always were related to Communism or criticism of the United Nations. Several headlines warned against "race-mixers" and left-wing subversives. In the midst of such news stories, the white South's objections to desegregation and political rights for black Southerners seemed to make practical sense. The collection of news items could also serve to galvanize subscribers (many of whom by virtue of being subscribers were already sympathetic to the council's message) into sustained resistance activities. In short, the council's newsletter placed local civil rights activities in a national and global context, challenging white Southerners to halt international trends toward Communism and race-mixing. Even in this most predictable of resistance activities, the council's approach sought to draw its white Southern audience beyond provincial concerns and make the South's predicament seem less unique.

The second (and more broadly reaching) strategy in the council's public relations campaign sought to move the message of resistance outside of the South altogether. As stated in the newsletter's mission, the Citizens' Council wanted to open up a conversation with Northern critics and friends alike to explain why the South felt as it did about desegregation. Leaders of the organization perceived criticism of Southern racial mores as misunderstandings that could easily be corrected with appropriate explanations. If these explanations could be circulated through venues like *The Citizens' Council*, Americans (presumably white) would sympathize and agree that the South's position was representative of how most white Americans felt about matters of race.[7]

The national scope of council activities, while begun with the publication of its newsletter, really got under way after the establishment of the Citizens' Council of America (CCA) in 1956. The CCA was to serve as an umbrella organization for council-like groups throughout the South—groups seeking to halt federal intervention in matters of race. Despite the attempt to unify resistance under the CCA, however, the council movement remained strongest in Mississippi. In December of that same year, the Educational Fund of the Citizens' Council received nonprofit status, allowing for tax-exempt donations. The establishment of this status shifted all public relations activities to the Educational Fund. The most appropriate venue for such activities was the mass media. This fact was true not only because it provided the greatest access to diverse audiences but also because council publications often blamed the national media for distorting the South's position.[8]

Ultimately, the Educational Fund's most significant investment was *Forum*, a weekly radio and television broadcast that served as a public affairs program. Running from 1957 until 1966, the program became one of the longest-standing and most impressive endeavors in which the council engaged. Initially, *Forum* was a 15-minute television program that ran on Jackson, Mississippi's NBC affiliate, WLBT. By December 1957 the council made audio recordings of the television broadcast available to radio stations.[9] In May 1958 the program relocated to Washington, DC, significantly broadening its access to national public figures.

It is impossible to determine with any kind of certainty how broad *Forum*'s audience was at any given time. *The Citizens' Council* listed radio and television stations that allegedly aired the program each month in 1958–59 in its column, "Citizens' Council *Forum* on TV and Radio." Even after the column was removed in April 1959 (abruptly and without explanation), council spokes-men consistently claimed that the scope of *Forum*'s distribution was growing exponentially. In February 1963 the council claimed 420 television and radio stations as carriers of the weekly program, but provided no evidence of these claims.[10]

When *Forum* debuted in 1957, the civil rights movement was well under way. The Civil Rights Act of 1957, the first federal civil rights law since Recon-struction, had been passed, giving federal sanction to a full-fledged assault on discriminatory voting practices. The ultimate push for sweeping legislation, however, was still several years away, and the 1950s represented a period during which *Forum* guests were still feeling out the contours of resistance. The local nature of its broadcasts during these early years had a severe impact upon the language of racism that prevailed. Guests often emphasized the lack of interest among local Negroes in the NAACP, embracing traditional paternalistic rheto-ric as a way to defend segregation and voting restrictions.

The consistent denial of agency within the black community was a com-mon thread throughout *Forum* broadcasts, especially in its first two years of programming. When guests discussed the emerging civil rights movement, the black community was virtually nonexistent in their remarks. Culpability for racial unrest could be attributed to a number of groups, but local blacks were not among them. Georgia congressman E. L. Forrester, during a 1958 appear-ance on *Forum*, argued that there was a fundamental misunderstanding about who was responsible for civil rights activity: "[M]ake no mistake about it . . . if you think it's a colored man . . . you are entirely wrong . . . [It is] the result of pressure brought upon the President of the United States by minority groups in the country who expect everything and give nothing. And if you want to know who they are, I want to tell you. They are white people."[11]

The "white people" Representative Forrester identified were often described on *Forum* as left-wing Communist sympathizers who cooperated with the NAACP to create racial disturbances throughout the South. In referring to civil rights activists as "racial agitators" or, more simply, as "outsiders," *Forum* guests were not unique in their consistent denial of an organic civil rights cam-paign. The South's confrontation with criticism of its racial practices led most white Southern political leaders to deny any discontent among "their" Negroes, blaming leftist propaganda machines for creating a theater of instability. Any local blacks that joined the NAACP were described as victims of such propa-ganda. And even though the NAACP was a black-dominated organization, the assumption prevailed that they were outsiders to the Southern black commu-nity, corrupted by liberal Communist-leaning whites.

Local black participation and leadership grew, however, and the approach toward race that *Forum* guests took in the 1960s reflected this reality. In its earlier programs, guests skirted racial prejudice through the demonization of outsiders and the depiction of local blacks as victims of propaganda who would otherwise be content with the system of white paternalism. The pressures of local activists through protests and boycotts brought more media attention to the South and support for further federal legislation. Confronted with the inevitability of racial change, *Forum* guests started employing more direct denouncements of the black race as a whole. Its guests were more diverse, with a number of them coming from outside of the South and, in some cases, from other countries. The variety of guests on *Forum* and the sympathy they exhibited toward Southern racial mores helped the council shed its provincial image without compromising its message.

In 1961 the program hosted Joseph Mitchell, the city manager of Newburgh, New York. Newburgh had recently made national news after his city's attempt to scale back its welfare program met with resistance. In a two-part feature, Mitchell explained how welfare costs had negatively affected his city—namely, through growing financial burdens and the spread of slum areas. He did not mention race in his description of the welfare system in Newburgh. When *Forum*'s host, Dick Morphew, questioned him about the racial demographics of his city since the implementation of the welfare system, Mitchell stated that race was "of no consequence." If the numbers were evaluated, he qualified, one could easily see that since the start of the program, the city of Newburgh gained three thousand "nonwhites" and lost four thousand "whites," a transition that divested the city of "the higher taxpaying, higher educated . . . more constructive or productive citizens" and replaced them with people "who have contributed to the rise of the slums and all that go with the slums."[12]

Mitchell's remarks foreshadowed a coming debate about entitlement programs, one that helped galvanize the conservative base over the next two decades. His description of the welfare issue, however, is instructive of the ways in which the Citizens' Council began to tap into wedge issues as a way to mask racial prejudice. Even though Mitchell explicitly denied his interest in race, his qualification about more productive white citizens moving out as nonwhites moved in is significant. Welfare reform debates alluded to the inferiority of blacks while insinuating that federal or state programs designed to alleviate this inferiority were damaging to the white community, whom he described as "higher taxpaying, higher educated" and "more productive."[13]

Not all of *Forum*'s guests were as careful to dismiss race. *Forum* hosted a number of "race experts" in the 1960s who approached their discussions of race with scientific arguments. These experts were the most direct critics of racial equality to appear on the program, but their claims to scientific legitimacy represented a similar approach to that of other guests. The states' rights argument and critiques of entitlement programs softened racial language and attached segregation to broader political traditions. Scientific theory created a connection that enabled the support of racial inequality as a proven fact. This claim to natural inequality was made even more legitimate when made by non-Southern "experts," who had no purported stake in the argument.

In 1962 Dr. W. C. George, author of *Biology of the Race Problem*, appeared on *Forum* to discuss his findings regarding innate racial difference. George labeled scientists who rejected his argument "equalitarians" who had "captured" the American Anthropological Association and the American Association of Physical Anthropologists. The equalitarian trend among such scientists, he argued, had led publishing houses and scientific journals to marginalize anyone who did not accept this theory. Dr. Robert Gayre, another *Forum* guest billed as a race expert, compared the current trends rejecting racial difference to the fissure between the Catholic Church and scientists during the Middle Ages, stating, "I would say this [equalitarian] teaching of today is a doctrine and those who conflict with it are heretics and that means not only those of us sitting around this table but the majority of scientists who wrote books and made speeches up to 1939."[14]

Dr. Henry E. Garrett, former president of the American Psychological Association and a professor at the University of Virginia at the time of his *Forum* appearance in 1964, made even more explicit comments about attempts to equalize the races. He agreed that the scientific community was largely to blame for the culture of conformity that underscored support for the civil rights movement. Such a sentiment, he explained, could not persist under practical circumstances. The North was operating under the false assumption that the black man was "a white man with dark skin," who, if treated like a white man, would behave accordingly. As white Northerners familiarized themselves with the realities of the race, however, they would quickly realize that "we are dealing with a different breed, a different sort of person." This realization would inevitably lead to a more "sensible" approach to racial difference.[15]

The appearance of these guests, all of whom appeared more than once on *Forum* in the 1960s, is reminiscent of traditional arguments about racial hierarchy that prevailed at the turn of the century. Their application to white resistance ideology is, however, crucial in understanding the transformation into conservative ideology that was under way within the Citizens' Council by 1960. Conservative intellectuals writing in the 1930s and 1940s wrote extensively about the dangers of using ideology as a policy guide. The totalitarian impulses that led to World War II, they argued, were grounded largely in central ideas, many of them racially based. Although these intellectuals were not speaking directly about race, racial conservatives (like those in organizations like the council) co-opted these arguments and applied them to equalitarianism.[16] The forced conformity to which George, Gayre, and Garrett referred mirrored conservative denouncements of ideological unity that had led to global war. Failure to question intellectual and scientific trends, they argued, was creating a blind faith among white Americans that contributed to impractical racial policies.

Other guests echoed these fears. In 1963 Virginia journalist John Synon appeared on *Forum*. Reflecting on pending legislation that would become the Civil Rights Act of 1964, Synon described support of the civil rights movement as "over-larded with emotion." The moral value attached to denouncements of segregation discouraged anyone from objecting to legislation for fear of being labeled a racist. John C. Satterfield, a Jackson, Mississippi, attorney and former president of the American Bar Association, was a guest three weeks later and argued the same point. The spectacle of civil rights demonstrations throughout the South, he claimed, created a heightened emotional environment that legislators leveraged against the American people to push through more sweeping legislation. Once such emotionalism had subsided, he predicted, Americans would be shocked at the aftermath of such decisions.[17]

As *Forum* guests moved away from paternalism, they moved toward innate racial difference as a defense against integration. This shift took place in the crucible of the civil rights campaign. Mississippi, by 1963, found itself at the heart of the movement. The Freedom Rides, violent reaction to the integration of the University of Mississippi, and an organized boycott of downtown merchants in the state's capital were only a few examples of the unraveling racial hierarchy. Most threatening was the increasing certainty that sweeping civil rights legislation was looming. Prior to the Civil Rights Act of 1964, the South had experienced increasing scrutiny through the Civil Rights Commission and two civil rights bills (1957 and 1960) that dealt with voting oversight. A variety of court cases were pending regarding different levels of desegregation or obstruction to the same. In general, however, it was the growing demonstrations and the national media's coverage of those events that most likely motivated the sense of betrayal that *Forum* guests began to exhibit toward Southern blacks. The paternalism that had characterized so many early reactions to the movement began to morph into white victimhood.

The Citizens' Council dedicated a number of programs to the Civil Rights Act of 1964. Previous legislation did not pose the same threat that this bill seemed to, according to *Forum* guests. Discussions about the Civil Rights Act of 1957 and 1960 had existed, but in 1963 it was clear that the system of segregation was about to be dismantled. This looming threat coincided with a more structured approach to resistance as it appeared through the council's radio program. Guests who appeared to discuss their opposition to the legislation described it as a bridge to federal power. Building from earlier arguments about the "emotionalism" associated with support of the civil rights movement, guests accused the federal government of exploiting such feelings as a means to expand its own power. The obvious victims of this power grab, in their minds, would be white majorities. Whether as a political tactic or out of sheer denial, these discussions failed to address black Americans in any comprehensive way.

Guests acknowledged two entities: whites and the federal government. More significant, however, is the fact that by 1963, direct references to conservatism began to appear regularly.

Connecting Segregation with Conservatism

Forum guests used political ideology in an attempt to attach opposition to racial change to a broader set of principles. Until 1961, however, much of this ideology revolved around two themes: the dangers of left-leaning political leaders and the well-worn mantra of states' rights. These two themes never disappeared completely from *Forum* discussions, but more frequent identifications of conservative ideology (and more specific calls to abandon the Democratic Party altogether) absorbed traditional defenses. The conservative label became a more sophisticated, structured, and marketable version of white resistance.

In 1961 one of the South's leading spokesmen for segregation, Senator Harry F. Byrd from Virginia, explained why he identified himself as a conservative, stating, "I want to preserve the fundamental principles of our government . . . [M]y conservatism is along the lines of conserving those things that have [made] this country, in a very short space of time, the greatest nation in the world." Centralization of government could only come, he argued, at the expense of states' rights and individual freedoms, the very foundations of American political theory.[18]

John G. Tower, a Republican senator from Texas, appeared on *Forum* several times, always as a spokesman for conservatism. Tower's appearances are revelatory in their deliberate attempt to marry white resistance (through the Citizens' Council's audience) to broader themes of political conservatism, a move that would simultaneously illuminate non-race-related issues. It is also noteworthy that Tower was one of the first Southern Republicans elected to national office during this period, a trend that would begin to spread throughout the region.

Tower offered a detailed definition of what he believed conservatism meant: "[A] conservative is one who believes in accommodating change and progress within the framework of existing institutions. That is to say, he recognizes that by virtue of evolutionary progress over centuries we have developed certain political and legal and economic institutions and they have served us very well and we think that they have provided us with not only an element of progress but an element of stability in our society and therefore, should be preserved . . . [T]he conservative is one who wants to preserve maximum individual liberty and freedom of choice." Tower went on to explain contemporary issues and how conservatives exemplified these principles. Central to conservative ideology was opposition to federal power at the expense of states' rights. Conservatives, Tower explained, preferred that power be disseminated among state and local governments. Their economic theory emphasized low taxes and low spending, giving individuals and communities more power over their money. Conservatives preferred a free-market approach to federal subsidies, specifically as they were applied to farmers. It was inaccurate, he explained, to perceive conservatives as a negative force against progress. Liberals were actually much closer to that definition because they sought to eliminate everything Americans valued through the growth of federal programs. Conservatives, he countered, were "for" the preservation of freedom, individual liberty, and freedom of choice.[19]

Tower's definition of conservatism matched the anti–federal government sentiment that infused so much of white resistance rhetoric. Conservatism was a broad label that did not have to explain the nature of resistance to civil rights legislation, though it easily could. Opposition to federal regulation was enough to insinuate that this ideology was the ideology of white resistance. No clearer example of this exists than the pointed discussions of party politics that appeared on *Forum* in the 1960s.

The Citizens' Council never formally endorsed any political candidates or spoke candidly about partisanship. This was true partly because of the existence of the one-party system that had dominated much of the South since Reconstruction. Locally, the council worked to identify sympathetic segregationist candidates but never pursued visibility during election seasons. Because most *Forum* broadcasts took place in Washington, DC, however, a majority of its guests were national political figures, both Republican and Democrat. It is also significant that a number of these guests were not members of the Citizens' Council and had no affiliation with the organization other than their appearance on the program. Many of them saw in the white resistance movement an opportunity to facilitate a political revolution where ideological identity could replace party identity. Sympathy for the white South's position, to put it another way, promised to pull white resistance from the margins of political theater into the mainstream.

The political shift that *Forum* guests envisioned was not only occurring in the South, they argued. Republican congressman and John Birch Society leader John Rousselot of California appeared on the program in 1962 to explain his home state's recent political revival of conservatism. His constituents, Rousselot explained, were realizing that not all problems could be solved at the federal level and that local and state authorities were, in fact, much better qualified to address many issues. More importantly, he argued, it was "the individual" who must begin to solve his own problems, not the federal government. The "revival of conservative philosophy" that Rousselot perceived would, at some point, lead to a "realignment of party activity" in which Southern Democrats would begin to migrate out of the Democratic Party and into the Republican camp. Similarly, left-leaning Republicans might find themselves more comfortable as Democrats.[20]

William K. Shearer, a conservative California journalist, felt that if conservatives from both parties could "all get in under one roof" there could exist a viable conservative majority that would "control the government." He identified the current racial crisis in the South as a catalyst to moving Southern Democrats into the Republican Party, where they would be welcomed, "because we know the great constitutional issues which are involved [in resistance] and which go beyond any individual questions."[21]

It was not just outside interest that brought attention to party alignment in the South. Southerners also appeared on the show to discuss the region's political options regarding federal support of civil rights activity. Weeks after the violence that erupted at the University of Mississippi upon James Meredith's admission in 1962, George Wallace, Alabama's segregationist governor and one of the most recognizable faces of resistance, appeared on *Forum*. President Kennedy's decision to maintain a military presence in Oxford, Wallace claimed, left many Southerners feeling "indignant and disturbed." Seven Southern states had pledged their electoral votes to Kennedy in 1960, and his recent approach to racial unrest left many Southern Democrats feeling abandoned. Wallace argued that this sense of abandonment had become visible in recent congressional elections in Alabama, where two Republican legislators were elected, evidencing "increased Republican sentiment." Perhaps, he reflected, Southerners were beginning to sort through their political choices through the binary of liberal versus conservative instead of Republican versus Democrat.[22]

Each of these guests presented conservatism as the solution to white Southern losses. Sold in this way, *Forum* provided a platform that made explicit the relationship between conservatism and the preservation of white privilege. The value its proponents placed on small government and local control alluded to disapproval of federal programs regarding racial equality, among other things. Regardless of how diverse its topics and guests were, the Citizens' Council funded *Forum* as a public affairs program that would sell the South's message of racial separation to the rest of the nation. Discussions of conservatism were clearly meant to connect that message to nonracial issues. Criticism of the Civil Rights Act of 1964 was an ideal example of how this connection developed.

In their discussions of what became the Civil Rights Act of 1964, *Forum* guests largely ignored the demands of civil rights activists. Instead, they tended to focus on the way in which the legislation would enable the federal government to exercise even more power over individuals. John Satterfield referred to the bill as a "Trojan Horse" that the federal government was using to destroy individual rights and property rights. Texas congressman John Dowdy claimed that even though the bill's supporters referred to it as a protection of civil rights, it was actually a violation of them. William K. Shearer saw the legislation as a direct attack on "the rights . . . and interests of the majority."[23]

The majority argument was one of the ways in which *Forum* guests promoted the idea of white victimhood without speaking directly about race. It emphasized the polarity of racial interests by moving discussions of whites' rights away from the rights being granted to black Americans. The extension of protection given in the Civil Rights Act of 1964 was, in these men's opinion, being taken at the expense of majority (white) interests. These same men argued that conservatism was the answer to such violations. Conservatism, as it appeared in *Forum*, was a political ideology that suited the needs of disaffected whites.

The successful implementation of the civil rights legislation that *Forum* guests railed against in 1963 and 1964 coincided with an escalation of racial unrest both within and outside of the South. Southern segregationists linked these riots to the evolving atmosphere of tolerance and special privileges the civil rights movement had popularized. The timing of these riots was instructive, guests argued, of the consequences of federal interference into matters of race.

Senator Strom Thurmond, one of the South's most outspoken opponents of integration, pointed out in an appearance in 1964 that the wave of riots that had recently plagued non-Southern cities occurred in areas that for several years had had laws preventing discrimination. Recent violence in these areas proved that legislation was not the answer for racial unrest. "Whatever adjustments are going to come," Thurmond declared, "are going to come in the hearts of people and they are going to come because of good will. You can't just pass a law and that's the end of it." Racial violence, he believed, was, in fact, a natural consequence of the tolerance the federal government had shown toward blacks during the course of the civil rights movement. The more attention given to civil rights activists, the more likely was for blacks in general to feel "oppressed" and resentful about so-called discrimination and for them to retaliate in a violent way.[24]

The participants in the riots that happened in 1964 and 1965 were not the passive, content Negroes early *Forum* guests claimed to be typical of the South. Even though these riots were happening outside of the South, guests insinuated that the movement had created discontent and cultivated an atmosphere of entitlement and lawlessness within black communities. Representative Joe D. Waggoner (D-LA) said as much in 1965: "'Obey those laws which you feel are right and disobey those laws which you feel are wrong' has been a common preaching and teaching of far too many people." Waggoner blamed this trend on "fuzzy social thinkers" who had successfully convinced blacks that they deserved preferential treatment.[25]

No institution was guiltier of perpetuating this kind of deceit than the national media. In *Forum*'s earliest broadcasts it was not uncommon for guests to denounce the media's coverage of Southern racial practices. Southern guests (who tended to dominate the programs in the 1950s) accused the national media outlets of misrepresenting the system of segregation in the South according to their own biases against the region. Journalists from the North, they argued, oversimplified white resistance to *Brown*, voting rights, and desegregation, without investigating *why* white Southerners felt so strongly about their racial institutions. These accusations appeared during the earliest days of organized resistance and fully reflected the sense of isolation that Southern segregationists felt as the nation turned a critical eye upon their way of life.[26] *Forum* was explicitly described as an alternative to these biases, an outlet that would allow Southerners an opportunity to justify their racial practices and explain to a national audience how similar their views were to the rest of the nation.

By the 1960s, much of the message of segregation had been lost among a myriad of political issues that sought to tie white resistance to broader issues of constitutional integrity and conservatism. The media remained a target, but guests connected it with the ideological polarization so many of them identified in their arguments. In 1962 Senator John Tower explained that journalists seemed to be unduly impressed by "liberal intellectuals." This fact could be seen in their tendency to "put forth that side of the argument more than they have tended to put forth the conservative side of the argument." The media had, in Tower's words, taken "a somewhat liberal orientation." George Wallace blamed the media for intimidating good Americans from being honest about how they truly felt about race. He described these Americans as "good conservative people who believe in progress . . . but also believe in individual liberty and freedom and . . . the property ownership system." Whenever conservatives tried to discuss these values, he claimed, the "liberal left-wing news media" immediately labeled them racist and ignorant.[27]

As racial violence escalated in 1964 and 1965, *Forum* guests attributed this "radical" turn of the civil rights movement to the anticonservative bias present in earlier coverage of demonstrations. The media had been most helpful, they argued, in cultivating a sense within the black community that they were discriminated against and deserved special treatment. This coverage had begun with the misrepresentation of white resistance in the South and had now resulted in a non-Southern strand of the civil rights movement that was, at its core, antiwhite. Blacks throughout the country, council administrator William J. Simmons argued, had been victims of a "barrage" of newspaper, radio, and television reports touting "so-called discrimination" as the root of civil rights demonstrations. The South had long understood, he continued, that greater forces were motivating these demonstrations. Now that the movement had moved out of the South "where everything that the mind of man could conceive has been done to grant special privileges to the very large

Negro minority there," the media seemed confused as to the causes of such antiwhite bias. Clearly, discrimination could not be the reason.[28]

The smugness with which Simmons and other guests discussed racial violence outside of the South, however, did not last long. In 1965 another wave of violence accompanied a voter registration campaign in Selma, Alabama. The media's coverage of the violence in Selma directly impacted the passage of the Voting Rights Act of 1965, which effectively prohibited state and local governments from obstructing an individual's access to voting because of their race. *Forum* guests immediately blamed the media's presence for inciting the demonstrations and subsequent violence. The situation in Selma had not been adequately investigated in the media's explanation of the events there, they argued, and white Southerners had once again been misrepresented. Alabama congressman James Martin described the confrontation as one that demonstrators carefully orchestrated in order to get media coverage, waiting until cameras were present to "reach the crescendo." Strom Thurmond predicted that racial unrest would continue until the media refused to cover it.[29]

From its inception, council literature blamed liberal media outlets for marginalizing the South by misrepresenting its racial system. When growing civil rights agitation became difficult to deny, however, the media became the actual cause of racial unrest. Different tactics signified the same message, however. In both approaches, as well as the variety of ways in which white resistance has been demonstrated above, denial of black participation was consistent. Despite changing circumstances, proponents of white resistance continued to marginalize the black community as a nonentity. It was white sympathizers—whether acting through the media, abstract federal power, or liberal ideology—who were responsible for enabling the movement. The contested territory during the period of resistance, at least in the eyes of *Forum* guests, was race, but it was not black identity that they chose to confront.

The 1960s saw the cultivation of resistance ideology into a marketable form. The Citizens' Council's reputation as the leading white resistance organization in the South during this period obscures the breadth of activity in which it invested. It fought civil rights activity successfully on the local level and obstructed progress in Mississippi for several years. Despite this delay, racial change came to its birthplace. The passage of landmark legislation eliminated state-sponsored discrimination throughout the country and, on the surface, signaled the failure of organized resistance. The process of resisting racial change, however, made much deeper footprints on the political landscape than a simple failure to maintain the racial hierarchy.

The council's public relations campaign sought to sell the message of segregation within a package of conservative values. In marketing its ideology, however, the council had to establish a venue that was representative of nonracial principles that could support its existing system. Denying organic black protest was foundational to these principles. If blacks did not want these changes, however, other causes had to be explained. Institutional culpability filled this void. Civil rights legislation represented federal growth at the expense of individuals. Liberal intellectuals captured both political and scientific theory, marginalizing anyone who disagreed with them. Racial violence was not an escalation of actual black discontent; it was a natural outgrowth of negative coverage of race relations. All of these arguments placed the blame upon white-dominated groups and institutions. More importantly, *Forum* marketed the message that none of these groups was representative of most white people who preferred a common-sense approach to government, politics, and race.

Conservatism became the antidote to these concerns. It represented a hands-off approach that valued individual achievement over government-enforced equality, an approach that comfortably encapsulated white resistance. Conservative spokesmen that appeared on *Forum* did not have to mention race in their definitions of conservatism. Their support of its principles through a white resistance venue, however, was clear in its intent. Conservative ideology welcomed white empowerment, not through the preservation of overt racist tirades but through sophisticated political language that valued the existing system, a system that had historically excluded blacks.

Overtures to conservative ideology had long been exchanged among disaffected Southern Democrats chafing under what they perceived as the excesses of the New Deal. These leaders had a familiarity with its merits that enabled them to carry that message to constituents at a time when white Southern unity seemed uncertain. *Forum* provided an opportunity to promote these ideas to an audience capable of real grassroots change. The actual effect of such attempts cannot be known with any certainty, but the Citizens' Council's investment in public programs like *Forum* went beyond political exchanges to the heart of their greatest hope, the conservative majority.

White resistance did not disappear because its immediate objectives were a failure. Racial polarization persisted in the political atmosphere that emerged during and after the civil rights movement. A number of factors were responsible for this persistence, but the transformation of segregationist ideology into conservative rhetoric is significant in understanding how white identity emerged alongside the arguments for racial equality. By denying black participation in civil rights gains and plotting out political ideology that ignored race altogether, venues like *Forum* enabled white resistance to remain relevant long after the Citizens' Council's publicity campaign ended.

Notes

1. Howard Zinn, *The Southern Mystique* (New York: Simon and Schuster, 1959), 218.
2. For a history of the Citizens' Council, see Neil R. McMillen, *The Citizens' Council: Organized Resistance to the Second Reconstruction, 1954–64*, 2nd ed. (Urbana: University of Illinois Press, 1994).
3. Clive Webb, ed., *Massive Resistance: Southern Opposition to Reconstruction* (New York: Oxford University Press, 2005) provides an anthology of contemporary historiographical perspectives on opposition to the civil rights movement. For more on anticommunism, see Jeff Woods, *Black Struggle, Red Scare: Segregation and Anti-Communism in the South, 1948–1968* (Baton Rouge: Louisiana State University Press, 2004); and Joseph Crespino, *In Search of Another Country: Mississippi and the Conservative Counterrevolution* (Princeton, NJ: Princeton University Press, 2007). Earl and Merle Black, *Politics and Society in the South* (Cambridge, MA: Harvard University Press, 1987); Kari Frederickson, *The Dixiecrat Revolt and the End of the Solid South, 1932–1968* (Chapel Hill: University of North Carolina Press, 2001); and Joseph E. Lowndes, *From the New Deal to the New Right: Race and the Southern Origins of Modern Conservatism* (New Haven, CT: Yale University Press, 2008) discuss white Southern discontent with the national Democratic Party. Matthew D. Lassiter, *The Silent Majority: Suburban Politics in the Sunbelt South* (Princeton, NJ: Princeton University Press, 2006), and Kevin M. Kruse, *White Flight: Atlanta and the Making of Modern Conservatism* (Princeton, NJ: Princeton University Press, 2005) are good recent studies of suburbanization in the South.
4. Lowndes, *From the New Deal to the New Right*, 26–34.
5. Association of Citizens' Councils, "The Citizens' Council" pamphlet (Winona, MS: Association of Citizens' Councils, 1954), cover, 2–3, Citizens' Council of America Collection, Mississippi Department of Archives and History, Jackson, MS.
6. Fred Jones, "Letter to Citizens' Council Members," October 15, 1954, Subject file, Citizens' Council College, Mississippi Department of Archives and History, Jackson, MS; "To All Citizens' Council Members," *The Citizens' Council*, October 1955, 1, Citizens' Council Publications, Special Collections, Mitchell Memorial Library, Mississippi State University.
7. "To All Citizens' Council Members."
8. McMillen, *The Citizens' Council: Organized Resistance*, 118–21; C. E. Powell to Ellett Lawrence, December 14, 1956, Citizens' Council Publications, 1952–1960, Mississippi Department of Archives and History, Jackson, MS; Association of Citizens' Councils, "The Educational Fund of the Citizens' Councils," (Greenwood, MS: Association of Citizens' Councils, 1957), 4, Citizens' Council Publications, 1952–1960.
9. "Council Offers Radio Program," *The Citizens' Council*, December 1957, 4, Citizens' Council Publications, Special Collections, Mitchell Memorial Library, Mississippi State University.
10. "An Airwaves Anniversary," *The Citizen*, February 1963, 2, Citizens' Council Publications, Special Collections, Mitchell Memorial Library, Mississippi State University.
11. E. L. Forrester, "Trend toward Centralization Cause," Citizens' Council *Forum* #5810, 1958, Citizens' Council *Forum* Collection (CCFC), Mitchell Memorial Library, Mississippi State University.

12. Joseph Mitchell, "Welfare Program in Newburgh, #2," Citizens' Council *Forum* #6134, 1961, CCFC.

13. Ibid.

14. W. C. George, "Biology of the Race Problem," Citizens' Council *Forum* #6248, 1962, CCFC; Robert Gayre, "Press Coverage of Race Problem in the Republic of South Africa," Citizens' Council *Forum* #6250, 1962, CCFC.

15. Henry E. Garrett, "The Race Problem Attitudes," Citizens' Council *Forum* #6437R, 1964, CCFC.

16. For examples of conservative intellectual ideology from the 1930s through the 1950s, see Albert Jay Nock, *Our Enemy the State* (New York: William Morrow, 1935); Friedrich Hayek, *The Road to Serfdom* (Chicago: University of Chicago Press, 1944); Ludwig Von Mises, *Omnipotent Government: The Rise of the Total State and Total War* (New Haven, CT: Yale University Press, 1944); and Russell Kirk, *The Conservative Mind: From Burke to Eliot* (Washington, DC: Regnery Publications, 1953). Nancy McClean writes extensively about the connection between Neo-Confederate romanticism and conservative intellectuals, particularly their contributions to *National Review*. See Nancy McClean, "Neo-Confederacy versus the New Deal: The Regional Utopia of the Modern American Right," in *The Myth of Southern Exceptionalism*, eds. Matthew D. Lassiter and Joseph Crespino (New York: Oxford University Press, 2009), 308–30.

17. John Synon, "Civil Rights Bill Opposition," Citizens' Council *Forum* #6342, 1963, CCFC; John C. Satterfield, "Effects of Civil Rights Act on Average Americans," Citizens' Council *Forum* #6346, 1963, CCFC.

18. Harry F. Byrd, "Meaning of 'Conservative,'" Citizens' Council *Forum* #6113, 1961, CCFC.

19. John G. Tower, "Conservative Views vs. Liberal Views (Economy)," Citizens' Council *Forum* #6210, 1962, CCFC; "Conservative Influences in the Government," Citizens' Council *Forum* #6212, 1962, CCFC.

20. John Rousselot, "Is There a Conservative Revolution in American Politics?," Citizens' Council *Forum* #6225, 1962, CCFC.

21. William K. Shearer, "Local Views of Oxford Incident," Citizens' Council *Forum* #6240, 1962, CCFC.

22. George Wallace, "Effect of Kennedy's Sending Federal Troops into Ole Miss on Future National Elections," Citizens' Council *Forum* #6246R, 1962, CCFC.

23. John Satterfield, "Civil Rights Bill," Citizens' Council *Forum* #6345, 1963, CCFC; John Dowdy, "Civil Rights Legislation," Citizens' Council *Forum* #6347R, 1963, CCFC; William K. Shearer, "California's View on the Civil Rights Act," Citizens' Council *Forum* #6404, 1964, CCFC.

24. Strom Thurmond, "Race Problems in the North," Citizens' Council *Forum* #6432, 1964, CCFC; "Causes of the L.A. Riots," Citizens' Council *Forum* #6536, 1965, CCFC.

25. Joe D. Waggoner, "Causes of Riots in the Large Cities," Citizens' Council *Forum* #6538, 1965, CCFC; Joe D. Waggoner, "Racial Riots," Citizens' Council *Forum* #6539, 1965, CCFC.

26. Robert A. Everett, "Centralization of Power," Citizens' Council *Forum* #5809, 1958, CCFC; Noah Mason, "Federal Aid to Education," Citizens' Council *Forum*

#5814, 1958, CCFC; F. Edward Hebert, "High-Ranking Military Officers Taking Jobs with the Defense Department," Citizens' Council *Forum* #6012, 1960, CCFC.

27. Tower, "Conservative Views vs. Liberal Views (Economy)"; George Wallace, "Wisconsin Presidential Primary," Citizens' Council *Forum* #6415R, 1964, CCFC.

28. William J. Simmons, "Trend of Racial Disturbance in Northern Cities," Citizens' Council *Forum* #6431, 1964, CCFC.

29. Armistead Selden, "News Coverage of Selma," Citizens' Council *Forum* #6508, 1965, CCFC; James D. Martin, "Selma," Citizens' Council *Forum* #6509, 1965, CCFC; Strom Thurmond, "Voting Rights Act," Citizens' Council *Forum* #6517, 1965, CCFC.

CHAPTER 2

"Inequality for All and Mint Juleps, Too"

White Social Sororities and "Freedom of Association" in the United States

Margaret L. Freeman

On June 23, 1964, Tom Charles Huston, national chairman of Young Americans for Freedom (YAF), a conservative political activist organization, delivered an address to the national convention of Alpha Gamma Delta sorority in Portsmouth, New Hampshire. A member of Phi Kappa Psi fraternity, Huston spoke passionately about what he termed, "'Operation Greek'—the effort to destroy the fraternity system." He explained that the program was "well financed" and led "by the same prophets of equalitarianism who are dedicated to the extermination of all those institutions and traditions which are part of the American way of life." These alleged enemies of the fraternity system, Huston argued, "clothed" their criticisms "in the sacred garment of 'civil rights.'"[1]

Huston and many others in the white Greek-letter community found themselves on the defensive in the decades following World War II, as they engaged with critics who claimed that sororities and fraternities were discriminatory organizations. While fighting fascist regimes during World War II and subsequently waging a Cold War to ensure the preservation of "American democracy" around the globe, United States leaders had inadvertently trained a spotlight on the racial injustices persisting within the country's own borders.[2] Greek-letter advocates, such as Huston, asserted what they claimed were their constitutional rights of "voluntary association" as a form of rebuttal to those who pressured sororities and fraternities to remove discriminatory clauses from their organizations' constitutions and bylaws. To Huston and other conservative-minded fraternity and sorority members, the federal government and the Supreme Court capitulated to the demands of civil rights activists and the so-called Liberal Establishment during the late 1950s and early 1960s. Federal legislation and Supreme Court decisions in this period fostered a spate of social reforms that seemed to conservatives to threaten to undermine "traditional" social values, including "freedom of association." As a result, Greek-letter advocates became increasingly vocal in their critiques of federal government and Supreme Court "anticonstitutionality," while complaining that the political establishment was operating to deny their individual rights of private property.

The alliance between the national conservative movement and historically white Greek-letter organizations has not received much attention from historians of modern American conservatism, but white sororities and fraternities played a critical role in the formation of a conservative, "color-blind" ideology that combined anti-Communism, patriotism, and defense of property rights in an attempt to maintain the racial status quo. As a fraternity alumnus, Huston's outspoken opposition to federal interference in intimate social relations and matters of private property reflected the ideology that the National Panhellenic Conference (NPC), the umbrella organization for the 18 white, national social sororities, had been proclaiming for more than a decade.[3] In line with other conservative thinkers of the period, many of whom regularly contributed to the *National Review*, Huston and other Greek-letter alumni feared that US leaders and "liberal" interest groups were stripping Americans of their individual rights, forcing a national policy of collectivism, and leading the nation down the road to Communism.

The Formation of the NPC's Conservative Ethic

NPC sororities reacted to the increased attention to civil rights in the United States in the years following World War II by adopting a conservative platform and outlook that influenced national sororities' subsequent policy decisions and their member education programs. The NPC's hard-line anticommunist and pro-America stance, its insistence on individual freedoms, and its disdain for US federal government intervention in what it viewed as private matters paralleled the rhetoric of the growing conservative intellectual movement of the late 1950s and early to mid-1960s. Like many conservative leaders, the NPC used its appeals for rights and freedoms to disguise its interest in maintaining social segregation of the races.[4] Both Greek-letter groups and conservatives would find a haven for these beliefs in the South, as massive resistance to federally mandated desegregation propelled many white Southerners toward the conservative movement.[5]

Throughout the twentieth century, national sororities fought against criticisms that they were elitist organizations. In an effort to "sell" their groups to campus administrators and potential pledges, sororities claimed to offer specific social training designed to create "graceful ladies." In the post–World War II period, these training programs explicitly extended their goal to include the manufacture of good citizens. Amid prevailing beliefs that Communism posed an immediate threat to American society, sororities' national officers created programs of citizenship training within sorority chapters to teach their members to champion the "all-American" values of individual freedom, private property rights, free enterprise, and adherence to the Christian faith. The sorority alumnae, who served as national officers and NPC delegates, disseminated their propaganda throughout their respective national organizations. In effect, through their educational programs and membership policies, which taught that power and privilege were reserved for a select few, national sororities defined acceptable US citizenry as composed of white, and for the most part Protestant, members of the middle and upper classes.

The NPC and its member groups designed their policies to be implemented on a national scale, meaning that college sorority members and alumnae in chapters all across the country would learn that conservative beliefs were integral to the existence of their sororal organizations. As early as 1949 the NPC emphasized, in reference to "freedoms" guaranteed by the US Constitution and the Bill of Rights, that it was "vital that educated women understand and have convictions about these fundamental rights in American democracy."[6] Sorority alumnae painted their critics as Communist-influenced civil rights "agitators," as they envisioned their national organizations as crucial participants in a showdown between democracy and Communism. At the same time, sororities' use of patriotic appeals to explain what they saw as their "fundamental right" to segregate removed the issue of race from discussions of sorority membership policies. While alumnae were the architects of this conservative propaganda, they imparted their messages to college members through their sororities' educational programming.

In the late 1940s, the NPC formed the Research and Public Relations Committee, primarily to deal with what NPC leaders termed "'discrimination' hysteria." In 1949, amid congressional debate over the Federal Employment Practices Commission (FEPC) bill proposed by President Harry S. Truman, the NPC committee reiterated the "facts about so-called discrimination," tracing it to FDR's initial establishment of the FEPC by executive order in 1941 and the resultant "agitation . . . over jobs in industry . . . at the close of the war." This federal power to investigate charges of discrimination, the NPC explained, "broadened to include jobs in government" and "recognition in public or semi-public groups." Eschewing any public racial animosity, however, the committee took pains to frame its argument in race-neutral rhetoric, stating, "The heart of discrimination is not racial but an effort to preserve deeply rooted American freedom." They claimed that Greek-letter groups were "private groups of friends as private as a family." They held that the organizations did not "choose [their] friends on the basis of disliking others," and asserted that "the right to choose our friends and associates is the most dynamic private right in our democracy. The forces trying to destroy that right want to destroy democracy."[7]

For the NPC and for many white Southerners, further evidence of "discrimination hysteria" would come from three Supreme Court decisions, handed down on June 5, 1950: *Sweatt v. Painter*, *McLaurin v. Oklahoma State Regents*, and *Henderson v. United States*, all of which outlawed forms of racial segregation. The rulings in the first two cases concerned professional and graduate education, while the third dealt with railway dining cars. The legal decisions signaled a shift in social norms, as understood by many white Southerners as well as the NPC, and helped to solidify, in their minds, the "liberal" position of the Supreme Court. Fearing that the court would continue to overturn provisions for "separate but equal" facilities, white Southerners and the NPC saw their states' rights and private rights, respectively, at stake.[8]

In December 1957, on the heels of the Civil Rights Act of 1957 and the formation of the Civil Rights Commission and three years after (and in response to) *Brown v. Board of Education* (1954), the NPC linked its concerns about Communism and "agitators" critical of sororities in *The NPC Declaration of Freedom*, a pamphlet commenting on individual rights granted by the Constitution. Like many conservatives and Southern segregationists, the NPC believed that these federal legislative and judicial actions unlawfully gave greater power to the federal government to limit activities that the NPC felt were guaranteed by the Bill of Rights. As a result, the NPC women conducted their conservative proselytizing on a more visible level, publishing a pamphlet for members and supporters that asserted the NPC's "responsibility to contribute to accurate and thorough knowledge about the Constitution of the U.S. and the Bill of Rights and to know the ideologies destructive of our Country." First and foremost, the NPC sought to demonstrate that the First Amendment "right of people peaceably to assemble" guaranteed sororities' rights as "voluntary associations" to choose their members. Although left unsaid, the NPC also interpreted this as the right to *deny* membership to those with whom they did *not* wish to associate. The connections made by the NPC among civil rights "agitators," restrictions on freedom for "rightful" citizens, and the role of Communism in this realignment of society were unmistakable.[9]

The NPC Allies with the Conservative Movement

The NPC's shift to a more forthright conservatism, demonstrated by its increasing reliance on conservative literature and willingness to collaborate with conservative groups, signaled sorority alumnae's identification with key aspects of conservative movement ideology. Sororities sought to ally themselves with conservative, patriotic organizations, including the Daughters of the American Revolution, the American Legion's All-American Conference to Combat Communism, and YAF, to publicly demonstrate their commitment to anti-Communism. They also gained access to conservative literature and contacts in the movement. By partnering with such conservative organizations, sororities forged a support network to fight the "liberal" critics who protested sororities' and fraternities' denial of membership to individuals based on race or religion. More important, by framing their critiques of liberal agitators in the rhetoric of the Cold War, sororities were able to link those who challenged their racially exclusive policies to the national threat posed by Communism, effectively removing race from the centerpiece of their calls for "freedom of association."[10]

The NPC drew on materials produced by the conservative movement's increasingly powerful network of intellectuals and organizations devoted to the popularization of conservative thought in post–World War II American politics and society. By presenting conservative magazines such as *Human Events* and *National Review*, along with radio broadcasts such as Clarence "Pat" Manion's *Manion Forum of Opinion*, as important informational sources in the late 1950s, the NPC leaders simultaneously trained their college and alumnae membership to adopt conservative frameworks for engaging the questions of "freedom of association" and "anti-Communism."[11] NPC leaders recited conservative movement ideology nearly verbatim as they reiterated the dangers of Communist infiltration and reminded sorority members and alumnae of the conservative NPC view, which held that "liberal" organizations and individuals were soft on Communism. In addition, they highlighted the importance of individuals' rights and freedoms as "traditional" American values that were integral to the fight against Communism, while pointing to federal interference in those rights and freedoms as movement toward a totalitarian regime in the United States. Significantly, even as the crux of their arguments in support of freedom and democracy hinged on concerns over racial integration, the NPC divorced race from its appeals, thus pioneering a "color-blind" approach in its conservatism.

If the sorority women reading the NPC's *Declaration of Freedom* somehow failed to see that the Research and Public Relations Committee was drawing a connection between civil rights, desegregation, and Communism, a three-page segment of recommended reading and a listing of "creditable organizations fighting to preserve various American fundamentals in accord with the Constitution" directed the women to an extensive listing of books by conservative intellectuals, conservative magazines, and conservative and American patriotic organizations. The pamphlet suggested a number of "special articles and editorials," including several of David Lawrence's "Opinion of the Editor" segments in *U.S. News & World Report* from 1957, titled "Civil Rights that Breed Civil Wrongs," "There Is No Fourteenth Amendment!" and "Illegality Breeds Illegality." In these pieces, Lawrence argued against the overreach of federal power into individual states and posited that instances of military enforcement of school desegregation, which he characterized as federal despotism, were based on illegal precedent and blatant disregard for the Constitution as originally written. Lawrence and other conservative movement leaders also held that the Fourteenth Amendment to the Constitution, which guaranteed rights of citizenship and equal protection under the law, should be "considered null and void" because of their belief that it was ratified by illegal measures during Reconstruction. Thus they contended that the Supreme Court's decision in *Brown v. Board of Education*, which found that segregated public schools were in violation of the Fourteenth Amendment's equal protection clause, was *also* invalid, as they believed the Fourteenth Amendment did not and should not exist.[12]

Significantly, the push by NPC leadership and conservative intellectuals in the mid- to late 1950s to uphold individual rights and protect private property allowed for some whites' engagement in racial discrimination to meet those goals. Many conservatives in this period saw the fight by white Southern segregationists to maintain their states' segregation laws as a prime example of individual rights endangered by the overreach of federal government. Some conservative movement leaders, like William F. Buckley Jr., used blatant white supremacist appeals in support of what they believed was the right of localities to uphold public school segregation in the wake of the *Brown v. Board* decision. Others, such as Buckley's colleague at *National Review* L. Brent Bozell, sought to couch the explosive issue of race in "color-blind" language, just as the NPC did—a tactic that made the conservative agenda palatable to a larger portion of the American population.[13] By moving conservative rhetoric toward the preservation of (white) American rights and freedoms and away from the denial of African American civil liberties, the NPC and conservative intellectuals obscured the critical role of race in their ideology.

The NPC proclaimed its devotion to the cause of the Southern prosegregationists, identifying similarities in their respective situations. In 1957 the NPC included as suggested reading material for its constituents a *National Review* book review and essay by University of Chicago professor and native Southerner Richard M. Weaver, titled "Integration is Communization." Weaver argued that the "racial collectivism" fueled by Communism was "being used as a crowbar to pry loose rights over private property." In a *National Review* article from 1960, Nashville Agrarian Donald Davidson explained that the Supreme Court would "not stop with school desegregation" and that "every section, North or South" was "under a threat that would not lift" until conservatives came together to "take action."[14] The NPC, having concluded that the next step in the attack would be the prohibition of sororities' and fraternities' abilities to privately choose their own members, would stand with conservatives against that threat.

Since the early 1950s, a number of university students and administrators across the United States had been pressuring their campuses' Greek-letter groups to remove their discriminatory membership clauses.[15] The NPC viewed the gains by "liberal" agitators, described in Weaver's essay, as a sign that the federal government was increasingly overstepping its bounds to interfere in the private lives of US citizens. As a result, the NPC feared that the federal government would give critics of Greek-letter groups the necessary legal power to undermine sorority and fraternity membership policies. Reports from meetings of the NPC and the individual sororities during this period demonstrate the alumnae's widespread belief that critics who questioned the organizations' membership selection or threatened "freedom of association" must be soundly refuted.[16]

In 1952, as an offshoot of her work for the Research and Public Relations Committee, Chi Omega alumna and Pennsylvania native Mary Love Collins formed the Edgewater Conference, a group that led the fight to uphold discriminatory membership clauses. An organization composed of sorority and fraternity alumni from a number of NPC and National Interfraternity Council (NIC) member groups, the conference first met at the Edgewater Beach Hotel in Chicago, Illinois, where they passed a conference resolution stating that the organization held "the common interest of the belief in the inherent values of collegiate fraternal organizations and the right of self-determination in the selection of members thereof."[17]

Edgewater participants saw Communism "as the basis of [their] trouble" and clearly connected it to forced racial integration as well as to a breakdown of what they understood as their freedom of choice as American citizens. Set in their belief that social integration of the races was "the ultimate end and the ultimate goal" of the "so-called liberals" and "campus authorities . . . who enforce[d]" nondiscrimination by Greek-letter groups and other student organizations, Edgewater members hoped to devise legal means to challenge those critics who wanted Greek-letter groups to do away with the discriminatory clauses. Harking back to ideas expressed in *Plessy v. Ferguson* (1896), which had established that the Fourteenth Amendment's equal protection clause did not extend to social arenas, the alumni tried to make an important distinction in their closed membership by stating that there was "nothing undemocratic" or unconstitutional about discrimination on any basis in "purely social realms." "Such discrimination shows only that we prefer to associate with *our own kind*, and it does not show that we desire to deny anyone a natural right" (emphasis mine), explained a lawyer speaking to the group in 1953. His reasoning, which was shared by Southern segregationists and many conservative writers of the period, identified segregation as an individual right. Indeed, leaders of the conservative movement emphasized this position by the 1950s as part of their scheme to appeal to the interests of white Southerners.[18]

Conservative intellectuals, Southern segregationists, and NPC leaders cloaked the issues of civil rights and racial discrimination in the language of the Red Scare, suggesting that anyone advocating for social equality likely had Communist tendencies. In the early 1950s, the Research and Public Relations Committee created the All-American Conference to Combat Communism. Spurred on by the American Legion's All-American Conference, the NPC formed its committee to "inform those with whom we come in contact, of the national danger of communism." The committee sent NPC delegates a newsletter containing lists of books, magazines, and pamphlets that might aid the sororities in presenting the lessons of anti-Communism to their members and urged their assistance in the "nation wide crusade." The newsletter recommended as useful tools in the crusade *The Coming Defeat of Communism* (1950) by James Burnham, who would soon become a regular contributor to *National Review*; anticommunist literature written by former members of the Communist Party; and a pamphlet titled *New List of Subversive Organizations*, prepared and released by the House Committee on Un-American Activities in 1951.[19]

While sororities' national leadership sought to shield their members from liberal influences in the name of anti-Communism, the leaders' primary concern was that sorority women might begin to view their organizations' membership restrictions as morally wrong and as a result seek to change the membership selection system. In particular, the NPC members and their male counterparts in the NIC saw the National Student Association (NSA), an organization that sought to secure equal rights for all students, as a distinct threat to their restrictive membership clauses. The NSA sat left of conservative organizations, but it was not the Communist front group suspected by the NPC and NIC. In the fall of 1962, a Duke University sorority woman wrote to thank the NPC's area advisor for hosting her as a guest during the summer and for "letting [her] read the NSA material."[20] Quietly, behind the scenes, NPC delegates and sororities' national officers fed anti-NSA propaganda to trusted college sorority women and chapter officers to disseminate throughout the collegiate membership.

While the NPC feared that any organization standing up for equal rights could threaten the membership selection processes of sororities, some associations, conventionally understood as "liberal," remained in the favor of the

NPC. In 1949, the NPC still approved of the Federal Council of Churches and the United Nations (UN), even though both organizations were moving to support human rights. "In both cases," the committee noted, the organizations had "declare[d] against discrimination in jobs, in government, and in the administration of law, but both declare[d] *for* the right of association" (emphasis mine). As late as 1957, the NPC remained an accredited observer at the UN and sent a delegate to Women United for United Nations, but these may have been strategic placements to keep an eye on UN activities. The NPC, like conservative movement leaders, was highly suspicious of the UN. Both groups saw the United States' membership in the UN as a yielding of American autonomy and believed that other nations could use the UN's influence to press for changes in US domestic affairs. In particular, many conservatives feared that the UN could somehow force desegregation of schools and social establishments in the United States at the desire of foreign countries, which again betrayed the underlying racial fears in their suspicions of statism.[21]

The circulation of conservative thought within the sorority community flowed from the NPC and its committees to the national leadership of each sorority and down to the regional alumnae and college chapter levels. At a Kappa Kappa Gamma national convention around 1960, the program included a "Leadership School" organized by Mary Turner Whitney, Kappa's NPC representative, and Edith Reese Crabtree, chair of the Fraternity Research Committee. A young woman leaving "the protection of home and college today," Crabtree noted, "will enter a world full of problems. There will be choices to be made, and her wisdom in making these choices will depend upon her ability to think for herself after she has the facts in hand." The "facts," presented by Whitney and Crabtree, detailed the conservative NPC position, which saw Greek-letter groups as being under attack by "pressure groups trying to drown out the voice of reason" with the "ultimate goal" of destroying the fraternity system and eroding American freedom. The women closed their session with "one more word from Senator [Barry] Goldwater's *Conscience of a Conservative*," which suggested that Goldwater's 1960 book, an influential tract for grassroots conservatives, had been a key text at the Kappa convention. "If they were made aware of the facts," Whitney and Crabtree quoted Goldwater, "all thinking Americans would recognize the extreme seriousness of the impending danger to the survival of American Freedom."[22]

The Conservative Movement Supports Greek-Letter Organizations

Writers and organizations associated with the conservative movement took up the cause of sororities' and fraternities' "freedom of association," presenting the groups as prime examples of private entities whose rights of private property were under attack by "liberal" critics and the federal government. In 1957 conservative commentator Russell Kirk had written a two-part essay in the *National Review* titled "In Defense of Fraternities." Although not a fraternity alumnus, Kirk stood up for the groups' rights to private membership. "Regardless of your feelings and my feelings toward Negroes, Jews, and Catholics, it is not you and I who have a right to say what qualities a fraternity should establish for membership." In addition, Kirk argued, "If a fraternity should admit *only* Negroes, Jews, and Catholics, you and I—taking us as members of the general public— would have no right to object . . . For a fraternity is not public property." Following this logic, Kirk contended that, like the general public, a college administration also did not "ordinarily have a right to regulate the conditions of membership in fraternities."[23]

By the 1960s, the newly formed YAF spoke directly to Greek-letter groups about the importance of standing up for their "rights" as private organizations. A supposedly nonpartisan, conservative, youth organization formed under the auspices of William F. Buckley Jr. in 1960, YAF shared the NPC's and NIC's critique of the NSA as a liberal agitator. Tom Charles Huston, a young fraternity alumnus from Indiana University, became YAF's national chairman in 1965. He traveled to many fraternity and sorority national conventions and was a featured speaker at the NPC's annual convention that year. Huston's rhetoric spoke to the fears of sorority alumnae who wanted to keep their associations closed to the types of people they felt would damage the reputation of the entire group. In his 1964 speech to Alpha Gamma Delta's national convention, Huston referred to the NSA as the "left-wing confederation of college and university student governments," directing the "anti-Greek drive . . . in the name of civil rights." With the NSA portrayed as the "radical" enemy, YAF joined the NPC and the NIC in their attempts to remove campuses from NSA affiliation.[24]

The YAF and the *National Review* also appealed to college sorority and fraternity members. In January 1964 Buckley wrote a piece in the *National Review* about his university speaking tour. He noted a recent trip to the University of Texas where a "typical day" of meeting with a political science class, debating at the law school, and having coffee at a professor's home also included lunch at a sorority as well as an evening meeting at a fraternity. Indeed, Buckley was also lodged at a fraternity house during his visit.[25] Buckley's apparent welcome by sororities and fraternities during his speaking tour suggests that they may have been integral in booking his speaking engagements and that members may have learned from their organizations that they should be supportive of Buckley's views as well as those of other conservatives who spoke out about the rights of individuals to maintain private property and to associate only with those whom they chose.

The "Color-Blind" Rhetoric of the NPC and the Conservative Movement in the 1960s

The NPC firmly embraced a conservative ethic by the early 1960s, expanding its critiques of the civil rights movement and suspected Communist activity in the guise of "color-blind" ideology, while looking to the South as a model of resistance in the fight to preserve discriminatory membership practices. The Research and Public Relations Committee worked to keep NPC delegates and their respective sororities abreast of current events, composing internal briefings on US domestic and foreign policy issues from a decidedly conservative viewpoint. The committee's news briefing from April 18, 1960, covered items such as the recent 1960 Paris Summit, UN resolution 1514 on decolonization in Africa, and "sit-ins" in the United States organized by the Congress of Racial Equality (CORE) and the National Association for the Advancement of Colored People (NAACP), all issues that the committee members clearly viewed with skepticism. To the committee, these developments signaled that "liberal" forces were exerting undue influence on the American public and their governing officials.

In line with conservative and American nationalist ideology that promoted a strong US military and encouraged limits on US involvement in international coalitions, the NPC found fault with the American foreign and domestic policy decisions of the Eisenhower Republicans, whom it deemed too liberal and too willing to cede American power on the world stage. A meeting between President Dwight D. Eisenhower and Soviet Premier Nikita Khrushchev at the 1960 summit, conservatives believed, would show that the United States was willing to negotiate with Communists. The NPC's committee report explained, "It is thought by some well-informed persons that 'The Summit' will scheme disarmament which would be fatal to our country." Like the NPC, many conservatives and segregationists believed that any sign of cooperation with the Soviets could signal a move toward the United States' infiltration, and eventual domination, by Communist forces. Such an event, these groups feared, would result in the end of states' rights and private property and organizations and—most important—would eliminate their ability to exclude individuals from schools, businesses, or clubs on the basis of race, if they so desired. Thus, in their estimation, Communism was at the heart of the current civil rights agitation in the United States.[26]

The NPC committee viewed the UN's work to secure human rights throughout the world as a harbinger of things to come in the United States. The committee report obliquely referred to the UN "resolution on Africa," which the committee termed "an internal matter." The resolution (1514) sought to uphold freedom and equal rights by "granting independence to colonial countries and peoples" throughout the world, an exercise in judgment that the NPC committee felt should be left to the colonial government and not accorded to an external governing body. Echoing the concern of conservatives at *National Review* who feared that the UN could pass resolutions enforcing racial integration in the Southern United States, the committee approached the resolution with alarm, asking, "Is that a prelude to what the UN could do in any one of the states of the United States?"[27]

In the US domestic realm, the Research and Public Relations Committee alerted delegates to the developments by civil rights "agitators" to reinforce the need for a continued defense against these "attacks" on national sororities' "freedoms." The committee likened student sit-ins organized by CORE and the NAACP to "student revolutionary activities in foreign countries," which, they argued, "reflected *political* forces." Meanwhile, the committee scoffed at press releases that revealed the NAACP's intention to use the First Amendment right of citizens "peaceably to assemble" to defend those arrested in sit-in activities. The NPC saw the invocation of the Bill of Rights by those whom it believed were guilty of attempting to destroy American freedom and the rights of private individuals as an ironic turn of events. In discussing the sit-ins, the committee again proposed a link between civil rights activism and Communism, noting a "wire by twenty-four persons to the President asking whether it would be necessary to appeal to the UN, a la the UN Resolution in the case of Africa," as evidence of "red influences to the 'sit-ins.'" Concluding their report, the committee noted what was, for them, a ray of hope in the midst of disinformation perpetrated by what they saw as "the Communist press with its own interpretations and its mastery of the technique to create confusion!" "Fortunately," the committee wrote, "great numbers of Americans find refreshing the clarity of U.S. Senator Barry Goldwater in his speech [to] the Senate, March 15, [1960]. He calls his words 'hard counsel'—the choice between freedom and surrender."[28]

While some conservative writers initially adhered to racist arguments in their defense of individual rights, by the early 1960s they had softened their rhetoric to espouse a race-neutral strategy. By shifting their talking points away from race and segregation and toward anti-Communism and a concentration on individual rights and freedoms, the conservative movement was able to gain greater support outside the South. Employing the race-neutral approach, the NPC and conservative writers publicly explained their efforts to preserve "freedom of association" as beneficial to *all* citizens, regardless of race, and not as intended to deny the rights of any individual or group. By upholding "freedom of association," they reasoned, Americans would ensure the primacy of the Constitution and the continuation of the freedoms it granted to all citizens. The "freedom of association" argument, however, still catered to whites interested in maintaining their freedom to keep from associating with African Americans and maintaining their privileged position in relation to them. While this appeal drew many Southern whites to the conservative movement, it likewise galvanized white citizens across the nation who feared the supposed loss of their own "rights" to minority groups who pressed to receive their fair share of constitutionally granted civil rights. Properly dispensed, the "color-blind" rhetoric, used by the NPC leaders since the late 1940s, would enable conservatives to gain a foothold at the grassroots level and issue a serious challenge to take over the GOP by the mid-1960s.[29]

The 1960s were a highly contentious time for Greek-letter organizations, as the federal government and university administrations sought to enforce nondiscrimination by sororities and fraternities. Like conservative movement leaders who saw mid-twentieth-century white Southerners as an untapped conservative force awaiting mobilization, the Edgewater Conference—and NPC and NIC groups in general—perceived sorority and fraternity chapters at Southern universities as the last line of defense against the federal incursions. Members considered chapters at the remaining segregated universities in the South to be the last strongholds of conservative sentiment.

In a February 11, 1964, editorial for the University of Georgia (UGA) student newspaper, the *Red and Black*, staff writer Neil Aronstam lampooned the image of UGA sororities by drawing parallels between the exclusive membership practices of the groups and the white supremacist legacy of the Old South. In the satirical piece, Aronstam interviewed the president of the fictional "Alpha Alpha" sorority, who explained that the organization was founded "just after the War of Northern Aggression on the principles of 'inequality for all and mint juleps, too.'" She noted that the sorority "has striven throughout the years to maintain the same standards, traditions, and outlooks that our forefathers had during the South's most glorious era." When Aronstam asked if she "didn't feel that was a bit outdated," she responded by "muttering something about damnyankees."[30] Clearly, however, to an increasing number of Americans who identified as conservatives, this veneration of the South and its system of social hierarchy was not outdated in the least.

With Southern university campus culture largely mirroring that of Southern society in general, social segregation of the races in Greek organizations seemed almost certain to continue indefinitely. Questioned about any problematic developments at the UGA during the 1960 Edgewater Conference, one member responded, "Down in that general area I don't think we need to be concerned too much, although that is not an absolute assurance we can dismiss it."[31] For the most part, national fraternity and sorority alumni felt confident that their Southern chapters were safe from liberal critics who might influence university officials to investigate membership restrictions. On the other hand, colleges and universities in non-Southern regions of the United States that had already been desegregated or had always been open to nonwhite students appeared to produce the most discussion at the Edgewater meetings. Conference members, who continued to use their "color-blind" rhetoric of individual freedom of choice to hide their segregationist agenda, believed that chapters at these schools would be the first to face serious challenges to their membership selection practices.

With the passage and enforcement of the Civil Rights Act of 1964, the federal government demonstrated a commitment to ending discrimination and desegregation in higher education. For conservatives, the 1964 act was yet another federal signpost on the road to a communistic society. Initially, the Meader amendment to the Civil Rights Act had prohibited interference in the functioning of private organizations, including sororities and fraternities. In 1965, however, Francis Keppel, US commissioner of education, made it clear that the Civil Rights Act charged individual universities with the task of eliminating discrimination by their campuses' Greek-letter societies. Citing Title VI of the act, which disallowed federal funding to programs or activities that fostered discrimination on the basis of race, color, or national origin, Keppel announced that he would cut federal funding to universities that allowed fraternities to continue discriminating on the basis of race.[32]

In order to comply with Keppel's enforcement of Title VI, universities would have to ensure that no student organizations allowed discriminatory clauses. In the cases of Greek-letter groups, university administrators requested assurances from national sorority and fraternity officers that their respective organizations' constitutions and bylaws were free of clauses that restricted membership on the basis of race. In doing so, the universities also attempted to convince themselves that by simply asking sororities and fraternities to affirm that their membership selection processes were not bound by discriminatory clauses, they could eliminate racial discrimination by the groups. In reality, a national sorority could claim that their organization did not have any discriminatory clauses even while adhering to an unwritten policy of barring blacks or Jews from membership.

By the mid-1960s, for example, Chi Omega had removed all discriminatory clauses from its constitution and bylaws, but as Guion Griffis Johnson, a traveling advisor for the sorority, explained, "[T]he [Chi Omega] Governing Council still insists upon 'the right to choose its own members' as guaranteed by the Bill of Rights of the Federal Constitution and withdraws chapters rather than give in on this point." This meant that Chi Omega's unwritten rule on discrimination remained in effect. Johnson thought it was "foolish to lose chapters on this basis" and noted her belief that both Mary Love Collins and Elizabeth Dyer (who became Chi Omega's national president in 1952) were "reactionary persons who are using 'the right to choose' as a stick with which to fight off integration."[33]

In the late 1960s, fraternity members in YAF complained that the NPC and NIC had failed to successfully coordinate their efforts against critics of Greek-letter groups. The image of fraternities as "a snooty bunch of beer drinkers, party goers, and woman chasers" and of sororities as a snobbish group of women who condoned and supported this behavior had tainted the system in the minds of many Americans. As a result, college administrators were shutting down chapters at "name colleges." "That is the way we lost the Ivy League," one national fraternity officer noted. "You know as well as I do we are losing ground in the North and parts of the Midwest and West; and the East is practically gone. The South alone remains loyal and true."[34] Even chapters in the South, where social conservatism thrived, had to comply with their universities' new regulations or face expulsion from campus. National sororities and fraternities found it necessary to adapt their constitutions to remove discriminatory membership clauses, even if it did not actually mean changing their behavior.

While some college sorority and fraternity members exercised opinions on social equality issues that were at odds with the rhetoric espoused by their national leaders and alumni, Greek-letter groups, by and large, attracted more conservatively oriented students.[35] Even if women joined a sorority without a particular political or ideological affiliation, the NPC and national sorority leaders worked to ensure that members received the lessons of citizenship according to a conservative worldview. At the 1964 World's Fair in New York, the NPC and the NIC sponsored an exhibit on the college sorority and fraternity titled "Free Enterprise in Action." By choosing this key tenet of conservatism as the theme for their representative display, Greek-letter groups underscored their continued fight to uphold rights of private property. "These voluntary organizations," the exhibit's pamphlet read, "represent the true spirit of free enterprise. They bring together young people of diverse interests, working toward a common goal."[36] That common goal, the NCP and NIC seemed to hope, was the popularization of conservative social and political agendas that were also favorable to Greek-letter groups. Through their publicly apolitical but ideologically conservative organizational platforms, sororities conditioned members to accept a common worldview that championed individual liberties for a select few and thereby assured their continued existence as restrictive membership groups.

Notes

1. Tom Charles Huston, "Operation Greek: The Attempt to Destroy the American Fraternity System," in Tom Charles Huston, "Fraternities and Freedom," 1965, 7–8, "Young Americans for Freedom, 1965, 1967–1968" folder, box 19, Wilson

Heller Papers, 1937–1984 (41/2/52), Student Life and Culture Archives (SLC), University of Illinois at Urbana-Champaign (UIUC).

2. Mary L. Dudziak, *Cold War Civil Rights: Race and the Image of American Democracy* (Princeton, NJ: Princeton University Press, 2000), 6–11.

3. The NPC formed in 1902 as a way for the national sororities to handle issues arising from rushing season. It became a conference where sorority alumni from the various national groups could discuss issues of mutual concern. Each national sorority that held a membership in the NPC had an alumnae delegate to the organization. The chairmanship of the NPC rotated among the member sororities.

4. Joseph E. Lowndes discusses this practice by writers at *National Review* and within the 1964 Barry Goldwater presidential campaign in *From the New Deal to the New Right: Race and the Southern Origins of Modern Conservatism* (New Haven, CT: Yale University Press, 2008), 44, 51–57.

5. Recent studies such as Kevin Kruse, *White Flight: Atlanta and the Making of Modern Conservatism* (Princeton, NJ: Princeton University Press, 2005); Matthew Lassiter, *The Silent Majority: Suburban Politics in the Sunbelt South* (Princeton, NJ: Princeton University Press, 2006); and Joseph Crespino, *In Search of Another Country: Mississippi and the Conservative Counterrevolution* (Princeton, NJ: Princeton University Press, 2007) illuminate the importance of race in the mobilization of grassroots conservatism in the South. For a party-level analysis of race as it influenced the Southern political shift toward the conservative movement and the GOP, see Lowndes, *From the New Deal to the New Right*. George Lewis, *The White South and the Red Menace: Segregationists, Anticommunism, and Massive Resistance, 1945–1965* (Gainesville: University Press of Florida, 2004) shows how Southern white supremacists used anticommunist rhetoric to remove race from debates over segregation policies.

6. NPC Proceedings, 1949, 117, box 1, record series NPC Proceedings, 1902–1989, 1994–1998, 2000–2001 (41/82/10), National Panhellenic Conference (NPC) Archives, SLC, UIUC.

7. NPC Proceedings, 1949, 116–18.

8. Numan Bartley, *The Rise of Massive Resistance: Race and Politics in the South During the 1950s* (Baton Rouge: Louisiana State University Press, 1967), 37–38.

9. "The NPC Declaration for Freedom," December 1957, "Declaration for Freedom, 1957" folder, box 1, NPC Fraternity Affairs File (41/82/9), NPC Archives. Lowndes argues that white supremacists gravitated toward conservatism as a means to combat what Southern white supremacist Charles Wallace Collins described as "the dual dangers of 'Negro equality and State capitalism.'" See Lowndes, *From the New Deal to the New Right*, 1–10 (quotation, p. 2).

10. George Lewis, "White South, Red Nation: Massive Resistance and the Cold War," in *Massive Resistance: Southern Opposition to the Second Reconstruction*, ed. Clive Webb (New York: Oxford University Press, 2005), 122.

11. "The NPC Declaration for Freedom." On the Manion Forum, see Rick Perlstein, *Before the Storm: Barry Goldwater and the Unmaking of the American Consensus* (New York: Hill and Wang, 2001), 3–16.

12. David Lawrence, "'Civil Rights' That Breed 'Civil Wrongs,'" *U.S. News & World Report*, July 19, 1957; David Lawrence, "There Is No 'Fourteenth Amendment'!"

U.S. News & World Report, September 27, 1957, quotation from p. 139; David Lawrence, "Illegality Breeds Illegality," *U.S. News & World Report*, October 4, 1957; and Nancy MacLean, "Neo-Confederacy versus the New Deal: The Regional Utopia of the Modern American Right," in *The Myth of Southern Exceptionalism*, ed. Matthew D. Lassiter and Joseph Crespino (New York: Oxford University Press, 2010), 318–19.

13. MacLean, "Neo-Confederacy versus the New Deal," 312–13; William F. Buckley Jr., "Why the South Must Prevail," *National Review*, August 24, 1957; Donald Davidson, "The New South and the Conservative Tradition," *National Review*, September 10, 1960; Richard M. Weaver, "The Regime of the South," *National Review*, March 14, 1959; and L. Brent Bozell, "The Open Question: Mr. Bozell Dissents from the Views Expressed in the Editorial, 'Why the South Must Prevail,'" *National Review*, September 7, 1957.

14. Richard M. Weaver, "Integration Is Communization," *National Review*, July 13, 1957; Matthew D. Lassiter, "De Jure/De Facto Segregation: The Long Shadow of a National Myth," in *The Myth of Southern Exceptionalism*, 29; and Davidson, "The New South."

15. In particular, the "Michigan Plan" became the standard adopted at many universities by the 1960s. The plan, which had been proposed by the University of Michigan's student legislature in 1950, required that fraternities and sororities remove discriminatory clauses from their constitutions by a certain date (usually within five years) or face removal from campus. For example, the University of Chicago had set October 15, 1954, for its deadline, while the University of Wisconsin and Columbia University aimed for removal by July and October 1960, respectively. Southern universities typically set the deadlines for their campuses' Greek-letter groups to remove discriminatory clauses within a year or two of the universities' racial desegregation. See Alfred McClung Lee, *Fraternities without Brotherhood, A Study of Prejudice on the American Campus* (Boston: Beacon Press, 1955), 62–68, 72–73.

16. Annadell Craig Lamb, *The History of Phi Mu: The First 130 Years* (Atlanta: Phi Mu Fraternity, 1982), 65–66; Genevieve Forbes Morse, *A History of Kappa Delta Sorority, 1897–1972* (Springfield, MO: Kappa Delta Sorority, 1973), 251–52; and Report of the 31st National Panhellenic Conference, 1949, 22–23.

17. Edgewater Conference Resolution, "Edgewater Conference (J. B. Baird), 1967–1982," folder, box 13, Wilson Heller Papers (41/2/52), SLC, UIUC.

18. Edgewater Conference Minutes, 1962, 26, box 1, Edgewater Conference File, 1953–1993 (41/93/31), SLC, UIUC; Edgewater Conference Minutes, 1953, 26; Bartley, *The Rise of Massive Resistance*, 28–57; Pete Daniel, *Lost Revolutions: The South in the 1950s* (Chapel Hill: University of North Carolina Press for Smithsonian National Museum of American History, 2000), 241; Kruse, *White Flight*, 9; Lassiter, *The Silent Majority*, 26–30; Crespino, *In Search of Another Country*, 81–83; Lowndes, *From the New Deal to the New Right*, 54–68; and MacLean, "Neo-Confederacy versus the New Deal," 316.

19. Lewis, *The White South and the Red Menace*, 47–50; Crespino, *In Search of Another Country*, 49–57; and "News Letter," [1951?], "All-American Conference to Combat Communism, 1951–1962" folder, box 1, NPC Fraternity Affairs File (41/82/009),

NPC Archives. The House Committee on Un-American Activities report cited was released May 14, 1951.

20. "United States National Student Association," 1950–1951, "All-American Conference to Combat Communism, 1951–1962" folder, box 1, NPC Fraternity Affairs File, 1941–1985 (41/82/9), NPC Archives; Duke Sorority Woman to Eileen Rudolph, September 28, 1962, box 2, Duke Panhellenic Council Records, 1936–1993, Duke University Archives, Duke University. In fact, since 1952, the financially strapped NSA had been funded by the U.S. Central Intelligence Agency in an effort to deter the group from accepting Communist subsidies. See "NSA Contemplates Its Shattered Image," *Washington Post*, February 20, 1967; Eugene G. Schwartz, ed., *American Students Organize: Founding the National Student Association after World War II: An Anthology and Sourcebook* (Westport, CT: American Council on Education/Prager Publishers, 2006), 219; and J. Angus Johnston, "The United States National Student Association: Democracy, Activism, and the Idea of the Student, 1947–1978" (PhD diss., City University of New York, 2009), 226.

21. NPC Proceedings, 1949, 118; NPC: An Historical Record of Achievement," (c. 1957), NPC Archives, NPC Publications (41/82/800), box 1, SLC, UIUC, 15; Lisa McGirr, *Suburban Warriors: The Origins of the New American Right* (Princeton, NJ: Princeton University Press, 2001), 176–79; "From the NPC-RPA Committee," April 18, 1960, "NPC Research and Public Relations Committee, 1957–58, 1960" folder, box 1, NPC Committee File (41/82/50), NPC Archives; and Sam M. Jones, "It Could Happen Here," *National Review*, December 28, 1955, 2.

22. "Dedicated to What?" n.d. [c. 1960], Stewart Howe Papers (26/20/30), box F-28, Kappa Kappa Gamma, Historical Clippings, SLC, UIUC.

23. Russell Kirk, "In Defense of Fraternities: Part II," *National Review*, May 18, 1957.

24. Gregory L. Schneider, *Cadres for Conservatism: Young Americans for Freedom and the Rise of the Contemporary Right* (New York: New York University Press, 1999), 32–33; Huston, "Fraternities and Freedom," 8; and "NSA Contemplates Its Shattered Image."

25. William F. Buckley Jr., "What Johnny Doesn't Know," *National Review*, January 14, 1964.

26. McGirr, *Suburban Warriors*, 67–68; "From the NPC-RPA Committee," April 18, 1960; and Lowndes, *From the New Deal to the New Right*, 49.

27. "Resolutions Adopted by the General Assembly During Its Fifteenth Session," Dusan J. Djonovich, ed., United Nations Resolutions, Series I: Resolutions Adopted by the General Assembly. (Dobbs Ferry, NY: Oceana Publications, 1974), 3:188–89; Jones, "It Could Happen Here," 2; and "From the NPC-RPA Committee," April 18, 1960.

28. "From the NPC-RPA Committee," April 18, 1960.

29. MacLean, "Neo-Confederacy versus the New Deal," 320; McGirr, *Suburban Warriors*; Lowndes, *From the New Deal to the New Right*, 55–70; Kruse, *White Flight*; Lassiter, *The Silent Majority*; and Crespino, *In Search of Another Country*.

30. Neil Aronstam, "Southern Sorority Toured," *Red and Black*, February 11, 1964.

31. Edgewater Conference Minutes 1960, 52.

32. Anthony James, "The Defenders of Tradition: College Social Fraternities, Race, and Gender, 1945–1980" (PhD diss., University of Mississippi, 1998), 102–4;

Nicholas L. Syrett, *The Company He Keeps: A History of White College Fraternities* (Chapel Hill: University of North Carolina Press, 2009), 256; and Wallace Turner, "Colleges Face U.S. Aid Cutoff If They Permit Fraternity Bias," *The New York Times*, June 18, 1965, 1, 24.

33. Guion Johnson to Mrs. Judson D. [Alice] Willis Mease, March 3, 1964, "Chi Omega Correspondence, 1964" folder, box 32, series 3.1, Guion Griffis Johnson Papers, Wilson Library, University of North Carolina at Chapel Hill.

34. "In Our Image," n.d., "YAF, 1965, 1967–1968" folder, box 19, Wilson Heller Papers (41/2/52).

35. Alfred McClung Lee suggests that the opinions of national fraternity and sorority leadership were not representative of the total membership of the groups. Those alumni who sought leadership roles were "caricatures of the worst aspects of the system and are completely wedded to the fraternity *status quo*." Students who wished to change membership standards had little recourse, for the alumni leaders kept the organizations tightly controlled. See Lee, *Fraternities without Brotherhood*, 13; and Syrett, *The Company He Keeps*, 237.

36. "Free Enterprise in Action," 1964, "Publications on Fraternities and Educational Associations, 1952–57" folder, box 1, NPC Fraternity Affairs File (41/82/9), NPC Archives.

CHAPTER 3

"Build, Baby, Build"

Conservative Black Nationalists, Free Enterprise, and the Nixon Administration

Joshua D. Farrington

"Black Americans who believe in jobs rather than welfare; who want a piece of the action, not a part of the dole, who want a political leader who does not promise more than he can deliver, do have somewhere to go," Floyd McKissick, the former national director of the Congress of Racial Equality (CORE) and one of the nation's most instantly recognizable faces of Black Power, told a group of African Americans in a fall 1972 campaign speech. The place he insisted they turn was to "the President of the United States, Mr. Nixon." The story of McKissick and other conservative nationalists and black businessmen has been left out of almost all the scholarly literature on the conservative movement that arose in the 1960s; the conventional historiography suggests that Barry Goldwater and the Southern Strategy left the Republican Party a lily-white wasteland that was anathema to any self-respecting African American. Similarly, the traditional narrative of Black Power has tended to portray it as a movement exclusively of the radical Left.[1]

In recent years, however, conservative nationalists and other black supporters of Richard Nixon and the Republican Party in the late 1960s and early 1970s have been the subject of some of the most innovative studies of the Black Power movement. The works of Thomas Sugrue, Manning Marable, Robert Weems, and Devin Fergus have revealed convincing evidence of not only the existence of conservative strains within Black Power but also their vitality in shaping the Republican Party's domestic initiatives. There has been little dialogue, however, between scholars of the white conservative movement and historians of Black

Power. Though they never represented a majority of African Americans, conservative black nationalists and their supporters in the black business community were an influential force that helped shape Richard Nixon and the Republican Party's domestic policy agenda—a force that included hundreds of millions of dollars directed toward black businesses.[2]

The black capitalism movement of the late 1960s drew on a black entrepreneurial spirit that had existed since the beginning of slavery. During the antebellum period, freed slaves like "Free Frank" McWhorter, when given the means and opportunity, created their own self-sufficient towns and communities. After the Civil War and Reconstruction, Booker T. Washington served as a conservative and pragmatic voice in black political life, advocating a bootstrap philosophy that appealed to both the dignity of black men and women and also to white Southerners who found comfort in its accommodationist nature. During the 1910s and early 1920s, Marcus Garvey proclaimed black self-reliance as the key to racial advancement. Garvey's central message of "race first" particularly applied to black-owned businesses. He called for self-determination and encouraged his followers to work within the capitalist system to create and support black stores, banks, insurance companies, and other business ventures. Though socialists and Communists denounced him as a "petty bourgeois misleader," Garvey's Universal Negro Improvement Association (founded in 1914) grew to over two million members by the early 1920s.[3]

By the time of the Great Depression of the 1930s, economic Garveyism, like all forms of conservatism, had fallen out of favor among most African Americans, who embraced the Democratic Party and New Deal liberalism as the solution to their economic plight. Though some African Americans continued to vote for the Republican Party through the rest of the 1940s and 1950s, the presidential election of 1964 resulted in the desertion of most remaining loyalists. Goldwater, who voted against the Civil Rights Act of 1964 and promised that he would "bend every muscle to see that the South has a voice in everything that affects the life of the South," received strong support from white Southern segregationists. At that year's Republican National Convention, there were almost one hundred members of the ultraright John Birch Society serving as delegates, compared to only 14 African Americans (who represented less than 1 percent of the total number of delegates). Because Goldwater embraced a philosophy that sheltered segregationists and made no effort to welcome African Americans, his conservatism was rejected almost unanimously by African Americans across the country. On Election Day, an estimated 95 percent of African Americans voted for Lyndon Johnson.[4]

Many Americans viewed the election as a significant turning point by a nation that had firmly committed itself to the ideals of liberalism. These same Americans were stunned the following year in the wake of the widespread destruction of the Watts neighborhood in Los Angeles. Occurring only days after the signing of the Voting Rights Act—the ultimate triumph of the civil rights movement and American liberalism—many white Americans were confused by the black community's continued anger and frustration. Just as many whites would be driven to embrace a conservative "law and order" philosophy as the decade of the 1960s continued, the failure of mainstream liberalism in solving deep-seated racial inequalities drove many blacks to embrace versions of militant Black Power that ranged from far-left Marxism to a conservative embrace of the free enterprise system.

Though *Black Power* remains the defining term in characterizing black political activism in the mid- to late 1960s, it was an elastic concept that covered a plethora of ideologies, ranging from the revolutionary nationalism of the Black Panthers to the conservative nationalism of black capitalists. Conservative black nationalists drew on the self-help ideology of Booker T. Washington and Marcus Garvey and joined with many members of the black business community in rejecting liberalism and integration as failures, instead embracing self-determination and "black capitalism" as the solutions to the economic woes of African Americans.

The first major indication that conservative black nationalism had become a viable tenet of black political thought came at the 1967 Black Power Conference in Newark, New Jersey. The conference was organized by one of the ideological leaders of conservative black nationalism, Nathan Wright. A former Episcopalian priest, Wright formed a consulting firm in the late 1960s called Empowerment Associates, and later become the founding chairman of the department of African and Afro-American studies at the State University of New York at Albany. Attracting 1,300 attendants, the conference concluded with a statement demanding that blacks get a "fair share of American capitalism." The emerging notion of "black capitalism" was fully embraced the following year at the 1968 Black Power Conference in Philadelphia. Again organized by Nathan Wright, who had established ties to white corporate society in part because of his affiliation with the Republican Party, the conference was officially sponsored by a white-owned company, Clairol. Like many white Republicans, Wright railed against welfare and integration as the answers to problems faced by black communities. Calling integration "an insult on its face" because it implied black men needed whites to progress, Wright called for black control of black communities, particularly their businesses. Instead of accepting welfare from the white-dominated government, the only assistance that blacks should accept from white America was that which furthered the black community's ability to serve itself. Echoing the rhetoric of many white conservatives, Wright argued that "all men should have some kind of responsibility . . . before they receive any money. Earning for self spells dignity."[5]

Like Wright, other black Republicans also endorsed black capitalism. Massachusetts senator Edward W. Brooke, who in 1966 became the first African American elected to the US Senate since Reconstruction, consistently pressed the Johnson administration to include greater emphasis on self-reliance and business initiatives in its Great Society programs. During his first year in the Senate, Brooke endorsed the nascent black capitalism movement and called for the Small Business Administration (SBA) to focus on black businesses and significantly increase their grants and loans to black entrepreneurs. Also in 1967, Arthur Fletcher, a lifelong Republican who would later become one of the most powerful African Americans in the Nixon Administration, organized the Self-Help Cooperative Association in East Pasco, Washington. By 1968, the association, which was funded by blacks themselves, had built a service station, begun construction on a shopping center, and formed its own credit union to fund future business endeavors. According to Fletcher, the goal of the organization was to ease black dependence on federal assistance and to teach "people what they can do for themselves."[6]

Another grassroots supporter of black capitalism was Harlem's Cora T. Walker. Running as the Republican Party's candidate in a 1964 state senate race, Walker's campaign emphasized self-help and was highly critical of what she perceived as black welfare dependency. During the Nixon years, Walker further solidified her conservative credentials by opposing busing, arguing that residents of Harlem should maintain and attend their own separate schools. In 1972 she appeared alongside Senator James L. Buckley, who had recently been elected on the Conservative Party ticket, on a slate of Republican National Convention delegates approved by the Manhattan Republican Organization.[7]

Prominently displaying a picture of herself with Malcolm X in her home, Walker was an unflinching advocate of black self-determination, once telling a reporter that African Americans "must begin to own some of this real estate called Harlem." In 1967, she spearheaded the creation and opening of the first black-owned supermarket in Harlem. By 1968, Walker had sold five-dollar shares to 2,550 individual shareholders (98 percent of whom lived in Harlem) and opened the 10,000-square-foot Harlem River Cooperative Supermarket. At its grand opening, one shopper remarked that the air-conditioned grocery store—which featured automatic doors, soft music, and fluorescent lighting—was "lovely" and that "you don't find this except in the suburbs."[8]

On the national level, the venerable civil rights institution CORE was the most vocal and prominent organization to support black capitalism in the late 1960s. Floyd McKissick succeeded James Farmer as national director in 1966. Unlike Farmer, who was a mainstream liberal, McKissick represented the emerging radicalism of the civil rights movement by the mid-1960s. A Durham, North Carolina, lawyer and former Freedom Rider, McKissick was a personal friend of Malcolm X, served as a lawyer for the Nation of Islam, and embraced the economic self-help ideology of the religion's leader, Elijah Muhammad. He was also the favorite candidate of CORE's nationalist members, second only to Stokely Carmichael as the most recognizable national advocate of Black Power. Under McKissick's leadership, CORE moved its national office from downtown Manhattan to Harlem, dropped the term "multiracial" from the organization's constitution, and drove out leading white members.[9]

Like the left-wing advocates of Black Power, McKissick believed the root of the problem in African American communities was economic. However, unlike Black Power's left wing, McKissick attacked welfare, claiming that "handouts are demeaning. They do violence to a man, strip him of dignity, and breed in him a hatred of the system." In opposition to the Marxism advocated by the Black Panther Party and others, who McKissick claimed only wanted "to tear down, burn down, [and] destroy," black capitalism was CORE's solution to African Americans' economic plight. In the words of Clarence Hodges, the chairman of the organization's St. Louis branch, their embrace of black capitalism meant "[B]uild, baby, build."[10]

McKissick left CORE in the fall of 1968 to focus exclusively on promoting black capitalism through his own consulting firm, McKissick Enterprises. Headquartered in Harlem, the company started a job-training consortium and funded the creation of black-owned restaurants, a shopping center, a publishing company, and numerous other business ventures. In an introductory brochure, McKissick wrote that the solution to "Black America's struggle" was "for Economic Power and Self-determination . . . These bring respect to those who gain them." McKissick then assailed liberalism, noting that while "many of the efforts [had] been sincere," they had not been successful and that "additional millions poured into unplanned poverty programs and welfare will not solve the dilemma posed by our ghettos." Instead, "the best solution" was self-reliance, personal responsibility, and "Black Economic Independence." Instead of receiving the "leftovers in the kitchen" (welfare), African Americans "want to sit at our own table and carve the financial turkey with all its trimmings." Whether one agreed with it or not, argued McKissick, capitalism was a reality in America. Rather than attempting to reform the economic system, as many on the Left sought to do, blacks had "no alternative at this time other than full participation as entrepreneurs."[11]

After McKissick's departure from CORE, an equally conservative black nationalist, Roy Innis, took the helm of the organization that was by 1968 the loudest advocate of black capitalism. Born in Saint Croix, Innis moved to Harlem as a small child and frequently compared himself to another Caribbean-born leader—Marcus Garvey. In 1968 Innis and CORE submitted the "Community

Self-Determination Bill" to various congressmen and the Republican National Convention. Among its numerous recommendations, the bill attacked welfare, which Innis believed created "perpetual serial welfare recipients" who had lost their dignity and self-respect because they did not work for what they earned. Innis's bill argued that blacks should form a "partnership" with the "private enterprise system and the independent sector" to promote and invest in the future of black businesses. The bill called for the federal government to encourage and provide assistance in the "establishment of community development corporations, community development banks, and other supporting programs and provisions in order to mobilize the talents and resources" of black communities. Though the bill was introduced by 36 Republican congressmen—and was endorsed by Richard Nixon, who played a prominent role in its initial drafting—it failed to find widespread support from the Democrat-controlled congress. However, the failure of the bill did not weaken CORE's attachment to conservative black nationalism, and by October 1969 it had created model economic development programs in Cleveland and Baltimore. According to Innis, "[T]he total thrust of CORE's endeavors to build a viable and positive black minority [was] directed toward self-help bootstrap efforts."[12]

Much of the rhetoric of conservative black nationalists paralleled that of many conservatives in the Republican Party, particularly in its denunciation of welfare. The handful of African Americans in the official party apparatus had contacts with black communities that white politicians did not have, and they were vital in bringing the notion of black capitalism to fellow Republicans. Clarence L. Townes Jr., head of the Republican National Committee's Minority Division, spoke before a Republican urban workshop in Washington, DC, and described the new focus of his department: "Never before has the Negro community been more insistent upon self-determination; and the Minorities Division presents the Republican philosophy to the Negro community's leadership in this light." In order to reach those disillusioned with liberal programs and policies, Townes advocated that the party promote "individual self-determination." Moreover, the only way for black capitalism to succeed would be for the white leadership of the Republican Party to join with conservative black nationalists and for both sides "to work together for their common interests."[13]

Through the prompting of Clarence Townes and other African American Republicans, Richard Nixon became the first white politician to embrace black capitalism on the national stage. Indeed, by the end of 1968, Nixon was the only presidential candidate to openly endorse the term "Black Power." Because of the fluidity of "Black Power" and the disenchantment of many African Americans with traditional liberal answers to racial conflict, Nixon believed he could form an alliance between conservative nationalists, black businessmen, and white Republicans, who all placed a similar emphasis on self-reliance.[14]

In March 1968 Nixon first stated his support for "Black Power," which he defined as "the power that people should have over their own destinies, the power to affect their own communities." The following month, in an April 25 radio address, he put forth his proposal and endorsement of black capitalism. He first attempted to pacify the concerns of white listeners by suggesting that "much of the black militant talk these days is actually in terms far closer to the doctrines of free enterprise than to those of the welfarist '30s" in its usage of the "terms of 'pride,' 'ownership,' private enterprise,' 'capital,' 'self-assurance,' [and] 'self-respect.'" Nixon further argued that new emphasis should be placed on "black ownership" and promised a new age of Black Power "in the best . . . constructive sense of that often misapplied term." If African American communities controlled their own small businesses and had local control of their own schools, then the country would see a "rebirth of pride and individualism and independence." This rhetoric was almost identical to the language used by McKissick, Innis, and other conservative black nationalists. According to James Farmer, the former leader of CORE who later accepted a position in Nixon's administration, Nixon's speech was a "supreme act of co-optation" in taking up the banner of Black Power by appealing to its most conservative strain.[15]

Despite Nixon's fears of being "skinned for this in the South," the only significant Southern conservative to express skepticism toward black capitalism was Strom Thurmond, who later argued that it was hard to support a program "whereby a businessman who is a member of the minority race is to be given preferential treatment." However, many conservative whites were quick to embrace the program as an alternative to traditional liberal responses to civil rights. The *National Review* declared that "hard work and self-discipline" were the keys to black economic betterment and praised Booker T. Washington for teaching that "respect and access to jobs must be earned by the Negroes themselves." Barry Goldwater declared before the Republican National Convention that his party would offer not liberal "pie-in-the-sky" promises but a real chance at "a piece of the action." He further stated his ardent support for "people power," be it "Black power, white power, green power, red, white and blue power . . . [O]ur Republican administration—will unleash all of *that* power." Numerous corporations like Clairol, the sponsor of that year's Black Power Conference, also embraced black capitalism as the safe alternative to the more militant demands of left-wing Black Power advocates. The basic principles behind black capitalism appealed to the worldview of mainstream American society whereby one could achieve the American dream through hard work, determination, and personal accountability. It also provided a way for blacks to play a greater part in the free market economy without forcing integration upon white neighborhoods and school districts.[16]

Less than a month after delivering his radio address endorsing black capitalism, Nixon met with McKissick and Innis in his New York apartment. During the private meeting, Nixon endorsed CORE's Community Self-Determination Act and restated his support of black capitalism. True to his word, Nixon later provided CORE two of his staffers to help shape the direction of the bill. His law firm helped draft its most legally technical sections, and Nixon himself pressed many conservative Republicans to cosponsor the legislation when it was brought to the House. Throughout the rest of the campaign, neither McKissick nor Innis publicly endorsed Nixon, but they frequently praised his support for black capitalism. When asked on *Meet the Press* if he supported Nixon, Innis remarked that he had "no choice for President" but was careful to add, "I praise Nixon when he said that black nationalism is relevant . . . I praise him when he endorses CORE's plan." Even without an explicit endorsement it was clear that Innis favored the Republican candidate. The militant black publication *Liberator* even noted, "The conservative is the natural ally of the moment for the Black man. Today, as Roy Innis of CORE has attested to, only Richard Nixon is . . . hospitable to Black Power."[17]

Nixon continued to advocate black capitalism through the rest of the campaign. In September he made an appearance in North Philadelphia alongside Leon Sullivan, who had long called for local government to provide job training and financial assistance to black entrepreneurs and businesses, at the only major black-owned shopping center in the country. The Nixon-Agnew Campaign Committee also purchased a two-page advertisement in *Jet* magazine on November 7, 1968. The first page featured a photograph of a young black man in a college setting holding a stack of books ("Homer Pitts"). The second page asked where he would work after getting his degree: "laborer . . . factory job . . . or his own business?" It then stated, "A vote for Richard Nixon for President is a vote for a man who wants Homer to have the chance to own his own business. Richard Nixon believes strongly in black capitalism. Because black capitalism is black power in the best sense of the word . . . And that's what the free enterprise system is all about."[18]

Though more than 80 percent of African Americans voted for Hubert Humphrey, the estimated 12 to 15 percent of the black vote garnered by Nixon was a marked improvement from Goldwater's showing four years earlier. It also revealed that while there was a sizable group of conservative black nationalists, the bulk of black political thought remained on the side of traditional liberalism or the militant Left. Indeed, following Nixon's support of black capitalism, the idea was widely criticized by the nation's left wing. The AFL-CIO denounced it as "a dangerous, divisive delusion." Black Panther Eldridge Cleaver called the program's supporters "puppets" of colonialists who promised them a "vested interest in the capitalist system." The militant publication *Soulbook* referred to conservative black nationalism as "cullud [*sic*] nationalism" and concluded that "their seeming militancy . . . can only be interpreted as 'loud-mouth' conservatism." Bayard Rustin argued that black capitalism's adherents "are not progressive," and Roy Wilkins opposed black capitalism on the grounds that it would replace white exploiters with black counterparts.[19]

Regardless of opposition by mainstream black leaders, the Nixon administration lived up to its promise to conservative black nationalists and adopted numerous programs to expand black capitalism. Less than two months into his presidency, Nixon signed Executive Order 11458, creating the Office of Minority Business Enterprise (OMBE) to carry out his policy of black capitalism and to expand "the free enterprise system at all levels." The agency was to provide information and training to black businessmen and entrepreneurs and, most important, to provide them with needed capital and loans. According to Nixon, the OMBE's main goal was to "encourage pride, dignity and a sense of independence" in black communities.[20]

Though the OMBE struggled to find adequate leadership and funding throughout its first year, it became a viable program by the early 1970s due to the diligence of African Americans inside and outside of the Nixon administration. After initial worries over limited funding for the OMBE, McKissick turned to Robert Brown to press the administration to live up to the promises of the executive order. Brown, Nixon's liaison with the black community, was a former public relations man from High Point, North Carolina, who had previously worked with McKissick in the state's CORE branch. Throughout the rest of 1969, Brown was relentless in convincing influential cabinet members like Leonard Garment and Maurice Stans of the importance of supporting the OMBE. Outside of the administration, black businessmen also pressed the administration to provide greater resources to its black capitalism efforts. *Black Business Digest* endorsed the OMBE's objectives and reminded Nixon that "the ultimate answer is not in the Welfare System but in programs of self-help—revenue-producing systems rather than revenue-draining programs." The most influential group, however, was the National Business League (NBL). Founded by Booker T. Washington in 1900 as a self-help organization that promoted black businesses, the NBL grew exponentially under Berkeley Burrell's leadership in the late 1960s. During the Nixon administration, Burrell, a Republican and successful entrepreneur, secured millions of dollars in OMBE grants to the NBL and by 1972 served as vice chairman of the OMBE's Advisory Council. By the mid-1970s, the NBL had expanded to 113 chapters (up from 30 chapters in 1962), and had a total membership of more than 10,000. Called by one contemporary an "updated version" of Booker T. Washington, Burrell was an adamant proponent of bootstrap self-help. He advised blacks to embrace the self-reliance ideology of the Republican Party because "every businessman is a Republican . . . Get up early and work hard—that's what the Republican party is all about."[21]

Through continued pressure by conservative nationalists and black business-men, the OMBE's budget grew exponentially from 1970 to 1974. In 1970 the program's budget was just more than $1 million; by 1972 its operating budget was $43.5 million. By 1974 the OMBE was operating at more than $91.3 million annually. Moreover, by pooling the resources of other federal agencies, particularly the Small Business Administration, the amount of loans and guar-antees given to black businesses through the OMBE rose from $20 million in 1969 to more than $400 million by 1971. The OMBE also guided many exist-ing businesses through the maze of procuring federal contracts, and by 1973 the federal government had purchased more than $200 million in black-owned services and products. The administration also worked outside of the OMBE to further its agenda of black capitalism. Through another executive order, Nixon expanded black-owned banks by waiving restrictive bank-chartering safeguards, and by the end of 1971 the government had deposited more than $100 mil-lion in banks owned by blacks. So prevalent was the notion of black capitalism in the political consciousness of the early 1970s that one of the decade's most watched television shows, *The Jeffersons*, featured a black Republican and self-made businessman from Harlem, George Jefferson. The show's theme song, "We're Movin' on Up," epitomized the hopes that many conservative national-ists and businessmen had placed in black capitalism.[22]

While the majority of the focus of Nixon's black capitalism programs tar-geted small businesses, Floyd McKissick obtained the support of the admin-istration for one of the most ambitious endeavors of the late 1960s and early 1970s: "Soul City." McKissick first proposed the project in January 1969. The idea was to create a model city where blacks controlled all the town's businesses, courts, utilities, and real estate. The town was established in Warren County, North Carolina, an ideal place for the grand experiment of black capitalism and self-determination. It was a majority-black rural county and one of the poorest in the state. McKissick believed that would-be investors would flock to the city to tap into the region's large supply of cheap labor and that African American entrepreneurs would welcome the chance of operating in a black-owned city. Though the fate of Soul City rested in the hands of the federal government, which could provide the needed financial incentives to attract businesses to the area, McKissick bought the first two thousand acres through a personal loan. Indeed, most of the costs of the entire project were paid by McKissick Enter-prises, which invested and borrowed more than $1 million for the city.[23]

In his campaign to receive federal funding for Soul City, McKissick contin-ued to appeal to the antiwelfare conservatism and self-help philosophy of many white Republicans. In fact, he had publicly switched his party affiliation from independent to Republican and formed the first official Republican Party orga-nization in Warren County. In addition to black control of the city's businesses, he also advocated the idea of "sweat equity" in order to provide the county's poor blacks affordable housing. Through this program, the home's future owner would provide his own labor to cut down on construction costs. Further appealing to the national and state Republican Parties, he openly embraced North Carolina's right-to-work laws. So adamant was McKissick in his promotional brochures that the city would be free of unions that Bayard Rustin publicly chastised him for using A. Philip Randolph's name on the city's massive industrial park. Rather than seeking to appease his liberal critic, McKissick simply renamed the structure "Soul Tech." By the end of 1969, McKissick had placed the stakes of Soul City in the hands of his Republican allies, promising President Nixon, North Carolina's Republican governor, and Republican National Committee chair George H. W. Bush that a political and economic investment in Soul City could grow the party exponentially among black voters over the next twenty years.[24]

Robert Brown and Samuel C. Jackson, both in frequent contact with McKissick, pushed for executive support of Soul City from their positions as leading African Americans inside the Nixon administration. Additionally, from the Senate, Edward Brooke served as one of the project's most adamant supporters. Brown claimed that the city "would be one of the great achievements of the American free-enterprise system" and would free those "held in bondage as the present welfare system has done and still does." Inside the Department of Housing and Urban Development (HUD), Jackson helped secure hundreds of thousands of dollars in grants to Soul City during its early development.[25]

Powerful white members of the Nixon administration were swayed by the pressure and arguments used by Soul City's black supporters. In a private memo to HUD officials, Leonard Garment, special assistant to the president, advised, "If we say 'no' to McKissick, we will stand accused not only of reneging on specific commitments to him, but of reneging on the President's commitment to the whole minority enterprise concept . . . We should give Soul City the green light." The director of the OMBE, John Jenkins, told McKissick that "Soul City can make a tremendous contribution to minority enterprise and to the total welfare of black people" and instructed him to "let me know of your needs and I will form the various groups to assist you with Soul City."[26]

The program received significant support from the executive department. In fact, by 1972 it was the largest publicly financed project ever developed by an African American and was the first new town not affiliated with another urban area to receive a federal loan guarantee. In July 1972, HUD secretary George Romney signed off on a $14 million guaranteed loan for Soul City. Over the course of the following three years, HUD provided grants for the creation of a health care company, a sewage system, and a water plant. Republican support continued throughout the rest of the decade. By the end of the Gerald Ford administration, approximately $8 million of state and local funding had been diverted to Soul City by the state's Republican governor, on top of more than $19 million in federal investments.[27]

The election of 1972 represented the peak of the relationship between conservative black nationalists and the Republican Party. One black delegate to the Republican National Convention (RNC) told President Nixon, "This is the first time since my efforts in your behalf of 1960, that I believe that there is a real break through to ge[t] the Black vote." The number of black RNC delegates had increased 115 percent from four years prior, which was the largest increase since Reconstruction. African Americans represented at least 10 percent of the delegations of Southern states like Arkansas, Louisiana, and Virginia, and five states had a higher percentage of black delegates than the percentage of blacks in their state's population. Though the number of African American representatives at the Democratic convention still far outnumbered those at the Republican convention, the increased number of black faces on the convention floor was a visible sign of the tentative alliance of conservative nationalists, black businessmen, and Richard Nixon.[28]

By the time of the election, McKissick had also become one of the Republican Party's most recognizable black supporters. No longer silent regarding his support for Nixon, as he was in 1968, McKissick contended that "Self Determination is a goal that the Republican Administration understands . . . The Democrats are still talking about *old goals*, not those of Self Determination." That year, McKissick served alongside Berkley Burrell on the Black Executives Advisory Committee of the Committee to Re-Elect the President (CREEP) and campaigned across the country on behalf of Nixon, wearing a "'72 Self-Determination" lapel button that pictured a solid black version of the GOP elephant surrounded by the black, red, and green stripes of the Pan-African flag. *The New York Times* and *Chicago Tribune* both went so far as to claim that McKissick was a "chairman emeritus of President Nixon's campaign organization."[29]

One of the largest campaign events for black supporters was a June fundraising dinner in Washington, DC, sponsored by the National Black Committee for the Re-Election of the President. More than 2,500 African Americans attended the $100-per-plate dinner to express their support for Nixon's black capitalism program. Prominent attendees to the fundraiser included the president of Malcolm X College, Charles G. Hurst; baseball star Jackie Robinson; football player and actor Jim Brown; and Betty Shabazz, the widow of Malcolm X. Lionel Hampton provided the entertainment, creating a new dance step called "the Nixon" to accompany his song "We Need Nixon." McKissick delivered the main address. The former farm boy from North Carolina told the audience that African Americans had too long "been sucking the sugar tit" of the Democratic Party and labor unions. "If you were a Southerner, and you knew what a sugar tit really is," he continued, "it ain't milk—it is a substitute for milk, and it's a pacifier, and it is something that makes you think you have got something when you ain't got it."[30]

In addition to gaining the endorsement of James Brown and other influential black luminaries, Nixon also earned the endorsement of 30 percent of the country's African American newspapers and magazines, including the *Cleveland Call and Post, Atlanta Daily World, Oakland Post,* and *Black Business Digest.* However, after Election Day, it was apparent that the majority of African American voters could not embrace the Republican candidate. While a few select cities went above the national average (for instance, 30 percent of Louisville's blacks voted for Nixon), only an estimated 13 percent of African Americans nationwide cast their ballots for him. This was only a marginal improvement from Nixon's showings in 1968. Though favored by many conservative nationalists and black entrepreneurs, Nixon's record on black capitalism was not enough to sway the vast majority of other African American voters, who remained committed to traditional liberalism and were leery of his Southern strategy and poor record on a number of other domestic issues.[31]

From today's vantage, the legacy of black capitalism is mixed. Many African American entrepreneurs, such as Elaine Jenkins, claim that "black business thrived under the Nixon Administration." In the 1980s, 64 of the 100 largest black corporations had been founded after 1970, and the total number of black-owned banks had more than doubled from 21 in 1970 to 45 by 1975. On the other hand, even at the height of administration support for black capitalism, black-owned companies represented only 1.7 percent of the gross income of all American businesses. The types of businesses supported by black capitalism were usually small and could not compete with the ever-expanding corporate structure of American society. In 1972, only 26 black businesses profited more than $5 million, and the largest one hundred black businesses combined would have ranked two hundred and eighty fourth on *Fortune 500*'s list of American corporations. While black capitalism did help many individual black entrepreneurs, the small-business nature of most black endeavors was inadequate to address the economic woes that plagued African American communities.[32]

The fate of Soul City as the 1970s progressed is particularly revealing of trends that broke the alliance between conservative black nationalists and the Republican Party. First elected in 1972, North Carolina Senator Jesse Helms was part of a new wave of conservative white politicians who rejected public funding for black capitalism. As a freshman senator in 1975, Helms called for an investigation into and audit of the expenditures of McKissick and Soul City, accusing them of the "greatest single waste of public money that anyone in North Carolina can remember." Though the General Accounting Office cleared both McKissick and Soul City of any major misconduct, the damage had already been done, and private funding for the already tenuous project came to a standstill. Finally, in 1979, under the leadership of Jimmy Carter—who had no political need to appease the Republican McKissick—HUD pulled all of its promised funds from Soul City, leaving it helpless to attract future investors.[33]

The miles of weed-lined paved roads and cul-de-sacs void of houses, the empty buildings in the multiacre industrial park, and the other skeletal remains of Soul City reflect the promise and failure of the relationship between black capitalists and whites in the Republican Party. By the early 1980s, the OMBE no longer existed and McKissick had abandoned the GOP to become chairman of the Warren County Democratic Party. Though Ronald Reagan attempted to revive black capitalism by creating the Minority Business Development Agency, the agency's average budget was barely half of what the OMBE's had been a decade prior under Nixon. Moreover, by the early 1990s, numerous programs requiring federal agencies to conduct business with minority companies had been ruled unconstitutional by the Supreme Court—a court that was largely constructed by Nixon and Reagan.[34]

Though the relationship between conservative nationalists and the Republican Party diminished from its heyday under Richard Nixon, stalwarts like Roy Innis and Nathan Wright continued to endorse Ronald Reagan, George H. W. Bush, George W. Bush, and other Republican candidates through the 2000s. In 2011, Innis continued to work behind the scenes in conservative circles, serving on the executive board of the National Rifle Association and establishing ties to the black presidential primary candidate Herman Cain. Cain, whose political action committee donated an estimated $100,000 to CORE, was the keynote speaker at that year's annual dinner honoring Martin Luther King Jr. After Cain temporarily achieved front-runner status in the early polls of fall 2011, Innis praised the candidate as representing "an idea that was trying to be expressed for a long time" by conservative black nationalists.[35]

Despite black capitalism's limitations, conservative black nationalists were a significant force in the late 1960s and early 1970s that temporarily united a conservative segment of Black Power to the nascent white conservative movement, a partnership that still reverberates into the twenty-first century. Conservative black nationalists were not members of the "Silent Majority," but their alliance with Richard Nixon and the Republican Party transformed the direction of the Congress of Racial Equality and helped direct hundreds of millions of dollars to black-owned businesses.

Notes

1. The author would like to thank Amanda Higgins and Megan Powers, who both went out of their way to assist with the development of this essay. "Statement— F. B. McKissick," September 1, 1972, folder 7638, Floyd B. McKissick Papers #4930, Southern Historical Collection of the University of North Carolina at Chapel Hill and the African American Resources Collection of North Carolina Central University; Manning Marable and Leith Mullings, *Let Nobody Turn Us Around: Voices of Resistance, Reform, and Renewal* (Lanham, MD: Rowman and Littlefield, 2000), 373; Rick Perlstein, *Nixonland: The Rise of a President and the Fracturing of America* (New York: Scribner, 2008); Matthew Lassiter, *Suburban Politics in the Sunbelt South: The Silent Majority* (Princeton, NJ: Princeton University Press, 2006); Peniel E. Joseph, *Waiting 'Til the Midnight Hour: A Narrative History of Black Power in America* (New York: Henry Holt, 2008); Jeffrey Ogbonna Green Ogbar, *Black Power: Radical Politics and African American Identity* (Baltimore: Johns Hopkins University Press, 2004).

2. Thomas Sugrue, *Sweet Land of Liberty: The Forgotten Struggle for Civil Rights in the North* (New York: Random House, 2008); Robert Weems Jr., with Lewis A. Randolph, *Business in Black and White: American Presidents and Black Entrepreneurs in the Twentieth Century* (New York: New York University Press, 2009); Devin Fergus, *Liberalism, Black Power, and the Making of American Politics, 1965–1980* (Athens: University of Georgia Press, 2009); Manning Marable, *Race, Reform, and Rebellion: The Second Reconstruction and Beyond in Black America, 1945–2006*, 3rd ed. (Jackson: University of Mississippi Press, 2007); Manning Marable, *Black Liberation in Conservative America* (Boston: South End Press, 1997).

3. Hanes Walton Jr., "Black and Conservative Political Movements in U.S.A.," *Political Science Review* 10 (July–December 1971): 107; Louis Harlan, *Booker T. Washington: The Wizard of Tuskegee, 1901–1915* (New York: Oxford University Press, 1986); Theodore G. Vincent, *Black Power and The Garvey Movement* (Baltimore: Black Classic Press, 2006).

4. Robert Alan Goldberg, *Barry Goldwater* (New Haven, CT: Yale University Press, 1995), 154–55, 202, 233; Hanes Walton Jr. and Robert C. Smith, *American Politics and the African American Quest for Universal Freedom*, 2nd ed. (New York: Longman, 2003), 142.

5. Douglas Martin, "Nathan Wright Jr., Black Power Advocate, Dies at 81," *The New York Times (NYT)*, February 24, 2005; "Nathan Wright Jr.," *Los Angeles Sentinel*, March 24–30, 2005; Marable, *Race, Reform, and Rebellion*, 95; Ashraf H. A. Rushdy, *Neo-slave Narratives: Studies in the Social Logic of a Literary Form* (New York: Oxford University Press, 1999), 52, 95–96; Marcus Pohlmann, *Black Politics in Conservative America*, 2nd ed. (New York: Longman, 1999), 270; Nathan Wright Jr., "The Social Arena of Black Political Action," in *What Black Politicians Are Saying*, ed. Nathan Wright Jr. (New York: Hawthorn Books, 1972), 200–201; Nathan Wright, Jr., *Let's Work Together* (New York: Hawthorn Books, 1968), 94–95.

6. Edward Ashbee, "The Republican Party and the African-American Vote since 1964," in *Black Conservatism: Essays in Intellectual and Political History*, ed. Peter Eisenstadt (New York: Garland, 1999), 237; Edward W. Brooke, Speech to the Annual Convention of the National Insurance Association in New Orleans, LA,

July 19, 1967, Clarence L. Townes Jr. Papers, Special Collections and Archives, James Branch Cabell Library, Virginia Commonwealth University; "Art Fletcher: His Self-Help Program Works," *Ellensburg [WA] Daily Record*, August 6, 1968; Lawrence Davis, "Negro's Hopes Rise in Coast Race for Lieutenant Governor," *NYT*, October 19, 1968; "Negro Wings State Primary on Coast," *NYT*, September 22, 1968.

7. "Cora Walker Pushing Bid for 21st Senatorial Seat," *Pittsburgh Courier*, April 18, 1964; "Black Profile," *Sacramento Observer*, May 14, 1970; "Cora T. Walker, Pioneering Female New York Attorney, Succumbs at 84," *Jet*, August 7, 2006, 35; "Cora Walker, 84, Dies," *NYT*, July 20, 2006; Constance Baker Motley, *Equal Justice Under Law: An Autobiography* (New York: Macmillan, 1999), 206; Martha Biondi, *To Stand and Fight: The Struggle for Civil Rights in Postwar New York City* (Cambridge, MA: Harvard University Press, 2003), 24, 284; Thomas Ronan, "Buckley Is Named as G.O.P. Delegate," *NYT*, April 12, 1972.

8. "A Great and Mighty Walk for Cora Walker," *New York Amsterdam News*, February 11, 1999; "Residents of Harlem Open Their Own Supermarket," *NYT*, June 5, 1968; Rudy Johnson, "Harlem Market Thrives as Co-Op," *NYT*, August 11, 1968; Theodore L. Cross, *Black Capitalism: Strategy for Business in the Ghetto* (New York: Atheneum, 1969), 43–44.

9. Floyd McKissick, "Statement on the Death of the Honorable Elijah Muhammad," February 27, 1975, folder 7316, McKissick Papers; Clarence E. Jones, "From Protest to Black Conservatism: The Demise of the Congress of Racial Equality," in *Black Political Organizations in the Post-Civil Rights Era*, ed. Ollie A. Johnson III and Karin Stanford (New Brunswick, NJ: Rutgers University Press, 2002), 87–88; Christopher Strain, "Soul City, North Carolina: Black Power, Utopia, and the African American Dream," *Journal of African American History* 89 (Winter 2004): 58; Manning Marable, *How Capitalism Underdeveloped Black America: Problems in Race, Political Economy and Society* (Boston: South End Press, 1983), 181; William L. Van Deburg, *New Day in Babylon: The Black Power Movement and American Culture, 1965–1975* (Chicago: University of Chicago Press, 1992), 133–34.

10. Floyd McKissick, "The Way to a Black Ideology," *Black Scholar* 1, no. 2 (December 1969): 15; Dean Kotlowski, "Black Power—Nixon Style: The Nixon Administration and Minority Business Enterprise," *Business History Review* 72 (Autumn 1998): 417; Wayne King, "McKissick Is Succeeding Although Not 'Supposed To,'" *NYT*, December 22, 1974; Kenneth Jolly, *Black Liberation in the Midwest: The Struggle in St. Louis, Missouri, 1964–1970* (New York: Routledge, 2006), 138.

11. D. L. Waller, "Floyd B. McKissick Enterprises, Inc.," n.d., folder 6442, and "The Corporate Goals of McKissick Enterprises," October 1968, folder 6444, McKissick Papers; Floyd McKissick, "Black Business Development with Social Commitment to Black Communities," in *Black Nationalism in America*, ed. John H. Bracey Jr., August Meier, and Elliott Rudwick (Indianapolis: Bobbs-Merrill, 1970), 492–93; Devin Fergus, "Black Power, Soft Power: Floyd McKissick, Soul City, and the Death of Moderate Black Republicanism," *Journal of Black History* 22, no. 2 (2010)," 152; Fergus, *Liberalism*, 199–200; Timothy Minchin, "'A Brand New Shining City': Floyd B. McKissick Sr. and the Struggle to Build Soul City, North Carolina," *North Carolina Historical Review* 82 (April 2005): 130; Deburg, *New Day in Babylon*, 134–35.

12. Alex Poinsett, "Roy Innis: National-Builder," *Ebony*, October 1969, 170, 176; Roy Innis, "Truth, Lies, and Consequences," in *Black Voices in American Politics*, ed. Jeffrey M. Elliot (New York: Harcourt Brace Jovanovich, 1986), 241, 244–45, 259; Weems, *Business in Black and White*, 116; Robert L. Allen, *A Guide to Black Power in America: An Historical Analysis* (London: Victor Gollancz, 1970), 155; Sugrue, *Sweet Land of Liberty*, 380; Deburg, *New Day in Babylon*, 137; Roy Innis, "Community Self-Determination Bill: A Summary," [New York?]: Congress of Racial Equality, 1969, 1–2; Jones, "From Protest to Black Conservatism," 94–95.

13. Clarence Townes, Speech to the Republican Big City County Chairman's Workshop in Washington, DC, March 23, 1968, Clarence L. Townes Jr. Papers; Clarence Townes, "'The Friendship of Black Citizens and Other Americans': 1969–1970 Program of the Minorities Division, Republican National Committee," folder: 1965–70, box 642, Papers of Edward W. Brooke, Manuscript Division, Library of Congress.

14. Weems, *Business in Black and White*, 110; Allen, *A Guide to Black Power in America*, 191; Kotlowski, "Black Power—Nixon Style," 411–12; Marable, *Black Liberation in Conservative America*, 217; Matthew Rees, *From the Deck to the Sea: Blacks and the Republican Party* (Wakefield, NH: Longwood Academic, 1991), 298.

15. Nixon for President Committee, "'Bridges to Human Dignity': An Address by Richard M. Nixon on the CBS Radio Network," April 25, 1968, folder: Nixon, Richard M., 1968 (1), box 14, Special Name Series, DDE: Post-Presidential Papers, Dwight D. Eisenhower Presidential Library; Marable, *Race, Reform, and Rebellion*, 95–96.

16. Dean Kotlowski, *Nixon's Civil Rights: Politics, Principle, and Policy* (Cambridge, MA: Harvard University Press, 2001), 38, 126; Sugrue, *Sweet Land of Liberty*, 442; Gerald and Deborah Strober, *Nixon: An Oral History of His Presidency* (New York: HarperCollins, 1994), 112; George H. Nash, *The Conservative Intellectual Movement in America Since 1945* (New York: Basic Books, 1976), 282; Congressional Quarterly Service, *The Presidential Nominating Conventions 1968* (Washington, DC: Congressional Quarterly Service, 1968), 71; Leah Michele Wright, "The Loneliness of the Black Conservative: Black Republicans and the Grand Old Party, 1964–1980" (PhD diss., Princeton University, 2009), 188–89; Ashbee, "The Republican Party and the African-American Vote since 1964," 237.

17. John McClaughry to John Conyers, October 29, 1968, folder 6199, McKissick Papers; Weems, *Business in Black and White*, 115–18; Allen, *A Guide to Black Power in America*, 194.

18. Nixon-Agnew Campaign Committee, "This Time, Vote Like Homer Pitts' Whole World Depended on It," *Jet*, November 7, 1968; Stephen Ambrose, *Nixon*, vol. 2, *The Triumph of a Politician, 1962–1972* (New York: Simon and Schuster, 1989), 187.

19. James M. Hund, *Black Entrepreneurship* (Belmont, CA: Wadsworth Publishing, 1970), 143; "Eldridge Cleaver Discusses Revolution: An Interview from Exile," in *The Black Panthers Speak*, ed. Philip S. Foner (New York: Da Capo Press, 1995), 108–9; Ernie Allen, "Black Nationalism on the Right," *Soulbook* 1 (Winter 1964): 8, 13; Sean Dennis Cashman, *African Americans and the Quest for Civil Rights, 1900–1990* (New York: New York University Press, 1991), 230; Kotlowski, *Nixon's Civil Rights*, 132; Bayard Rustin, "Negroes and the 1968 Elections," in *Down the*

Line: The Collected Writings of Bayard Rustin (Chicago: Quadrangle Books, 1971), 251; Walter Rugaber, "Stans to Promote a Minority Business Enterprise," *NYT*, March 6, 1969; Timothy Mason Bates, *Black Capitalism: A Quantitative Analysis* (New York: Praeger, 1973), 1; Ashbee, "The Republican Party and the African-American Vote since 1964," 235.

20. Jonathan Bean, *Big Government and Affirmative Action: The Scandalous History of the Small Business Administration* (Lexington: University Press of Kentucky, 2001), 72–73; Ellen Boneparth, "Black Businessmen and Community Responsibility," *Phylon* 37 (1976): 28–29; Weems, *Business in Black and White*, 127; Kotlowski, *Nixon's Civil Rights*, 134.

21. Floyd McKissick to Robert Brown, April 4, 1969, folder 6201 and Floyd McKissick to Jack Ford, August 1, 1972, folder 7732, McKissick Papers; "Robert Brown, Man in the News," *Sacramento Observer*, January 9, 1969; Theodore Cross, *The Black Power Imperative: Racial Inequality and the Politics of Nonviolence* (New York: Faulkner Books, 1984), 333–34; Hund, *Black Entrepreneurship*, 8; Kotlowski, *Nixon's Civil Rights*, 141; "As Black Business Digest Sees It: The November Election," *Black Business Digest*, October 1972, 4; "The National Business League," *Black Enterprise*, June 1972, 38, 41; "Black Publishers to Honor Berkeley Burrell at S.F. Confab," *[San Francisco] Sun Reporter*, June 7, 1975; "Berkeley Burrell," *Toledo Blade*, August 31, 1979; Paul Delaney, "Minority Capitalism: Only Game in Town," *NYT*, December 1, 1973; "Berkeley G. Burrell, NBL Pres., Dies of Heart Attack," *Jet*, September 20, 1979, 16; A. Wright Elliot, "'Black Capitalism' and the Business Community," in *Black Economic Development*, ed. William Haddad and G. Douglas Pugh (Englewood Cliffs, NJ: Prentice-Hall, 1969), 75; Bean, *Big Government and Affirmative Action*, 61–62, 77–78.

22. Warren Brown, "Nixon and McGovern Battle for Black Votes," *Jet*, November 2, 1972, 90; Maurice Stans, "A Piece of the Action: Report of the President on Minority Business Enterprise," June 30, 1970, folder: Commerce Dept. Minority Business Enterprise 1969–1971, box 130, John Sherman Cooper Collection, Margaret I. King Library, University of Kentucky; Weems, *Business in Black and White*, 227; Frank Toner to Art Fletcher, September 6, 1974, folder: Fletcher, Arthur, box 11, Robert T. Hartmann Files, Gerald R. Ford Library; Kotlowski, *Nixon's Civil Rights*, 136, 151; Cross, *The Black Power Imperative*, 171; Wright, "The Loneliness of the Black Conservative," 208.

23. Floyd McKissick, "Making Black Capitalism Work," in *Black Voices in American Politics*, 282; "Blacks: Soul City," *Newsweek*, August 14, 1972; "Negroes to Build Their Own 'New Town' in North Carolina," *NYT*, January 14, 1969; Harold Woodard, "Floyd McKissick: Portrait of a Leader" (MA thesis, University of North Carolina, 1981), 40; Deburg, *New Day in Babylon*, 135; Minchin, "A Brand New Shining City," 125; Fergus, *Liberalism*, 197; Fergus, "Black Power, Soft Power," 153.

24. Strain, "Soul City, North Carolina," 63, 65; Fergus, *Liberalism*, 119, 228; Fergus, "Black Power, Soft Power," 153, 172.

25. Floyd McKissick to Bob Brown, October 9, 1969, folder 6199, McKissick Papers; Robert Brown, Speech delivered in Soul City, NC, July 21, 1972, folder: 721/72—Soul City (Brown, Robert J.), box 25, Stanley S. Scott Papers, Ford Library;

"Blacks: Soul City"; Simeon Booker, "Washington Notebook," *Ebony*, January 1977, 26; "Homecoming for Sam Jackson," *Ebony*, July 1971, 66.

26. Leonard Garment to Mel Laird, June 21, 1973, folder: Soul City [2 of 3], box 64, White House Central Files, Staff Member and Office Files, Bradley H. Patterson Papers, Richard Nixon Presidential Library and Museum, Yorba Linda, CA, National Archives and Records Administration; John Jenkins to Floyd McKissick, September 28, 1971, folder 6129, McKissick Papers.

27. "Blacks: Soul City"; Fergus, *Liberalism*, 26; Minchin, "A Brand New Shining City," 125–26; Woodard, "Floyd McKissick," 40–41.

28. Elaine B. Jenkins to RMN, June 12, 1972, folder: Citizens—Blacks II (Fund-Raising) (1 of 4), box 26, Committee for the Re-Election of the President Collection: Frederic Malek Papers. Series II, Nixon Library; Walton and Smith, *American Politics and the African American Quest for Universal Freedom*, 142; Fergus, *Liberalism*, 208, 212. This was also the convention where the infamous picture of Sammy Davis Jr. hugging Richard Nixon was taken.

29. Floyd McKissick to Bob Brown, May 29, 1972, folder 6201, McKissick Papers; King, "McKissick Is Succeeding"; "Blacks: Soul City"; Strain, "Soul City, North Carolina," 65; Fergus, "Black Power, Soft Power," 158–59; Fergus, *Liberalism*, 197–98.

30. "F. McKissick Lauds Nixon," *Tri-State Defender*, June 24, 1972; "Blacks Meet in D.C.," *Cincinnati Herald*, June 24, 1972; "Black Republicans Plan Rally to Support Nixon," *NYT*, June 1, 1972; "McKissick: It's Time to Give Up the Sugar Tit," *The Black Advocate*, August 1972, folder: Blacks II (14 of 14), box 23, CREEP Collection: Frederic Malek Papers. Series II, Nixon Library; Committee for the Re-Election of the President, "Black Nixon Supporters," April 24, 1972, folder 7550, McKissick Papers.

31. Stan Scott to Herb Klein and Ken Clawson, November 10, 1972, folder: Black Vote in 1972—General (5), box 6, Scott Papers, Ford Library; Joint Center for Political Studies, "News Release," November 10, 1972, folder: Black Vote in 1972—General (5), box 6, Scott Papers, Ford Library.

32. Elaine Brown Jenkins, *Jumping Double Dutch: A New Agenda for Blacks and the Republican Party* (Silver Spring, MD: Beckham House, 1996), 42; Thomas D. Boston, *Race, Class and Conservatism* (Boston: Unwin Hyman, 1988), 36; Joan Hoff, *Nixon Reconsidered* (New York: Basic Books, 1994), 97; Rees, *From the Deck to the Sea*, 298; Cashman, *African Americans and the Quest for Civil Rights*, 228–29; Kevin Yuill, *Richard Nixon and the Rise of Affirmative Action: The Pursuit of Racial Equality in an Era of Limits* (Lanham, MD: Rowman and Littlefield, 2006), 177; Peter Carroll, *It Seemed Like Nothing Happened: The Tragedy and Promise of America in the 1970s* (New York: Holt, Rinehart and Winston, 1982), 48; Cross, *The Black Power Imperative*, 268.

33. "2 in Congress Ask Inquiry On McKissick's Soul City," *NYT*, March 9, 1975; Fergus, *Liberalism*, 16–17, 218; Fergus, "Black Power, Soft Power," 165–67; Minchin, "A Brand New Shining City," 127, 139, 148, 153.

34. Floyd McKissick to Robert Morgan, August 22, 1979, Folder 7729, McKissick Papers; Simeon Booker, "Washington Notebook," *Ebony*, October 1978; Omar H. Ali, *In the Balance of Power: Independent Black Politics and Third-Party Movements*

in the United States (Athens: Ohio University Press, 2008), 153; Weems, *Business in Black and White*, 219–20, 227.

35. Herb Boyd, "Black Power Advocate Dr. Nathan Wright, 81, Passes," *New York Amsterdam News*, March 3–9, 2005; Josh Horwitz, "Herman Cain's Reverend Wright," *Huffington Post*, November 3, 2011, http://www.huffingtonpost.com/mobileweb/josh-horwitz/herman-cains-reverend-wri_b_1073956.html.

PART 2

Shaping Conservative Ideology

CHAPTER 4

Fellow Travelers

Overlap between "Mainstream" and "Extremist" Conservatives in the Early 1960s

Samuel Brenner

In March 1962 a member of the John Birch Society (JBS)—the infamous ultraconservative organization that Massachusetts candy manufacturer Robert Welch had founded in 1958 to combat Communism and promote what Welch referred to as "Americanism"—wrote a "Member's Monthly Message" (MMM) to society headquarters in Belmont, Massachusetts, asking the society to rush him its "[s]tand on fluoridation of water." Aficionados of Stanley Kubrick's classic 1964 film *Dr. Strangelove*, in which the insane General Jack D. Ripper denounces fluoridation as the "most monstrously conceived and dangerous Communist plot we have ever had to face" just before firing off a hail of bullets at US military personnel whom the general believes are Communist agents, might be surprised by the society's response. "As you will recall, the objectives of the Society are for 'less government, and more responsibility,'" replied the society's research department. "We are opposed to the fluoridation of public water supplies on grounds that the government has no right at any level to administer what in effect is, compulsory dental care . . . [F]luoridation of all water supplies is certainly a massive wedge for socialized medicine, and certainly establishes a precedent which could prove to be extremely dangerous . . . to our individual liberties."[1] While by the end of the 1960s Welch would—like General Ripper—come to suggest that fluoridation was a Communist plot designed to harm the health of America's youth, the society's stance in the early 1960s was more measured and less hysterical.

The apparent dissonance of the society's response in the light of its reputation highlights a historical fact generally overlooked by scholars: in the early

1960s, the "extremist" ultralibertarian, ultraconservative, anticommunist conspiracists (or, as they labeled themselves, "Americanists") embraced a coherent
ideology that actually had a great deal in common with the ideology that motivated more "mainstream" conservatives—and, for that matter, that would in
large part be recognizable to significant numbers of mainstream conservatives
in the United States today.

The emergence of modern American conservatism in the 1950s and 1960s
was accompanied by the development of "Americanist" organizations and the
proliferation of "Americanist" leaders and writers. Welch helped coin and popu-
larize the term *Americanism* in a conscious attempt to provide a "useful . . .
constructive opposite of Communism." "The very name by which we identify
ourselves defines our objective," Welch argued. "It is to conserve as much as we
can . . . from the encroachments and destructiveness of this advancing collectivism." (Although, as Michael Kazin and Joseph A. McCartin have observed,
the term *Americanism* had been used by others, including the American Legion
early in the twentieth century, Welch's *Americanism* referred to a specific and
unrelated ideology.)[2] In general terms, the Americanists of the late 1950s and
1960s enshrined what they saw as the traditional institutions of the American
political system and Constitution and embraced free-market economics, individualism, and states' rights. They strenuously denounced Communism, maintaining that international Communism was a direct threat to the American way
of life and practice of religion, and they sought to expose policies they saw as
potentially favorable to Communists as well as direct Communist influence on
individual American politicians and the American political system as a whole.
The Birch Society was by far the most influential Americanist organization, and
Welch, its controversial founder, was perhaps the most influential Americanist
leader; the thoughts and activities of the Birchers are fairly accurate reflections
of the thoughts and activities of Americanists more generally.

While contemporaries reacted to Americanism with a mixture of fear and
ridicule, in recent years, scholars have increasingly come to believe that Americanists played an important role in the development of modern American conservatism. In some cases, that belief is linked to the view that the Birch Society
and its allies brought grassroots organization to a movement that had lacked
coherence and that Americanist organizations helped galvanize those who
would go on to become critical "mainstream" conservative actors. (One point of
this chapter is to argue that it is hard to draw clear distinctions between "mainstream" and "extremist" conservatives during this period and that who was a
"mainstream" conservative has become clear only in hindsight. For the purposes
of this chapter, "mainstream" conservatives in the early 1960s were those who
explicitly embraced the ideology of "conservatism," especially during the Goldwater presidential campaign, and who were considered intellectually respectable

by later conservatives).[3] "The Birch Society took all the disparate problems of American politics, sorted them out, and provided JBS members with a comprehensive program that connected the dots in American life based on the theory that Communists were busily infiltrating every corner of American society, and offered them an alternative to ultimate Communist domination," wrote Alfred S. Regnery, the son of the influential conservative publisher Henry Regnery, in his *Upstream: The Ascendancy of American Conservatism* (2008). "But as nutty as its views may have been, the John Birch Society was a model of efficient organization."[4] This view of the Americanist Right as a catalyzing agent is not incorrect. By viewing Americanists primarily as well-organized conspiracists who brought grassroots organization to conservatism, however, writers like Regnery are overlooking or in some ways obscuring the very real similarities between early Americanist ideology and the ideology of "mainstream" conservatism. Indeed, even some of the most heavily derided Americanist campaigns, including the drive to impeach Supreme Court Chief Justice Earl Warren and to oppose fluoridation and the civil rights movement, were initially in part predicated on libertarian and constitutionalist arguments.

In recent years, scholars and historians have begun to reevaluate the importance of Americanist ideas, individuals, and organizations. The individuals at the grass roots who "organized study groups, opened 'Freedom Forum' bookstores, filled the rolls of the John Birch Society, entered school board races, and worked within the Republican Party," argued Lisa McGirr in 2001, "became the ground forces of a conservative revival—one that transformed conservatism from a marginal force preoccupied with Communism in the early 1960s into a viable electoral contender by the decade's end." "Often dismissed as a fringe group composed of conspiracy theorists," agreed Jonathan Schoenwald, "the JBS was far more complex, played a historically understated role as a faction in the conservative movement, and helped to chart the course of postwar conservatism in America." "The Birchers are just the kind of persistent outliers that have always had their effect on American politics, but who must ever remained doomed . . . to suffer only the enormous condescension of consensus-addled elites who only know how to think about political actors that poll higher than 15 percent," wrote Rick Perlstein, the author of *Before the Storm: Barry Goldwater and the Unmaking of the American Consensus*, in an article for *In These Times*. "It is true that the John Birch Society has worked remarkably hard to make it remarkably hard for anyone but a partisan to take it seriously. But it has also put a discernable imprint on American political culture for more than 40 years."[5]

Even as scholars such as McGirr, Schoenwald, and Perlstein have addressed how the Birch Society and its allies played a greater role than previously understood in the development of modern American conservatism, however, historians have not fully explored exactly what it was the "extremists" believed and what set those extremists apart from their more "mainstream" conservative fellows. In part this may be because, with conservatism and the eventual rise of Ronald Reagan at the center of their focus, many historians have reasonably addressed Americanism largely in terms of its impact on mainstream conservatism rather than as an ideology and a movement in its own right.[6] Shifting the focus slightly, however, and examining and comparing the early public writings of Americanist elites, such as Welch, and some of the MMMs, which were sent by rank-and-file Birchers and intended only for the eyes of fellow Americanists, reveals that many Americanists had, and viewed themselves as having, a coherent ideology that closely mirrored the ideology of "mainstream" conservatism and that they viewed their grassroots campaigns to restore the United States to the silver standard, oppose fluoridation, and defeat the civil rights movement as reflections or embodiments of that ideology.

In the early 1960s, then, Americanists were on the cusp of being a significant part of the rise of modern American conservatism, at both the grass roots and the polls. Instead, however, the Americanists were effectively marginalized and ostracized by both the mainstream Right and the mainstream Left, neither of which embraced Americanist conspiracism. That fellow conservatives helped to isolate Americanists, and the Birch Society in particular, is well understood by historians. In the mid-1960s, mainstream conservatives such as philosopher Russell Kirk, *National Review* publisher William F. Buckley Jr., and Senator Barry Goldwater, disgusted by some Americanist conspiracist beliefs and worried about the effect on conservatism of being allied with perceived extremists, consciously attempted to distinguish between "conservatives" and "extremists" and ultimately moved to cut all ties between modern American conservatism and Americanism. What is less well understood, however, is that their ultimate success has masked the historical fact that, in the early 1960s, the ideological distinctions between "mainstream" and "extremist" conservatives were not always so clear.[7]

This chapter describes how Americanist elites such as Welch viewed Americanist ideology, analyzes samples from MMMs sent by ordinary Americanists in the Birch Society to demonstrate that Americanists at the grass roots were motivated by the same ideological concerns as were their leaders, and examines how in the mid-1960s Buckley and the *National Review* helped to expurgate Americanism from conservatism and in the process left the impression that "mainstream" conservatism and Americanism had always been more distinct than was in fact the case.

Americanist Ideology

In broad terms, Americanism as an ideology was composed of five parts: traditional constitutionalism, libertarian individualism, religion, anticommunism, and conspiracism. Of these, anticommunism and conspiracism were predominant, with at least some part of the concern for traditional constitutionalism, libertarian autonomy, and religion being based on the belief that such philosophies would help to sustain the strengths of the American political, social, and economic system and oppose the spread of Communism and the victory of the great Communist conspiracy.

By far the most important unifying element of Americanist ideology was anticommunism. While there was nothing unusual about American political and ideological movements in the 1950s and 1960s expressing philosophies of anticommunism, the core foundational Americanist texts reflect an anticommunism that was as vigorous as, or more muscular than, any expressed elsewhere on the American political spectrum. Anticommunism was, in particular, the major focus of *The Blue Book of the John Birch Society*, which was supposed to be required reading for every new or prospective member. "For *our* enemy is the Communists, and we do not intend to lose sight of that fact for a minute," Welch wrote in the foreword to the fourth printing of the text. Despite the Americanist focus on anticommunism, however, from their very inceptions groups such as the Birch Society made it clear that anticommunism was an important step on a longer road. "It is our purpose . . . to inspire and to coordinate greater efforts on the part of all men and women of good conscience and good will, who want to bring about 'less government, more responsibility, and a better world,'" Welch wrote. The Society's goals, he added, were "not negative, but positive," but "[w]e know, however, that under present circumstances a preponderant part of our efforts must be directed to turning back the Communists, as a prerequisite to all else we wish to accomplish."[8]

The second philosophy expressed powerfully by Americanists was conspiracism, which took two forms: The first was the belief that Communism was neither an ideology, nor a governing national principle of the Soviet Union, but rather a vast international disease-like conspiracy designed to take over the world, destroy freedom, and undermine religion. The second form was the belief that this international Communist conspiracy had extended its tentacles deep into US society and government in order to "soften" the country for conquest. It was this belief, that the greatest danger to the United States lay in the threat of internal subversion rather than in the threat of outside conquest, on which Americanists ultimately differed most starkly from mainstream conservatives. The difference was not merely cosmetic: in the end, this conspiratorial thinking drove a wedge between Americanists and conservatives such as Russell Kirk, who criticized those who expressed such ideas for "silliness and injustice of utterance."[9]

The concern that the Communist conspiracy was attempting to infiltrate American society and culture heavily informed the three other main elements of Americanist ideology. The overriding concern for many Americanists was that the great strengths of American society were being perverted and twisted so as to ease the path for Communist conquest. "Here are the Communists' aims for the United States—to be achieved, they hope, through the leftward momentum of the attitude induced by Sputnik and all of its auxiliary propaganda," Welch wrote, listing the following:

> (1) Greatly expanded government spending . . . as wastefully as possible. (2) Higher and then much higher taxes. (3) An increasingly unbalanced budget . . . (4) Wild inflation of our currency, leading rapidly towards its ultimate repudiation. (5) Government controls of prices, wages, and materials, supposedly to combat inflation. (6) Greatly increased socialistic controls over every operation of our economy and every activity of our daily lives. This is to be accompanied, naturally and automatically, by a correspondingly huge increase in the size of our bureaucracy, and in both the cost and reach of our domestic government. (7) Far more centralization of power in Washington, and the practical elimination of our state lines . . . (8) The steady advance of federal aid to and control over the educational system, leading to complete federalization of our public education. (9) A constant hammering into the American consciousness of 'modern warfare,' the beauties and the absolute necessity of 'peace,'—peace always on Communist terms, of course. And (10) the consequent willingness of the American people to allow the steps of appeasement by our government which amount to the piecemeal surrender of the rest of the free world and of the United States itself to the Kremlin-ruled tyranny.[10]

Americanists were also deeply concerned with the importance of religion—*any* religion. Welch, for example, bemoaned the dearth of all "true" fundamentalism in the United States. "[T]he same trend of worldly disillusionment and loss of true faith is visible among Catholics, among Jews, among Moslems, among Buddhists, and among the formerly devout believers of every great religion in the world," Welch wrote. "Except for the diminishing number of fundamentalists of all religions, and the increasing but still comparatively small percentage of the human race which has fervently accepted Communism as a religion, all faith has been replaced, or is rapidly being replaced, by a pragmatic opportunism with hedonistic aims." As Welch made clear, he—and thus the Birch Society—did *not* distinguish between Christians and Jews, Buddhists and Muslims, but rather between those who believed in a divine being and those who did not. "[W]e are merely urging Protestants, Catholics, Jews or Moslems to be better Christians, better Jews, or better Moslems, in accordance with the deepest and most humanitarian promptings of their own religious beliefs," Welch argued. "Yet the evangelical fervor, with which we expect our members to fight forces of evil and work for a better world, makes certain principles with regard to religious groups apply to ourselves."[11]

The fourth element of Americanist ideology was what might be called traditional constitutionalism. Traditional constitutionalism meant adherence to traditional understandings of the limitations of federal power, the preeminence of states' rights, and the sort of independence and sovereignty—even the semi-isolation—prevalent in the United States before the upheaval of the Great Depression and the New Deal. "We believe that a Constitutional Republic, such as our Founding Fathers gave us, is probably the best of all forms of government," Welch wrote in the June 1962 *Bulletin*, which was designed as a restatement of the Birch Society's beliefs. "We believe that a Democracy, which they tried hard to obviate, and into which the Liberals have been trying for fifty years to convert our Republic, is one of the worst of all forms of government." A part of the plan for Communist conquest, Welch wrote, "is the conversion of the United States into a socialist nation, quite similar to Russia itself in its economy and political outlook, before police-state enforcement is ever introduced." In the eyes of Americanists, the Communists in attempting to conquer the United States would first try to convert the country into a socialist nation—with some part of this conversion to come through the actions of the Supreme Court. Writing in 1964 in the Birch Society publication *American Opinion*, for example, Revilo P. Oliver, a professor of classics who for years stood as one of the leading intellectual lights of Americanism before moving firmly into the anti-Semitic, white supremacist Right, emphasized the importance of "pornographic filth, now officially sanctioned and protected by the Warren Court in the International Communist Conspiracy's over-all strategy for corrupting and stultifying American children by exciting . . . precocious sexual lusts."[12]

A significant part of the Americanist concern about traditional constitutionalism was that increasing collectivism in American society—along with the weaknesses inherent in the United States' republican system—would together bring the United States closer to Communism. Among these weaknesses, in Welch's view, was the American public's willingness to go along uncaringly with whatever programs were suggested by the federal government, especially, ironically, when they were presented as part of an anticommunist campaign. For years, Welch concluded, "we have been taken steadily down the road to Communism by steps [such as foreign aid programs] supposedly designed, and presented to the American people, as ways of *fighting* Communism." The Americanist concern over traditional constitutionalism was also inextricably bound up with the belief that the United States should not be in any way answerable to international organizations such as the United Nations—especially since these organizations were, in the eyes of Americanists, dominated by Communists and dupes.[13] Such beliefs, of course, led to the identification of the Americanist Right with the sorts of absolutist anti–United Nations messages signaled by the ubiquitous Americanist bumper stickers and highway signs encouraging readers to "Get US Out of the U.N.!"

The fifth element of Americanist ideology was a form of libertarian individualism. This element was expressed in two ways: first, as a rejection of the increasing power of the federal government and the perceived increasing dedication of leading American politicians and policy makers to social welfare programs, which Americanists believed would have the effect of weakening the United States before the agents of Communism, and second, as an assertion that increased government regulation of such elements of American life as the economy would simply prove harmful to the United States. The Americanist concern over libertarian individualism thus influenced Americanist positions on such issues as the "socialization" of medical care, the fluoridation of public water supplies, and the move away from pure free-market and laissez-faire economics. As Welch explained, "[T]he whole essence of our purpose, and the guiding principle for our action, covering not only our fight *against* collectivism but our fight *for* our constructive replacement, can be summarized in the objective expressed by just five words: *Less government and more responsibility.*"[14]

Individual Americanists

The words of ordinary Americanists in the early 1960s, as revealed in a sampling of the Birch Society's MMMs, demonstrate that Americanists at the grass roots were similarly expressing mainstream conservative ideas. This is not to say that Americanists and Birchers were *only* concerned with such ideas; in fact, most MMMs concerned the minutiae of the society's operations, updates on the society's campaigns to impeach Earl Warren and get the United States out of the United Nations, and reports about the dangers posed by Communists. Some were racist or anti-Semitic, and others were simply incoherent. What these selected messages demonstrate, however, is that in the early 1960s, ordinary Americanists—the "extremists"—were *also* concerned with the same sorts of fiscal, philosophical, moral, and social concerns that were motivating "mainstream" conservatives.

Critical for many Americanists were financial concerns, which were often informed by a free-market sense that the increasingly regulated economic system was strangling growth. Writing in September 1961, for example, a Bircher from Santa Maria, California, asked the society to place more emphasis "on the fact that the Free Enterprise system will fail unless people, especially the young people, and a lot of business people cease abusing it." Perhaps the most popular single target for Americanists interested in economics was the income tax—which many Americanists considered a grave harm to freedom. "The public will have to be educated in the sources of Federal Gov't income if the income tax is ever to be abolished," wrote Carroll R. Sorenson of Alamogordo, New Mexico, in consternation. A Bircher from Newington, Connecticut, wrote to suggest that the society shift its primary effort to elimination of the income tax "and getting the government out of business." "[I]s there anything more fundamental than government finance, nor anything more destructive to our solvency than the Federal Reserve Act?" asked a Bircher from San Marino, California, in November 1964. "Do you think it would help anything to ask our members to refuse federal reserve notes and demand silver certificates?" added Dave Smith two weeks later. "Would it not be in order to mention the plan lately proposed by the Administration for stopping the drain of gold from the Treasury; taxing investments made by Americans in foreign securities?" asked Sid Cochran Jr., an attorney in Tyler, Texas. "This proposed tax would trample further upon the historic freedom of the Yankee trader to go where he thought the grass was greenest and make hay."[15]

Other Americanists were more concerned with what they viewed as attempts by the federal government to encroach upon individual liberties and local authority. In January 1965, for example, a female Birch Society member from Midland, Texas, wrote to Belmont to suggest that the society "stress the dangers of Medicare, especially to the small businessman and the reasons we are fighting medicare [*sic*], and what it will lead to." George W. Lynch of Southampton, Pennsylvania, was worried about the creation of local planning commissions, which would have the effect of reorganizing counties and towns. "I have watched with alarm while my county, Bucks County, PA has presented the first 'County-wide comprehension plan' in Pennsylvania," Lynch wrote. "From viewing it, it appears that this plan erases every township and borough line in the county and points the way to elimination of local government."[16]

Americanists were also clearly focused on what can be considered socially and morally conservative concerns. A female Bircher from Inverness, Mississippi, for example, wrote in October 1961 to complain that the society had "never mentioned the fact that the Bible is being taken out of our Sunday Schools—is being ridiculed and denounced." In January 1965, Lillian Chastain of Houston, Texas, wrote to suggest that the society's members "encourage all women to dress, act, and talk more feminine and men dress, act, and talk more masculine. Encourage parents to raise their children to be feminine or masculine. The sexes are encouraged to dress and act the same in China and Cuba for psychological reasons, and look what the liberals in Washington are doing and encouraging." Americanists were also raising concerns about Communist and liberal influence in public education and what they saw as the failure of the public education system to teach personal responsibility. "It seems in our own area, at least, that the Public school teachers have been indoctrinated with some key words that arouse an absolutely blinding emotion," wrote a society member from Tigard, Oregon. "To a conservative American of my limited mental stature this poses a formidable hurdle."[17]

Some Americanists, inspired by regional concerns, sought to bring attention to their concerns about illegal immigration and racial turmoil. Writing in November 1961, for example, Leslie M. Ward of La Crescenta, California, suggested that the society mount a campaign for stricter enforcement of immigration and naturalization laws. "If [Attorney General] Robert Kennedy could be shown that the people *want* enforcement of the immigration laws," Ward wrote, "there might be a change in official attitude on down the line, and some of the subversive aliens would leave the country." A Bastrop, Louisiana, Birch Society member was worried about the effects of outside organizers on Southern attempts to respond to the civil rights movement. "Also in this time of great international stress we should start a concerted section to ask our leaders (President Kennedy, et al) to ask for a cease in the internal strife caused by freedom rides," he wrote. "I realize much of this strife is Communist inspired, but an appeal from what people consider the 'proper' quarters might have some good effects." R. H. Whittick of Bull Shoals, Arkansas, wrote just after the 1964 election to ask when the Birch Society was going to "do something about the Hart-Kennedy Immigration bill, that would allow 1 million immigrants per year into this country." The bill, Whittick added, made "the Civil Rights Act look like a joke, in comparison." A few weeks later, Jess Urban complained about the Supreme Court's power, suggesting that the Birch Society press "for curtailing the Supreme Court's jurisdiction thru state legislature action regarding apportionment and the prayer decision."[18]

"Mainstream" Distancing

Before the 1960s there was often overlap between the ideas and activities of the Americanists and more "mainstream" conservatives such as Buckley. In October 1959, for example, Buckley shared a Chicago stage with former Utah governor J. Bracken Lee, Revilo P. Oliver, Medford Evans, Dan Smoot, and Welch— all Americanists—at a meeting organized by Kent and Phoebe Courtney, the ultraconservative publishers of *The Independent American*. "That adds up to a lot of right-wing firepower," declared the *National Review* in November, as it expressed the "hope" that the event "will help to rally conservative sentiment."[19]

Throughout 1961, even as the Birch Society became the target of choice for mainstream journalists and liberal politicians who viewed the society as part of what the Anti-Defamation League's Arnold Forster and Benjamin R. Epstein later termed the "Danger on the Right," Buckley and the *National Review* continued to defend the society and even Welch. The liberals and the Communists, Buckley explained, "to the extent their programs coincide," felt threatened by the rise of conservatism, and "accordingly they have taken hold of a vulnerable organization and labored to transform it into a national menace." Buckley explicitly distinguished his own views of the dangers of Communism from Welch's conspiracist views, criticized *The Politician* (a book in which Welch claimed that Eisenhower was "a dedicated, conscious agent of the Communist conspiracy"), and argued that the differences between *National Review*'s and Welch's "views of the world situation" were critical, insomuch as *National Review* conservatives "certainly do not believe [the Communist conspiracy] is in control of the Government." Buckley, however, was carefully attempting to stake out an important middle ground in denying Welch's views while retaining the support of Birchers. "I myself have never met a single member [of the Birch Society] who declared himself in agreement with certain of Mr. Welch's conclusions," Buckley wrote. "Certain elements" of the press, Buckley added, were using Welch "to anathematize the entire American right wing."[20]

Buckley was not alone in providing support for Americanists throughout 1961: in June, for example, *Time* quoted Goldwater as saying of the Birch Society, "I only know one chapter, the one in my home town. They are the finest people in my community." In September, L. Brent Bozell (who later ghostwrote Goldwater's *Conscience of a Conservative*) wrote that the Americanist campaign to impeach Warren was misguided—only because impeachment was the *wrong* remedy for what he perceived as Warren's "grand sins" in promulgating unconstitutional rulings and making "war against the public order."[21]

Early in 1962, however, the *National Review* stunned Americanists by directly attacking Welch—a move that Buckley in 2008 explained was part of a concerted "plot" by conservative leaders, including himself, Kirk, and Goldwater, to cull ultraconservatives from conservatism. Buckley began his article by noting that a number of conservative and anticommunist leaders had recently criticized Welch as unfit to lead a national anticommunist and antistatist movement. "[T]heir opinion—our opinion," he wrote, "is that Robert Welch is damaging the cause of anti-Communism." Welch's problem, Buckley concluded, lay in refusing to "make the crucial moral and political distinction" between "1) *an active pro-Communist*, and 2) *an ineffectually anti-Communist Liberal*." Buckley took care to distinguish Welch from the Birch Society. The society's members "include, in our judgment, some of the most morally energetic, self-sacrificing, and dedicated anti-Communists in America," Buckley wrote.[22]

Leading conservatives quickly stepped in to express their agreement with Buckley. "[The editorial] is a courageous and responsible analysis, and I wish to associate myself with its conclusions," wrote Senator John Tower of Texas.

"With [this article] you have once again given voice to the conscience of conservatism," applauded Ronald Reagan. We must "make it plain that we do not intend to depart from the truth in the pursuit of aims we believe are in the best interests of the American people," Goldwater added. "Mr. Welch is only one man and I do not believe his views, far removed from reality and common sense as they are, represent the feelings of most members of the John Birch Society." The best thing that Welch could do "to serve the cause of anti-Communism," Goldwater concluded, "would be to resign."[23]

The *National Review*'s campaign to distinguish between mainstream and extremist conservatives escalated in the fall of 1963, after New York senator Jacob Javits, a liberal Republican, launched into a powerful attack on the politicians (including Goldwater) he believed supported the "radical right." Javits's attack prompted a furious response from Buckley. "[The] truth is this," Buckley wrote, "that Senator Goldwater has never been a member of the [Birch] Society, that he scarcely knows its leader Mr. Welch, that he has consistently repudiated Mr. Welch's spectacular theses, that Mr. Welch has no hold on him whatever, and that on several occasions he has called upon Mr. Welch to resign his leadership as the result of his manifest disqualifications as a political analyst. For he knows Mr. Welch is seized of an unreal vision." Buckley, however, again took care to defend some Americanist beliefs. "Because Robert Welch believes in a cluster of political unrealities," Buckley argued, "it does not thereby follow that taxes aren't too high, or that our foreign policy is not inadequate." For the first time, moreover, Buckley began to criticize *members* of the Birch Society. "They are not, in fact, all of them 'good' people," he wrote. That said, Buckley added, it would be unreasonable to judge a society on the excesses of one member. "And so I stand by my statement . . . [that] I have a considerable admiration for the majority of those members of the John Birch Society."[24]

Controversy over Goldwater's ties to extremism came to a head after the Republican National Convention in July 1964, where, in his speech accepting the party's nomination, Goldwater issued a ringing defense of what he saw as the proper sorts of extremism. "I would remind you that extremism in the defense of liberty is no vice!" Goldwater famously declared. "And let me remind you also that moderation in the pursuit of justice is no virtue!" In the weeks after the convention, as he increasingly came under fire from Democrats and liberal Republicans who had interpreted his words as an endorsement of the Birch Society and its Americanist allies, Goldwater tried to backpedal from his comments. In the end, of course, Goldwater was unable to shake off allegations of extremism or to overcome Johnson. In the wake of Goldwater's devastating electoral defeat in November 1964, *National Review* conservatives increasingly identified the presence of extremists in the conservative movement as a cause of Republican weakness. For example, in June 1965, in an article titled "How to Beat a Good Congressman," Neal Freeman bitterly observed that the answer was "simple": "Just keep repeating Birch . . . Bircher . . . Birchest."[25]

By this time, moreover, the problem for mainstream conservatives was not only that they were being tarred by liberals with the Bircher brush but also that some Birchers and Americanists were developing ideas and theories that seemed increasingly absurd to observers. In 1965, for example, Baptist minister David A. Noebel, a longtime Bircher who was at the time an associate evangelist in Billy James Hargis's Christian Crusade, published a pamphlet titled *Communism, Hypnotism and the Beatles.* In this pamphlet, Noebel—citing copiously from articles in *American Opinion*, the Birch Society's magazine—argued that the Beatles were part of "an elaborate, calculating and scientific technique directed at rendering a generation of American youth useless through nerve-jamming, mental deterioration and retardation." In February 1965, *Newsweek* reported on Noebel's anti-Beatles lecture tour of California and used Noebel's own words to ridicule the minister. "In the excitatory state that the Beatles place these youngsters into," Noebel declared, "these young people will do anything they are told to do . . . One day when the revolution is ripe, [the Communists] could put the Beatles on TV and [they] could mass hypnotize the American youth."[26]

Having walked a fine line between courting Americanists and excoriating Americanist leaders, in mid- to late 1965—in part because of opinions like Noebel's Beatles-as-Communist-hypnotizers theory, and in part because of the Birch Society's developing opinions on the civil rights movement and US intervention in Vietnam—Buckley and the *National Review* conservatives finally began to try to separate themselves entirely from Welch, the Birch Society, and all Americanist and conspiracist organizations. Soon after the appearance of a 1965 edition of *American Opinion* in which Welch and the society claimed that the United States was now "60% to 80% in Communist control," for example, Buckley published several syndicated columns in which he implied that the existence of the society was a danger to conservatism. On October 19, 1965, moreover, he and fellow *National Review* editors James Burnham and Frank S. Meyer published a devastating series of articles in a special issue further attacking the society as harmful to conservatism. "However worthy the original motivations of those who have joined [the JBS]," warned Meyer, "it is time for them to recognize that the John Birch Society is rapidly losing whatever it had in common with patriotism and conservatism—and to do it before their own minds become warped by adherence to its unrolling psychosis of conspiracy." In his article, Meyer argued that while there "was, in fact, a Communist conspiracy of some significance acting domestically," the real danger to the conservative program was posed by *liberals* and that the conspiracist view of Communism detracted attention from the true enemy. "Responsible conservatives have long tried to believe that the JBS, though 'misguided,' was 'going in the same direction,' and therefore an 'ally,'" added Burnham. "But unfortunately, under the years of brainwashing . . . the Society as a collective body . . . has become a suitable ally only for confusion and sterility."[27]

"Buckley's articles cost the Birchers their respectability with conservatives," Richard Nixon declared in 1967. Being marginalized on charges of extremism set up something of a feedback loop for Americanists: the more they were painted as extremists, the greater the number of Americanists who left to join mainstream movements—thus leaving only the actual extremists to make policy decisions for Americanist organizations. Adding to the increasing extremism of the Birch Society was the increasing conspiracism and paranoia of Welch, who in 1966 lost the support even of many staunch Americanists when he concluded that the "Communist movement," as bad as it was, was in fact "only a tool of the total conspiracy" and that the *true* culprits were "the Insiders," a shadowy group of conspirators who traced their roots back to the Bavarian Order of the Illuminati, which had been founded by Adam Weishaupt in 1776. By the end of the 1960s and the beginning of the 1970s, even some Americanists and former Americanists believed that organizations such as the Birch Society had become irrelevant. "I do not know of anything that could make the John Birch Society rise to any position of importance," declared Tom Davis, the former Birch Society East Coast director of public relations, in October 1967.[28] Nonetheless, the fact remains that, during the early 1960s, there was far more overlap between the ideologies of "mainstream" conservatism and of Americanism than *National Review* conservatives really wanted to admit.

"Mainstream" and "Extremist" Overlap

"Recently," Frank Meyer wrote in the 1965 *National Review* attack on the Birch Society "the practical political positions of the Society have less and less represented the general consensus of the conservative outlook, as they have sometimes done in the past, if in a distorted form, and begun consistently to express the underlying paranoid theories of Robert Welch."[29] Meyer's critique masked the fact that Americanist ideology in the early 1960s in many ways closely tracked and resembled "mainstream" conservative ideology. In other words, the Americanist viewpoint was not so much a "distorted form" of the "consensus of the conservative outlook" as it *was* that consensus—albeit with an added focus on conspiracism. This is not, of course, to say that the Americanists, and in particular the Birchers, did not also express what appeared to many observers, including *National Review* conservatives, to be outlandish ideas. That said, however, it is clear that as of the mid-1960s it served the goals of the *National Review* conservatives to suggest that there had always been an even greater difference between "mainstream" conservatives and Americanists than was in fact the case. Put another way, while Americanism certainly became increasingly marginalized and extreme over the course of the 1960s and 1970s, the historical reality is that in the early 1960s, at least in terms of ideology, the conservative spectrum did not always divide as easily into "extremists" and "mainstream" camps as many contemporary and subsequent observers and scholars have suggested.

Notes

1. JBS MMM, [name expurgated], Chapter QOBC, Secane, PA, March 1962, "1962" and "MMM, '62 Continued" folders, box 7, JBS Papers, John Hay Library, Brown University, Providence, RI; Letter from John Birch Society Research Department to [name expurgated], Secane, PA, March 1962, "1962" and "MMM, '62" folders, JBS Papers.

2. Robert Welch, *The Blue Book of the John Birch Society* (Boston: Western Islands, 1961), 128, 150; Michael Kazin and Joseph A. McCartin, eds., *Americanism: New Perspectives on the History of an Ideal* (Chapel Hill: University of North Carolina Press, 2006).

3. For one example of an important conservative thinker helping to identify intellectually respectable 1960s conservatives, see George H. Nash, *The Conservative Intellectual Movement in America since 1945* (New York: Basic Books, 1976). My thanks to Dan Williams for suggesting this definition of "mainstream" conservatism.

4. Alfred S. Regnery, *Upstream: The Ascendency of American Conservatism* (New York: Threshold Press, 2008), 77, 80. For works that cover Americanists' role in the development of postwar conservatism, see Donald T. Critchlow, *The Conservative Ascendancy: How the GOP Right Made Political History* (Cambridge, MA: Harvard University Press, 2007), 57, 59; Lisa McGirr, *Suburban Warriors: The Origins of the New American Right* (Princeton, NJ: Princeton University Press, 2001), 4, 337; Cas Mudde, "The Rise (and Fall?) of American Conservatism," *Journal of Politics* 72 (April 2010): 588–94; and Jonathan M. Schoenwald, *A Time for Choosing: Extremism and the Rise of Modern American Conservatism* (New York: Oxford University Press, 2001), 9. For the Americanists' role in mobilizing people who later became "mainstream" conservatives, see Regnery, *Upstream*, 77, 80.

5. McGirr, *Suburban Warriors*, 4; Schoenwald, *A Time for Choosing*, 98; Rick Perlstein, "Fringe Benefits: Do the John Birch Society and Ralph Nader Have Anything in Common?," *In These Times*, January 8, 2001.

6. See, for example, William Rusher, "Toward a History of the Conservative Movement," *Journal of Policy History* 14 (2002): 321–30 (addressing the role of the John Birch Society in the development of modern conservatism).

7. Ironically, given that historians have tended to distinguish between "mainstream" and "extremist" conservatives, the close ideological similarities between the two were first noted by two of the harshest critics of conservatism and Americanism. In *The Radical Right* (1967), Arnold Forster and Benjamin R. Epstein, respectively the national director and the general counsel of the Anti-Defamation League of B'nai B'rith, argued that the *National Review* attacks were more about form than substance, and that the borders between the extreme conservatives and the Radical

Right were "hazy." On these hazy borderlines, they added, extreme conservatives and Radical Rightists "mingle in common causes . . . because the basic philosophical differences did not matter to those involved, or were not clearly recognized to begin with." Benjamin R. Epstein and Arnold Forster, *The Radical Right: Report on the John Birch Society and Its Allies* (New York: Random House, 1967), 62.

8. Raymond E. Wolfinger et al., "America's Radical Right: Politics and Ideology," in *Ideology and Discontent*, ed. David Apter (London: Free Press of Glencoe, 1964), 263; Welch, *The Blue Book*, x; JBS *Bulletin*, March 1960, 4.

9. Welch, *The Blue Book*, 20–21; Russell Kirk, cited in William H. Honan, "Russell Kirk Is Dead at 75; Seminal Conservative Author," *The New York Times*, April 30, 1994. For a conspiracist view of international Communism, see also Fred Schwarz, *You Can Trust the Communists (...to Be Communists)* (Englewood Cliffs, NJ: Prentice-Hall, 1960), 2.

10. Welch, *The Blue Book*, 23–24.

11. Ibid., 48–50, 155.

12. Robert Welch, JBS *Bulletin*, June 1962, 4; Welch, *The Blue Book*, 20; Revilo P. Oliver, article on "Brainwashing," *American Opinion*, November 1964, 37.

13. Robert Welch, JBS *Bulletin*, April 1960, 3; Welch, *The Blue Book*, 19–22, 33.

14. Robert Welch, JBS *Bulletin*, June 1962, 4; Welch, *The Blue Book*, 117.

15. JBS MMM, [name expurgated], Santa Maria, CA, September 1961; JBS MMM, Carroll R. Sorenson, Alamogordo, NM, October 1961; JBS MMM, [name expurgated], Newington, CT, October 1961; all in "Tim Welch" folder, box 6, JBS Papers, John Hay Library. JBS MMM, [name expurgated], San Marino, CA, November 10, 1964; JBS MMM, Dave Smith, quoted in Laurence Swanson, MMM Summaries, week of November 23, 1964; both in "64" folder, box 7, JBS Papers, John Hay Library. JBS MMM, S. A. Cochran, Jr., Tyler, TX, week of August 5–9, 1963, "Members Letters, Sent to Welch" folder, box 6, JBS Papers, John Hay Library.

16. JBS MMM, Mrs. [name expurgated], quoted in MMM Summaries, week of January 4, 1965, "MMM's 1965" folder, box 7, JBS Papers John Hay Library. At this time, the Medicare legislation was under consideration and had not yet been passed. Johnson ultimately signed the bill into law in July of 1965. JBS MMM, George W. Lynch, Chapter 760, Southampton, PA, May 1962, "1962" and "MMM, '62 Continued" folders, box 7, JBS Papers, John Hay Library.

17. JBS MMM, Mrs. [name expurgated], Inverness, MS, October 1961, "Tim Welch" folder, box 6, JBS Papers, John Hay Library; JBS MMM, Lillian Chastain, Houston, TX, quoted in MMM Summaries, week of January 11, 1965, "MMM's 1965" folder, box 7, JBS Papers John Hay Library; JBS MMM, [name expurgated], Tigard, OR, October 1961, "Tim Welch" folder, box 6, JBS Papers, John Hay Library.

18. JBS MMM, Mr. Leslie M. Ward, La Crescenta, CA, November 1961; JBS MMM, [name expurgated], Bastrop, LA, September 1961, "Tim Welch" folder, box 6, JBS Papers, John Hay Library; JBS MMM, week of November 9–13, 1964, included in memo to Welch; JBS MMM, R. H. Whittick, Home Chapter, Bull Shoals, AR, week of November 9–13, 1964, included in memo to Welch; JBS MMM, Jess Urban, quoted in Laurence Swanson, MMM Summaries, week of November 30, 1964, "64 folder," box 7, JBS Papers John Hay Library.

19. "Rally in Chicago," *National Review*, November 7, 1959, 450.

20. Arnold Forster and Benjamin R. Epstein, *Danger on the Right* (New York: Random House, 1964); William F. Buckley Jr., "The Uproar," *National Review*, April 22, 1961, 241–43.

21. "Salesman for a Cause," *Time*, June 23, 1961; L. Brent Bozell Jr., "Should We Impeach Earl Warren?" *National Review*, September 9, 1961, 153.

22. William F. Buckley Jr., "Goldwater, the John Birch Society, and Me," *Commentary*, March 2008; William F. Buckley Jr., "The Question of Robert Welch," *National Review*, February 13, 1962, 83–88. "The wound we . . . plotters delivered to the John Birch Society proved fatal over time," Buckley later wrote.

23. Senator John Tower (R-TX), letter to the editor, *National Review*, February 27, 1962, 140; Ronald Reagan, letter to the editor, *National Review*, March 13, 1962, 177; Senator Barry Goldwater (R-AZ), letter to the editor, *National Review*, February 27, 1962, 140.

24. Jacob K. Javits, "To Preserve the Two-Party System," *The New York Times*, October 27, 1963; William F. Buckley Jr., "Goldwater and the John Birch Society," *National Review*, November 19, 1963, 430. Buckley and the *National Review* viewed Schwarz and the CACC as non-extremist conservatives. See, for example, "The Impending Smear of Fred Schwarz," *National Review*, June 5, 1962, 398. Schwarz himself had notably refused to criticize (or praise) the Birch Society, even when he was challenged to do so on the television program *Meet the Press*. Frederick Schwarz, *Beating the Unbeatable Foe* (Washington, DC: Regnery, 1996), 3–14.

25. Tim Wicker, "Convention Ends; Extremism in Defense of Liberty 'No Vice,' Arizonan Asserts," *The New York Times*, July 17, 1964; "Transcript of Goldwater's Speech Accepting Republican Presidential Nomination," *The New York Times*, July 17, 1964; Neal Freeman, "How to Beat a Good Congressman," *National Review*, June 29, 1965, 547. For immediate responses to Goldwater's speech, see, for example, "Editorial Comments from Across the Nation Appraising the Nomination of Goldwater," *The New York Times*, July 17, 1964.

26. David A. Noebel, *Communism, Hypnotism and the Beatles—An Analysis of the Communist Use of Music—the Communist Master Music Plan* (Tulsa, OK: Christian Crusade Publications, 1965), 1; "Beware the Red Beatles," *Newsweek*, February 15, 1965. See also Mark Sullivan, "'More Popular Than Jesus': The Beatles and the Religious Far Right," *Popular Music* 6 (October 1987): 313–26.

27. "The John Birch Society and the Conservative Movement," *National Review*, October 19, 1965, 914; Frank S. Meyer, "Principles and Heresies: The Birch Malady," *National Review*, October 19, 1965, 919–20; James Burnham, "The Third World War: *Get US Out!*," *National Review*, October 19, 1965, 927.

28. "The Sniper," *Time*, November 3, 1967; McGirr, *Suburban Warriors*, 222; Robert Welch, "The Truth in Time," *American Opinion*, November 1966; Richard Stone, "John Birch Blues: Many Top Aides Quit Right-Wing Group, Say Funds, Members Decline," *Wall Street Journal*, October 6, 1967. For another story on the Birch Society decline, see Gordon Hall, "Top Is Falling Out of the Birch Society," *Washington Post*, December 24, 1967.

29. Meyer, "Principles and Heresies," 919.

CHAPTER 5

From Without to Within the Movement

Consolidating the Conservative Think Tank in the "Long Sixties"

Jason Stahl

On May 19, 1976, the foremost conservative think tank in the United States held its annual dinner at the Madison Hotel in Washington, DC. There was much to celebrate. Over the previous decade, the American Enterprise Institute (AEI) had seen explosive growth, no matter the metric. During this period, AEI's operating budget had increased almost tenfold and would rise as high as $13 million annually by the early 1980s.[1] Likewise, its staff of researchers had multiplied by tenfold. By 1976 the institute could boast of an Academic Advisory Board that showcased some of the premier conservative intellectuals of the period, including Irving Kristol and Paul McCracken. Thus the dinner—despite the tenuous state of conservative political organizing in the mid-1970s—served to mark the triumph of this unabashedly conservative institution. Here was a public policy planning center that gave conservatives hope for the future.

Indeed AEI was now so prominent that the dinner's featured guest was none other than the president of the United States, Gerald Ford. Ford had utilized AEI's research staff and their publications since his early congressional years in the late 1940s and was a longtime friend of AEI's president, William (Bill) Baroody. Speaking to the gathered institute's staff, Ford bestowed praise on the group and noted how "in the Congress, as Vice President and now as President, my staff and I have relied on AEI's pioneering work." Ford also noted that AEI's conservatism made the institution great, as it ensured "that there [was] a vital competition in the realm of ideas. Competition of ideas is absolutely essential to the continuation of a free society, for it is diversity which is the strength of our democracy."[2] Through Ford's promotion of "ideological diversity," he was, as will be seen in this chapter, explicitly adopting the language that AEI itself used to achieve relevance as an explicitly conservative institution offering a "conservative voice" in political and public policy debates. By the mid-1970s AEI and other conservative think tanks like the Heritage Foundation were explicitly positioning themselves *within* the conservative movement. However, this was not always the case. Even in the early 1960s these institutions were not comfortable with such a positioning, given that it implied an inherent bias in their research product. To understand this transformation—from *without* the conservative movement to *within* it—we must turn to the "long sixties," roughly 1960 to 1972. Examining this time period will help bring a full understanding of how, why, and through what means think tanks and their participants were able to move from a marginal position of political power outside the conservative movement to political powerbrokers as explicitly ideologically conservative institutions.

A Three-Stage Transition

By the mid-1970s, conservative think tanks were—and still are—best understood as research and public relations institutions, populated by conservative intellectuals and largely financed by wealthy and corporate donors. They theorize and "sell" conservative public policy and ideologies to both lawmakers and the public at large. From the mid-1970s onward—the heyday of the modern conservative think tank—such institutions were instrumental in the turn away from New Deal liberalism and the concomitant rise of conservatism. They have helped plan a wide variety of conservative public policies and have been instrumental in getting more and more Americans to adopt the identity "conservative" through their promotion of conservative identities.

However, when AEI first emerged in 1943 as the American Enterprise Association (AEA), such an understanding of what a conservative think tank was and what it did simply did not exist. When AEA tried to formulate such a conception in the late 1940s, it immediately came up against the main barrier to its relevance: the notion that its wealthy and corporate funders were making it hopelessly biased toward conservative policies and political economy. Thus the story of the consolidation of the modern conservative think tank in the long '60s is primarily a story about how such a barrier was overcome. Such a story contains roughly three parts.[3]

First, in the early 1960s, worry over appearing "biased" led AEI to explicitly position itself *outside* of the conservative movement and instead to assert its wholesale objectivity in public policy debates. Even after it came under the presidency of conservative Bill Baroody in 1962, and even as it employed many conservatives, the institute consistently adhered to the idea that it was not a part of the conservative movement. It would only "provide the facts" of public policy debates to lawmakers and let these lawmakers arrive at their own position.[4]

Such an orientation, one that situated the conservative think tank outside of the conservative movement, would not change until 1964, when Baroody and his AEI associates experienced true conservative activism for the first time. In this second part of the modern think tank consolidation, Baroody and his researchers went outside of their institution to run the presidential campaign of Barry Goldwater. In Goldwater's campaign, which was unabashedly funded by wealthy conservative interests, the think tank researchers felt they could finally have what they wanted: a venue to promote their unabashed conservatism without the need to assert "objectivity." Although this would end in a failed effort, these AEI researchers would take the lessons they learned as an internal think tank on the campaign and use them to reform the conservative think tank into its modern composition. This initially resulted in a failed effort to create a new, explicitly conservative think tank, the Free Society Association (FSA)—one that would promote conservatism to policy makers and the public at large. However, after the failure of the FSA, Baroody and others rededicated themselves to making AEI into the modern conservative think tank model.

The third and final part of the consolidation of the modern think model came in the late 1960s and early 1970s, when Baroody moved AEI from outside the conservative movement to within it. To do so, Baroody and AEI worked to normalize their corporate and wealthy funders in a new way that would not only place them outside of the realm of critique but also engage them as an *asset* in entering political debates with a forthright conservative ideological project. The most obvious result of this move was that during the late 1960s and early 1970s conservative think tanks saw a massive increase in the amount of funding they received. These new monies, obtained largely from very wealthy families and corporations, had the clear effect of increasing the political and cultural power of these institutions. More research could be produced, more media appearances could be made, and more conservative legislation could be prepared as a result of the increased funding.

However, beyond this obvious linking of the material and institutional power of the think tank, the two worked together in a far more powerful way. In essence, the drastically increased funding of conservative think tanks in this period and the way in which this funding was justified created a whole new discourse of public policy expertise that greatly benefited conservatism as a political movement. This new discourse brought about a shift where ideological differences and "balancing" these differences in a "marketplace" became values in and of themselves. Indeed, they became the highest valued commodities of all in the two decades in which Americans became increasingly skeptical of liberalism as a governing ideology. As conservatives at AEI and elsewhere in the late 1960s and early 1970s worked to drive home the point that so-called liberal institutions—academia, foundations, the media, and liberal think tanks—were dominating a "marketplace of ideas," they opened up a new avenue to their own relevance, one that positioned institutions like conservative think tanks as necessary "competition" to a liberal intellectual monolith.

Thus not only did the corporate and wealthy funding of conservative think tanks not harm their credibility, but the bias created by it was actually *highly sought after* in the name of an ideological competition. This created a massive shift to a new language of public policy argumentation, which would greatly aid in shifting policy discussions to the right in that it would allow conservatives entrance into public policy debates by virtue of their identity as "conservatives" rather than of the specific content of their beliefs per se. It was enough that they could "create competition" with other institutions that were declared hopelessly liberally biased. This shift—from belief to being—created a new dominant discourse of public policy expertise and debate that exists to this day and, arguably, continues to shift such debates rightward.[5] In the late 1960s and early 1970s this discourse would be the necessary solution for conservatives at AEI and other conservative think tanks seeking to bring their institutions fully inside of the conservative movement.

Ideological Objectivity

Such a discourse had not always been operative in policy debates. When AEI emerged in 1943 as the "American Enterprise Association" there existed a deep suspicion of any organization that spoke on behalf of big business. With the memory of the Great Depression not far from Americans' minds, a "business association," as the think tank was then known, had to tread lightly when advocating for corporate interests to policy makers and the public at large. AEA's head, Lewis H. Brown, who was also the president of the Johns Manville Corporation, understood this well. He knew that his organization, a partnership of top executives of leading business and financial firms, would have this bias immediately taken into account when it put forth public policy recommendations. Thus, in his opening speeches for the organization, Brown tended to couch the nascent think tank's interests in diplomatic language such as the need to "re-educate every man, woman, and child to a deep faith . . . in the American way." He also engaged in one of the most acceptable forms of conservative discourse at the time, anticommunism, when he declared that all liberal reform could be a Trojan horse for "Marxism itself." Finally, Brown took up a familiar and somewhat popular conservative cause for the think tank's first public policy pronouncement—that of foreign aid. After visiting postwar Germany, Brown and AEA commissioned a 250-page report for the government, which, according to *Business Week*, suggested "rebuilding Germany as the economic heart of Western Europe . . . as fast as possible to get Germany off the backs of American taxpayers."[6]

Nevertheless, even such small interventions in policy making and political advocacy drew the ire of federal regulators disciplined by the Depression to be skeptical of business organizations. Thus in 1950 the House Lobby Investigating Committee began an investigation of the think tank that, in turn, led to it being named a "'big business' pressure organization," as the committee cited correspondence among its officials to indicate it promoted a "Republican-Southern Democrat coalition favorable to large corporations." The committee also said that AEA should have to "register under the Federal Lobby Act given that it met the tests for lobbyists."[7] In addition to this collective memory of the Depression, there had also by the 1950s and early 1960s emerged what historians now call a period of "liberal consensus" within the federal government whereby social scientists and politicians were deemed capable of defining social problems and then coming up with solutions to those problems through "scientific" techniques. The elite intellectual and cultural hegemony of a liberal consensus ideology during the 1950s and early to mid-1960s is hard to overstate. Numerous scholars have interpreted this hegemony in different ways. What is important for this chapter, however, is the point on which these scholars agree—that is, that within elite policy-making circles, contesting the idea of policy-making as an "objective," "rational," and "scientific" endeavor would have been extremely hard.[8] This dominant understanding of liberal technocratic expertise meant that business-oriented groups such as AEA would have trouble inserting themselves into policy discussions, given that they were immediately deemed too biased to come up with "scientific" solutions to the nation's problems. Baroody knew this liberal consensus discourse well and fully understood just how hard it would be to challenge this specific ideology from the inside in the early 1960s. Thus, when he became president of AEA in 1962, he immediately changed the name to the American Enterprise Institute so as to distance the think tank from any "business association" understandings while simultaneously adopting the more academic "Institute."

Despite his deeply conservative personal orientation, Baroody attempted to reposition the organization within the liberal technocratic ideal in order to make it newly relevant. A 1962 letter Baroody sent to AEI's director of special projects Karl Hess is instructive in this regard. He writes, "The Institute does *not* press any particular policy position or even attempt to form, suggest, or support any particular policy position. The Institute *does* attempt to provide the research assistance which will bring to bear upon any policy consideration the most pertinent facts available and the most knowledgeable considerations by acknowledged authorities in the field."[9] In this way, and at this time, Baroody made a political calculation—that the foundations of the liberal technocratic ideal were not to be challenged; a new path to relevance for AEI would be found through a strict adherence to the ideal rather than an aggressive expression of conservative politics and public policy. Hess—a staunch conservative—needed immense discipline from Baroody in this regard. Baroody went on to tell Hess, "The Institute has no position except to serve. You can anticipate that, as in the past, the originators of requests for Special Projects research will occupy positions all along the political spectrum. Our job is neither to form nor to change those positions but only to provide materials appropriate to them."[10] In some ways this tactic of providing technocratic expertise worked to enhance AEI's relevance. The Institute was very much revived in the early 1960s through its production of issue primers dedicated to presenting rigorously balanced interpretations of legislation. However, such a positioning came at the expense of Baroody and Hess's own conservative politics. By attempting to remove any taint of corporate or wealthy interest bias from the institution, these men effectively conceded that the institution of the think tank would not have anything to do with the promotion of conservative and corporate ideological causes. Thus in the mid-1960s both would effectively abandon the institution in order to practice their conservatism elsewhere—most notably in Barry Goldwater's 1964 run for the presidency.

An Activist Awakening

In Goldwater's campaign, Baroody, Hess, and other AEI intellectuals such as Edward McCabe saw, as many other conservatives did at the time, an outlet for their conservative politics that the think tank could not provide. Whereas in AEI they were dedicated to the liberal technocratic ideal and to distancing themselves from the interests of their corporate and wealthy funders, in the Goldwater campaign they could embrace this same funding and forthrightly promote their conservative politics through Goldwater. However, in many ways their experience on the campaign provided the foundation for a new understanding of the conservative think tank after the campaign was over. It was in Goldwater's campaign that Baroody and his AEI associates saw a perfect venue for inserting a forthright conservatism into the political "marketplace of ideas." The most comprehensive source detailing this effort by AEI associates is Stephen Shadegg's 1965 memoir *What Happened to Goldwater?*[11] Shadegg was a member of Goldwater's inner circle who had run his 1952 campaign for the Senate. He was an advisor on the 1964 campaign, but he ultimately felt he was phased out for the Baroody's AEI "brain trust." Thus while historians should view Shadegg's memoir with some suspicion, given his jaded outlook, it is invaluable at providing insight into the role of AEI associates in the Goldwater campaign and the lessons they would draw from this experience for the overall project of political conservatism. While Shadegg's sometimes Rasputin-like portrayal of Baroody is undeniably hyperbolic, it is nevertheless clear that Baroody and at least six AEI "associates" played key roles in the Goldwater campaign's "brain trust." In fact, this is one of the first sources available in the postwar period that describes conservative activism of this type using the phrase "think tank." More important, Shadegg's portrayal, as we will see, is backed up by Goldwater's own autobiographies and archival material regarding the role of AEI associates on the campaign.

Baroody, ever the entrepreneur, clearly understood the Goldwater moment in which his new "think tank" could advocate for conservatism in a way he thought impossible within AEI itself. From the beginning of the campaign Baroody and his associates attempted to take over all aspects of campaign policy making, speechwriting, and strategy. According to Goldwater himself, Baroody leaked an unflattering report to *The New York Times* that indicated that the campaign was in the process of being taken over by "far right" intellectuals William F. Buckley Jr. and L. Brent Bozell of *National Review*. In his 1988 autobiography, Goldwater asserted he was "now convinced that Baroody quickly slammed the door because he saw a possibility that he might have to share power with the two men, both of whom were highly intelligent and very political." After this coup, Baroody and his associate Edward McCabe immediately began providing polling research for Goldwater. However, this was just a precursor to their main role as key advisors and speechwriters for the campaign. By 1964, Shadegg argued, Baroody was "dictating the content of the speeches."[12] In this role, Baroody, McCabe, and Hess were most interested in promoting the unabashed conservatism that they had curbed within AEI.

At the Republican nominating convention, Shadegg argued that Baroody, McCabe, Hess, and four other AEI-affiliated individuals—Warren Nutter, Harry Jaffa, Chuck Lichtenstein, and Glenn Campbell—made up Goldwater's "brain trust." This group worked as a committee to come up with Goldwater's speech, including the widely quoted line, "[E]xtremism in the defense of liberty is no vice, and moderation in the pursuit of justice is no virtue"—words, according to Shadegg, "which attracted national attention which added to the disunity in the party, and which were to be interpreted and explained in a dozen different ways." Shadegg bitterly asserted that "the manner in which the acceptance speech was written became the pattern for the Goldwater statements during the campaign—ideas and phrases gathered together under Baroody's supervision, edited by McCabe, Kitchel, and Hess, until all unity of thought and style was completely destroyed." Goldwater's autobiographies back up this portrayal from the convention onward, asserting that Baroody wrote "our ideological speeches with the help of others. Hess wrote the daily material." Moreover, Goldwater also argued that after the convention speech, he, Baroody, and Goldwater's campaign manager Denison Kitchel alone decided the speech would mark the start of a campaign where "for better or worse, I would be myself—a straight-shooting, down-the-line conservative—for the entire campaign."[13] Baroody and his AEI associations now had the conservative ideological project that they thought they could not have at the think tank itself.

After the convention, Baroody consolidated his power, brought in more of his AEI people, and took on more activities in the campaign. Shadegg argued that Baroody's group took up the "third floor in an office reserved for the Senator and his brain trust, forty speech writers, stenographers, and clerks, all selected by Bill Baroody[, who] were busily framing major policy statements, planning the content of television presentations, and developing the over-all strategy." Now explicitly describing the group as a "think tank," Shadegg argued that they were "responsible for the preparation of speeches and statements to be released through the PR department and on nationwide television." Goldwater agreed with this interpretation, arguing that after the nomination speech "Baroody saw himself as the head of a new brain trust around me. He would gather the research, direct the speechwriters, and be our resident intellectual with a team of his own bright young assistants. Baroody was classicist, almost an ancient Greek or Roman. He was also a man who enjoyed power."[14]

In this role, the think tankers were instrumental in producing more ideologically conservative speeches like the nominating convention speech. Gone was any need to present "balanced" portrayals of issues like at AEI—on the campaign they could create an internal think tank to directly express conservatism to the masses. Thus they wrote a speech on "checks and balances" that dogged Goldwater on the campaign trail after they inserted the line, "I weigh my words carefully when I say that—of all three branches of government—today's Supreme Court is the least faithful to the constitutional tradition of limited government, and to the principle of legitimacy in the exercise of power." A common staple of conservative discourse today, at the time—in the context of Supreme Court decisions on school prayer and state legislature reapportionment—it was seen by many, especially Shadegg, as too ideological for a presidential campaign. Likewise, toward the end of the campaign, Goldwater gave a televised address written by Baroody and his associates titled "The Free Society," which spoke out against busing, "racial quotas," and government intervention to alleviate private sector discrimination. In this address, Goldwater also spoke out against street demonstrations for civil rights and conflated them with everyday street crime. He asserted, "Above all, no Administration should, as [Johnson's] has, call men into the streets to solve their problems. The leadership of this nation has a clear and immediate challenge to go to work effectively and go to work immediately to restore proper respect for law and order in this land—*and not just prior to election day either!*" This exhortation came directly after Goldwater asserted in the speech that "our wives, all women, feel unsafe on our streets. Crime grows faster than population, while those who *break* the law are accorded more consideration than those who try to *enforce* the law." Shadegg asserted that this second section of the speech was widely declared to be excessive and contributed to the perception that Goldwater was nothing but an authoritarian. He argued that in the end, the "conflict between the practical politicians on the second floor and the elite members of Bill Baroody's 'think tank' on the third floor" was too much for the campaign. Goldwater himself agreed, stating in his first memoir, "My critics have remarked, and in retrospect I must agree with them, that my inner circle of advisers had very little experience in the politics of campaigning. Baroody, an intellectual, had devoted his career to dealing in abstracts," while "Hess was a good writer, a strongly conservative ideologue, but no politician."[15]

After the campaign, Baroody and his associates were despondent, but their experience as the campaign's internal think tank would provide the foundation for a reformation of AEI into a modern conservative think tank. No longer content to position AEI within the liberal technocratic ideal, Baroody and his associates began to think of new ways to centralize think tanks as an institution *of* and not *outside of* the postwar conservative movement. They would have to find a way to legitimate the kind of policy planning and conservative political theorizing they had done as the campaign's internal think tank within their old institution.

Legitimizing Partisan Advocacy: The Development of the "Marketplace"

How to structure a reformation of the think tank remained an open question. How could Baroody and other elite conservative activists reorient their think tank toward conservative causes without being seen as inherently biased toward the interests of the corporations and wealthy individuals who funded it? On the Goldwater campaign, this wasn't a problem, but within the technocratic world of policy planners in the mid-1960s, it was still an enormous barrier to relevancy.

At first, Baroody thought the answer would be to start a new think tank that would be entirely independent of AEI and that could then be free to advocate for conservative ideology and policy. Named the "Free Society Association," Baroody's new think tank took its title from Goldwater's "Free Society" speech. To raise funds for this unabashedly conservative think tank, Baroody enlisted the help of Goldwater himself. In a 1966 fundraising letter for the organization, Goldwater argued that the think tank was "set up as a nationwide, non-partisan crusade to promote the cause of freedom." While he used the letter to describe the organization as "non-partisan," it clearly had the contours of the modern conservative think tank, dedicating itself "to use the mass media, and most of all to mount a hard-hitting [educational] program among the nation's young people."[16] In this think tank emerged the modern goal of the conservative think tank—attempting to reform the identities of the public toward conservatism while at the same time boosting conservative causes in the mass media. To do so, in its brief period of relevancy in 1965 and 1966, the think tank enlisted not only Goldwater but also other conservative luminaries to write for its publications and give speeches. The group especially attempted to target young conservatives on college campuses to enlist them in the cause.

However, this new think tank would almost immediately falter and become unsustainable as an institutional project, primarily because there was never an entirely clear institutional mission for the organization. Moreover, it seems as if by 1967 and 1968 it became something of a slush fund, often supporting former Goldwater employees who could not find jobs after his campaign. Goldwater wrote a series of increasingly hostile letters to Baroody letting him know of his dissatisfaction with the progress of the nascent think tank. In one he noted that he had "made payments toward $20,000 which I never anticipated at all in the beginning." In another he lamented that "a lot of money was raised and a lot of money went down the drain and there was the time when good judgment said to close it down" but that he could not do so in 1967 in the midst of a tough Senate reelection bid, arguing it would "not be good to either conservatism or to my efforts" to have the think tank dismantled.[17] Thus it was not until after his election that the faltering endeavor would shut its doors.

During this same mid-1960s period, AEI was having its own share of troubles. After the 1964 presidential campaign, Lyndon Johnson, not one to ignore his political opponents, used his power against AEI. In 1965 a House select committee began an inquiry into "whether the involvement of AEI's staff in the campaign violated the institute's tax-exempt status." Thus they "subpoenaed its financial records, prompting a two-year investigation by the Internal Revenue Service." Ultimately, because Baroody and his associates had taken official leave of AEI, the investigation resulted in no punishment, but Baroody "never forgot that think tanks and politics can be a dangerous mix."[18]

Chastened by these two experiences in the mid-1960s, it was not until the late 1960s that Baroody began to rethink the foundations of their institutional model. This was particularly the case as the nation went through the collective convulsions that are now known simply as "1968." As liberal technocrats increasingly came to be blamed for a whole host of problems including urban blight, rioting, fiscal and monetary problems, and the war in Vietnam, conservatives began to identify the whole liberal technocratic edifice as the fundamental problem. Such a shift in thinking regarding the very legitimacy of the liberal technocratic model meant that more conservative understandings of policy making would be more readily accepted. Thus the personnel of AEI would not have to change—it still could house the same conservative intellectuals, who would now be free to offer a direct critique of the liberal technocratic ideal. A July 1968 letter from Baroody to corporate funders of AEI demonstrates this newly emerging critique. While still making an appeal to the "objective, non-partisan" research of AEI, Baroody nevertheless situated liberal technocrats as the main source of the nation's problems:

> Much of our thinking at AEI is conditioned by a conviction that the intellectual community plays an increasingly major role in the formulation of public policy—in short the conviction that most governmental programs, for example, enacted in the last thirty years did not originate either in the mind of a politician or from the overwhelming demand of the people or from the planks of a party platform. They were born in and can trace their origins through the thought and writings of an academic or a group of academics whose views concerning the organization of a society may not necessarily coincide with yours or mine.[19]

It is in quotes such as this one that we begin to see the shift to the "marketplace of ideas" discourse that conservative institutions like AEI would use to gain new power as explicitly conservative institutions within the conservative movement. Baroody began to position the conservative think tank as a counter to academia, liberal think tanks such as the Brookings Institution, and foundations such as the Ford Foundation, arguing that because liberal technocrats in these organizations had planned policy without the conservative counterpoint, the nation now had the problems that it did. Moreover, he made the explicit case that these technocrats were in no way democratically accountable to the electorate—that they could merely impose their will on the nation.

This critique of a "liberal establishment" began to emerge in full force from AEI and numerous other conservative entities. Within the White House itself, Nixon issued an order in 1969 that "all White House staff people . . . as well as Cabinet people . . . are not to use the Brookings Institution because of its bias against conservatives and the administration." Referencing future scandals associated with the Watergate break-in, Nixon aide Tom Huston suggested an IRS audit of Brookings or even a break-in to "go after the classified material which they have stashed over there." In the end, however, it was suggested that the White House "play the Brookings game ourselves" through the development of a counterestablishment of conservative think tanks and foundations designed to promote conservative causes. Additionally, the memo suggested that they "scare the living hell out of Brookings and paint it as pro-Hanoi and anti-American."[20]

It was with this counterestablishment project that AEI and conservative think tanks more generally would come into play. In a 1970 internal memo, a writer for AEI declared that liberal technocrats at Brookings had been engaging in "an assault on the political, economic and social structure of the country" that was "largely financed by major infusions of financial resources from the Ford Foundation." By 1971 letters to corporate and conservative foundation donors from Baroody were stressing this need for a counterestablishment:

> Essentially, what is required is a serious effort to right the imbalance reflected by the continuing and even accelerating impact on public opinion formation and public policy determination. This cannot and ought not to be attempted through an action against such existing centers. It can only be achieved by assuring similar resources to institutions and centers not similarly oriented. *The goal of such an effort would be to make certain that the American people are exposed to varying points of view on public policy issues. It is essential that fair competition exists in the arena of idea formation.*

Here we see the liberal technocracy under assault and a drastic shift away from the idea held in earlier AEI years that the institution should be concerned with "objectivity." Instead, the entire liberal technocratic ideal is deemed the problem, one that can only be remedied by a shift to a "marketplace of ideas" as opposed to a monopoly. Under such a discourse, then, the bias of conservative and corporate funders—who are being targeted with this letter—is not a problem, but rather a *solution* that is needed to balance what is seen as a monolithic liberal establishment. Indeed, this particular discursive formation actually presents corporate and wealthy interests as fundamentally *powerless*—as the "little guys" struggling to make their voices heard. One of these wealthy interests—conservative John Merrill Olin, who in this period was doing much to fund AEI and other conservative causes—felt so aggrieved that in April 1972 he often wrote to Baroody himself requesting that specific studies be produced that supported his goals of keeping in check "new tax legislation on corporations and wealthy individuals," particularly "estate and gift tax regulations." In responding, Baroody noted that AEI had done several studies but would not release them to the public "until the appropriate time." Olin replied tersely: "So far as I'm concerned the appropriate time is now."[21] The studies were then produced in early 1973. This type of explicit research buying and producing became much more possible as the new marketplace discourse effectively legitimized the bias of the wealthy funders of AEI and other conservative institutions.

By the time of Nixon's reelection in 1972, this establishment/counterestablishment critique had fully crystallized, and a wholesale shift in conservative funding priorities—as well as a shift to the broader "marketplace" discourse—was under way. In late 1972 Nixon aide Pat Buchanan wrote a memo to the president arguing for the creation of a "new 'cadre' of Republican governmental professionals who can survive this Administration and be prepared to take over future ones"—a conservative "government-in-exile" centering on institutes that could "serve as the repository of [conservative] political beliefs." While Buchanan was skeptical that AEI could fill the bill, assuming it was still wedded to nonpartisanship, Baroody was at the same time giving a talk titled "The Corporate Role in the Decade Ahead" to a Business Council meeting that stressed the same points, albeit in language more concerned with corporate, rather than Republican, interests. In his speech Baroody argued that the "corporate class had abdicated the intellectual arena" and was giving money to institutions like Brookings, the Ford Foundation, and universities that did not support its values. Returning to the marketplace metaphor, Baroody argued that corporations needed to break an intellectual monopoly: "To break this monopoly requires a calculated, positive, major commitment—one which will insure that the views of other competent intellectuals are given the opportunity to contend effectively in the mainstream of our country's intellectual activity. There are such people. They can be encouraged and mobilized. Their numbers can increase. But, that can hardly happen without reordering priorities in the support patterns of corporations and foundations—at least by those corporations and foundations concerned with preserving the basic values of this free society and its free institutions."[22] A mere decade after writing a letter declaring that AEI would take no position on any issue, Baroody had openly declared that this was now the institute's sole purpose. Whereas his 1962 letter was technical in its advocacy of "objectivity," the 1972 speech was more akin to one given at a political rally, urging corporations to stand up for their values in an intellectual and monetary marketplace. The clear shift from outside to inside the conservative movement had taken place.

As for the "reordering of priorities" advocated by Baroody in this speech, such reordering quickened in the early 1970s as corporations and conservative individuals, through their own foundations, began to add their money and voices to the "marketplace of ideas." To take but one example of where this money was coming from, from the middle of 1969 to the middle of 1973 AEI received almost half of its $8 million budget from a single source—conservative millionaire Richard Mellon Scaife, who, along with Joseph Coors and John Merrill Olin, used his own foundation to pour money into think tanks like AEI and the Heritage Foundation (another conservative think tank that formed in 1973). Additionally, vast new resources were pouring into AEI coffers as corporations sought to add their voice to the "marketplace of ideas." By the middle of 1974, Baroody had honed his pitch to these corporations in a new fundraising form letter that drew from his earlier Business Council speech:

Paul McCracken recently said: "A free society can tolerate a monopoly in the production of widgets but it cannot survive a monopoly in public policy idea formation." The results of such a near-monopoly in the intellectual community are clearly evident. It is certainly safe to say that the long-term trendline in public policy has been toward more rather than less regulation of business, toward higher rather than lower taxes on business—in short, toward more rather than less government intervention in the private sector. And—growing public hostility to business is a fact. Effective competition of ideas is the American Enterprise Institute's approach to the problem.[23]

Once again, Baroody used the discourse of the market to defuse a critique of corporate donations; such donations were welcome and necessary to create competition. Thus the donations, far from being something to be ashamed of, were cause for celebration as the corporate "little guy" was finally having his voice heard, for instance, in debates over regulation and taxes.

Consolidation

The success of the AEI and others in promoting the new public policy marketplace discourse was evident as such language and actions moved beyond the confines of conservative institutions. Even the institutions of the so-called liberal establishment began to internalize this critique and sought to remedy it by "leveling the marketplace." Thus, from 1972 to 1975, the Ford Foundation gave AEI $480,000 in grants. This gave both institutions credence to declare that they were working to "level the marketplace" by adding self-identified conservatives to the "competitive field." Likewise, traditional media sources, which were often situated by conservatives as part of the liberal establishment, began to turn to conservative think tanks in their stories in the name of "balancing the marketplace." Many of these same sources also began to do full stories on AEI, adding to its marketing and branding strategies. The New York Times, Newsweek, Business Week, the Los Angeles Times, Esquire, Time, and U.S. News & World Report, among others, did lengthy promotional stories for the institute, all of which stressed the "competition of ideas" framework. One Newsweek piece helpfully sold AEI as the necessary "counter-Brookings" for right thinking. Brookings itself began to hire Republicans, as well, to show that it too was interested in "diversity."[24] In short, the so-called liberal establishment fully internalized the conservative marketplace discourse of public policy. Brookings sought corporate donations in the name of ideological and material balance; it hired Republicans, including its president, to offset concerns that it was too one-sided and to add "diversity" to the institution; and there was a full "flipping of the discourse" from the previous decade, in that the new "voice to be suspicious of" was not the voice of corporations but rather of liberally aligned institutions.

This new acceptance of the marketplace metaphor by the very institutions that conservatives critiqued is what truly led to the hegemony of the new discourse.

It was this hegemonic discourse that ultimately allowed conservative think tanks to become part of the conservative movement by the early 1970s. No longer needing to place their institutions outside of the movement, as Baroody did with AEI in the early 1960s, and no longer needing to go outside of places like AEI to practice their conservative politics, as elite activists did on the Goldwater campaign, the new trope of ideological diversity allowed AEI to become part of the conservative movement. Moreover, it allowed conservative institutions to be centrally placed in the American national political scene with immense power that they could have only imagined in the early 1960s. First and foremost, the discourses of "competition," "ideological diversity," and a "marketplace of ideas" allowed for the dissipation of any concerns regarding the funding of the ideological project of the modern conservative think tank. Corporations and the extremely wealthy were merely positioned as another voice in a level "marketplace of ideas." Second, there was a shift from belief to being—or from the content of policy to political identity—as the most important value in public policy debates. This constituted the germination of the elite media discourse within which Americans live today, where "balancing" public policy debates between "two sides" in a "marketplace of ideas" effectively takes precedence over policy content. In such an arena, the modern conservative think tank would benefit greatly. No longer needing to maintain the pretense of objectivity or to go outside of the think tank to advocate for conservative policies, conservatives within think tanks could use their institutional apparatus to sell conservatism.

Notes

1. James Allen Smith, *The Idea Brokers: Think Tanks and the Rise of the New Policy Elite* (New York: Free Press, 1991), 179.
2. Background information, President's drop-by at American Enterprise Institute's Dinner, May 19, 1976, folder: TR1, 5/19/76-5/20/76 Executive, White House Central Files, Gerald R. Ford Library, Ann Arbor, MI.
3. Historians of elite conservatism must contend with a problem not known to the social historians of the Right who have come before us: how to document elite political movements. Whereas social historians had numerous archival resources of grassroots movements and oral histories of grassroots participants, historians of elite conservatism often contend with a dearth of sources. For instance, in this project it should be noted that while there are a small number of smaller defunct think tanks with accessible archives, the main conservative think tanks such as AEI and Heritage do not have accessible institutional archives. This, of course, presents a problem for historians, given the primacy awarded to archival research within the profession. Without access to such resources, historians are forced to try to piece together the history of elite movements from a wide variety of sources.

4. Here this essay explicitly disagrees with James Allen Smith's interpretation that the entrance of Baroody into AEI began its explicitly conservative reorientation (Smith, *The Idea Brokers,* 167–89). New evidence provided in Baroody's papers and examination of AEI publications at the time suggest that it was not until the late 1960s that AEI made an explicit shift to operating inside the conservative movement.

5. For more on the shift from belief to being and how it played out in the larger politics of the Left and Right in the 1960s and 1970s, see Timothy Brennan, *Wars of Position: The Cultural Politics of Left and Right* (New York: Columbia University Press, 2006). James Allen Smith also perceptively notes the development of this new discourse at AEI in the 1960s and early 1970s (Smith, *The Idea Brokers,* 179). This chapter pushes Smith's analysis further. Whereas Smith argues that such a counter-positioning of AEI against "liberal" institutions gave AEI an "institutional mission" and "helped to rally more contributors," Smith's analysis misses the larger significance of what was occurring. More important is the way that the development of the discourse removes earlier concerns of "biased" funding—the factor that had been the most useful bludgeon against conservative think tanks. Instead, what the new discourse does is turn the bias into an *asset*—a way to enter political debates as opposed to being excluded from them.

6. Lewis H. Brown, "Private Business Agencies to Achieve Public Goals in the Postwar World," *American Economic Review* 33 (March 1943): 81; "The Brown Plan," *Business Week,* October 25, 1947, 25.

7. "Lobby Inquiry Finds 'Big Business' Group," *The New York Times,* December 30, 1950.

8. This essay's understanding of "postwar liberal consensus" is guided by Godfrey Hodgson's still relevant understanding of the phrase. Hodgson's understanding essentially gives scholars the following definition of the beliefs that constituted the liberal consensus: (1) American free enterprise is now different than older forms of capitalism as it has revolutionary potential for social justice; (2) Tenet 1 is true because the federal government has found a way to sustain unending economic growth, so no class conflict over resources will ever be needed again; (3) The United States is moving towards social equality and abolishing social classes, as all workers are becoming middle class and business is controlled by enlightened management; (4) Social scientists and politicians within the government are capable of defining social problems and then coming up with solutions to those problems; (5) Communism is the main threat to this American system just described, so the United States will have to engage in a prolonged struggle against Communism at home and abroad; (6) It is the duty of the United States to help spread such a system abroad (Godfrey Hodgson, *America in Our Time: From World War II to Nixon, What Happened and Why* [New York: Doubleday, 1978], 67–98). For my own understanding of the hegemony of liberal technocratic expertise, I am in debt primarily to scholars like Hodgson who have since interpreted the liberal consensus ideology as being intimately related to the early Cold War and the re-articulation of various academic disciplines during this period. See Thomas Bender and Carl E. Schorske, eds., *American Academic Culture in Transformation: Fifty Years, Four Disciplines* (Princeton, NJ: Princeton University Press, 1997), esp. 243–308; K. A. Cuordileone, *Manhood and American Political Culture in the Cold War* (New York: Routledge, 2005), esp. 1–36; Ellen Herman, *The Romance of American Psychology: Political Culture in the Age of Experts* (Berkeley: University of

California Press, 1996); Elaine Tyler May, *Homeward Bound: American Families in the Cold War Era*, rev. ed. (New York: Basic Books, 2008).

9. William J. Baroody to Karl Hess, November 30, 1962, folder 7, box 13, William J. Baroody Papers, Manuscript Division, Library of Congress, Washington, DC. Emphasis in original.

10. William J. Baroody to Karl Hess, November 30, 1962, folder 7, box 13, Baroody Papers.

11. Stephen Shadegg, *What Happened to Goldwater?: The Inside Story of the 1964 Republican Campaign* (New York: Holt, Rinehart and Winston, 1965).

12. Barry M. Goldwater with Jack Casserly, *Goldwater* (New York: Doubleday, 1988), 147–48; Shadegg, *What Happened to Goldwater?*, 120.

13. Shadegg, *What Happened to Goldwater?*, 132, 165–66. Glenn Campbell by this time was at the Hoover Institution at Stanford University, another conservative think tank which emerged as such in the late 1950s (Shadegg, *What Happened to Goldwater?*, 165–66; Goldwater and Casserly, *Goldwater*, 156, 190).

14. Shadegg, *What Happened to Goldwater?*, 190, 194; Goldwater and Casserly, *Goldwater*, 188.

15. "Campaign Speech before the American Political Science Association, Chicago, Illinois," September 11, 1964, folder 8, box 133, Series 2: 1964 Campaign, Personal and Political Papers of Senator Barry M. Goldwater, Arizona Historical Foundation, Tempe, AZ; "Nationwide TV Address on 'The Free Society,'" October 22, 1964, folder 18, box 133, Series 2: 1964 Campaign, Goldwater Papers (emphasis in original); Shadegg, *What Happened to Goldwater?*, 250, 253; Barry M. Goldwater, *With No Apologies: The Personal and Political Memoirs of United States Senator Barry M. Goldwater* (New York: William Morrow, 1979), 163–64. For more on the development of "law and order conservatism" in the 1960s, see Michael W. Flamm, *Law and Order: Street Crime, Civil Unrest, and the Crisis of Liberalism in the 1960s* (New York: Columbia University Press, 2007).

16. Direct mail from Barry Goldwater, June 3, 1966, folder 20, box 48, Series 1: Personal Papers, Goldwater Papers.

17. In Goldwater's files, the placement of Karl Hess seems to be a particular source of problems in this regard. See multiple letters in box 48, folder 20 for more on the Hess placement. Barry Goldwater to William J. Baroody, March 13, 1967, folder 20, box 48, Series 1: Personal Papers, Goldwater Papers; Barry Goldwater to William J. Baroody, June 15, 1967, folder 20, box 48, Series 1: Personal Papers, Goldwater Papers.

18. Smith, *The Idea Brokers*, 178; Lee Edwards, *The Power of Ideas: The Heritage Foundation at 25 Years* (Ottawa, IL: Jameson Books, 1997), 5.

19. William J. Baroody to Orville E. Melby, July 8, 1968, folder 4, box 59, Baroody Papers.

20. Tom Charles Huston to H. R. Haldeman, July 16, 1970, in *From: The President; Richard Nixon's Secret Files*, ed. Bruce Oudes (New York: Harper and Row, 1989), 29; H. R. Haldeman to Ken Cole, May 1, 1969, in Oudes, ed., *From: The President*, 147–48.

21. Draft memo, "The Brookings Institution," August 12, 1970, folder 1, box 62, Baroody Papers; William J. Baroody to John Swearingen, November 16, 1971, folder 7, box 56, Baroody Papers (emphasis in original); John Merrill Olin to

William J. Baroody, April 12, 1972, folder 8, box 60, Baroody Papers; William J. Baroody to John Merrill Olin, April 24, 1972, folder 8, box 60, Baroody Papers; John Merrill Olin to William J. Baroody, April 27, 1972, folder 8, box 60, Baroody Papers; John Merrill Olin to William J. Baroody, February 20, 1973, folder 8, box 60, Baroody Papers.

22. Patrick Buchanan to Richard Nixon, November 10, 1972, in Oudes, ed., *From: The President,* 558–68; William J. Baroody, "The Corporate Role in the Decade Ahead," delivered at a Business Council meeting, October 20, 1972, folder 6, box 86, Baroody Papers.

23. American Enterprise Institute to Commissioner of Internal Revenue Service, May 6, 1974, folder 4, box 44, Baroody Papers; William J. Baroody to Lewis A. Lapham, May 31, 1974, folder 5, box 56, Baroody Papers.

24. AEI financial records, 1972–1975, folder 8, box 58, Baroody Papers; "The Conservative's Think Tank," *Business Week,* May 2, 1977, 80–81; "The Other Think Tank," *Time,* September 19, 1977; Kenneth Lamott, "Right-Thinking Think Tank," *The New York Times,* July 23, 1978; Steven Rattner, "A Think Tank for Conservatives," *The New York Times,* March 23, 1975; Peter Steinfels, "The Reasonable Right," *Esquire,* February 13, 1979, 24–30; "Celebration on the Right," *Newsweek,* May 17, 1976, 81; "Two 'Think Tanks' with Growing Impact," *U.S. News & World Report,* September 25, 1978, 47–48; "Brookings Needs Help," *Los Angeles Times,* date unknown, found in folder 5, box 86, Baroody Papers.

PART 3

God and Country

CHAPTER 6

The Righteousness of Difference

Orthodox Jews and the Establishment Clause, 1965–71

Robert Daniel Rubin

Jewish Americans played a significant role in the rights revolution of the 1960s. Amid that decade's upheavals, Jews continued the liberal activism that they had carried out throughout the twentieth century. Yet historians ought not to assume that American Jewry acted as a monolith or held uniformly liberal attitudes, even regarding the constitutional politics of church and state. To be sure, the strong majority of Jewish Americans supported the federal courts' recognition of a "wall of separation" between religion and government; indeed, Jewish lawyers and scholars played a prominent role in such efforts. Yet not all Jews supported "strict separationism." Nor did their collective attitude on the matter remain constant. Divergence and change marked the group's stance.

To grasp more fully Jewish Americans' political orientations during the 1960s, historians must consider the actions of a largely neglected subgroup. Orthodox Jews—those complying with the strictest and least modern codes of ritual observance—increasingly acted out of interests distinct from those of their more liberal counterparts. Orthodox Jews' worldview diverged from liberals' over the course of this decade. Whereas non-Orthodox Jews continued to assimilate into mainstream American society and to capitalize on the Constitution's guarantees of full civic and religious inclusivity, the Orthodox cast their lot as outsiders. Before long, Orthodox Jewry formed a cultural enclave.

Through its focus on the constitutional politics of church-state separation in education, this essay addresses crucial fissures within the public life of America in the 1960s, when, somewhat under the radar, conservative religion influenced

society and politics in surprising ways. The differences in constitutional politics between liberal and Orthodox Jews shed light on the gradual-but-certain
discrediting of the "melting pot" concept and dissolution of political centrism.
By examining right-wing Jews' initial attempts to influence federal case law on
schooling and religion, we learn much about how morally orthodox citizens
helped undermine the ideological center of American political life. We gain
insight as well into the distinctive unfolding of American Jewry, whose recent
history registers biting internal divisions. And we glimpse the emergence of an
Orthodox subculture, at once modern and antimodern, determined to close
itself off from the wider society by trumpeting one of that society's most prized
postmodern verities, the righteousness of difference.

Educating for Equality

Jewish Americans have generally throughout modern history held liberal attitudes on the relationship between government and religion. In the decades
following World War II, Jewish community leaders campaigned for the most
liberal of positions, a "strict separation" between church and state. Rabbis representing the largest Jewish-American denomination, the Reform movement,
declared that America's greatness lay in its record of disestablishment—the distance kept between government and religious sects. Jews continued to see their
history in America as marked by profound freedom, and freedom, in the Jewish lexicon, denoted freedom from religious compulsion, as well as from the
second-class status that had accompanied their struggles against compulsion. A
sturdy wall cleaving government from religion has meant nothing less than an
opportunity to live openly, without fearing violence or forced exile.[1]

Jewish American support for church-state separation derives from Jews'
experience as a minority group. Throughout centuries in diaspora, Jews world-
wide assumed their fundamental difference from the ethnic and religious
majorities that enveloped them. Historically, they maintained legal and political
order within their own communities, constituting semiautonomous enclaves,
relatively unassimilated alien entities amid surrounding nations and empires.[2]
Minority status in the United States has been accompanied by rather different
conditions and opportunities. Here, Jews have happily discovered that fellow
Americans offered more than mere tolerance. Since World War II, the United
States government has interpreted its charter to require that the nation's public institutions honor the liberty and dignity of those citizens whose minority
status disadvantages them politically. To protect religious minorities from mis-
treatment within public institutions such as schools, the United States Supreme
Court applied its civil-rights constitutionalism specifically to religion in a series
of rulings from 1947 to 1963, mandating that a sturdy "wall of separation"

cleave church from state. Two of these decisions most fully expressed the court's notion that fairness and neutrality required the secularization of public institutions. In *Engel v. Vitale* (1962), the justices determined that government had no business composing prayers for classroom recitation; a year later, in *Abington v. Schempp*, they declared that devotional Bible reading and recitation of the Lord's Prayer in public schools likewise violated the First Amendment's Establishment Clause. Because most Jews have benefitted from robust protection of the rights of religious minorities, most Jews have sought to preserve, as vital to their interests, the court's doctrine of church-state separation.[3]

Toward their goal of civic equality, Jews have long championed nonsectarian public schools. If religious practices were prohibited from the classroom, they reasoned, then schools could promote the one legitimate public "faith"— Americanism, an ethos of thick religious impartiality and inclusivity. Following World War II, Jews spearheaded a movement to commit courts and legislatures to church-state separationism. This effort was led by the American Jewish Congress and especially by the chief counsel for its Commission on Law and Social Action, Leo Pfeffer, whose numerous amicus briefs looked to ban organized, spoken religious exercises from the public schools. Pfeffer became the civil-libertarian face of American Jewry, crafting a separationist doctrine that found its way, in more-or-less whole cloth, into the court's opinions of the late 1940s through 1970s. At the highest echelons of constitutional law, organized Jewry, with Pfeffer in the lead, realized its vision of an impartial, nonsectarian, universally inclusive classroom.[4]

Pfeffer's briefs in the postwar Establishment Clause cases suggest the centrality of constitutional politics to the era's liberalism. Pfeffer seconded assertions made by the American Civil Liberties Union and the National Association for the Advancement of Colored People in insisting that government not abridge any citizen's right to full membership within public life. This included a citizen's religious rights, which must, Pfeffer believed, be guarded by a strict separationism keeping religion "outside of the cognizance of political government." He acknowledged that implementing the Establishment Clause would remain a political activity, overseen by judges responding to persuasive attorneys, scholars, and government officials. However, Pfeffer insisted, church-state law must never be circumscribed by the potential tyranny of a political majority. The freedom and dignity of unpopular religious minorities needed to be defended against majoritarian suppression. Pfeffer maintained that "there are some areas of man's life that are too important and sacred to be assigned to the coercive arm of the state," most notably "the area of the mind and conscience, and, above all, of man's relationship to God."[5]

To help protect unpopular minorities from coercion and preserve their dignity, Pfeffer and Jewish liberals turned to a powerful government institution—the public education system—to inculcate citizens with an equal respect for all their fellows. Liberals championed an ostensibly all-inclusive, religiously neutral, secular public sphere. Those who dwelled therein, despite their many differences, would be steeped in open-mindedness and would learn to speak across their differences by recognizing the fundamental worthiness of students from varying backgrounds and with varying beliefs. The ideal of assimilating schoolchildren into a culture based on tolerance sat at the center of Chief Justice Earl Warren's opinion in *Brown v. Board*. The primary value of public education, Warren suggested, was as an "instrument in awakening the child to cultural values . . . and in helping him to adjust normally to his environment." Like all other students, "children of the minority group" deserved the opportunity to assimilate. Only thereby might they achieve civil equality and overcome any "feeling of inferiority as to their status in the community."[6]

Pfeffer subscribed to the assimilationist ethic behind the civil-rights jurisprudence of the Warren Court. Only public education based on universal citizenship, he suggested, incorporated Jews into American society without requiring that they act as Christians. His views influenced Justice William Brennan, whose concurring opinion in *Abington v. Schempp* offered the court's fullest application of the assimilationist ethic to the question of religion in public schools. Brennan contended that public education could properly acculturate only by remaining religiously neutral. And religious neutrality, in turn, required a thoroughgoing secularism. "It is implicit in the history and character of American public education," Brennan wrote, "that the public schools serve a uniquely public function: the training of American citizens in an atmosphere free of parochial, divisive, or separatist influences of any sort." Only such an environment would permit schoolchildren to "assimilate a heritage common to all American groups and religions," a "heritage neither theistic nor atheistic, but simply civic and patriotic." Brennan's opinion signaled that the public-sphere secularism of organized American Jewry had indelibly impacted the nation's fundamental law. Through their constitutional efforts, Jews had secured their legacy as the nation's foremost proponents of the secularized classroom.[7]

Cultural Conservatism and the Court

The rights revolution provoked a bitter reaction among those who considered themselves its nonbeneficiaries—indeed, its victims. Critics charged the court with usurping the rights of individual states and their citizens to fashion laws based on their prejudices. White racism attained "principled" expression in a republican majoritarianism that condemned the federal government, and especially its courts, for trammeling over local opinion. Had this anticourt populism targeted only the justices' desegregation rulings, its appeal would have remained somewhat limited. Instead, the court's critics applied their majoritarian theory to the full range of minority-rights case law. In their diatribes against judicial activism, issues such as race, religion, crime, and public decency blurred together. The content of their complaints became secondary to the political theory that afforded those complaints nationwide resonance. Thus arose a newly invigorated conservative movement, alarmed at what it considered a court-sponsored ethos of moral laxity and contempt for social tradition.[8]

Central to this emerging movement was religious conservatism. Following World War II, nationalism acquired a strongly religious hue, as conservative Christians looked to the public schools as a primary site at which the nation's citizens and their society could be fortified through a curriculum featuring an explicitly devotional content. The court's religion-in-schools decisions frustrated supporters of school prayer and caused them to redouble their efforts by sponsoring a series of school-prayer amendments. In the quarter century after *Engel*, Congress entertained more than six hundred such amendments. The testimony and public commentary on these bills registered much more than concern for children's moral instruction. Prayer supporters gave voice to a political critique of the court, which they accused of violating democratic principles. As historian Aaron Haberman finds in his study of the school-prayer movement, conservative critiques "accused the Court of subverting the intent of the Founders and taking away a clear right guaranteed to the majority." Numerous proponents of the 1964 Becker Amendment to legalize classroom prayer echoed the witness who warned the House Judiciary Committee that "unless positive action is taken [to restore prayer in schools] it appears likely that in the name of religious freedom the will of the majority may very well be subjected to the will of the minority." Throughout the House testimony, the court was identified as a tyrant forcibly recasting American government.[9]

Congressional sponsors of prayer amendments achieved no success. Frustration only confirmed their suspicion that the public schools, with the help of the Supreme Court, had become factories for inculcating students with an un-American, antireligious worldview. Religious conservatives vilified the schools as hotbeds of "secular humanism," a comprehensive ideology contrary to their own understanding of religion. As the federal courts continued to desegregate and secularize public education, large numbers of white Christian parents moved their children into the largely all-white, conservative Christian private academies that suddenly dotted the nation's landscape in the late 1960s and 1970s. These parents were having nothing of the liberal, assimilationist ethos given the force of law by the Warren Court. If public schools were no longer guided by the clean, "American" values of the alleged majority of citizens, then the God-fearing legions would start their own schools.[10]

The place of American Jews amid these changes is complicated and hard to trace with precision. Largely because of their association with liberal politics, Jews do not appear often in studies on conservative politics—especially those on the growing popular hostility toward public education and the rights revolution. In scholarly accounts Jewish Americans remain steadfast champions of the church-state separationism that their leaders helped craft. A closer look, in fact, reveals a situation that defies plain categorization. No one ideology describes Jewish Americans from the mid-1960s onward. They cannot be located as a singular bloc, squarely within either the era's anticourt reactionary politics or the clear-cut liberal assimilationism lauded since the 1940s by most prominent Jewish legal activists.[11]

Assimilationism and Its Discontents

While most Jewish intellectuals of the postwar era echoed the liberal positions advanced by the major Jewish organizations, exceptions could gradually be heard. Early on, one notable figure, theologian-sociologist Will Herberg, cautioned that separationism had become a "religion" among Jews and that government could not flourish if shorn of traditional religious content. Herberg depicted separationism as a symptom of liberal Jews' attempt to assimilate into mainstream American culture—to adopt a generalized "American way of life." Like other Americans, he complained, most Jews had sloughed off the demands of prophetic religion and instead adopted a religion of personal adjustment and cultural conformity. This troubled Herberg, who considered American civic culture sufficiently robust to support a true pluralism among differing religious groups—each, in its way, commanded by God. Jews enjoyed a historic opportunity: to be true to their religion and yet full members of their society. Each of the "minorities within the national community," he insisted, could "pursue its own particular concerns without impairing the overall unity of American life." Surely, there was "no need for . . . the anxious search for injuries and grievances that ha[d] characterized so much of the Jewish 'defense' psychology."[12]

Herberg's attack on assimilationism and separationism would resonate with a small but important part of the Jewish community, Orthodox Jews. Committed to a lifestyle that distinguished them from their fellow Americans, Orthodox Jews could hardly have imagined any aspect of their daily routine not steeped in observance to Jewish law. As Herberg recognized, Pfeffer's notion of religious devotion as a private matter made little sense to these Jews. When they began to stake out their own political positions in the 1960s, they traveled down the pathway cleared by Herberg—a pathway diverging from the political trajectory of mainstream American Jewry.[13]

Like morally conservative Christians, Orthodox Jews recoiled at what they considered the decadence and anarchy polluting American culture. In 1962 the Union of Orthodox Jewish Congregations of America (OU) decried "the rising tendency to disregard any standards of decency in the field of publication, motion pictures, and television" and called on "all responsible forces within American society to join in combating this onslaught upon the moral health of this nation." The OU did not express an isolated sentiment; by middecade, every prominent Orthodox organization stood publically against the moral anarchy supposedly rampaging through society, including liberal Judaism. These groups feared that women's liberation and the youth movement indicated an obscene, licentious culture with which no God-fearing man or woman should have any sustained contact. By middecade Orthodoxy had slid precipitously to the ideological right.[14]

Orthodoxy diverged from mainstream Jewry in another important respect. Whereas the latter retained its historical support for public education, Orthodox Jews became more determined than ever to educate their children in the private Jewish day schools and *yeshivos* proliferating in the northeastern United States. As the Orthodox community turned inward during the 1960s and 1970s, it used its private schools for "contra-acculturation," to purge its young of the mainstream's habits and beliefs. Orthodox leaders sought government funding for their school system; this, in turn, led them to break from the separationist view that would bar government from supporting religion. After years of falling in line with the liberal civic agencies on constitutional matters, the chief Orthodox groups disassociated themselves from the litigation and amicus briefs generated by Leo Pfeffer.[15]

Notwithstanding their revulsion toward the radical 1960s, Orthodox Jews did not adopt the entire agenda of the Christian Right. The Orthodox were a minority within a minority, guarding their antimodern Judaism against an alien society. They rarely invoked the populist rhetoric common among morally conservative non-Jews. The "Silent Majority" may have shared Orthodox Jews' disdain for licentiousness, but it wasn't pressing to have Talmud instruction incorporated into the public-school curricula. Most important, the Orthodox did not wholly oppose the religion-clause activism of the Supreme Court. The legal issue that compelled them—government aid to parochial schools, or "parochaid"—required the court to protect their free-exercise rights, sometimes against state laws supported by electoral majorities. Ultimately, they felt ambivalence toward the rights revolution. They may have loathed the pornographers and criminals whose rights the court guarded, but they would increasingly turn to that same court to protect their own right to difference.[16]

Orthodoxy Finds Its Voice

Although a handful of Orthodox Jews lauded religious exercises in public schools, that issue found little traction overall within the community, whose members cared primarily about education of the traditionally Jewish variety.[17] Only when

Congress and President Kennedy considered including religious academies in a comprehensive attempt to fund all needy schools did Orthodoxy see its own interests at stake. Only with the parochaid debate did the community find its political voice. In March 1961 Rabbi Morris Sherer, director of the ultra-Orthodox Agudath Israel of America, testified affirmatively before Congress, insisting that government ought to treat religious schoolchildren no worse than it treated nonreligious students. Simple fairness required "equal treatment" in the matter, Sherer reasoned. Four years later, he and historian William Brickman gave similar testimony to the House subcommittee that shepherded to passage the Elementary and Secondary Education Act (ESEA), which President Johnson signed into law in April 1965. A new church-state controversy was born.[18]

Organized American Jewry responded to the passage of the ESEA. The new law alerted Jewish liberals, who immediately sought to limit its reach. Pfeffer urged the court to strike down sections of the ESEA, and similar parochaid measures, as assaults on the rights of minorities. Meanwhile, Orthodox scholars and lawyers were galvanized by the act's passage. Orthodoxy had long remained unheard in the politics of church and state; hereafter, it stood independently on such matters. The parochaid issue gave its leaders a newfound confidence in their ability to persuade governmental officials. Its members were learning, in the words of Orthodox constitutional law professor Marvin Schick, that they "could benefit by acting on their own behalf." For the first time, Schick wrote, Orthodox Jewry evinced a "new vigor and confidence . . . as it [went] about its business." No longer, it seemed, would liberal organizations speak for the interests of Orthodox Jews.[19]

In the summer of 1965, Sherer, Schick, and attorney Reuben Gross created a new organization to represent Orthodoxy's constitutional interests. The National Jewish Commission on Law and Public Affairs (COLPA) would speak whenever a consensus appeared to exist within the community. The group set out to counter the liberals—especially Pfeffer—who crowned themselves representatives of all American Jewry. "Sad experience of the past has shown," Sherer complained, "that where Orthodox institutions were not united, the non-Orthodox took advantage of this division to step in and claim rights to represent Yeshivos for whom they have no right to speak." COLPA intended to repair this breach. Schick believed that Pfeffer exerted a pernicious influence within the Jewish community and upon the world of constitutional law. Not only had Pfeffer "attempt[ed] to perpetuate the myth of a monolithic Jewish position on church-state affairs" but, worse, he and his collaborators had led the "the bulk of the organized and articulate Jewish community" into idolatry, Schick charged, as, "robot-like," their minions "invoked the holiness and oneness of the First Amendment and proclaimed their opposition to any 'breach in the wall separating church and state.'"[20]

Notwithstanding its general revulsion toward mainstream society, COLPA was led by professionals expert in understanding American society and government. Among its early members were men accomplished in law and academe, including Schick, a scholar of constitutional law; Brickman, a renowned historian of comparative education; and Jacob Landynski, a political scientist. Also among COLPA's founders was its vice president, Nathan Lewin. One of Washington, DC's most prominent trial lawyers, Lewin had clerked for Justice John Harlan and assisted solicitors general Archibald Cox and Thurgood Marshall. Presently, he served as deputy to the assistant attorney general in charge of the Civil Rights Division of the Justice Department. Lewin's leadership would bring gravitas to COLPA as it set about litigating on behalf of the First Amendment rights of Orthodox Jews.[21]

COLPA aimed to increase governmental deference to the interests of Orthodoxy. According to Sherer, denial of parochaid had effectively cast a *cherem*, or decree of excommunication, on Orthodox children. By obstructing any possible funding for the schools that they attended, separationist doctrine signaled those children's relative unimportance. The recently passed ESEA articulated what Sherer called a "principle of recognition" to *yeshiva* students. Were their education to become as well funded as that of public-school students, they would learn that they, too, mattered. "It is this *principle of recognition* accorded to the Yeshiva student, over and above any immediate financial advantages," Sherer averred, that "makes the President's education bill a document of major importance to the Jewish community." COLPA, it seemed, prioritized its members' civic inclusion as much as their cultural separatism.[22]

Although COLPA promoted its constituents' status in the public sphere, it by no means sought assimilation into the mainstream culture. The group, as Schick explained, was "especially keen on the need to promote Orthodox unity." COLPA walked a fine line: while engaging judges and legislators, it viewed that engagement in instrumental terms, as the cost of doing business in a country not entirely its own. It might solicit government aid, but it would not send its children to state-run schools. Beyond all else, COLPA looked to craft a rabbinic church-state position. While COLPA appealed to the constitutional right of Jews to an affordable education, it understood its *raison d'être* in terms of Jewish obligation to fulfill God's commands. Passage of the ESEA was a gift that obligated COLPA's founders to provide a service for its people. "Dialectically," Schick explained, "success often creates responsibilities that otherwise would not be incurred." And so the group set out to meet what it considered a specifically Jewish responsibility, to ensure that children of the community received a full, high-quality education and that their parents be accorded full recognition under the law, even as they remained relative foreigners settled along society's margin.[23]

COLPA and the Constitution

At its first annual conference in September 1967, COLPA anticipated that the Supreme Court would soon hear arguments in the initial two cases for which the group had written briefs. The cases, *Flast v. Cohen* and *Board of Education v. Allen*, had been launched by a coalition led by Leo Pfeffer, who hoped to disable those sections of the ESEA permitting public funding of religious schools. COLPA opposed Pfeffer's efforts. The papers and comments at its inaugural conference gave voice to a constitutional ideal of citizenship based on religious expression, not one that bracketed or deferred religious expression.[24]

To realize that ideal, COLPA challenged the court's long-standing presumption that religious education needed to be cordoned off from any influence or assistance by the state.[25] The group contended that private religious schools should be eligible for assistance because they served the public function of producing good citizens. Comments made at the conference echoed Herberg's earlier assertion that "the promotion of religion" by schoolteachers fulfilled "a major 'secular' purpose of the state in its furtherance of the common good of the civil order." Brickman painted Orthodox schools as factories for Americanism. Sherer agreed, holding that a school did not need to be stripped of its religious content in order to contribute to society's well-being. "What we are operating in the Yeshiva world are public schools," he averred, schools "not for anyone's private gain." As Sherer saw the matter, the "secular studies programs" in "our Yeshiva public schools" provided as complete of a civic education as the public schools and were therefore "equally entitled to the help received by the humanist [public] schools."[26]

Because its constituents' educational needs differed so profoundly from those of other Americans, its constituents deserved accommodation, COLPA claimed. The state-run schools could not meet the most fundamental needs of the Orthodox community, because those schools were products of a distinctly secular culture with its own narrow worldview. Conference papers and comments suggested that Orthodox schools were no more parochial than the public schools and that all schooling relied on one "religion" or another—including the nontheistic, humanistic variety—to provide the necessary ideological lens through which students understood their world. "Where education is not set in the context of the transcendent *Weltanschauung* of the Jewish-Christian faith," Herberg had written, "it will quite inevitably operate from the standpoint of a secularist-humanist counter-religion." COLPA applied this reasoning to its constituents' situation, arguing that the state was obligated to fund religious private schools so that citizens of faith could freely choose the "religion" into which they wanted their children indoctrinated. Orthodox students had to avoid the fate of the public school student, "guided most of his waking hours, five days a week by professionals in whose eyes religion does not seem to matter." Such a student, according to Landynski, would inevitably understand his or her own religion as trivial, unrelated to citizenship or factual knowledge, possessing the "status of a weekend chore comparable to the mowing of the lawn." The other leaders of COLPA agreed. Entitled to equip their children with their community's worldview, Orthodox parents deserved the same state assistance enjoyed by the parents of public-school students.[27]

Society's interests were also at stake, COLPA maintained. Only by funding religious private schools would government foster the ideological diversity valued by Americans. "In this pluralistic society," Sherer said, there could be no "monolithic educational plant." Instead, "the humanistic-secularistic public schools and the religious-oriented public schools" had to function as "partners, side by side." According to Lewin, the state needed to nurture society's diversity by ascertaining its citizens' legitimate educational needs and aiding in their fulfillment. With its already "enormous range of educational programs," he pointed out, government rightly "eschews conformity and appears evenhandedly to support diverse educational ventures and expressions of view." Could it possibly be appropriate for the state to "stay its hand when what is being taught is religion?" Society's strength was its pluralism, Landynski agreed, and public schools alone could not nurture the full range of that pluralism. "The history of America has been one long chapter of diversity *within* unity," he reminded his colleagues, and "it would be wrong to assume that national unity is in any [more] impaired by religious diversity in education" than by diversity "in any other sphere of life."[28]

Anticipating liberal objections, Lewin averred that state funding of religious academies in no way indicated an establishment of religion. Merely to fund a school was not to establish its preferred worldview, he held—especially if government were to fund all schools regardless of worldview. "One religion or all religions may be considered '*established*' in the constitutional sense only when the government" places "its prestige and authority behind the activity which is affected." The state no more put its imprimatur on religion by funding religious schools than it endorsed the purpose behind every other project to which it awarded a grant. Indeed, by funding the secular-humanist public schools but not those associated with other religions, the state was endorsing one worldview at the expense of its competitors. The state was violating Brennan's requirement that it exhibit genuine neutrality by showing no hostility toward religion.[29]

COLPA soon applied these arguments to its first Supreme Court brief, submitted January 1968 in *Flast*. The group again depicted itself as the protector of rights and secularists as the violators. Although it paid lip service to the majoritarianism of Solicitor General Erwin Griswold, whose brief countered Pfeffer's civil libertarianism by calling on the people's elected representatives—rather than the courts—to determine expenditures on education, COLPA appealed primarily to the justices' activist tendencies by seeking protection for the rights of its own constituents. Pfeffer, it alleged, offered "no clear statement" about how the ESEA deprived liberals and secularists "of *their* constitutional rights." Pfeffer's only purpose in bringing suit, rather, was to "tarnish a major congressional enactment" intended only "to help hard-pressed local educational systems and educationally disadvantaged children." The civil rights of Orthodox Jews, and not Pfeffer's clients, had been trod upon. COLPA implied that it alone remained "committed to the preservation of constitutional rights for all Americans"; it alone "support[ed] the advancement of educational opportunity for all American children," including the secular education of religious students at private schools. Alongside the language of civil libertarianism, it spoke that of civic republicanism. It quoted *Brown* on "the importance of education . . . in the performance of our most basic public responsibilities" and as "the very foundation of good citizenship." Government's "public responsibility," according to COLPA, "include[d] the obligation to provide quality education," so "that the students develop their fullest potential and thereby maximize their contribution to society." The brief urged the justices not to let "separation of church and state . . . obstruct the state's recognition of its responsibilities to parochial school children who are in need of special educational services."[30]

In *Allen*, six weeks later, COLPA again challenged Pfeffer on his own civil-libertarian ground. Like him, the group declared its resolve "to combat all forms of religious prejudice and discrimination" and to preserve "the principles of the First Amendment, in the belief that thereby Americans of the Jewish faith, in common with all Americans, will enjoy the blessings of liberty." Once again, COLPA emphasized its commitment to the rights of minorities and the well-being of the civic sphere. The group appealed to government's "responsibility for the proper education of children," which remained necessary for "develop[ing] their potential" to meet "the needs of our growing society." It was up to the justices to enforce this commitment, just as it was up to them to ensure that government show a "wholesome neutrality" in its dealings with religion, as required by *Schempp*. COLPA implored the state to maintain a genuinely "neutral role in religious affairs by extending public benefits to children attending parochial as well as other private schools in an effort to promote the general welfare and insure full educational opportunity for all schoolchildren." It was Pfeffer, COLPA insisted, who looked to squash society's robust religious diversity—whose "distortion of the separation principle" had "poison[ed] the air of pluralism."[31]

The court's decisions together composed a draw. Pfeffer and his allies scored a victory in *Flast*, while in *Allen*, the court ruled in favor of COLPA's associates. The opposing Jewish groups faced off a third time in *Lemon v. Kurtzman*

(1971), the case that would determine parochaid law for the foreseeable future. COLPA's brief was prepared by its leading expert on constitutional law, Nathan Lewin, who aimed to drive a wedge between the enforcement of minority rights and the strict separation of church and state. If the court wished to protect the rights of a marginal minority such as Orthodox Jews, he suggested, then it needed to make good on its own commitment to ensuring "benevolent neutrality" between government and religion—to treating religious institutions no worse than their nonreligious counterparts. The Free Exercise Clause required the court to uphold all "neutral and nondiscriminatory" statutes sanctioning parochaid. Such laws, Lewin opined, "offer[ed] no advantage to religious schools or students on account of their religion," but, rather, cultivated "an equality which is consistent with this Nation's great tradition of voluntarism," while spreading the costs of education more equitably among all families. Meanwhile, to exclude "religiously affiliated institutions" from public assistance, Lewin claimed, would be to "disqualify from public benefits those institutions or individuals who, by reason of religious belief, deem it essential to provide a comprehensive religious education for their children . . . in the same institution and as part of the same school day as is given over to secular training." Nothing could more egregiously transgress benevolent neutrality. Any "statute which explicitly conditioned State aid on an individual's disbelief in thorough and rigorous religious training" surely must "be invalid," Lewin reasoned.[32]

The *Lemon* ruling did not go in COLPA's favor. Nor would COLPA have any success in subsequent parochaid cases, as, over the next decade, the justices would strike down law after law sanctioning government assistance to religious schools. Still, COLPA's amicus briefs left behind examples of the sort of civil-libertarian arguments on which religious conservatives would build successfully from the 1980s onward. Beginning in the mid-1960s, Orthodox Jewish lawyers, rabbis, and intellectuals had organized themselves, contested the strict separationism with which Jewish Americans had been exclusively associated and advanced a concept of minority rights requiring government to treat religious individuals and institutions no worse than it treated their nonreligious counterparts. First Amendment jurisprudence did not change as an immediate result. But future decades would bring greater success for groups such as COLPA.[33]

An Unlikely 1960s Artifact

In opposing the era's church-state jurisprudence, COLPA revealed itself as a product of that era. Orthodox leaders concluded, by the mid-1960s, that the American legal establishment had accorded them inadequate respect. The Warren Court had interpreted the Establishment Clause in ways that diminished the quality of education that they could offer their children, they believed; the liberal Jewish agencies—claiming to speak for all American Jews—had articulated principles and supported laws that allegedly trampled the needs of the Orthodox community. With no organization promoting their interests, Orthodox leaders formed COLPA. Although the new group contested the strict-separationist interpretation of the First Amendment's religion clauses, it did not oppose "judicial activism" in general or the rights regime to which it had given rise. To the contrary, COLPA, too, advocated for a kind of constitutional activism, one in keeping with the norms advanced within sacred Jewish text.

In traditional Jewish law, rabbis function much as judges function in contemporary American law. Although Jewish law places great significance on the will of the communal majority, rabbis must balance majoritarian impulses against a kind of individual rights, what constitutional theorist David Dow calls "the magisterial notion of human dignity." Every member of the Jewish community, no matter how lacking in influence, inherently deserves to be respected by the rest of the community, and if the majority's will would trample over the dignity of the least powerful person, then the rabbis must intervene on his behalf. It was this notion of rights to which COLPA appealed. Orthodox Jews saw themselves as a minority within a minority, and they turned to the nation's supreme judges to intervene as rabbis might, to provide them a modicum of dignity. Liberal Jews belonged to an American majority unwedded to the commands of the Bible, they believed, while they themselves lurked along society's God-fearing margin—consigned, in Rabbi Sherer's words, to *cherem*, or excommunication, by the "doctrinaire devotees of Church-State separation."[34]

COLPA was a product of the 1960s also in that the group's founding was sparked by Orthodox Jews' revulsion toward the decade. They recoiled from a mainstream culture increasingly divorced from the strict morality normative within their community—a morality on which their free exercise of religion supposedly depended. The Constitution needed primarily to honor God's law, they believed; if First Amendment guarantees meant anything at all, they meant to protect the wisdom of the devout over the impulses of the licentious. Although Jewish law prioritizes a person's dignity, Jewish law does not recognize personal entitlement. The basis of rights under rabbinic law is to help the individual fulfill his or her obligation to God, not to indulge his or her desires. Traditionally, Jews have experienced law heteronomously, as a commandment from a God to whom they are obligated. In this important sense, Orthodox Jews rejected the rights revolution. They appealed to the Free Exercise Clause on "legitimate" grounds: they were seeking assistance in their worship of God, not in their pursuit of comfort. Horrified by the supposed decadence engulfing their community, they separated themselves as never before, their schools serving as islands of purity where they could guide the development of their children and propagate their culture. "Their heightened anxiety about Jewish continuity and integrity," according to sociologist Samuel Heilman, propelled them to take "an antagonistic, powerfully contra-acculturative stance toward contemporary society, its values and lifestyle."[35]

COLPA was a product of the 1960s in still another respect. A deep cultural pluralism accompanied the rights revolution. Ever more diverse, American politics and law accommodated groups such as the Orthodox and efforts such as theirs to remain a subculture apart. Orthodoxy protected its boundaries and asserted its interests with newfound effectiveness in America of the 1960s, whose society was concerned for the dignity and rights of dissenters. America's moral multiplicity may have alarmed Orthodox Jews; it may have compelled them to keep their children far away from public schools. That same moral pluralism also made possible their politicization, including their assault on the assimilationist model of religion-clause jurisprudence. Within American society of the 1960s, historian Haym Soloveitchik points out, "the 'melting pot' now seemed a ploy of cultural hegemony, and was out; difference, even a defiant heterogeneity, was in." However repulsed Orthodoxy was by the surrounding culture's permissiveness and decadence, Orthodoxy benefitted from society's celebration of deep difference. Orthodoxy's increasingly doctrinaire adherence to sacred text marked its difference, which placed it in good stead amid the emerging ethos of cultural fracture. Soloveitchik explains that "for those who sought to be different and had something about which to be genuinely different, the Sixties in America were good years."[36]

When Lewin wrote that "those who are actively erecting the Wall Between Church and State seem to be burying under . . . it the religious minorities it was designed to protect," he did more than espouse rhetoric. Lewin understood that, at its apparent peak, America's culture of assimilation was hemorrhaging credibility. One unintended result of the rights revolution was its sanctioning of defiant right-wing heterogeneity, even at the expense of liberal constitutionalism. In demanding state assistance for their private schools, Orthodox Jews recognized that the vital ideological center no longer held. To opt out was to belong. By simultaneously rejecting mainstream culture and demanding government accommodation, COLPA affirmed its provenance as an artifact of the 1960s, a decade whose precise meaning continues to elude our grasp.[37]

Notes

1. Lance J. Sussman, "Reform Judaism, Minority Rights and the Separation of Church and State," in *Jewish Polity and American Civil Society: Communal Agencies and Religious Movements in the American Public Sphere,* ed. Alan Mittleman, Jonathan D. Sarna, and Robert Licht (Lanham, MD: Rowman and Littlefield, 2002), 261–82; Gregg Ivers, *To Build a Wall: American Jews and the Separation of Church and State* (Charlottesville: University Press of Virginia, 1995).

2. H. H. Ben-Sasson, *A History of the Jewish People,* trans. George Weidenfeld (Cambridge, MA: Harvard University Press, 1976), 388–89, 593–611.

3. Stephen J. Whitfield, "Declarations of Independence: American Jewish Culture in the Twentieth Century," in *Cultures of the Jews: A New History,* ed. David Biale (New York: Schocken, 2002), 1099–1146; Gregg Ivers, "American Jews and the Equal Treatment Principle," in *Equal Treatment of Religion in a Pluralistic Society,* ed. by Stephen V. Monsma and J. Christopher Soper (Grand Rapids, MI: Eerdmans, 1998), 158–78; Ivers, *To Build a Wall,* 1–6; Gregg Ivers, "Religious Organizations as Constitutional Litigants," *Polity* 25 (Winter 1992): 249–51; Everson v. Board of Education, 330 U.S. 1 (1947); McCollum v. Board of Education, 333 U.S. 203 (1948); Engel v. Vitale, 370 U.S. 421 (1962); Abington v. Schempp, 374 U.S. 203 (1963). The Supreme Court first began actively to protect vulnerable minorities with its doctrine of "preferred freedoms," which it first advanced in Palko v. Connecticut, 302 U.S. 319 (1937), 327–28; and United States v. Carolene Products, 304 U.S. 144 (1938), 153 n4.

4. Naomi W. Cohen, *Jews in Christian America: The Pursuit of Religious Equality* (New York: Oxford University Press, 1992), 79–87, 123–24; Marc Dollinger, *Quest for Inclusion: Jews and Liberalism in Modern America* (Princeton, NJ: Princeton University Press, 2000), 129–63; Stuart Svonkin, *Jews against Prejudice: American Jews and the Fight for Civil Liberties* (New York: Columbia University Press, 1997); Frank J. Sorauf, *The Wall of Separation: The Constitutional Politics of Church and State* (Princeton, NJ: Princeton University Press, 1976), 158–62; David G. Dalin, "Introduction," in *American Jews and the Separationist Faith,* ed. David G. Dalin (Washington, DC: Ethics and Public Policy Center, 1993), 1–3; Jonathan D. Sarna, "Church-State Dilemmas of American Jews," in *Jews and the American Public Square: Debating Religion and Republic,* ed. Alan Mittleman, Jonathan D. Sarna, and Robert Licht (Lanham, MD: Rowman and Littlefield, 2002), 57–63; Ivers, *To Build a Wall,* 100–145.

5. Leo Pfeffer, "The Case for Separation," in *Religion in America: Original Essays on Religion in a Free Society,* ed. John Cogley (Cleveland: Meridian, 1958), 92, 94.

6. Brown v. Board of Education, 347 U.S. 483 (1954), 493–94.

7. Pfeffer, "Case for Separation," 54; Synagogue Council of America (SCA) and National Community Relations Advisory Council (NACRAC), *amici curiae* brief, *Vashti McCollum v. Board of Education of School District No. 71, Champaign County, Illinois,* United States Supreme Court, October term 1947, case no. 90 (Oct. 24, 1947), 26; ibid., *Engel v. Vitale,* United States Supreme Court, October term 1961, case no. 468 (Mar. 5, 1962), 9–11, 23. *Abington v. Schempp,* 374 U.S. at 241–42 (Brennan, J., concurring).

8. George H. Nash, *The Conservative Intellectual Movement in America since 1945,* 2nd ed. (Wilmington, DE: ISI, 1996), 185–87, 199–203; Lucas A. Powe, *The Warren Court and American Politics* (Cambridge, MA: Belknap, 2000), 59–60, 187–89, 361–63; John Morton Blum, *Years of Discord: American Politics and Society, 1961–1974* (New York: Norton, 1991), 190–98; Dan Carter, "A World Turned Upside Down: Southern Politics at the End of the Twentieth Century," in *The Southern State of Mind,* ed. Jan Nordby Gretlund (Columbia: University of South Carolina Press, 1999), 57; David Goldfield, *Southern Histories: Public, Personal, and Sacred* (Athens: University of Georgia Press, 2003), 55–58; Allan J. Lichtman,

White Protestant Nation: The Rise of the American Conservative Movement (New York: Atlantic Monthly, 2008), 278–80.

9. Conrad Cherry, ed., *God's New Israel: Religious Interpretations of American Destiny* (Chapel Hill: University of North Carolina Press, 1998), 303–27; Cohen, *Jews in Christian America*, 131–32, 159–62; Aaron Louis Haberman, "Civil Rights on the Right: The Modern Christian Right and the Crusade for School Prayer, 1962– 1996" (PhD diss., University of South Carolina, 2006), 77, 92–94, 61–100, 115– 16; Edward Keynes with Randall K. Miller, *The Court vs. Congress: Prayer, Busing, and Abortion* (Durham, NC: Duke University Press, 1989), 174.

10. Keynes with Miller, *Court vs. Congress*, 1, 146, 169–71, 188–89. The spreading of secular humanism was decried in Rousas John Rushdoony, *The Messianic Character of American Education: Studies in the History of the Philosophy of Education* (Vallecito, CA: Ross House, 1963). Rushdoony's critique was later fleshed out in Francis A. Schaeffer, *How Should We Then Live: The Rise and Decline of Western Thought and Culture* (Wheaton, IL: Crossway, 1976); John W. Whitehead and John Conlan, "The Establishment of the Religion of Secular Humanism and Its First Amendment Implications," *Texas Tech Law Review* 10 (Winter 1978), 1–66; Tim LaHaye, *The Battle for the Mind* (Old Tappan, NJ: Revell, 1980); and Francis A. Schaeffer, *A Christian Manifesto* (Wheaton, IL: Crossway, 1981). On the rise of all-white Christian academies, see Peter Skerry, "Christian Schools versus the IRS," *Public Interest* 61 (Fall 1980): 18–41; Godfrey Hodgson, *The World Turned Right Side Up: A History of the Conservative Ascendancy in America* (Boston: Houghton Mifflin, 1996), 170–78; and Joseph Crespino, "Civil Rights and the Religious Right," in *Rightward Bound: Making America Conservative in the 1970s,* ed. Bruce J. Schulman and Julian E. Zelizer (Cambridge, MA: Harvard University Press, 2008), 90–105.

11. Portions of American Jewry are depicted as politically conservative in Jonathan Rieder, *Canarsie: The Jews and Italians of Brooklyn against Liberalism* (Cambridge, MA: Harvard University Press, 1985); and Samuel G. Freedman, *Jew vs. Jew: The Struggle for the Soul of American Jewry* (New York: Simon and Schuster, 2000). On the contradictions plaguing the liberal activism of American Jews, see Dollinger, *Quest for Inclusion*; and Michael E. Staub, *Torn at the Roots: The Crisis of Jewish Liberalism* (New York: Columbia University Press, 2002).

12. Will Herberg, "The Sectarian Conflict over Church and State," *Commentary* 14 (November 1952): 451–61; Will Herberg, "Religious Education and General Education: A Jewish Point of View," *Religious Education* 48 (May/June 1953): 135–39; Will Herberg, "Religion, Democracy, and Public Education," in *Religion in America: Original Essays on Religion in a Free Society,* ed. John Cogley (Cleveland: Meridian, 1958), 118–47; Will Herberg, *Protestant, Catholic, Jew: An Essay in American Religious Sociology* (1955; Garden City, NY: Anchor, 1983), 254–81; David G. Dalin, "Will Herberg in Retrospect," in *From Marxism to Judaism: Collected Essays of Will Herberg,* ed. David G. Dalin (Princeton, NJ: Markus Weiner, 1989), xi–xxv.

13. Herberg, "Sectarian Conflict over Church and State," 457–58. The ascending prominence of Orthodox Jews within American Jewry is discussed in Jonathon Amont, *United Jewish Communities Report Series on the National Jewish Population*

Survey, report 10, *American Jewish Religious Denominations*, February 2005, 5–8, http://www.jewishfederations.org/page.aspx?id=108513. See also Dana Evan Kaplan, *Contemporary American Judaism: Transformation and Renewal* (New York: Columbia University Press, 2009), 141–42.

14. Samuel C. Heilman, *Sliding to the Right: The Contest for the Future of American Jewish Orthodoxy* (Berkeley: University of California Press, 2006), 96–101. The OU is quoted in Lawrence Grossman, "Mainstream Orthodoxy and the American Public Square," in *Jewish Polity and American Civil Society: Communal Agencies and Religious Movements in the American Public Sphere*, ed. Alan Mittleman, Jonathan D. Sarna, and Robert Licht (Lanham, MD: Rowman and Littlefield, 2002), 301.

15. Heilman, *Sliding to the Right*, 78–81, 101–4; Jack Wertheimer, "The Jewish Debate over State Aid to Religious Schools," in *Jews and the American Public Square: Debating Religion and Republic*, ed. Alan Mittleman, Jonathan D. Sarna, and Robert Licht (Lanham, MD: Rowman and Littlefield, 2002), 227. The concept of contra-acculturation is explained in Heilman, *Sliding to the Right*, 11–12.

16. On the "Silent Majority," see David Farber, "The Silent Majority and Talk about Revolution," in *The Sixties: From Memory to History*, ed. David Farber (Chapel Hill: University of North Carolina Press, 1994), 291–316; Jeff Roche, "Political Conservatism in the Sixties: Silent Majority or White Backlash," in *The Columbia Guide to America in the 1960s* (New York: Columbia University Press, 2001), 157–66; and Robert Mason, *Richard Nixon and the Quest for a New Majority* (Chapel Hill: University of North Carolina Press, 2004), 37–76, 82–86, 142–46.

17. Grossman, "Mainstream Orthodoxy and the American Public Square," 299–300; Wertheimer, "Jewish Debate over State Aid to Religious Schools," 218. For examples of Orthodox Jews advocating for nondenominational prayer in the public schools, see Menachem Schneerson, "Letter from the Lubavitcher Rabbi on the Need for Public School Prayer," in *Religion and State in the American Jewish Experience*, ed. Jonathan D. Sarna and David G. Dalin (Notre Dame, IN: University of Notre Dame Press, 1997), 215–16; Michael Wyschogrod, "Second Thoughts on America," *Tradition* 5 (Fall 1962): 28–36; and William W. Brickman, "The School and the Church-State Question," *School and Society*, May 6, 1950, 272–82.

18. Agudath Israel of America, *Daring to Dream: Profiles in the Growth of the American Torah Community* (New York: Agudath Israel, 2003), 269; Morris Sherer, "The Great Society and Aid to Religious Schools," *Jewish Observer* 2 (January 1965): 3–5; William W. Brickman, "The New Education Bill and Church-State Relations," *Jewish Life* 47 (May–June 1965): 22–37; Ivers, *To Build a Wall*, 146–51; Sarna and Dalin, eds., *Religion and State in the American Jewish Experience*, 256–59.

19. Ivers, *To Build a Wall*, 152; Grossman, "Mainstream Orthodoxy and the American Public Square," 294–98; Heilman, *Sliding to the Right*, 6–12; Marvin Schick, ed., *Governmental Aid to Parochial Schools: How Far?* (New York: National Jewish Commission on Law and Public Affairs, 1967), 4–6.

20. Schick, ed., *Governmental Aid to Parochial Schools*, 6–8, 11; Sherer, "Great Society and Aid to Religious Schools," 5. COLPA member William Brickman launched an extensive broadside against the American Jewish Congress and its liberal allies. See Brickman, "New Education Bill and Church-State Relations," 28–34.

21. Schick, ed., *Governmental Aid to Parochial Schools*, 4–8; Marvin Schick, "Forty Years Ago," *Cross-Currents*, September 15, 2005, http://www.cross-currents.com/

archives/2005/09/15/forty-years-ago; Aryeh Solomon, "William Brickman's Legacy in Jewish Education Worldwide," *European Education* 42 (Summer 2010): 85–101; Jacob W. Landynski, "Governmental Aid to Non-Public Schools: A Proposal for an Experiment," in *Governmental Aid to Parochial Schools,* ed. Schick, 27–43; Nathan Lewin, "'Government Financing' and the Establishment Clause," in *Governmental Aid to Parochial Schools,* ed. Schick, 44–53; Elie Zirkind, "A Lawyer, a Legend—Interview with Nathan Lewin," *What Where When* (Baltimore, MD), November 2009, http://www.wherewhatwhen.com/read_articles.asp?id=626.

22. Sherer, "Great Society and Aid to Religious Schools," 3 (emphasis in original).

23. Schick, ed., *Governmental Aid to Parochial Schools,* 6–7, 17; Grossman, "Mainstream Orthodoxy and the American Public Square," 297–98.

24. Flast v. Cohen, 392 U.S. 83 (1968); Board of Education v. Allen, 392 U.S. 236 (1968). On Pfeffer's role in these two cases, see Ivers, *To Build a Wall,* 146–64.

25. The court indicated the unconstitutionality of direct aid to religious schools in *Everson v. Board,* 15–16. Two concurring opinions by Justice Douglas built on this finding. See *Engel v. Vitale* (Douglas, J. concurring), 437; and *Abington v. Schempp* (Douglas, J. concurring), 229.

26. Will Herberg, "Religion and Public Life," *National Review,* August 13, 1963, 104; Schick, ed., *Governmental Aid to Parochial Schools,* 57–58, 67.

27. Herberg, "Religious Education and General Education," 137–38; Landynski, "Governmental Aid to Non-Public Schools," 37.

28. Schick, ed., *Governmental Aid to Parochial Schools,* 57; Lewin, "'Government Financing' and the Establishment Clause," 50–51; Landynski, "Governmental Aid to Non-Public Schools," 36 (emphasis in the original).

29. Lewin, "'Government Financing' and the Establishment Clause," 49, 50–52 (emphasis in the original); *Abington v. Schempp* (Brennan, J. concurring), 299.

30. Griswold's argument appears in the brief for appellees, *Florence Flast et al. v. John W. Gardner,* United States Supreme Court, October term 1967, case no. 416 (January 29, 1968); National Jewish Commission on Law and Public Affairs (COLPA), *amicus curiae* brief, *ibid.* (January 27, 1968), 9–10, 11, 4, 2, 1, 16, 17, 19 (emphasis in original).

31. National Jewish Commission on Law and Public Affairs, *amicus curiae* brief, *Board of Education of Central School District No. 1 v. James E. Allen Jr.,* United States Supreme Court, October term 1967, case no. 660 (March 29, 1968), 2, 4, 6, 21, 6, 21.

32. Lemon v. Kurtzman, 403 U.S. 602 (1971). National Jewish Commission on Law and Public Affairs, *amicus curiae* brief, *Lemon v. Kurtzman,* United States Supreme Court, October term 1970, case no. 89 (October 27, 1970), 7, 3, 10–11. On the court's own requirement of "benevolent neutrality," see Walz v. Tax Commission, 397 U.S. 664 (1970), 668–69.

33. Ivers, *To Build a Wall,* 179–88. Religious conservatives would effectively utilize civil-libertarian arguments in Widmar v. Vincent, 454 U.S. 263 (1981); Board of Education of Westside Community Schools v. Mergens, 496 U.S. 226 (1990); Lamb's Chapel v. Center Moriches Union Free School District, 508 U.S. 384 (1993); Rosenberger v. Rector and Visitors of University of Virginia, 515 U.S. 819 (1995); and Good News Club v. Milford Central School, 533 U.S. 98 (2001). A formidable endorsement of privileging benevolent neutrality in Establishment

Clause cases is made in Stephen V. Monsma, *Positive Neutrality: Letting Religious Freedom Ring* (Grand Rapids, MI: Baker, 1993).

34. David R. Dow, "Constitutional Midrash: The Rabbis' Solution to Professor Bickel's Problem," *Houston Law Review* 29 (Fall 1992): 572–73; Sherer, "Great Society and Aid to Religious Schools," 3.

35. Heilman, *Sliding to the Right,* 80–81, 96–101; Grossman, "Mainstream Orthodoxy and the American Public Square," 301; Robert M. Cover, "Obligation: A Jewish Jurisprudence of the Social Order," in *Law, Politics, and Morality in Judaism,* ed. Michael Walzer (Princeton, NJ: Princeton University Press, 2006), 3–6.

36. Haym Soloveitchik, "Rupture and Reconstruction: The Transformation of Contemporary Orthodoxy," *Tradition* 28 (Summer 1994): 77–78.

37. COLPA, *amicus curiae* brief, *Lemon v. Kurtzman,* 7.

CHAPTER 7

Richard Nixon's Religious Right

Catholics, Evangelicals, and the Creation of an Antisecular Alliance

Daniel K. Williams

E vangelical Protestants began and ended the decade of the 1960s by campaigning for Richard Nixon. Sixty percent of evangelicals voted for Nixon in 1960, 69 percent did so in 1968, and 84 percent did in 1972. They considered him a "man of destiny to lead the nation" and a man who was "in God's place," as Billy Graham told Nixon on more than one occasion.[1] But though evangelicals' faith in Nixon never wavered, their reasons for supporting him changed. In 1960 they viewed Nixon as a champion of Protestantism who would save the country from the dangers posed by a Catholic candidate. By the end of the decade, they began to view him not as a sectarian symbol, but as the champion of an antisecular, ecumenical coalition that was broad enough to include Catholics. Nixon's success in positioning himself as a transdenominational moral leader who could reach out to evangelicals without losing the Catholic vote laid the groundwork for the rise of a politically influential Religious Right and transformed the Republican Party. Though Nixon was never fully conscious of the degree of his success in creating an interdenominational religious coalition, it became one of his most enduring political legacies.

While many historians have examined Nixon's use of racial and cultural appeals to create a coalition of Sun Belt suburbanites, rural Southerners, and Northern workers, few scholars have given much attention to his use of religion to unite his denominationally divided supporters in a coalition against secularism. Even fewer have examined Nixon's transition from a representative of Protestantism to a leader of an interreligious coalition that included Catholics.

Yet knowledge of Nixon's use of religion is essential for a full understanding of his appeal. Though Nixon was far from personally devout, he had a visceral understanding of religion that too many historians have ignored, and he used that understanding to foster a movement that changed American politics.[2]

Evangelicals and Catholics before the 1960s

Prior to Nixon's presidency, the Republican Party had found it difficult to appeal to evangelicals and Catholics simultaneously, let alone to create a political coalition that united both of them in a common conservative goal. Evangelicals had long been staunchly opposed to Catholicism and deeply suspicious of Catholic politicians. In 1928 the presence of a Catholic, anti-Prohibitionist, Democratic presidential candidate on the ballot prompted Southern evangelical ministers who had been lifelong Democrats to abandon their party and campaign for the Republican candidate in order to keep a Catholic out of the White House. Southern states such as North Carolina, Tennessee, and Texas, which had not voted for a Republican presidential candidate since Reconstruction, cast their electoral votes for Herbert Hoover when a Catholic was the Democratic nominee.

It was thus hardly surprising that as evangelicals began moving into the Republican Party in the 1950s, they brought with them a deep suspicion of Catholics and often portrayed the GOP as the party of Protestantism. Evangelicals related to President Dwight Eisenhower primarily as a Protestant leader, and they believed that he was effective as a Cold Warrior because of his Protestant faith. They gave him a majority of their vote in both of the presidential elections in which he was a candidate. Billy Graham began building a political alliance with Eisenhower as early as 1951, and as soon as the general won the presidential election, he found a Presbyterian church in Washington for him to attend. Eisenhower's championship of a civil religion of anticommunism appealed to evangelicals. Eisenhower led a prayer at his own inauguration, regularly attended church throughout his presidency, and signed legislation adding the words "under God" to the Pledge of Allegiance. Though the ecumenically minded Eisenhower did not intend to privilege Protestantism in his laudations of religious faith, evangelicals viewed his religious rhetoric as endorsements of their own views. "Millions of Americans thank God for your spiritual leadership," Graham told the president. Eisenhower was uniquely suited, he said, to "contribute to a national spiritual awakening."[3]

Along with the Eisenhower presidency, the Cold War gave evangelicals an opportunity to link their defense of evangelical Protestant theology with the American ideals of freedom, patriotism, and anticommunism. Though evangelicals' suspicion of Catholics long predated their concerns about Communism, evangelical anti-Catholicism of the mid-twentieth century was thoroughly infused with Cold War rhetoric and the charge that Catholics were un-American and therefore unqualified to defend the nation or uphold the Constitution. It was a surprising charge to level against a church that was thoroughly opposed to Marxism and whose members loudly proclaimed their patriotism, but when evangelicals argued that the Constitution and the Bill of Rights were Protestant documents, they were implicitly claiming that the nation's heritage of liberty—and, by extension, its mission to uphold freedom and democracy around the world in the fight against Communism—depended on its Protestant religious identity. "America is a Christian country," fundamentalist radio broadcaster Billy James Hargis declared in 1960, a time when fundamentalists restricted the term "Christian" to evangelical Protestants. "The men and women who braved an uncharted wilderness to carve out this Republic, were rich in faith. With a Bible under one arm, and a musket under the other, they were willing to fight for their faith and their freedom."[4]

In the view of evangelicals, Catholics did not fit into the American tradition, and their increased political prominence in the mid-twentieth century threatened the nation's values and freedoms. When the National Association of Evangelicals (NAE) formed in 1942, it made opposition to Catholic political power one of its central aims. The NAE opposed state funding for parochial schools, which many Catholics favored, and its members worried about the influence of Catholic politicians. The NAE's anti-Catholicism was the principal reason that it allied itself with Protestants and Other Americans United for Separation of Church and State, an organization that also received strong support from the Southern Baptist Convention. Many evangelicals believed that their own political activity was the last remaining bulwark protecting the nation's government from the threat of the Catholic Church. "Either Christians who love the Lord are going to take Christ into the political life of the nation or the increasing infiltration of Roman Catholic power will take over," James DeForest Murch, editor of the NAE journal *United Evangelical Action*, wrote in 1956.[5]

Though evangelicals did not directly claim that Catholics would compromise American security, they did at times suggest that evangelical Protestants were uniquely qualified to maintain the nation's fight against Communism. In the early 1940s, evangelicals attacked liberal Protestant organizations, such as the Federal Council of Churches (later, the National Council of Churches), as insufficiently anticommunist.

In the early 1950s, the president of the NAE simultaneously headed the All-American Conference to Combat Communism. As late as 1960, the NAE contrasted its self-described "vigorous stance against the Red Menace" with the "silence or apologetic attitude of some religious organizations toward Communism." The battle against Communism was a spiritual struggle against an "enemy of righteousness," the NAE said, and it would have to be waged through "prayer, Bible study, and evangelism," a strategy that evangelical churches were uniquely qualified to adopt.[6] As evangelicals brought their anti-Catholic Cold War rhetoric into the Republican Party in the 1950s, national Republican Party leaders such as Eisenhower and Nixon found it difficult to win Catholic votes while simultaneously maintaining relationships with Billy Graham, the NAE, and other evangelicals.

Most Catholics were Democrats in the mid-twentieth century. Franklin Roosevelt's New Deal political coalition had been based largely on the votes of Catholics in Northern industrial cities, and his administration had given unprecedented power to Catholic Democratic politicians and even to church leaders. New Deal programs incorporated principles of Catholic social teaching and received strong support from American bishops. Though some Catholics who moved to the suburbs in the 1950s began voting Republican, most remained firmly committed to the Democratic Party through the end of the 1960s.[7]

Yet ironically, Catholics shared most of evangelicals' assumptions about the nation's Christian identity, the evils of Communism, and the religious basis for the public moral order. Though few in the 1950s would have envisioned a political alliance between evangelicals and Catholics, the idea was not as far-fetched as most assumed. Like many evangelical Protestants, Catholics believed that the nation's religious heritage was the key to its success in the Cold War. But unlike evangelicals, they viewed the Catholic Church as a primary defender of the nation's Christian political tradition, because they knew that the Catholic Church had long been staunchly opposed to Communism. Pope Pius XI's encyclical *On Atheistic Communism* (1937) depicted the struggle against global Communism as a spiritual battle in which Catholics would play a decisive role. During the 1950s, American Catholic laypeople held monthly "block rosaries" to petition the Virgin for the conversion of Russia and the end of atheistic Communism. Such prayer vigils, Catholics thought, were just as vital as the American military to national success in the Cold War. Increasingly, Catholics began to link their religion to the causes of the state, because both the church and the state were engaged in an international fight against evil. Though most Catholic voters still remained registered Democrats, some could be persuaded to vote for a Republican candidate when the GOP offered a strong Cold Warrior as a candidate. A near majority of Catholics voted for Eisenhower's reelection in 1956.[8]

But Eisenhower's personal popularity was not enough to bring Catholics and evangelicals together, and their mutual suspicion toward each other continued unabated. In 1960 the two groups faced off against each other in an election that both viewed as a test of the nation's religious identity. When John

F. Kennedy became the second Catholic in American history to win a presidential nomination from a major party, evangelicals mobilized against his candidacy, warning that his election would "spell the death of a free church in a free state and our hopes of continuance of full religious liberty in America." Many Catholics, on the other hand, were jubilant that one of their own finally had a chance to win the presidency. A vote for Kennedy, they thought, was a vote for their own legitimacy in the nation. Kennedy won more than 70 percent of the Catholic vote.[9]

Nixon's Evangelical, Anti-Catholic Coalition

Nixon's position as Kennedy's opponent and inheritor of the Eisenhower mantle guaranteed him the support of conservative Protestants in the 1960 presidential election. Evangelicals championed the vice president's reputation as a strong Cold Warrior and worried aloud about what Kennedy would do if he were to become leader of the free world. "This is a time of world tensions," Billy Graham said in May 1960, "and I don't think it is the time to experiment with novices." Nixon, on the other hand, was someone they knew they could trust. The vice president, Graham said, was a "splendid churchman" who was "most sincere." He was the "best qualified and best trained man for the presidency."[10]

Though evangelicals wanted to cast Nixon as an exemplar of Protestantism, just as they had with Eisenhower, they found it hard to make a convincing case that he fit that role. Nor did Nixon seem eager to make the case himself. A lapsed Quaker, he was not a frequent churchgoer. Graham encouraged him to go to church more often during the election, but Nixon resisted the invitation. Graham realized that if Nixon were not personally devout, he would need a running mate who was in order to mobilize the evangelical vote. "It becomes imperative for you to have as your running mate someone the Protestant church can rally behind enthusiastically," Graham told Nixon in the summer of 1960. He suggested the former missionary and Republican congressman Walter Judd for the role. "With Dr. Judd I believe the two of you could present a picture to America that would put much of the South and border states in the Republican column and bring about a dedicated Protestant vote to counteract the Catholic vote," Graham said.[11] But Nixon declined the advice and instead chose as his running mate Massachusetts Senator Henry Cabot Lodge, a person who had no special appeal for evangelicals. (Incidentally, a decade later, Lodge would become President Nixon's special envoy to the Vatican.)

Nixon knew that at a time of increasing religious tolerance in American society, he would be labeled a bigot and his political career would be over if he ran as an overtly anti-Catholic candidate, as evangelicals wanted. He repeatedly assured the public that he had no wish to make religion an issue in the campaign. He also tried to broaden his support among Catholics by relying on Catholic Republicans, such as Father John Cronin, to promote his campaign. When he solicited the support of evangelicals, he did so only through interme-diaries, such as Billy Graham or former Missouri congressman Orland K. Arm-strong, who secretly enlisted the support of prominent leaders in the Southern Baptist Convention, the Churches of Christ, and other conservative evangelical organizations that feared Catholic political power.[12] It was a delicate balancing act for Nixon, one that he never fully mastered. Building a conservative coali-tion through anti-Catholicism was a route fraught with perils.

In the absence of overt encouragement from the candidate, evangelicals were left to invent their own image of Nixon as a spiritual warrior, however reluctant he might be to take up the standard in the cause. Most of their pronouncements in the election were denunciations of Kennedy's religion rather than positive endorsements of Nixon, but even if they did not have a personal affinity for Nixon, they viewed him as an agent of righteousness simply because he was running against Kennedy. Immediately before the election, Graham assured Nixon that even though the polls were going against him, he had the "prayers of millions of Christians" on his side. By late October, Nixon had received sup-port not only from leaders of the Southern Baptist Convention but also from the NAE, independent fundamentalists associated with Bob Jones University, and traditionally apolitical Pentecostal denominations. Billy Graham sent a let-ter to the two million people on his mailing list encouraging them to "organize their Sunday school classes and churches to get out the vote." Nixon's support came from an unprecedented ecumenical coalition of religious groups who had never before worked together, but who found common cause in preventing a Catholic from becoming the nation's next president. "I am convinced that we are involved in a deep spiritual struggle," Graham said. "There is an unseen battle waging that does not show up in the polls and statistics."[13]

Evangelicals were despondent when Nixon lost the election, because they had viewed him as their last chance to stop a Catholic onslaught. Weeks after the elec-tion, some ministers, such as the Oakland, California, Baptist pastor G. Archer Weniger, were still placing their hopes in a recount that could swing the elec-tion to Nixon. When they finally had to admit defeat, they could scarcely come to terms with the deathblow that they felt the election had rendered to their dream of a Protestant nation. "We have felt like [a] death of a loved one has taken place—not the death of an individual, but the death throes of a nation," Billy Graham's father-in-law, L. Nelson Bell, said after the election. The country could now expect "a slow, completely integrated and planned attempt to take over our nation for the Roman Catholic Church." But Bell praised Nixon for his efforts on behalf of the Protestant cause. "You, Dick, stood for the things which have made America great, while Mr. Kennedy appealed to the most venal elements in individuals and society as a whole," Bell told Nixon. "I feel that the judgment of God hangs over a people to whom He has given so much and who have rejected spiritual values for those which are material . . . To see our nation in the hands of a conceited, arrogant and inexperienced young man is a frightening thing. But God may use it yet to bring us to our knees."[14]

Convinced that a Catholic president was un-American, many fundamentalists and evangelicals spent the next year looking for signs that Kennedy was selling out America's interests in the Cold War. The Bay of Pigs fiasco demonstrated to Bob Jones Jr. that Kennedy's foreign policy decisions had "cost us prestige among the nations of the world." "Unhappy [are] the people whose government is in the hands of a child," he told his university's students in a chapel talk. Billy James Hargis, whose *Christian Crusade* program was carried on hundreds of radio stations in the South and Midwest, told his listeners in the summer of 1961 that he was "convinced that the Kennedy administration is trying to neutralize the anti-Communist efforts of the United States." And John R. Rice, editor of the South's leading fundamentalist periodical, the *Sword of the Lord*, accused the Kennedy administration of "running America further and further in debt with wasteful, prodigal, wicked spending."[15] Everything that the Eisenhower administration had stood for seemed to be under attack.

Secularism and the Weakening of Evangelical Anti-Catholicism

Evangelicals' fear of Catholicism was so strong in the early 1960s that many of them ignored the threat of secularism, which would later become their principal concern. Immediately after Kennedy's election, the NAE spoke of the need to formulate a "Protestant strategy for the sixties" to win back the nation through politics, and a year later, a Southern Baptist business leader in Colorado, Gerri von Frellick, formed a new political organization, Christian Citizen, to elect born-again Christians to Congress. When the Supreme Court ruled against school prayer in *Engel v. Vitale* (1962), many evangelicals were so fixated on the possibility that Catholics would try to obtain federal money for their parochial schools that they viewed the ruling in favor of church-state separation as a victory for their cause. "Be very cautious about a constitutional amendment [to rescind *Engel*]," the Southwest NAE's newsletter cautioned in 1962. "Some that are being suggested carry some real dangers, not the least of which would be to open the gate to 'a whole convoy of Vatican trucks.'" Even the court's decision against devotional Bible ruling in public schools in 1963, which upset many Protestants, seemed to some Southern Baptists less threatening than the possibility of Catholic influence in the nation's schools. "If these laws [requiring the reading of the Bible in public schools] had been upheld, then the Catholics would have a right to insist that we erect the statues of their saints in our public schools in order to be reverent," the *Alabama Baptist* proclaimed.[16]

The nation's leading Catholic bishops, on the other hand, rushed to condemn the court's decision, because they viewed it as a sign that the nation had exchanged its traditional Christian heritage for secularism, a move that directly compromised America's security interests in the struggle against Soviet Communism. "All law comes from God," James Francis Cardinal McIntyre said in the wake of *Engel*. "Yet the court presumes to deny to the children of God in our schools the opportunity to speak to the Creator, the Lawmaker, the Preserver of mankind. This decision puts shame on our faces, as we are forced to emulate Mr. Khrushchev."[17]

Evangelicals were not yet ready to make peace with Catholics, but some of them did agree with the cardinal's assessment. Though the Supreme Court's rulings against school prayer and Bible reading did not alarm the editor of the *Alabama Baptist*, they disturbed the NAE, Billy Graham, and the South's leading fundamentalist radio broadcasters, all of whom echoed Catholic clerics' warnings about the dangers of a secular state. "A neutral or secular state, while preserving the nation from dominion by a denomination, leaves America in the same position as Communist Russia," Harold Ockenga, a founder of the NAE, declared immediately after the Supreme Court issued its ruling against public school Bible reading exercises in *Abington v. Schempp*. For many evangelicals, secularists—not Catholics—had become the nation's primary spiritual threat.[18]

In 1964 fundamentalist Presbyterian radio preacher Carl McIntire announced that he was going to support the Republican presidential ticket that year because the GOP platform endorsed a constitutional amendment to restore school prayer and Bible reading. When Republican presidential candidate Barry Goldwater selected a Catholic running mate, Representative William Miller of New York, McIntire did not express any objection, even though he had been one of the most vociferous critics of Kennedy's religion only four years earlier. Similarly, other formerly anti-Catholic Southern fundamentalists, such as John R. Rice and Billy James Hargis, endorsed the Goldwater-Miller ticket on the grounds that Goldwater was the strongest anticommunist in the race. By combining a strongly hawkish policy against Communism abroad with opposition to the Civil Rights Act of 1964, the Goldwater-Miller ticket appropriated the most powerful symbols of Southern Protestantism and linked them with a national conservative agenda that included Catholics. Even the most ardent fundamentalists in the South did not object.[19]

The culture wars over the sexual revolution brought Catholics and evangelical Protestants into a unified coalition and led them to discover the common moral and cultural values that they already shared. By the late 1960s, evangelicals were alarmed over the apparent breakdown in social morality, as a younger generation challenged traditional taboos against premarital sex and illicit drug use. Billy Graham's weekly radio broadcasts in 1967, which included sermons such as "Students in Revolt," "Conquering Teenage Rebellion," "Obsession with Sex," "The Shadow of Narcotics Addiction," "Flames of Revolution," "Rioting, Looting, and Crime," and "America Is in Trouble," described a nation on the verge of disintegration. Some evangelicals discovered that conservative Catholics who shared their concerns had already launched campaigns against cultural liberalism. In 1966 San Diego Baptist pastor Tim LaHaye, who would later become a household name among evangelicals as a bestselling author, joined Catholics and other conservatives in a coalition to pass restrictions on pornography in California. In 1968 Billy James Hargis's Christian Crusade joined the campaign against sex education that Southern California Catholics had started. He also invited Phyllis Schlafly's husband, Catholic conservative Fred Schlafly, to appear on his radio program. When Bob Jones Jr. rebuked Hargis for cozying up to Catholics, he responded that he was still "anti-Catholic" and "critical of the Pope and the hierarchy of the Roman Catholic Church" but that he could not ignore the fact that his anticommunist organization was receiving "some very generous support from Catholic laymen."[20]

Nixon's New Interreligious Coalition

Evangelicals' new political alliance with conservative Catholics worked to Nixon's advantage in 1968, because it allowed him to appeal simultaneously to Catholics and evangelicals rather than risk dividing the conservative coalition with separate appeals to each group. The role in which evangelicals now cast Nixon—as defender of the nation's morals against a liberal secular onslaught—came naturally to the Republican politician. He launched his bid for the White House in October 1967 with a *Reader's Digest* article calling for "national character and moral stamina." In a piece designed for churchgoing Middle America, Nixon criticized federal welfare policies that encouraged fathers to "stay away from the home" and lamented the rise in "lawlessness." For the previous two decades, evangelicals had argued that success in the Cold War depended on social morality, and Nixon's *Reader's Digest* article did the same. "A nation weakened by racial conflict and lawlessness at home cannot meet the challenges of leadership abroad," he wrote.[21]

Three months later, Nixon invited Billy Graham to his vacation home in Key Biscayne, Florida, to solicit the evangelist's official blessing for his presidential run. Graham was circumspect in his response, but Nixon nevertheless told socially conservative audiences that Graham's encouragement had been partly responsible for his decision to enter the race. He made it a point to attend one of Graham's crusades during the campaign and paid a personal visit to Graham's mother, who sported a Nixon campaign pin when she spoke with reporters after the event. Graham, for his part, was eager to preach the law-and-order message that formed the platform for Nixon's campaign. "We've got to have law and order, no matter how much force it takes," he said in October 1968. He praised Nixon as a "man of high moral principles," saying, "There is no American I admire more than Richard Nixon."[22]

Evangelicals believed the myth about Nixon because they were sure that America was on the verge of moral breakdown, and they were looking for someone to save the nation from destruction. As Graham's wife, Ruth Bell Graham, said, "If God does not punish America for its sins, He will have to apologize to Sodom and Gomorrah." With evangelicals sure that the nation was in danger of collapse or divine judgment, it was not hyperbole when Billy Graham announced in 1968, "I feel that the very survival of the country may be at stake in this year's election."[23]

A Gallup poll showed that 75 percent of Americans in 1970 thought that the influence of religion in the nation was declining, a view that only 14 percent of Americans had held in 1957. Evangelicals were alarmed. From small towns in the South and Midwest, stretching from the Kentucky coal country to rural Georgia and across to Oklahoma, Kansas, and other places in the nation's heartland, citizens wrote to Nixon about their fears of the increasing national influence of "atheists," "communists," "delinquents," and "hippies."[24]

But Nixon's election victory gave them hope. "I have heard that you are a man of strong faith," a woman from Campbellsville, Kentucky, wrote to Nixon during his first month in the White House. When Nixon launched a series of White House worship services on his first Sunday in office and invited Billy Graham to preach, evangelicals were overjoyed that the president had tapped one of their own as his pastor. "There is no doubt in my mind that you are a sincere, born-again Christian," Billy James Hargis declared. Pastors quoted the new president's religious pronouncements approvingly in their sermons and church bulletins, lauding him for such statements as "more preaching from the Bible rather than just about the Bible is what America needs." By 1972, evangelicals had become so enamored of the president that the Southern Baptist Convention's Carl Bates could declare Nixon a "born again Christian" and invite him to address the Southern Baptist Convention's annual meeting, marking the first time in its 125-year history that the denomination had asked an American president to speak at its annual convention. And for the first time in years, some began to believe that perhaps the nation's moral decline could be reversed. A Baptist pastor in Wichita, Kansas, spoke for many of his cobelievers when he told the president in a letter, "With your God-fearing attitude and spiritual insight I believe our nation is on the right track." Graham told the president in December 1971, "Under your administration, we have probably one of the great religious revivals of American history . . . I believe Christian people everywhere are praying for you . . . And they're thanking God for you."[25]

Evangelicals were ecstatic about Nixon because he positioned himself as a moral leader defending religious values against secular attack. "We have found ourselves rich in goods, but ragged in spirit," Nixon told Americans in his first inaugural address. "To a crisis of the spirit, we need an answer of the spirit." Marijuana use, he believed, was a "spiritual problem," and he resolved to take a tough line against it, just as he did on pornography. He vetoed a bill to provide federal funding for daycare because of its "family-weakening implications." Nixon was so successful in projecting the image of a moral traditionalist that even some of his critics conceded his sincerity on this point, attacking Nixon not for being hypocritical but rather for adhering to a moral code that was too stringent and parochial for an increasingly pluralistic and secular nation. "The tragedy of Mr. Nixon is not that of an evil man who has abandoned the public trust, but rather that of a moral man whose most cherished ideals are not commensurate with the realities of this time," Charles Henderson, a liberal Protestant chaplain at Princeton University, wrote in 1972.[26]

Nixon's image as a moral traditionalist was crucial in winning the evangelical vote, but it was also helpful in appealing to Catholics. In 1968 Nixon received only one third of the Catholic vote, and he resolved to increase that share in 1972. Kevin Phillips's *The Emerging Republican Majority*, which the Nixon campaign team treated as a political bible, cited the evangelical Sun Belt and the Catholic suburban North as the key to future Republican victories, and the Nixon White House was determined to make inroads in both constituencies. While H. R. Haldeman reached out to Graham to bolster the president's support among evangelicals, White House aide Charles Colson helped craft a "Catholic strategy" to pick up votes in the North. By the summer of 1972, Nixon's concerted effort to appeal to Catholics had attracted the attention of the national press. "The President, a Quaker, has been courting [Catholics] as if making his first communion were the most important thing in his life," the *Washington Star* remarked in June 1972.[27]

The Nixon administration's outreach to both evangelicals and Catholics relied on similar strategies, because in both cases the president portrayed himself as an opponent of secularism and licentiousness. "We have to remember that our primary base of support will probably be among the fundamentalist Protestants," Nixon told Haldeman in 1970, "and we can probably substantially broaden that base of support." In the spring of 1972, he told Haldeman that he wanted to make "dope," "abortion," "busing," "crime," and other moral issues the themes of his reelection campaign, rather than talk about issues—such as the environment—that some of the more liberal members of his party were touting. Haldeman carried out his boss's wishes by informing Nixon's campaign staff that the "real issue" in the election was "patriotism, morality, religion; not the material issues of taxes and prices. If those were the issues, the people would be for McGovern." Though George McGovern, Nixon's Democratic opponent in 1972, was the son of a Methodist minister, the Nixon campaign cast him as the secular candidate of cultural liberalism, who would legalize abortion and surrender in Vietnam.[28]

Colson framed his outreach to Catholics in similar terms. "Catholic voters tend to be more conservative on at least the social issue[s]," he wrote. Winning their support would require the president to "continue to take a hard line on obscenity, abortion, etc." White House speechwriter Pat Buchanan, a conservative Catholic, suggested a similar strategy for Nixon and inserted morally conservative rhetoric that he knew would appeal to fellow moral traditionalists, especially Catholics, into the president's speeches. In one conversation about a Catholic political strategy in the spring of 1972, Nixon and Colson highlighted two issues by which to reach conservative Catholics in the upcoming election— marijuana and abortion. At Buchanan's suggestion, the president wrote to Terence Cardinal Cooke to express his opposition to the liberalization of state abortion laws. Shortly thereafter, he sent a telegram of support to the National Right to Life Committee, which was still under the auspices of the Catholic Church. As Buchanan had hoped, Nixon quickly found that his defense of the "sanctity of life" won him plaudits from Catholic clerics. Nixon viewed his moderately conservative stance on abortion primarily as a way to appeal to Catholic voters, but as prolife articles in *Christianity Today* demonstrated, it may have also enhanced his reputation among some conservative evangelicals.[29]

Nixon may not have even realized the extent to which his political efforts succeeded in uniting Catholics and evangelicals, because at times he expressed concern that either evangelicals or Catholics would turn against him for appearing to favor one group over the other. After accepting an invitation to speak to the Southern Baptist Convention's annual meeting in Philadelphia in 1972, he canceled it, because he feared that speaking to Southern Baptists in a predominantly Catholic Northern city would alienate Catholics in the region. He worried that his administration's support for parochial school aid would attract opposition from "Billy Graham's fundamentalists." At times, his campaign aides plotted ways to divide the Protestant and Catholic vote, turning one group against the other to their advantage. But the battle between evangelicals and Catholics that Nixon had expected never came, and even parochial school aid proved to be far less divisive than he had feared. Although the Southern Baptist Convention passed a resolution against Nixon's proposal in 1971, that did not deter the convention's president from publicly supporting Nixon or inviting him to speak at the convention's annual meeting during his reelection campaign the following year.[30]

Nixon was able to reach out to both groups simultaneously not only because the events of the previous decade had brought Catholics and Protestants closer together on issues of public morality but also because he shrewdly positioned himself as an ecumenical defender of the nation's morals, so that Catholics and Protestants could both view him as one of their own. Though Watergate would cause many to wonder how evangelicals such as Billy Graham could have been so credulous as to view the profane and conniving Nixon as an exemplar of morality and a defender of the nation's religious heritage, the role may have suited Nixon better than the president's detractors thought. Though Nixon was not personally devout, he admired some of his religious supporters, even as he tried to manipulate them to win their votes. Their enemies were his enemies. In private conversations, he expressed anger at the sexual licentiousness and cultural liberalism of the era, and he portrayed evangelicals and conservative Catholics as his lone supporters in a world that was against him. Mainline Protestants and "ultraliberal Catholics" were both a "terrible bag," Nixon mused in one White House conversation during his first term in office. But "conservative Catholics" were different, he said, and "the Billy Grahams and all the rest, the Southern Baptists and so forth, they've got character. They've got guts to believe in something."[31]

Nixon won a higher share of both the evangelical and Catholic vote than any previous Republican presidential candidate had received in the postwar era. Though he continued to receive criticism from some bishops over the Vietnam War and economic issues, he was beginning to forge a coalition of conservative Catholics who liked what he said about drugs, abortion, and moral permissiveness. Perhaps most remarkably, many of the issues that he used to appeal to Catholics were the same ones that he employed to win the support of evangelicals. Evangelicals greeted Nixon's reelection with the jubilant expectation that his second term would bring the restoration of a Christian-based moral order in the nation. Graham assured his fellow believers that Nixon knew that the nation's "greatest problem" was "moral permissiveness and decadence," and he promised that the president would put "a lot more emphasis on moral and spiritual affairs" in his second term. *Eternity* magazine expressed "hope that the reelected President will not be known simply as a pragmatic politician who has achieved diplomatic success in thorny international issues, but one who by precept and example guided the nation out of its ethical morass."[32]

Nixon disappointed his supporters. Instead of guiding the nation out of an "ethical morass," he led the nation into one with the Watergate scandal. Graham, who believed that Nixon's "moral and ethical principles wouldn't allow him to do anything like that," tried to defend the president from political attacks as long as possible, but eventually, he came to the reluctant conclusion that the president had lied to him and the nation.[33]

But Nixon's downfall did not destroy the socially conservative coalition that he had helped to create. Though Nixon proved unable to deliver the moral revival that evangelicals had expected, the interdenominational coalition against secularism continued to grow stronger and maintained its alliance with the GOP. Six years after Nixon's resignation, conservative Catholics and evangelicals again came together to elect Ronald Reagan.

Nixon had arrived on the political scene at an opportune time, because in the late 1960s, when he ran for president the second time, evangelicals were beginning to join with Catholics in local moral campaigns. Nixon then transformed those fledgling coalitions into a powerful political juggernaut that would reshape the Republican Party. Desperate to win the Catholic vote and determined to increase his support among evangelicals, Nixon found a way to reach out to Catholics while simultaneously cultivating an alliance with Billy Graham. Having first united evangelicals in an anti-Catholic coalition in 1960, Nixon then transformed that coalition into a broader alliance against secularism ten years later. Nixon succeeded beyond what he could have imagined. Ultimately, the coalition that he helped to create would become the basis for the Religious Right, a movement that would reshape both the Republican Party and the nation's political agenda.

Notes

1. Lyman Kellstedt et al., "Faith Transformed: Religion and American Politics from FDR to George W. Bush," in *Religion and American Politics: From the Colonial Period to the Present*, ed. Mark A. Noll and Luke E. Harlow, 2nd ed. (New York: Oxford University Press, 2007), 272–73; Billy Graham to Richard Nixon, September 1, 1960, microfilm reel 1, collection 74, Billy Graham Center Archives (BGCA), Wheaton, IL (originals in Nixon Presidential Library [NPL], Yorba Linda, CA); Tape recording of telephone conversation between Richard Nixon and Billy Graham, December 19, 1971, WHT 16-124, NPL.

2. No historian has yet provided a detailed study of the way in which Richard Nixon helped to create an alliance between conservative Catholics and evangelical Protestants, although a few historians have examined his relationship with social conservatives, with a focus on his use of racial and cultural appeals. For these studies, see Robert Mason, *Richard Nixon and the Quest for a New Majority* (Chapel Hill: University of North Carolina Press, 2004); Steven P. Miller, *Billy Graham and the Rise of the Sunbelt South* (Philadelphia: University of Pennsylvania Press, 2009); Rick Perlstein, *Nixonland: The Rise of a President and the Fracturing of America* (New York: Scribner, 2008); Thomas J. Sugrue and John D. Skrentny, "The White Ethnic Strategy," in *Rightward Bound: Making America Conservative in the 1970s*, ed. Bruce J. Schulman and Julian E. Zelizer (Cambridge, MA: Harvard University Press, 2008), 171–92; and Bruce J. Schulman, *The Seventies: The Great Shift in American Culture, Society, and Politics* (New York: Free Press, 2001).

3. Kellstedt et al., "Faith Transformed," 272; Stephen J. Whitfield, *The Culture of the Cold War*, 2nd ed. (Baltimore: Johns Hopkins University Press, 1996), 88; Billy Graham to Dwight Eisenhower, December 3, 1951, February 8, 1954, and December 2, 1957, folder 1-12, collection 74, BGCA (originals in Eisenhower Presidential Library).

4. Billy James Hargis, *Communist America—Must it Be?* (Tulsa, OK: Christian Crusade, 1960), 31.

5. Barry Hankins, *Uneasy in Babylon: Southern Baptist Conservatives and American Culture* (Tuscaloosa: University of Alabama Press, 2002), 150–51; James DeForest Murch, *Cooperation without Compromise: A History of the National Association of Evangelicals* (Grand Rapids, MI: William B. Eerdmans, 1956), 137, 140, 150.

6. *United Evangelical Action*, February 1943, 2; Murch, *Cooperation without Compromise*, 161; "NAE Launches Anti-Communist Program," *United Evangelical Action*, June 1960.

7. Kenneth J. Heineman, *A Catholic New Deal: Religion and Reform in Depression Pittsburgh* (University Park: Pennsylvania State University Press, 1999); David J. O'Brien, *American Catholics and Social Reform: The New Deal Years* (New York: Oxford University Press, 1968); George J. Marlin, *The American Catholic Voter: 200 Years of Political Impact* (South Bend, IN: St. Augustine's Press, 2006), 192–237.

8. William B. Prendergast, *The Catholic Voter in American Politics: The Passing of the Democratic Monolith* (Washington, DC: Georgetown University Press, 1999), 120–31.

9. Herschel Hobbs, Statement to the Church, November 1960, folder 21-6, Herschel H. Hobbs Papers, Southern Baptist Historical Library and Archives (SBHLA), Nashville, TN; Associated Press, "Kennedy is Attacked," *The New York Times*, July 4, 1960; Marlin, *American Catholic Voter*, 257. For Catholic support of Kennedy in 1960, see Thomas J. Carty, *A Catholic in the White House?: Religion, Politics, and John F. Kennedy's Presidential Campaign* (New York: Palgrave Macmillan, 2004); and Shaun A. Casey, *The Making of a Catholic President: Kennedy vs. Nixon, 1960* (New York: Oxford University Press, 2009).

10. "Baptists Call Church Issue in Presidency," *Chicago Tribune*, May 21, 1960; William G. McLoughlin Jr., *Billy Graham: Revivalist in a Secular Age* (New York: Ronald Press, 1960), 117–18; Billy Graham to Richard Nixon, November 17, 1959, microfilm reel 1, collection 74, BGCA (original in NPL).

11. Richard Nixon to Billy Graham, August 29, 1960, microfilm reel 1, collection 74, BGCA (original in NPL); Graham to Nixon, June 21, 1960, microfilm reel 1, collection 74, BGCA (original in NPL).

12. Casey, *Making of a Catholic President*, 83–94, 102–22, 181–85.

13. Associated Press, "Arkansas Baptists to Oppose Kennedy," *The New York Times*, September 7, 1960; "Dr. Bob Jones Jr. Will Not Vote for Senator Kennedy," *Baptist Bible Tribune*, October 21, 1960; Associated Press, "A Catholic President Opposed," *The New York Times*, August 5, 1960; Associated Press, "Religious Issue Raised," *The New York Times*, September 3, 1960; Graham to Nixon, August 22, 1960, and November 2, 1960, microfilm reel 1, collection 74, BGCA (originals in NPL).

14. G. Archer Weniger, *Blu-Print*, November 22, 1960; L. Nelson Bell to Richard Nixon, November 11, 1960, folder 39-15, collection 318, BGCA.

15. "Cuba Handling Called 'Stupid,'" *Greenville News*, May 3, 1961; "'Stupid' Kennedy Assailed," *Greenville Piedmont*, May 2, 1961; "Hargis Hits Socialistic Legislation," *Columbia [SC] State*, February 7, 1962; John R. Rice, "Why Did God Allow Kennedy's Death?" *Sword of the Lord*, January 24, 1964, 7.

16. George L. Ford, "A Protestant Strategy for the Sixties," *United Evangelical Action*, December 1960, 5; John Wicklein, "Christian Group Aims at Politics," *The New York Times*, February 1, 1962, 23; *Time for Action: Report from Southwest NAE* (1962); "The Supreme Court Upholds the Constitution," *Alabama Baptist*, June 27, 1963, 3.

17. Alexander Burnham, "Churchmen Voice Shock at Ruling," *The New York Times*, June 26, 1962.

18. Burnham, "Churchmen Voice Shock at Ruling"; *Christian Beacon*, August 27, 1964, 8; "America Needs God No More?" *United Evangelical Action*, August 1963, 18.

19. *Christian Beacon*, August 27, 1964, 8; Rice, "Why Did God Allow Kennedy's Death?"; Donald Janson, "Rightist Pledges to Aid Goldwater," *The New York Times*, August 8, 1964.

20. Tapes of Billy Graham's *Hour of Decision* broadcast, collection 191, BGCA: "Students in Revolt," February 5, 1967; "Conquering Teenage Rebellion," April 9, 1967; "Obsession with Sex," May 14, 1967; "The Shadow of Narcotics Addiction," June 18, 1967; "Flames of Revolution," June 25, 1967; "Rioting, Looting, and Crime," July 30, 1967; "America is in Trouble," August 6, 1967; "California: The Men from CLEAN," *Newsweek*, September 5, 1966, 23; William Wingfield, "The Politics of Smut: California's Dirty Book Caper," *Nation*, April 18, 1966, 457; Lisa McGirr, *Suburban Warriors: The Origins of the New American Right* (Princeton, NJ: Princeton University Press, 2001), 226–27; William Martin, *With God on Our Side: The Rise of the Religious Right in America* (New York: Broadway Books, 1996), 103–8; Billy James Hargis to Bob Jones Jr., April 16, 1968, Fundamentalism File, J. S. Mack Library, Bob Jones University, Greenville, SC.

21. Richard M. Nixon, "What Has Happened in America?" *Reader's Digest*, October 1967, 49–54.

22. Nancy Gibbs and Michael Duffy, *The Preacher and the Presidents: Billy Graham in the White House* (New York: Center Street, 2007), 159–70; Religious News Service, "Graham to Candidates: Americans Wants Change in U.S. Moral Direction," *Western Voice*, November 7, 1968, 3.

23. T. W. Wilson, "America Facing God's Judgment," *Hour of Decision* tract (1970), BGCA; Louis Cassels, "Protestant Factions Join in Gun-Curb Drive," *Washington Post*, June 15, 1968.

24. Billy Graham to Leonard Garment, May 16, 1970, "Religious Matters, 1-69 / 12-70" folder, box 1, Subject Files—Religious Matters, White House Central Files (WHCF), NPL; Petition from Senior Citizens Group (Dahlonega, GA) to Richard Nixon, February 11, 1969, and Mrs. W. Ray Mings (Campbellsville, KY) to Nixon, February 3, 1969, "Religious Matters, begin 2-28-69" folder, box 1, Subject Files—Religious Matters, WHCF, NPL.

25. Mings to Nixon, February 3, 1969; Billy James Hargis to Richard Nixon, July 14, 1970, "EX TR 48-1, Knoxville, Tenn. to speak at Billy Graham's 'Crusade,'

Univ. of Tenn., 5/28/70" folder, box 38, TR, WHCF, NPL; Carl E. Bates to William Covington Jr., March 10, 1972, folder 1, Carl E. Bates Papers, SBHLA; Ken Adrian (Wichita, KS) to Richard Nixon, January 27, 1969, "RM 2-1 Religious Service in the White House, begin 2-5-69" folder, box 7, WHCF, Subject Files— Religious Matters, NPL; Tape recording of telephone conversation between Richard Nixon and Billy Graham, December 19, 1971, WHT 16-124, NPL.

26. Richard Nixon, First Inaugural Address, January 20, 1969, www.bartleby.com/124/pres58.html; John D. Skrentny, *The Minority Rights Revolution* (Cambridge, MA: Harvard University Press, 2002), 241; Charles P. Henderson, *The Nixon Theology* (New York: Harper and Row, 1972); Charles P. Henderson, "Mr. Nixon's Theology," *The New York Times*, July 3, 1972.

27. Marlin, *American Catholic Voter*, 276; Kevin Phillips, *The Emerging Republican Majority* (New Rochelle, NY: Arlington House, 1969); White House memo from Charles Colson to Peter Flanigan, February 18, 1972, "February 1972" folder, box 131, Colson Files, WHSF, NPL; White House memo from Charles Colson to H. R. Haldeman, June 15, 1972, "H. R. Haldeman, January 1972 [2]" folder, box 3, Colson Files, WHSF, NPL; Smith Hempstone, "Nixon, the Catholic Vote and the Megastates," *Washington Star*, June 14, 1972.

28. Richard Nixon to H. R. Haldeman, November 30, 1970, folder 3-7, collection 74, BGCA (original in NPL); Tape recording of White House conversation between Richard Nixon and H. R. Haldeman, Oval Office, April 10, 1972, Oval 705-3, NPL; H. R. Haldeman, White House memo, "General Philosophy and Themes," October 15, 1972, "H. Misc. Materials, 1972" folder, box 48, H. R. Haldeman Files, White House Staff Files (WHSF), NPL; White House memo from Charles Colson to Clark MacGregor, July 13, 1972, "July 1972" folder, box 132, Charles Colson Files, WHSF, NPL.

29. Colson to Flanigan, February 18, 1972; Patrick J. Buchanan, White House memo, [1972], "Abortion" folder, box 11, Patrick J. Buchanan Files, WHSF, NPL; Tape recording of conversation between Richard Nixon and Charles Colson, Executive Office Building, April 5, 1972, EOB 330-17, NPL; Edward B. Fiske, "After Five Years, Cooke Still Relishes His Pastoral Role," *The New York Times*, April 7, 1973; Richard Nixon to Terence Cardinal Cooke, May 5, 1972, "John Ehrlichman [2]" folder, box 7, Charles Colson Files, WHSF, NPL; National Right to Life Committee, Press Release, [June 1972], "National Right to Life Convention, June 16–18, 1972" folder, box 4, American Citizens Concerned for Life Papers (ACCL), Gerald R. Ford Presidential Library, Ann Arbor, MI; James T. McHugh, Press Release from the Family Life Division of the United States Catholic Conference, April 5, 1971, "Miscellaneous Reference Materials (3)" folder, box 3, ACCL, Ford Library; "The War on the Womb," *Christianity Today*, June 5, 1970, 24–25; "Abortion and the Court," *Christianity Today*, February 16, 1973, 32–33. For an analysis of Nixon's stance on abortion, see Daniel K. Williams, "The GOP's Abortion Strategy: Why Pro-Choice Republicans Became Pro-Life in the 1970s," *Journal of Policy History* 23 (2011): 513–39.

30. Tape recording of conversation between Richard Nixon and H. R. Haldeman, Executive Office Building, March 22, 1972, EOB 324-22; Tape recording of conversation between Richard Nixon and John Ehrlichman et al., Executive Office

Building, October 19, 1971, EOB 292-11, NPL; Lee Porter to Dwight L. Chapin, April 7, 1972, "[Ex] UT 1-3 Telephone 1/1/71-" folder, box 19, UT, WHCF, NPL; Tape recording of telephone conversation between Richard Nixon and Charles Colson, October 20, 1971, WHT 11-163, NPL; Southern Baptist Convention, Resolution on Public Funds and Non-Public Education, June 1971, www.sbc.net/resolutions/amResolution.asp?ID=946; Bates to Covington, March 10, 1972.

31. Tape recording of conversation between Richard Nixon and Russell Kirk, Oval Office, April 4, 1972, Oval 702-9, NPL.

32. Kellstedt et al., "Faith Transformed"; Marlin, *American Catholic Voter*, 282; "Personalia," *Christianity Today*, December 22, 1972, 39; Editorial, "'72's History, '73's Issues," *Eternity*, January 1973, 7.

33. Religion News Service, "Graham Says Nixon Not in Watergate," *Baptist Standard*, February 16, 1973, 18.

PART 4

The International Arena

CHAPTER 8

"Girded with a Moral and Spiritual Revival"

The Christian Anti-Communism Crusade and Conservative Politics

Laura Jane Gifford

Charles Sarvis, an anticommunist activist from Seattle, Washington, traveled to the Communist-controlled Indian state of Kerala in January 1959 to visit a friend named George Thomas. Thomas was working on the front lines of anticommunist efforts—not on behalf of the United States government, or even a mainstream aid organization, but under the auspices of the Christian Anti-Communism Crusade (CACC). Sarvis explained that Communists had won power in this southern Indian state a year and a half prior "by flooding the country with literature." The Communists published four daily newspapers and two weekly magazines, as well as a dozen "leftist" newspapers. At present, however, there was no publication that could "present the truth of the Communist party goals." The solution? The CACC must donate sufficient funds to enable Thomas to purchase the equipment he needed to publish a daily newspaper. Provided with the truth, Kerala citizens were sure to vote the Communist government out of power in 1962 and turn the tide of Communist expansion in this important Asian nation. Thomas was "the man of the hour in India." The CACC had forwarded $15,000 to Thomas already, executive director Dr. Fred Schwarz reported, but he needed $50,000 immediately. "Please continue to believe, pray and give that the goal may be reached," Schwarz exhorted. "We cannot afford to fail."[1]

While many scholars have dismissed the CACC as simply another right-wing organization prominent in the 1950s and 1960s, the crusade's work in Kerala is but one example of the very different manner in which some CACC leaders interpreted the fight against Communism. The ideology and program of the CACC combines a philosophy of anticommunism deeply steeped in religious motivations with a uniquely international approach to understanding—and combating—the Communist menace. This approach no doubt has its foundations in the Australian citizenship of its founder and guiding force, Dr. Frederick Schwarz. Schwarz viewed the United States as a bulwark that could protect less-powerful nations, Australia chief among them, from Communist expansion.[2]

Schwarz differed from other conservative proponents of religious anticommunism in his level of understanding of Communist thought and philosophy and his fundamentally internationalist conception of the anticommunist struggle. Many of the other putative experts who spoke at CACC-sponsored anticommunism schools, however, and the overweening political climate of the United States combined to produce outcomes more in line with the prevailing, nationalistic, anticommunist Right than with Schwarz's unique take on the international situation. Schwarz himself consistently distanced himself from the outcomes of his schools and educational enterprises, emphasizing his role as diagnostician and absolving himself of responsibility not only for the actions his "students" might take but also, in the name of academic freedom, for the individuals who spoke at CACC events.

Schwarz was a highly informed, articulate, internationally focused anticommunist activist; he was also an inveterate fundraiser, comparatively uninterested in supervising his Crusades' overall message or the activities undertaken by his "graduates." Consequently, the CACC represents a missed opportunity for an ideologically grounded, internationalist approach toward Christian anticommunism. Had Schwarz chosen to repudiate affiliation with internal-subversion advocates and instead grounded the CACC's approach wholly in the international sphere, his organization could have represented a uniquely Christian approach toward understanding of—and intervention in—the struggle for control and authority around the world. Instead, he remained prone to simplistic critiques of some of the Right's most prominent straw men, and he failed to close off his organization from more dubious appeals to fear and uncertainty. As a result, Schwarz straddles the line between servant and charlatan.

Becoming an Activist

The most pivotal event of Schwarz's formative years in Australia came when, as a representative of his university's Evangelical Union, he was nominated to debate a young Communist law student on the topic "Is Communism a Science or a Religion?" Schwarz, a devout Baptist, spent his time arguing that Communism did in fact possess all the key attributes of a religion. He went on to observe, however, that the Communist student entirely ignored the subject of the debate, launching instead into an attack on capitalism. The episode led Schwarz to begin an extensive program of self-education in Communist doctrine, immersing himself in philosophical tomes to the extent that, as he later put it, his wife "would sometimes shock some of our friends by stating that she frequently had four men in bed with her—Marx, Lenin, Stalin, and myself."[3]

Schwarz spent many a Sunday afternoon debating Communists in the Sydney Domain, where he claimed on one occasion to have completely befuddled the local Communist chairman by citing, in detail, the definition of dialectical materialism. He also maintained a regular speaking schedule at churches throughout New South Wales. At one such occasion, Schwarz caught the attention of two North American visitors—the Reverend Carl McIntire, head of the fundamentalist and separatist American Council of Christian Churches (ACCC) and International Council of Christian Churches (ICCC), and Dr. T. T. Shields, a Toronto minister and fellow member of the ICCC.[4]

McIntire and Shields were suitably impressed by their new Aussie acquaintance. They invited Schwarz to visit the United States, and following a series of ACCC- and ICCC-sponsored events in the United States and abroad, Schwarz recalled that Billy Graham, among others, "urged me to form an organization that would educate people about the Communist menace, and at the same time be in harmony with Christian evangelism." The Christian Anti-Communism Crusade was founded in May 1953, with Schwarz as executive director. He would spend the bulk of his working life in the United States, based in Long Beach, California, and traveling thousands of miles a year.[5]

A frequent criticism of Schwarz was that he was preaching to Americans without actually identifying himself, through citizenship, with Americans' cause. What right had this Australian doctor to tell the United States it was failing in the fight against the Communist enemy? Shouldn't he go back to his own homeland and fight his fight there? Alternatively, if he was trying to cast his lot with the Americans, why didn't he pledge his loyalty to Uncle Sam?[6]

Such criticisms, however, failed to appreciate the international lens through which Schwarz viewed his struggle. For him, the United States was a vital protectorate—as long as its citizens could be convinced of the significance of strenuous opposition to Communism. Schwarz exhorted audiences, "If you were prime minister of Australia, and Soviet submarines with nuclear weapons were stationed in the ocean waters near Brisbane, Sydney, Melbourne, Adelaide, Perth, and Hobart, and the Soviet commander phoned you and demanded surrender, what would you do?" Over half of Australia's population lived in these coastal cities. Australia had no technological means by which to oppose such a submarine force. The only obvious response was to call the president of the United States and plead for American protection. If the United States were unable—or unwilling—to help, Australians faced no alternative but surrender. "When asked how the Communists could conquer Australia, I would answer, 'By telephone.'" Schwarz believed he could best guarantee Australia's security by teaching Americans about the true nature and objectives of Communism.[7]

Much was written about Schwarz and his movement over the course of the 1960s and 1970s, but most observers remained preoccupied primarily with whether Schwarz and the CACC truly fit into either of two major blocs: the radical Right or fundamentalist Christianity. Schwarz proclaimed himself a "narrow-minded Bible-believing Baptist," and much of the rhetoric of the CACC, particularly in its early years, had a fundamentalist focus.[8] Schwarz's politics were clearly conservative, and he endorsed Barry Goldwater in 1964. By the late 1950s, with the inception of a program of Anti-Communism Schools, however, the organization's mission was more broadly focused. In any event, focusing on such distinctions dilutes the most significant component of the CACC's activism: its international approach. Billy James Hargis and Carl McIntire launched balloons across the border of the Iron Curtain, but Schwarz and the CACC sponsored missionaries around the world, printed newspapers abroad and waged so active a campaign against Communism in British Guiana that both Schwarz and CACC associate Dr. Joost Sluis were cast out of the protectorate as illegal immigrants.

Education is the Key

Schwarz's reaction to Communism stayed remarkably focused from the time of his first exposure to Communist tactics: education was the key to successfully combating this menace. Schwarz composed his first booklet-length tract, *The Heart, Mind and Soul of Communism*, in 1952. "Communism is a religion of promise," he declared, a promise that in one aspect appealed to the poor, ignorant, and underprivileged but in another aspect appealed to the wealthy, the educated, and the idealistic. For the poor, Communist "religion" promised a world free of material want. For the elite—and this represented a far more insidious force—the "religion" of Communist philosophy represented the potential of a "new and finer mankind." Schwarz's Christian audiences should have a special understanding of the appeal of such a promise: "They are dedicated to the redemption of man through the Gospel of the Grace of God revealed in Jesus Christ." The problem? Communists claimed to achieve humanity's redemption not through God, but through science—and the cornerstones of scientific Marxism were atheism, materialism, and economic determinism.[9]

Schwarz further developed his exposition of Communism in *Communism: Diagnosis and Treatment* (1956), using his analogical prowess to the fullest to refute the argument that Communism fulfilled the communal life profiled in the biblical book of Acts: "The word 'Studebaker' at one time indicated a covered wagon, but today it suggests a sleek, streamlined automobile. Communism is what its creators Karl Marx, Frederick Engels, Vladimir Lenin, and Joseph Stalin have stated and shown it to be, and what its present leaders manifest from day to day." Schwarz referenced Communist publications ranging from Engels' *The Origin of the Family, Private Property, and the State* (1884) to Lenin's *The State and Revolution* (1917) to construct a reader-friendly description of the diagnosis and symptoms of Communism—and, most alarmingly, the prognosis for survival of the free world without adequate treatment. "The Communists are deluging the world with books and directed them primarily to the minds of the young," he warned, again assigning paramount importance to education. Only "good books, clean books, well-printed books" about Christianity and democracy, provided to "the students of Asia, Africa, and South America," would prevent Communism's further spread.[10]

As the CACC grew in prominence, Schwarz was invited to speak before the House Committee on Un-American Activities (HUAC). The Allen-Bradley Company, a manufacturing firm headquartered in Milwaukee, Wisconsin, widely distributed the transcript of his 1957 testimony in an effort labeled "Operation Testimony." Allen-Bradley paid to have the transcripts printed in major newspapers throughout the country and gave 25 free copies to any individual who asked for them as well as unlimited free copies to churches and schools. At Christmas 1958, the firm printed copies in newspapers under the title "Will You Be Free to Celebrate Christmas in the Future?"[11]

By the mid-1950s, however, international distribution of the HUAC testimony and other CACC literature was a paramount focus. An Indian Christian Crusade was established with CACC help in 1956, and by the late 1950s translation and distribution of CACC materials took up a sizeable percentage of the organization's resources. As already noted, the CACC contributed thousands of dollars to the activities of George Thomas, a native of India who returned to Kerala in 1957. Members donated funds to provide literature for a CACC-affiliated organization in Taiwan and Korean-language copies of *The Heart, Mind and Soul of Communism* in Korea. Citing the gospel parable of the loaves and fishes, Schwarz exhorted newsletter subscribers to even greater heights of philanthropy: "If everyone [*sic*] of us gave all that we had, it still would be so little compared to the vast assets available to the enemy. Our confidence is in the power of God to multiply our gifts."[12]

The CACC responded to Vice President Richard Nixon's tumultuous 1958 Latin American trip by launching a $10,000 campaign to start a literature distribution program. The year 1959 saw requests from missionaries in the Sudan, Ethiopia, and Nigeria to reprint and distribute *Heart, Mind and Soul* as well as further evidence of the strong support the CACC enjoyed from conservative businessmen; Jack Danciger of Fort Worth, Texas, had thousands of copies of Schwarz's HUAC testimony translated and printed for Latin America. "Thank God for patriotic American businessmen," Schwarz pronounced in a tone that encouraged others among his readership to follow Danciger's lead. In June 1960 the CACC secured enough funds to make a down payment on a rotary press for the Kerala operation. The CACC even entered the world of comic books, publishing *Two Faces of Communism* in 1961 and including Spanish-language versions for the Latin American market. *Two Faces* told the story of an all-American father telling his all-American kids about being temporarily duped by Communist promises as a young man. Comics destined for distribution in Latin America depicted horrors like Catholic priests being murdered by Communists.[13]

By the early 1960s, books, pamphlets, and other publications were cascading out of CACC headquarters. Donald McNeil, a concerned observer of right-wing activity in Phoenix, Arizona, described the wide range of literature available at a 1961 Anti-Communism School, including seven Schwarz-authored works, large stacks of other speakers' volumes, and a wide variety of tape recordings. McNeil collected a number of CACC pamphlets that could be personalized by groups seeking to distribute tracts. CACC literature tables also included five-cent "Midget Missiles" and one-cent "Penny Projectiles" tailored for mass distribution as well as manuals outlining how to establish a study group.[14]

The most significant of the reams of literature coming out of Christian Anti-Communism Crusade headquarters was Schwarz's first full-length book, which hit the presses in 1960 as *You Can Trust the Communists (. . . to Do Exactly as They Say)* and was altered later in the decade to become the slightly less flamboyant *You Can Trust the Communists (...to Be Communists)*. Schwarz's mission was to expose Communism to the light of rational thinking. This was not some mysterious organization trading in undiscoverable secrets. Rather, Communists were people operating according to clearly defined principles that were both trustworthy and predictable. With solid grounding in Communist philosophy, language, and tactics, Communists could be successfully countered on their own terms—and defeated.[15]

Chief among the problems non-Communists, and especially Christians, faced was a tendency to interpret Communist phraseology in Christian terms. For example, Communists were entirely genuine in their desire for "peace" and their sponsorship of the "peace organizations" so often accused of or uncovered as being Communist fronts. The crux of the problem was that "peace" for Communists had a different *meaning* than "peace" for a Christian anticommunist.

In Communist philosophy, "peace" could only be achieved through Communist victory. Therefore, every action that would further a final victory for Communism was a peaceful action—even war. And make no mistake, Schwarz admonished—the Communists believed they were presently at war.[16] Schwarz spent the bulk of *You Can Trust the Communists* carefully explicating major tenets of Communist belief with frequent references to Marx, Lenin, Hegel, and the other philosophical antecedents of Communist thought. Schwarz placed trust in his readers to understand what was in many cases a fairly complex series of explanations, and as *Time* magazine put it in 1962, "his treatment of such a difficult subject as dialectical materialism is a model of instructive popularization." He also made it clear, however, that he intended his work to be a populist manifesto. Common people must lead the charge against Communism, because the very people most likely to be taken in by Communist logic were not the workers of the proletariat but *academics*. Communists successfully recruited young intellectuals because of four characteristics shared by much of the Western elite: disenchantment with capitalism, materialist philosophy, intellectual pride, and unfulfilled religious need.[17]

Marxist thought postulated that humans were entirely material creatures. There was no God; as well, there were no true spiritual qualities in humankind. Rather, environment was the sole determinant of human character and attribute. By altering human environments, those controlling the wheels of power—the scientific and intellectual elite—could control the dynamics of human society. Schwarz argued that human life continued to require a purpose. If God no longer provided that purpose for the Western intellectual elite, a philosophy based on organization, fidelity, and belonging would fill that vacuum of need.[18] This is why the Christian Anti-Communism Crusade was not just the Anti-Communism Crusade. Communism was what happened when people tried to play God.

Schwarz cited three elements as essential to success: motivation, knowledge, and organization. Grassroots efforts were of paramount importance—"the powers of multiplication are limitless." The role of government must be limited regardless of who was in power for the simple reason that a government has little access to deep, motivating forces like home, family, or faith. Christians should aid the poor and feed the hungry, but no quantity of foreign aid would automatically cause recipients to think the "right" thoughts—and believing it would was Marxist-materialist, not Christian. Above all, he promoted knowledge gained through reading, study, and careful spiritual preparation as "the foundations of freedom must be girded with a moral and spiritual revival."[19]

With the publication of *You Can Trust the Communists* in the second half of 1960, distribution efforts expanded apace. As of June 1962, paperback copies of the publication had been distributed to every priest, rabbi, and preacher in the United States, and the CACC increasingly turned its efforts toward Latin America. While a Spanish translation was already available, it was proving prohibitively expensive. Accordingly, the CACC planned to print 100,000 Spanish-language copies in Mexico City for distribution to university students throughout Latin America. "This project would cost us $35,000," Schwarz reported. "It could save this nation many millions."[20]

Donors to the CACC's international efforts demonstrated their absorption of Schwarz's international message. Not only did these donors offer financial assistance; they also personally identified with the struggles faced elsewhere in the world. Sister Mary Anthonette, OSB, for example, related her "interest and gratification" that the CACC was focusing on Mexico in 1963, commenting, "I suffer spiritually with those who are under Communist domination or who are being victimized by its diabolic author." Others who learned of the CACC's efforts took Schwarz's educational message to heart. Writing in response to a February 1962 *Time* profile of several right-wing organizations, Joseph C. Zengerle III, a West Point cadet, took aim at the magazine's criticism of Schwarz for failing to offer a detailed program of action: "Is it not enough that Schwarz arouses an intense desire in the American people to learn about Communism for themselves?"[21]

Reports from abroad indicated these publications were finding their intended audience and impacting local opinion. In November 1962, for example, Schwarz shared a letter from an activist in Puerto Rico who reported on the distribution of five thousand volumes: "The children just love them; Teenagers, and even old men. The farmers in the hills love them." A year later, Schwarz shared the good news that one of Rio de Janeiro's leading newspapers wished to serialize *You Can Trust the Communists*. Schwarz even enjoyed the imprimatur of the US government. In January 1963 he informed CACC supporters that the United States Information Agency (USIA) was assisting in the translation and publication of *You Can Trust the Communists* around the world, including the recent arrangement of a publisher for the book in Portuguese in Brazil.[22]

Anti-Communism Schools

As these reams of material made their way across the United States and around the world, the CACC turned its attention toward a new educational focus. Schwarz's first experience with anticommunism education outside the bounds of Bible-school audiences came in 1957 and 1958, when he was invited to speak at two St. Louis educational seminars organized by conservative activist Phyllis Schlafly. Schwarz used these seminars as a model to develop his own series of anticommunism schools. He also encouraged Schlafly and her husband, Fred, to organize their Cardinal Mindszenty Foundation in 1958.[23]

Speakers at the CACC Anti-Communism Schools ranged from former FBI double agent Herb Philbrick and anticommunist activist W. Cleon Skousen to government experts, including Representative Walter Judd (R-MN). In December 1958 the CACC held a weeklong school in Long Beach, California. As news of the program crossed the country, other localities invited Schwarz to hold similar events. At a Milwaukee school in early 1960, even a blizzard failed to prevent audiences of eight hundred attendees, and a Houston school scheduled for Saturdays in March drew more than one thousand. Schools were scheduled for Phoenix, Arizona, and Orange County, California in February 1961; Tyler, Texas, in March; St. Louis in April; and Miami in June. Schwarz and the CACC even hoped to hold schools in Jamaica and British Guiana in March and April. "These will be pioneering ventures of breath-taking potential . . . The Caribbean must not become a Communist sea."[24]

Schwarz professed a belief in the exercise of academic freedom, consistently disavowing responsibility for the remarks of particular speakers. He also claimed no responsibility for activities that might result from his schools, although he clearly endorsed further educational efforts. Critics of the CACC questioned these positions. Many argued that the CACC's efforts were having extremist consequences. McNeil, for example, reported that speakers in Phoenix "solemnly proclaimed that Franklin D. Roosevelt, Frank Sinatra, Linus Pauling, Robert Hutchins, psychiatrists, liberals, teachers, newspapermen, and clergymen were linked to Communist goals." McNeil's disapprobation extended to Schwarz himself, whom he observed speaking of Communist conspirators as "these strange personalities, these racketeers, these intellectuals" in a way that implied the terms were synonymous. Schwarz also made his claim, often repeated, that at the present rate of progress, Communists would conquer the United States by 1973.[25]

Five of the Phoenix school's seven steering committee members later told a reporter they were members of the John Birch Society (JBS). Following the school, Phoenix activists formed a Citizens Information Center to consolidate efforts to oppose Communism in the Phoenix metropolitan area. McNeil believed that the efforts of anticommunist conservatives were paralyzing progress in the region and that the CACC fed into this climate of paralysis and fear. Schwarz and the CACC's relationship to the JBS, in particular, was a fraught one. Despite the leading role Birchers took in organizing schools such as the Phoenix event, Schwarz disavowed any comparisons between the CACC and the society. However, JBS founder Robert Welch publicly lauded the CACC for its work and offered the JBS as a way to put the awareness brought by Schwarz's schools into action.[26]

The composition of the students at Schwarz's schools was essentially middle-class, and commentators remarked on the dedication of many attendees. Even the critical McNeil noted that he couldn't "remember seeing such an attentive, quiet audience for a long time." A survey of two 1962 San Francisco Bay–area schools revealed that the average income, education, and occupational levels of respondents were above the region's average. Average age was fairly similar to the region's overall demographics, and two thirds of attendees were self-identified members of the Republican Party. Students were significantly more engaged in political life than the average American, and the most conservative respondents also tended to be the most politically active.[27]

As the plans for schools in Jamaica and British Guiana indicate, Schwarz's outlook regarding the Communist threat was truly global. Often Schwarz's plans were bigger than the CACC's wallet, and the predicted Jamaica and British Guiana schools did not immediately materialize. Dr. Joost Sluis, an orthopedic surgeon and the regional director of the CACC's Northern California chapter, visited Central America in the spring of 1960. He reported that evidence of Communist influence in Latin America and the Caribbean was on the rise, especially in universities. To combat this growing problem, American students would be distributing 10,000 copies of *The Heart, Mind and Soul of Communism* in Spanish to their Mexican counterparts. Sluis saw a need for the development of Spanish-language films, literature, and radio and television programming to counter the "beautiful" Communist magazines and propaganda flooding the United States' neighbors to the south.[28]

Sluis increasingly focused his attention on British Guiana because he felt it would be a uniquely significant beachhead for Communist expansion. Generally, he argued, the Communist conquest of a country was dependent on the presence of a Communist government bordering that country. The only exceptions to this rule were Russia and Cuba. A third exception, however, might be British Guiana. Cuba was close enough to provide necessary support. If British Guiana went Communist, its shared borders with both Venezuela and Brazil would provide easy access to the largest, most influential countries on the continent. In an effort to forestall the efforts of nationalist Cheddi Jagan's People's Progressive Party (PPP), which Sluis labeled Communist, the orthopedist visited British Guiana on six separate occasions between 1961 and 1963. He led meetings with the assistance of East Indian aides from Kerala, distributed hundreds of copies of *You Can Trust the Communists*, and helped locals distribute other simple literature. In May 1962 Sluis and Schwarz were declared "prohibited immigrants" by British Guiana, which was still a British protectorate but led locally by Jagan. Sluis interpreted Jagan's calls for independence as a move toward Communist domination. He predicted an independent British Guiana would immediately align with Russia, using Cuban-trained members of the PPP's youth organization to enforce local order.[29]

While more recent scholarship has emphasized Jagan's nationalism and downplayed the risk of Communist expansion in the South American state, at the time of the CACC's activity in British Guiana, Schwarz and his colleagues were very much on the side of the American government—and some government officials explicitly acknowledged the success of the CACC's efforts. Ambassador deLesseps S. Morrison, US representative to the Organization of American States, for example, lauded the organization in a speech made in August 1962 to the Institute on World Affairs, arguing that Schwarz and the CACC "made a contribution to the downfall of Communism in British Guiana." It is likely that the CIA passed money to groups, including the CACC, who opposed the secularization of British Guiana's public schools in the early 1960s.[30]

The apex of the Anti-Communism Schools' success came in 1961 with a series of events held in Southern California, a bellwether for conservative activism. An Orange County School of Anti-Communism in the spring drew thousands, including a crowd of more than 7,000 young people on "Youth Day." From August 28 to September 1 the CACC held its largest school, drawing up to 10,000 people to an All–Southern California School of Anti-Communism held in the Los Angeles Sports Arena. Schwarz boasted of the formation of thousands of study groups throughout Southern California. On October 16, Schwarz followed up on the CACC's astounding success with a rally at the Hollywood Bowl, drawing 12,000 attendees and an estimated four million television viewers over 33 stations in six states. John Wayne, Jimmy Stewart, George Murphy, and Jack Warner were among the celebrities drawn to the event, which featured speeches by Senator Thomas Dodd (D-CT) and Walter Judd—and a public apology by *Life* publisher C. D. Jackson for an "over-simplified misinterpretation" of the CACC that the magazine had recently published. *The New York Times* reported following the rally that the CACC had outstripped the John Birch Society as the most popular right-wing organization among Southern California conservatives.[31]

Schwarz's Icarus Moment

On the heels of the CACC's greatest success, Schwarz attempted to move into the heart of the Eastern Establishment, New York City, for what he believed could be his greatest triumph. New York City was an important destination for many reasons. It was the headquarters of the national and international media, offering an unparalleled chance to counter "extremist" portrayals of the CACC. New York was the headquarters of the United Nations and therefore the locus point for international impressions of America. It was the national headquarters of the Communist Party. There were more than five hundred colleges and universities in the vicinity, some of which Schwarz planned to visit. It was home to minorities of all backgrounds. In short, "It is truly the City of Promise but giants lurk in the pathway." Three thousand enthusiastic supporters attended an opening rally in Manhattan Center on Friday, April 13. The undertaking as a whole would be very expensive, in part because Schwarz was focusing all his efforts on New York rather than continuing his usual revenue-producing pattern of speeches and rallies.[32]

By early 1962, however, success had heightened the organization's public profile, bringing Schwarz and his crusade under increasing media scrutiny. *The New Republic*, for example, reported in January on the activities of a local meeting in Southern California. Attendees were primarily "[s]olid-citizen type, community pillars; kind you can count on to aid civic projects." They listened to a recording of a Schwarz speech, which the magazine described as "mostly historical with emotional overtone, 'Communism' substituted for 'brimstone.'" The message put forth by the local leader? "Communism is engulfing us; it's in the air, everywhere; much of it put out by liberal newsmen and authors[,] . . . dupes. What to do? Refute everything not 100 percent American. United States must quit UN, contains 'known Communists' (baffling point not elaborated). End foreign aid; eliminate income tax. Leader very tolerant—told us not to call names . . . gratified approval; then everyone proceeded to call names." Following the leader's presentation, the audience was allowed to ask questions. Most, the magazine reported, showed deep fear of a threat perceived as real and imminent.[33]

Meanwhile, whispers of anti-Semitism grew throughout the spring. Schwarz was himself descended from a Jewish father who converted to Christianity. The term "Christian" in the CACC's name, however, opened the organization to charges of exclusivity. In early 1962, Schwarz appealed to the head of the Anti-Defamation League (ADL), Arnold Forster, asking him to investigate charges of anti-Semitism in an effort to clear his name. Instead, the ADL *Bulletin* published an article deriding Schwarz for the comments of some CACC speakers and casting the Australian as a charlatan out for profit. William F. Buckley Jr. and *National Review* leapt to Schwarz's defense.[34]

Forster had little regard for Buckley—he referred publicly to the *National Review* editor as an "eighteenth century egg-head" and "a quixotic beatnik in a Brooks Brothers suit"—but Buckley's prominence bolstered the public profile of the controversy. The *New York Herald Tribune* published a rebuttal letter by Schwarz countering Forster's charges that the CACC offered black-and-white solutions to complicated problems and distracted Americans with efforts to seek out domestic Communists while ignoring the international arena. "Why," asked Schwarz, "have I been declared an 'illegal immigrant' by the Left-leaning government of British Guiana? Would he suggest it is because I have been advising Americans to ignore Communism outside the borders of the U.S.A.?"[35]

Schwarz believed the controversy and ensuing publicity would help CACC efforts in New York. "There is now a rising tide of interest, enthusiasm and knowledge," he reported to his supporters, and he anticipated an "overflowing rally" on June 28 at Madison Square Garden, as well as an "outstanding" school at Carnegie Hall from August 27 to 31. The Madison Square Rally was a success, drawing eight thousand attendees, good newspaper coverage, and a memorable statement by pop sensation Pat Boone that "I would sooner see my four daughters blown into Heaven by an atomic bomb than taught into Hell by the Communists."[36] The school itself, though, attracted far fewer attendees. While enrollment was more than two thousand, only about four hundred consistently attended.

Schwarz called the school "an unqualified success." *The New York Times* and other papers reported on the CACC with "objectivity and honesty," among other things conducting a thorough and exonerating investigation of the organization's finances. Schwarz appeared on "Meet the Press" and acquitted himself well. Eight television broadcasts of the school garnered many additional viewers. "I found it difficult to walk on the street in New York without being constantly recognized and approached," Schwarz said. "The attitude of these viewers was almost invariably friendly and enthusiastic." Schwarz reported that the deficit from the New York School would total $75,000 but labeled it an "investment" in a battle "growing in intensity."[37]

Unfortunately for the CACC, the New York school proved to be a turning point. Never again would Schwarz draw as large an audience as he enjoyed in 1961. Schwarz blamed the Kennedy administration for his change in fortunes; he believed the administration had concluded his ministry was helping Republicans and had targeted him accordingly. The USIA reversed its policy of support for distribution of *You Can Trust the Communists* abroad, and the Internal Revenue Service investigated CACC activities. The CACC also suffered from news of the Reuther Memorandum, the product of a 1961 commission organized by Attorney General Robert Kennedy that investigated conservative organizations following the resignation of Major General Edwin Walker.[38] The CACC's change in fortunes was part of a larger reaction to the perceived growth of right-wing extremism. Despite Schwarz's optimism, the "extremist" label continued to be applied to his CACC, although not without significant challenges.

The success of the Goldwater-for-President movement in the early 1960s led to a flurry of books on the Right. Some authors viewed Schwarz as one among an extremist crowd, while others were more inclined to draw distinctions. Donald Janson and Bernard Eismann labeled Schwarz the "'Enry 'Iggins of the Right," emphasizing the number of financial appeals he made, the ambiguity they found in his lectures, and the disturbing statements made by some of his supporters. Schwarz's ADL nemesis, Arnold Forster, coauthored *Danger on the Right* in 1964 with fellow ADL leader Benjamin Epstein. Predictably, their treatment of Schwarz was less than favorable. As Schwarz consistently reminded his students, "knowledge is power"—but for Schwarz's students, Forster and Epstein argued, "it is also frightening and quite expensive," citing lists of materials for sale at Anti-Communism Schools that totaled as much as $689.10. The ADL leaders acknowledged Schwarz's scholarship but rued the waste of what could have been a positive contribution to the nation's political debate.[39]

Not every commentator was quite so condemnatory. Brooks Walker, a Unitarian minister, wrote in his 1964 book *The Christian Fright Peddlers* that Fred Schwarz did not like to be identified with the right wing—"and strictly speaking, he is correct." Schwarz commented only selectively on domestic issues, "and he [was] altogether unwilling to compile his private list of American subversives." Nonetheless, he drew his largest base of support from the Right. Schwarz shouldn't be blamed too extensively for his followers; after all, even Jesus had a Judas. "Schwarz's commitment to the right wing is qualified by a measure of good sense, a modicum of intellectual perception and an unwillingness to get involved publicly in naming names and denouncing particular instances of subversion," Walker concluded.[40]

Over the balance of the decade, Schwarz increasingly turned toward television and other media to transmit his message. Despite Schwarz's initial optimism, the financial fallout from the New York school was substantial. The CACC was having considerable trouble raising enough money to complete a Portuguese translation of *You Can Trust the Communists* for Brazil. The organization required $35,000 per month simply to maintain existing programs, including $10,000 in salaries for workers around the world.[41] An infusion of donations in late April lessened the organization's immediate financial troubles, and a televised "Anti-Communist Literature for Latin America Banquet" at the Hollywood Palladium on June 10 substantially bolstered Latin American outreach efforts. Even so, the CACC experienced increasing difficulties carrying out its plans. A Washington, DC, school was delayed and then further postponed in the wake of President Kennedy's assassination, although it was finally held in June 1964.

By 1965, some commentators observed a shift in the activities and ideological program of the CACC. Scholar Erling Jorstad argued that Schwarz was answering critics who faulted the CACC for using nonauthoritative "experts" and catering to older, wealthier citizens by recruiting new, more qualified speakers and reaching out more specifically to teenagers and college students. Jorstad perhaps overdrew his contrast; from the beginning, Schwarz was an eager proponent of youth outreach. Still, right-wingers such as W. Cleon Skousen did disappear from CACC itineraries, replaced by individuals including David N. Rowe, director of Yale's graduate program in International Studies; Edward J. Rozek, a Kremlinologist from the University of Colorado; Warren Nutter of the University of Virginia; and James David Atkinson of Georgetown University.[42]

By the 1970s, Schwarz's programs were increasingly concerned with linking perceived scourges like antiwar protests, women's liberation, and abortion rights to Communism. Even so, for Schwarz the signal threat continued to be external. "If the United States inhabited the planet alone, and the only danger was the American Communist Party, I think I could safely go home to Australia and enjoy my family," he told a reporter for the *Atlantic Monthly* in 1974. The CACC remained internationally active well into the 1980s; in October 1983, for example, three staffers held an anticommunist seminar in San Jose, Costa Rica, organized by a businessman and lay minister who first learned of the CACC via a Spanish-language edition of *You Can Trust the Communists*—evidence of the continuing success of literature distribution efforts.[43]

The CACC still exists but in greatly diminished form. Schwarz retired in 1998, passing the reins to Summit Ministries founder and fundamentalist activist Dr. David Noebel, an associate of Billy James Hargis who cut his political teeth campaigning against sex education and civil rights. This was an ironic choice for a man who had spent so many years attempting to differentiate his organization from unambiguously right-wing fundamentalists, but likely it reflects his increasing concerns about contemporary social trends.[44] Schwarz died in January 2009.

A Complex Legacy

Fred Schwarz and his Christian Anti-Communism Crusade, then, represented a complex tangle of ideology and outreach, strident anticommunism and international concern. Schwarz and his organization undoubtedly contributed to the growth of the Right. CACC schools and study groups heightened individuals' awareness of the Communist menace, but they also opened a door through which extremist groups including the John Birch Society might enter. Schwarz's claim to restrict himself to the pathology of Communism was not without credence, but it also neatly exempted him from responsibility for the results of his educational enterprises. There is no question that the CACC was a juggernaut of literature, tapes, and other educational material, although it is fairly evident that Schwarz did not seek personal financial gain. More disturbing is the simple disavowal of responsibility he routinely made for what came next. It was in this aspect that he most closely approached the role of charlatan, selling his audiences an experience without providing them sufficient guidance to avoid the shoals of extremism.

In the end, however, the CACC provided one signal service to its supporters: it helped to expand the terms of the Communist struggle beyond America's shores. Had he chosen to concentrate more wholly on this emphasis, the CACC could well have made a more substantial contribution. For Schwarz and the CACC, the threat of international Communism was just that—international. Even as he continued to belittle academics and caution against the folly of blinkered liberals, Schwarz consistently emphasized the international arena as the greatest and most significant stage for Americans' ideological battles. The financial, personnel, and publicity resources the CACC dedicated toward international efforts demonstrated their significance. As an Australian, Schwarz understood the complex interrelationships that governed international society. As head of the CACC, he attempted to bring this understanding to his supporters. In so doing, he added needed complexity to the conservative activism of the Cold War era.

Notes

1. Christian Anti-Communism Crusade (CACC) Newsletter, April/May 1959, http://www.schwarzreport.org/uploads/schwarz-report-pdf/schwarz-report-1959-05.pdf.
2. Many historians of modern American conservatism mention the CACC at least in passing; Lisa McGirr's work in *Suburban Warriors: The Origins of the New American Right* (Princeton, NJ: Princeton University Press, 2001) has been the most thorough. Angela Lahr's *Millennial Dreams and Apocalyptic Nightmares* (New York: Oxford University Press, 2007) also mentions the CACC in some detail. Political scientist Clyde Wilcox provides a quantitative analysis of the CACC's membership in *God's Warriors: The Christian Right in Twentieth-Century America* (Baltimore: Johns Hopkins University Press, 1992).
3. Dr. Fred Schwarz, *Beating the Unbeatable Foe: One Man's Victory Over Communism, Leviathan, and the Last Enemy* (Washington, DC: Regnery, 1996), 16–17, 21–24, 34.
4. Schwarz, *Beating the Unbeatable Foe*, 39–41; Shelley Baranowski, "Carl McIntire," in *Twentieth-Century Shapers of American Popular Religion*, ed. Charles H. Lippy (New York: Greenwood Press, 1989), 256–61.
5. Schwarz, *Beating the Unbeatable Foe*, 42, 70–71, 104–5.
6. See, for example, Arnold Forster and Benjamin R. Epstein, *Danger on the Right: The Attitudes, Personnel and Influence of The Radical Right and Extreme Conservatives* (New York: Random House, 1964), 47, 60; "Letters," *Time*, February 23, 1962.
7. Schwarz, *Beating the Unbeatable Foe*, 103–4.
8. "Organizations: Crusader Schwarz," *Time*, February 9, 1962.
9. Dr. Fred Schwarz, *The Heart, Mind and Soul of Communism* (Long Beach, CA: Christian Anti-Communism Crusade, 1952), 6–11.
10. Fred Schwarz, *Communism: Diagnosis and Treatment* (Los Angeles: World Vision, 1956), 5, 12, 21, 54.
11. CACC Newsletter, May 1958, http://www.schwarzreport.org/uploads/schwarz-report-pdf/schwarz-report-1958-05.pdf; CACC Newsletter, September 1958 http://www.schwarzreport.org/uploads/schwarz-report-pdf/schwarz-report-1958-09.pdf; CACC Newsletter, March 1959, http://www.schwarzreport.org/uploads/schwarz-report-pdf/schwarz-report-1959-03.pdf.
12. CACC Newsletter, December 1957, http://www.schwarzreport.org; CACC Newsletter, September 1958, http://www.schwarzreport.org/uploads/schwarz-report-pdf/schwarz-report-1958-09.pdf.

13. CACC Newsletter, November 1958, http://www.schwarzreport.org/uploads/schwarz
-report-pdf/schwarz-report-1958-11.pdf; CACC Newsletter, March 1959, http://
www.schwarzreport.org/uploads/schwarz-report-pdf/schwarz-report-1959-03.pdf;
CACC Newsletter, June 1960, http://www.schwarzreport.org/uploads/schwarz
-report-pdf/schwarz-report-1960-06.pdf; *Two Faces of Communism* (Corpus Christi,
TX: Citizens Alert, 1961).
14. Donald R. McNeil, "Anti-Communism in Phoenix: A Case History" (unpublished paper, n.d., ca. 1962), box 4, folder 4, Donald R. McNeil Papers, Wisconsin Historical Society; "Insurance Against Communism" (Houston: Christian
Anti-Communism Crusade, 1956), "Communism . . . a Disease!" (Houston:
Christian Anti-Communism Crusade, 1959), "Communism . . . a Monopoly!"
(Houston: Christian Anti-Communism Crusade, n.d.), "Communism . . . a Religion!" (Houston: Christian Anti-Communism Crusade, n.d.), all box 1, folder
9, Donald R. McNeil Papers, Wisconsin Historical Society; Donald Janson and
Bernard Eismann, *The Far Right* (New York: McGraw-Hill, 1963), 59. McNeil, a
resident of Mesa, Arizona, was working on an adult education survey financed by
the Carnegie Foundation. He became interested in conservative activities in the
Phoenix area as a result of the involvement of the John Birch Society and other
conservative organizations in local school board elections. He ran for a position
on the Mesa School Board in 1961 and was subjected to a series of unfounded
accusations of Communist connections (Edwin W. Davis, Confidential Report,
Mesa, Arizona, School Board Election in November 1961, box 1, folder 9, Donald R. McNeil Papers, Wisconsin Historical Society).
15. Dr. Fred Schwarz, *You Can Trust the Communists (. . . to Do Exactly as They Say)*
(Englewood Cliffs, NJ: Prentice-Hall, 1960), 1–2.
16. Schwarz, *You Can Trust the Communists*, 5–7, 16.
17. "Organizations: Crusader Schwarz," *Time*, February 9, 1962; Schwarz, *You Can
Trust the Communists*, 19–20.
18. Schwarz, *You Can Trust the Communists*, 28, 33, 36.
19. Schwarz, *You Can Trust the Communists*, 164, 169–70, 176, 178–80, 181.
20. CACC Newsletter, June 1962, Reel 20, Right Wing Microfilm Collection, California State Library.
21. CACC Newsletter, September 1963, www.schwarzreport.org/uploads/schwarz
-report-pdf/schwarz-report-1963-09.pdf; "Letters," *Time*, February 23, 1962.
22. CACC Newsletter, November 1962, www.schwarzreport.org/uploads/schwarz
-report-pdf/schwarz-report-1962-11.pdf; CACC Newsletter, November 1963,
www.schwarzreport.org/uploads/schwarz-report-pdf/schwarz-report-1963-11.pdf;
Fred Schwarz to "Friend," January 8, 1963, Reel 20, Right Wing Microfilm Collection, California State Library.
23. Donald T. Critchlow, *Phyllis Schlafly and Grassroots Conservatism: A Woman's Crusade* (Princeton, NJ: Princeton University Press, 2005), 67, 80.
24. CACC Newsletter, March 1960, http://www.schwarzreport.org/uploads/
schwarz-report-pdf/schwarz-report-1960-03.pdf; CACC Newsletter, June 1960,
http://www.schwarzreport.org/uploads/schwarz-report-pdf/schwarz-report
-1960-06.pdf; CACC Newsletter, November 1958, http://www.schwarzreport
.org/uploads/schwarz-report-pdf/schwarz-report-1958-11.pdf.

25. "Organizations: The Ultras," *Time*, December 8, 1961; McNeil, "Anti-Communism in Phoenix . . . ," box 4, folder 4, Donald R. McNeil Papers, Wisconsin Historical Society; McNeil, "Sessions of Christian Anti-Communism School," March 1, 1961, unpublished paper, box 1, folder 9, Donald R. McNeil Papers, Wisconsin Historical Society. Schwarz based this claim upon a report from officials of the Republic of China that Stalin and Mao had agreed upon this date in 1952 (Schwarz, *Beating the Unbeatable Foe*, 354).

26. The Citizens Information Center furnished information to interested parties, maintained book, film, and tape recording libraries, developed a speaker's bureau, printed pertinent literature, commissioned surveys and studies, and provided cooperation and assistance to governmental agencies and civic organizations (McNeil, "Anti-Communism in Phoenix"; Citizens Information Center statement of purpose, n.d., box 1, folder 9, Donald R. McNeil Papers, Wisconsin Historical Society; Merrill Folsom, "'Crusade' on Reds is Brought East," *The New York Times*, May 10, 1961, 38; Lawrence E. Davies, "Welch Sees Drive Against Military," *The New York Times*, January 13, 1962, 10).

27. Sheilah Rosenhack Koeppen, "Dissensus and Discontent: The Clientele of the Christian Anti-Communism Crusade" (PhD diss., Stanford University, 1967), 15–16, 27–30, 32–33, 37, 46–47, 49, 53–55.

28. CACC Newsletter, July/August 1960, http://www.schwarzreport.org/uploads/schwarz-report-pdf/schwarz-report-1960-08.pdf.

29. Joost Sluis, "An Alumnus and the Christian Anti-Communism Crusade," *Harvard Medical Alumni Bulletin*, Spring 1963, 2–4.

30. CACC Newsletter, November 1962, www.schwarzreport.org/uploads/schwarz-report-pdf/schwarz-report-1962-11.pdf; Stephen G. Rabe, *U.S. Intervention in British Guiana: A Cold War Story* (Chapel Hill: University of North Carolina Press, 2005), 83.

31. Schwarz himself considered 1961 to be the "zenith" of his movement (*Beating the Unbeatable Foe*, 197); McGirr, *Suburban Warriors*, 54; CACC Newsletter, September/October 1961, http://www.schwarzreport.org/uploads/schwarz-report-pdf/schwarz-report-1961-10.pdf; Bill Becker, "Right-Wing Groups Multiplying Appeals in Southern California," *The New York Times*, October 29, 1961, 43.

32. Fred Schwarz to "Friend," May 1962, Reel 20, Right Wing Microfilm Collection, California State Library.

33. "T.R.B. from Washington," *The New Republic*, January 1, 1962, 2.

34. "The Mad Attempt to Get Schwarz," *National Review*, July 31, 1962, 53–54.

35. CACC Newsletter, August 1962, Reel 20, Right Wing Microfilm Collection, California State Library.

36. Ibid.

37. Fred Schwarz to "Friend," September 6, 1962, Reel 20, Right Wing Microfilm Collection, California State Library.

38. Schwarz, *Beating the Unbeatable Foe*, 251–52; Jonathan Schoenwald, *A Time for Choosing: The Rise of Modern American Conservatism* (New York: Oxford University Press, 2001), 116–17.

39. Janson and Eismann, *The Far Right*, 55, 59–61, 68; Forster and Epstein, *Danger on the Right*, 47, 60, 67.

40. Brooks R. Walker, *The Christian Fright Peddlers* (Garden City, NY: Doubleday, 1964), 56, 62–67, 70, 78–79, 82.

41. Fred Schwarz to "Friend," March 1963, Reel 20, Right Wing Microfilm Collection, California State Library.

42. Erling Jorstad, "The Remodeled Right: Schwarz and Stormer on Campus," *Motive* 26 (November 1965): 29–30.

43. Sanford J. Ungar, "Ideology: The Christian Anti-Communism Crusade," *Atlantic Monthly*, June 1974, 8, 10–11, 14; CACC Newsletter, December 1, 1983, Loc. 147.I.13.7B, box 71, Walter Henry Judd Papers, Minnesota Historical Society.

44. Gary K. Clabaugh, *Thunder on the Right: The Protestant Fundamentalists* (Chicago: Nelson-Hall, 1974), 47, 100, 127.

CHAPTER 9

Disarming the Devil

The Conservative Campaign against a Nuclear Détente in the 1960s

Michael Brenes

In December 1963, Secretary of Defense Robert S. McNamara announced significant cuts to US defense spending, a decision that would leave thousands of out of work in defense plants across the Northeast and much of the Sun Belt South. McNamara and President Lyndon B. Johnson had no designs for a large-scale reduction of US military forces or plans for universal disarmament; the defense cuts were "purely related to obtaining the maximum defense at the lowest possible cost, and had no relationship whatsoever to changing the strength of our defense forces." Instead, the Johnson administration sought to revamp and streamline the American military in an effort to reduce tensions between the Soviet Union and the United States. While liberals such as Senator George McGovern (D-SD) welcomed McNamara's announcement, conservatives at the grassroots level and in Washington, DC, were incensed. Conservatives believed that the Soviet Union and global Communism were the premier threats to the United States and that military superiority was the only means to prevent a Communist attack. The American Right was unconvinced that McNamara did not desire universal disarmament of nuclear weapons. In McNamara, they saw evidence that liberals had accepted the notion that the arms race was obsolete and that they thus sought to weaken American military forces and expose America to Soviet aggression. To conservatives, the secretary of defense was the personification of liberalism run amok. McNamara's actions, they believed, jeopardized US national security and were sure to result in the United States losing the Cold War.[1]

This essay examines the conservative reaction to the Kennedy and Johnson administrations' attempts to achieve a nuclear détente in the 1960s by reducing the United States' reliance on nuclear weapons and a large defense budget. Grassroots conservatives, leaders of the American military, and sectors of American business that benefited from the Cold War aligned to prevent a nuclear détente between the United States and the Soviet Union during the 1960s by working to erode New Deal liberalism. They also made early, important inroads into securing the support of working-class defense industry employees in regions affected by potential cuts. Conservatives argued that liberals were too preoccupied with expanding the regulatory apparatus of the New Deal state and not worried enough about preventing the spread of Communism. Only if the federal government refocused its efforts away from social welfare programs, civil rights reform, and international institutions such as the United Nations could the United States protect itself against Communism. For conservatives, the course of American foreign policy was intertwined with domestic events, as their positions on national security were bound up within the politics of the New Deal.[2]

By the 1950s, conservatives had accepted the notion that the national security state established by Presidents Franklin D. Roosevelt and Harry Truman—the vast network of defense industries dispersed throughout the Sun Belt, Northeast, and Northwest and the workers and military personnel that relied on this industry to sustain their livelihood—needed to be enlarged in order to commit the United States to victory over Communism. The paradox for conservatives was that in order to do this, they had to use liberal means to achieve their desired ends: they had to expand the size of the federal state. As historian Julian Zelizer has noted, despite conservatives' ostensible support for reducing the federal government, its scale and scope has swelled even as conservatives have come into power in greater numbers.[3] Conservatives did not seek to reduce the size of the federal government so much as reinvent its purpose. Rather than "small-government" conservatives competing with "big-government" liberals, then, the central conflict between the Left and the Right in the second half of the twentieth century was between two divergent perceptions of the New Deal state in American politics and who would control that state in the future.

The Cuban Missile Crisis and Changing Terms of Debate

This fundamental tension between liberals and conservatives came to a head for the first time in the 1960s, after the Cold War was transformed in the wake of the Cuban missile crisis in 1962. For the first time since the 1940s, American policy makers seriously advocated a reduction in military forces and nuclear weapons. Plans for defense cuts and reductions in nuclear weapons signaled a crisis for conservatives, since up until the 1960s the Right believed it could use Cold War military spending as an instrument to weaken the welfare state. Conservative Republicans believed, as argued by Senator Everett Dirksen (R-IL) in 1961, that "with so many crises in faraway places, emphasis will have to be on guns" during the Cold War, and they sought to find "ways the domestic budget and so-called welfare items can be trimmed in view of the delicate international situation."[4] When McNamara announced defense cuts and proposals for disarmament in the early 1960s, conservatives feared that federal monies would be directed exclusively to liberal programs at the expense of fighting Communism. Conservatives thus embarked on a massive assault on New Deal liberalism by utilizing the resources of the national security state to their advantage.

By the mid-1940s, conservatives at the grass roots and in Congress saw the need for the United States to play a more active role in shaping global affairs. Far from being wholly isolationist and antistatist, a number of conservatives in the 1940s favored an internationalist foreign policy to defeat Communism. After 1949, isolationist holdouts like Senator Robert Taft (R-OH) faded into obscurity after the "loss of China" to Mao Zedong and the advent of the Korean War. Even the Old Right isolationist Frank Chodorov argued in the conservative magazine *Human Events* that the US government should reallocate spending on social welfare programs to add another two billion in defense spending for the war in Korea and place one million Americans "on the public payroll . . . [to] be put on the military assembly line" to defeat Kim Il-Sung and the North Koreans. Events on the battlefield as well as at home provided conservatives with fresh momentum. When General Douglas MacArthur was removed from command of UN forces in Korea—after MacArthur publically criticized Truman in the right-leaning magazine *The Freeman*—conservatives turned the event into a cause célèbre. The Right exploited the subsequent controversy over MacArthur's dismissal to justify their claim that liberal Democrats did not have the will or ability to take the measures necessary to roll back Communism.[5]

By 1952, conservatives became the staunchest proponents of interventionism as they proved unable to reconcile their antistatism with their anticommunism, and the latter won out over the former. As future *National Review* editor William F. Buckley Jr. wrote in 1952, conservatives had to "accept Big Government for the duration" in order to repel the spread of Communism. Republicans in Congress continued to allocate more tax dollars on defense, eventually overtaking the Democrats by the late 1950s in their support for more military spending.[6] The last vestiges of conservative isolationism faded when Eisenhower received the presidential nomination for the Republican Party. In Eisenhower, the Right saw a tough-minded general similar in character to Douglas MacArthur. Conservatives threw their support to Eisenhower's candidacy, which helped in his victory over Democrat Adlai Stevenson.

Eisenhower took office in 1953 with the mindset that American military preparedness was the most effective deterrent to Communist aggression. This conclusion had been echoed repeatedly by leading figures within the US government since 1945. While policy makers realized that the Soviet Union posed no considerable military threat to the United States considering the losses it suffered fighting Germany, they feared the spread of Communism to Western Europe and other strategic areas that had suffered immensely from the war. The publication of NSC-68 also convinced policy makers that the Communist "assault on free institutions is world-wide now" and required a buildup of American military power to marginalize its impact. Defense spending skyrocketed during the Korean War to more than 15 percent of GDP, while the ideology of "massive retaliation" put forward by Dwight Eisenhower's "New Look" in 1953 ensured that nuclear weapons would provide the basis for US Cold War foreign policy. Massive retaliation spurred an arms race between the United States and the Soviet Union in which military dominance was measured in terms of which nation possessed larger numbers of tactical missiles that could be used in destroying the other during a nuclear strike. Corporations across the country employed numerous Americans during the early Cold War to make products that would help to provide the bulwark against Soviet aims for global domination. Indeed, the arms race was a boon for the defense industry. But the arms race also contributed to heightened tensions between the two superpowers as nuclear escalation resulted in diplomatic gridlock between the United States and the Soviet Union. It was for these reasons that Eisenhower expressed apprehensions about the arms race and its repercussions for international politics.[7]

Unlike Eisenhower, conservatives had no reservations about the arms race, as they believed it was the sole deterrent to Communist expansion. But by the late 1950s and early 1960s the looming threat of nuclear warfare and the escalation of the arms race spurred activists on the left to work to ban the proliferation of nuclear weapons. The Committee for a Sane Nuclear Policy (SANE) was formed in 1957 to advocate "a permanent end to nuclear tests" as well as "comprehensive arms control." SANE was one among a number of groups established during this time whose purpose was to eradicate nuclear weapons. The movement to abolish nuclear weapons was global in scope, as France, England, Australia, and West Germany all had significant antinuclear movements. Organizations such as the World Council of Peace were at the forefront of the international call for disarmament, helping to convene the World Congress for General Disarmament held in Moscow in 1962. "Disarmament—general, complete and controlled, including the destruction of nuclear weapons—is the most urgent need of our time," the council claimed.[8]

The Cuban missile crisis legitimized the concerns expressed by antinuclear activists, as the event converted a minority opinion on the dangers of nuclear weapons into a majority. The Cuban missile crisis in October 1962 offered the first significant challenge to the arms race and the viability of nuclear weapons to preserve what historian John Lewis Gaddis has titled the "long peace."[9] After Soviet premier Nikita Khrushchev decided in 1962 to transport to Cuba missiles capable of launching nuclear weapons, the possibility that the two superpowers could kill a significant portion of the world's population over miscommunication and hubris became very real. Nuclear war was fatefully avoided when a secret deal was arranged between President John F. Kennedy and Khrushchev—Kennedy would remove American missiles in Turkey the following year if Khrushchev took Soviet missiles out of Cuba. After the crisis was resolved, the world breathed a collective sigh of relief as it stepped back from the brink of nuclear war.

Americans were largely satisfied with the peaceful resolution of the crisis, but many conservatives were not. Grassroots conservatives criticized the Kennedy administration for what they saw as its willingness to capitulate to Soviet intimidation. Groups such as the Committee for the Monroe Doctrine (CMD), headed by Captain Edward V. Rickenbacker, were formed weeks after the conclusion of the Cuban missile crisis. The organization derived its name from its belief that Kennedy had "invented a Monroe Doctrine in reverse" by bargaining with Khrushchev over the missiles. Rickenbacker and *National Review* editor William F. Buckley Jr. formed the CMD to express their view that Kennedy had abandoned Cuba to Communism. CMD members believed that Cuba still intended to attack the United States with nuclear weapons and that Castro secretly withheld missile shipments that were supposed to be returned to the Soviet Union. This sentiment was widespread among conservative activists in 1962, as they began to circulate bumper stickers with the slogan "Those Missiles are Still in Cuba."[10]

Conservatives also argued that the administration's handling of the Cuban missile crisis signaled the failure of liberals' management of foreign policy due to their preoccupation with civil rights and other domestic reforms. One conservative woman from Pennsylvania was furious that the United States, "while fanatically employing military force and violence" to carry out the "un-constitutional Supreme Court decision" in *Brown v. Board of Education* (1954), "ignored the Monroe doctrine, and allowed arms and ammunition to pour into Cuba from the Kremlin, in ships we 'loaned' them." Young grassroots conservatives who were members of the National Association of Americans for Goldwater viewed members of the Kennedy administration as "welfare whiz-kids" who were in office "peddling their frosted over fertilizer under the appealing title, 'New Fronteer' [*sic*]."[11]

While often resorting to hyperbolic rhetoric to express their concerns over possible remaining missiles in Cuba, conservatives did highlight a very real problem faced by American policy makers. During the last months of his life, President Kennedy and members of his national security team were consistently alarmed by their inability to verify that the Soviets had removed the entire arsenal of intercontinental ballistic missiles shipped to Cuba under Operation Anadyr. Kennedy also worried about the remaining Soviet troops in Cuba, receiving only the vague assurance from Soviet Ambassador Anatoly Dobrynin that all Soviet personnel would be evacuated in due time. But despite their misgivings and insecurities about the resolution of the Cuban missile crisis, the Kennedy administration sought to make sure such an event could not occur again. McNamara and President Kennedy reached the conclusion after October 1962 that a foreign policy based on the deterrence of nuclear warfare was irrational and unrealistic. Kennedy's national security advisors operated after 1962 on the presumption that nuclear weapons were irrelevant within the changing context of the Cold War. The only means to deter nuclear war was through international agreements that limited the proliferation of nuclear weapons. White House officials did not arrive at this decision easily, but they reasoned there were few options. Even after Communist China tested its first atomic bomb in 1964, McNamara and President Lyndon Johnson insisted that nonproliferation and disarmament were the best means to preserve peace.[12]

Policy makers like McNamara therefore decided that the creation of new weapons programs in preparation for an all-out war against the Soviet Union would waste federal dollars. The United States and the Soviet Union had achieved nuclear parity, McNamara argued, and allocating more monies to build conventional military weapons was not going to change these circumstances. It did not matter if the Americans had the Nike-Zeus missile and the Soviets did not. In the end, if war between the superpowers did come, it would surely come in the form of a nuclear war, and both countries would succumb to its consequences. Working from this premise, McNamara sought to drastically reduce defense expenditures and overhaul US foreign policy by squashing plans to fund extraneous weapons programs.[13]

The Kennedy administration's desire to reduce nuclear weapons had broad public support throughout the world by late 1962. Allies of the United States, such as Great Britain, responded to the Cuban missile crisis by trying to place pressure on Kennedy to push further for nuclear disarmament. Presidential speechwriter and Kennedy advisor Ted Sorensen claimed that Kennedy expressed "a desire to influence neutral and 'world opinion'" by proposing concrete plans for nuclear nonproliferation. Such overwhelming international support for disarmament terrified the New Right, and in response, conservatives went on the counteroffensive. The changes in the 1960s to both world and domestic affairs—particularly the civil rights revolution sweeping across the Jim Crow South—unhinged conservatives as they witnessed their positions on states' rights and the need for a muscular foreign policy fall increasingly outside the political norm.[14]

A Different Vision of the Federal State

While ideological reasons motivated conservatives to roll back liberals' attempt to achieve a nuclear détente, so did economic ones. Large sectors of American industry had a financial stake in preserving the Cold War status quo. A number of Sun Belt states and areas in Long Island and the Northwest relied on defense contracts to keep employment levels high. The federal government's investment in defense, dating from World War II, had led to vast economic growth in the South, and few Southerners wanted to return to a time when the region ranked last in per capita income, capital investment, and real estate values. The political economy of the Cold War ensured that the South would continue to experience rapid rates of industrial development for decades to come. The presence of the defense industry in strengthening the economic vitality of the Sun Belt also helped conservatives explain away the role of factors such as white racism in swinging Southerners behind the GOP. It allowed Goldwater as a presidential candidate to argue that his popularity in the South had nothing to do with his opposition to the 1964 Civil Rights Act. Southerners were growing increasingly conservative, Goldwater argued, because they "have roots in the new industrialization of a part of the country which from its earliest settlement has existed in an agricultural economy and society. They are related to the growing importance of business activity and concern for the interests of the business community." Sun Belt conservatism was "primarily an economic conservatism stemming from the growth in business activity." According to Goldwater, Southerners had come to terms with "the fact that integration is coming and it is not an overriding issue with them." As historian Bruce Schulman has argued, federal investment in the defense industry in the South also served its residents by "maintaining the separation between military spending, which it approved, and social spending, which it reviled."[15]

Any talk of defense cuts therefore deeply disturbed conservative Sun Belt politicians like Senator Strom Thurmond (R-SC). A leading conservative Republican known for his outspoken support for racial segregation in addition to greater military spending, Thurmond was not reluctant to tell leaders of the defense industry that his state relied on the Cold War for its continued prosperity. "Defense business means better employment, bigger payrolls, and general economic improvement," Thurmond said, and it was his political obligation to ensure that his Sun Belt constituents were "not discriminated against in the awards of government contracts." South Carolina's overwhelming reliance on the defense industry was therefore tied to Thurmond's and other Southern politicians' political futures. The economics of the Cold War also played a strong role in the development of Southern nationalism and in shaping conservatives' ideology toward Communism. Sun Belt conservatives combined their opposition to liberalism with their ardent anticommunism when they railed against McNamara's nuclear détente throughout the 1960s. Thurmond and other Sun Belt conservatives insisted that liberals failed to comprehend that the weapons their constituents built did not exacerbate tensions between the United States and the Soviet Union but averted Communist aggression.[16]

Manufacturers in the Sun Belt had perhaps the most to lose from a decline in the defense budget. Groups, such as the Southern States Industrial Council (SSIC), that were composed of various Sun Belt manufacturers—many of which also received defense contracts—helped to finance conservative efforts to expand American military forces and prevent defense cuts in the 1960s. Formed in the 1930s as a reaction to Franklin D. Roosevelt's New Deal, the SSIC billed itself as "The Voice of the Conservative South" and argued for a decrease in corporate tax rates, less government regulation, and a foreign policy that relied on "peace through strength." While the SSIC represented Southern business, it also solicited funds from business executives who operated in the North. The leading contributor to the SSIC was Pierre S. du Pont III of the chemical manufacturer E. I. du Pont de Nemours Co., based in Wilmington, Delaware. Pierre du Pont was the single largest donor to the SSIC, donating $21,000 between 1958 and 1964. An earlier generation in the du Pont family had founded the American Liberty League, an organization created in 1934 to overturn Franklin Delano Roosevelt's New Deal. Du Pont's father, along with his uncle Irénée and grandfather Lammont, spent thousands of dollars to promote free-market capitalism while at the same time making millions through defense contracts during and after World War II.[17] McNamara's cuts to the defense budget would hurt companies like DuPont as well as Southern manufacturers.

Other probusiness groups, afraid of a decline in profits if McNamara's plans for the military budget went forward, joined the chorus of conservatives opposing a drawdown of military forces. Organizations such as the National Association of Manufacturers (NAM) and the Chamber of Commerce included members of the defense industry who thought they had a lot to lose from a drawdown in the Cold War. Beginning in the 1960s, these defense executives partnered with grassroots conservatives and former military officers, many of whom received jobs with defense companies following their retirement, to pursue efforts for more defense spending. These individuals converged in NAM and the Chamber of Commerce, as well as groups with names such as the American Security Council (ASC), the National Security Industrial Association, the National Strategy Committee, and the National Strategy Information Center. These organizations were led by executives from companies such as Motorola and General Electric that received numerous defense contracts and recruited leading conservative intellectuals like William F. Buckley Jr. to attend conferences on the dangers of "relax[ing] our posture of readiness" for the sake of détente.[18]

These groups came out in force to oppose the 1963 Limited Test Ban Treaty that prohibited the atmospheric testing of nuclear weapons. Stanley Andrews, a former advisor to the defense hawk Senator Frank Lausche (D-OH), created the group Americans for National Security because he thought American taxpayer dollars were wasted on a Senate Arms Control and Disarmament Agency that was "being used as a tool of rash and fuzzy-brained pacifists in the State Department to unilaterally disarm the United States." Andrews told the Senate that the Limited Test Ban Treaty would "enhance the opportunities which the Kremlin is seeking to achieve its ultimate design for world domination." By denying passage of the treaty, the Senate would "put a block in the way of Communism's supreme objective—world domination." The euphemistic-sounding Americans for National Security was an organizational offshoot of the Liberty Lobby, a notoriously racist organization that believed the federal government should stop financing federal education and civil rights reform and redirect its attention toward building a strong national defense. Other grassroots conservative groups such as the Citizens Congressional Committee, headed by its legislative secretary Charles W. Winegarner, tried to rally conservative members of Congress against the "Treason Treaty." Winegarner stated in an issue of *The Cross and the Flag*, a magazine affiliated with the Christian Nationalist Crusade, another prosegregationist group, that he had the support of over "50 Ambassadors or Legation representatives" for his antidisarmament agenda. Conservatives in Washington, DC, also fought aggressively to defeat the treaty. Through their control of the Senate Preparedness Investigating Committee—a committee organized with the purpose of increasing military spending—conservatives such as Senator John Stennis (D-MS) and Thurmond held hearings where other conservatives, like the hawkish General Curtis LeMay, who had close ties to the ASC, testified against the treaty. When the Limited Test Ban Treaty was ratified in September 1963 by a Senate vote of 80 to 19 and with the backing of considerable public support, conservatives were demoralized. While the Limited Test Ban Treaty was unable to achieve a sustained détente between the Soviet Union and the United States during the 1960s, it was nevertheless a milestone in the Cold War. The treaty was the first major accord between the two superpowers in the postwar era with the intent to ameliorate the arms race. For these reasons, conservatives viewed the treaty's ratification as the beginning of a process that would culminate with a Communist takeover of the United States.[19]

The test ban and the settlement of the Cuban missile crisis were significant issues that recruited grassroots conservatives and members of the defense industry to Barry Goldwater's 1964 presidential candidacy. The conservative business consultant F. Clifton White, who advised many defense companies in the 1950s through the Richardson Foundation, used the treaty as an issue to solicit donations to a redesigned Draft Goldwater committee. An executive at Weyerhaeuser, a company with ties to the defense industry, expressed interest in donating to White's committee because he felt liberals' abandonment of the free market and states' rights would have repercussions for America's vulnerability in the world. If liberals remained in charge, their domestic policies would "move us inevitably toward less and less freedom and make us vulnerable to the development of ignorance and stupidity among our people, thus further weakening our national alertness and discernment so that we shall become easy marks for dictatorship and will ultimately lose spirit and fight and become a defeatable [sic] nation." He expressed the tenets of "big-government conservatism" when he stated he did "not believe in a strong federal power, subsidizing weaker and weaker and less and less effective state governments. On the other hand, I am firmly convinced we need a powerful well-organized military adequately backed with the best possible research and development activities and receptive to innovations which will keep them in a position of leadership." The lines between local and international politics were often blurred for Goldwater supporters. One conservative implied that the 1964 Republican National Convention should be viewed as another conflict in the Cold War, as the winner of "The 1964 Battle of San Francisco" would determine the course of international events for at least another four years.[20]

Rhetorically antistatist on domestic issues, the conservative critique of liberals' approach to foreign policy was not that the federal government was spending money but that it was not spending enough money on the right programs. Paul M. Heilman, a conservative businessman and Cuban exile, told the Coconut Grove Rotary Club in Coconut Grove, Florida, on May 29, 1963, about the need to be educated about the nature of Communism because the greatest threat is "our own apathy" toward the Communist menace. Heilman stated that Americans should not have been worried about a nuclear attack during the Cuban missile crisis, because they had unqualified missile supremacy "by nearly four to one." He went on to add, however, that "unless the leaders of our nation develop a will to win, a resolute plan to defend to our interest against that International Communism, unless we take a stand, all other items in anyone's plan fall flat." Adding to America's vulnerability, said Heilman, was the Kennedy administration's willingness to run up deficits for aid to the United Nations and the Peace Corps, two organizations that conservatives felt did not deter the spread of Communism. The only way to defeat the Communists was to redirect federal expenditures away from these programs and develop "a policy of strength and firmness" based on military preparedness.[21]

Conservatives grew further enraged when President Lyndon Johnson established the Gilpatric Committee, Johnson's contribution to continue the efforts of Kennedy to achieve nuclear nonproliferation. Phyllis Schlafly and Chester Ward of the ASC mounted the most visible challenge to the Gilpatric committee. In books with such titles as *The Betrayers* and *Strike from Space*, Schlafly and Ward argued that liberals had undermined the military superiority of the United States by seeking a reduction in nuclear arms. Schlafly and Ward argued that any form of détente with the Soviets spelled the end of the United States; the Soviet Union would use détente to build up its forces to carry out its long-term goal of destroying capitalism. A nuclear détente would be ineffective, as the only "two great guarantees of peace are the power of God and United States military strength." The "Gilpatric policy of refusing to engage in a military space race with Russia," the two conservatives wrote, had left the United States behind the Soviets in space technology. Schlafly and Ward also criticized Johnson for letting "the big money and the huge national effort go to prestige projects" like sending a man to the moon, while merely "crumbs are left for military space programs which could insure our survival and our freedom, as well as peace on earth." Other conservatives echoed Schlafly and Ward, believing that sending a man to the moon was akin to putting "the American taxpayer" through a "long roll in the lunar porkbarrel." While *National Review* editor Frank S. Meyer was critical of Schlafly's and Ward's bombastic style and reductionist thinking, he nevertheless agreed "that what they are fundamentally getting at is frightening."[22]

Defense Workers Join the Fight

Increasingly, defense workers also joined with grassroots conservatives to prevent a nuclear détente. Like their bosses, defense workers had a significant stake in the arms race, as it provided them with steady employment. Employees of the defense industry—particularly white-collar engineers and scientists—saw themselves as part of a growing middle class of Americans who prospered during the postwar economic boom because of the conflict with the Soviet Union. Defense workers were encouraged by employers to view themselves as global actors in the Cold War, carrying out the mission of spreading freedom to the world. In opening the Sperry Gyroscope plant on Long Island in 1943, President R. E. Gilmour told his employees that they were "the shock troops of the industrial second front" and that the building of the factory "symbolize[d] the determination of the American people to become invincible in military strength and to subordinate all else until that objective is accomplished." Gilmour also said that the defense industry was "as potent an element of military strength as a great legion or a mighty fortress of the past" and stood as an "[i]ndustrial challenge to the enemies of democracy." Such rhetoric helped imbue defense workers with a Manichean view of US foreign policy. These defense workers became Cold War conservatives, as they supported increased military spending to preserve their job security and believed that the Soviet menace represented the ultimate threat to their freedom.[23]

As a result, areas such as Southern California and Suffolk County, Long Island, where the defense industry dominated the economy, became bastions of postwar American conservatism. The *Orange County Industrial News* maintained the position as early as 1961 "that there will be no agreements on disarmament or on limitation of nuclear weapons." The Sun Belt benefited enormously from being a primary recipient of defense contracts, but many of its residents did not look favorably upon the federal government. Defense workers were present in the crowds at conservative rallies held by figures such as Billy James Hargis of the Christian Crusade and the disgraced General Edwin Walker, who was forced to resign after distributing John Birch Society literature to soldiers under his command. On their "Operation Midnight Ride" tour across the country, Hargis and Walker regularly lambasted plans of disarmament and the UN's control of US foreign policy.[24]

In the 1960s defense workers who were laid off because of budget cuts denounced those responsible for the job losses. The business of the Cold War touched everyone in communities that relied heavily on defense contracts from the federal government. When layoffs occurred, they affected not only those who worked at the plant but also restaurants, retail stores, and small businesses that relied on these workers to patronize these establishments. Nonunion defense workers suffered the most from the layoffs. Because of the industry's reliance on government contracts for profits, defense work was unpredictable and constantly subject to employment instability and fluctuations in profits. Unorganized workers therefore had no recourse when they lost their jobs. Several attempts by major unions such as the United Auto Workers and the International Union of Operating Engineers to organize workers employed at Grumman in the 1960s failed as the company managed to prevent unionization through welfare capitalism. Companies such as Boeing also fed workers a steady diet of "right to work" propaganda to marginalize the power of unions. General Electric, the second largest defense contractor in the nation in the 1960s, and other defense corporations involved in NAM were also at the forefront of anti-union campaigns in the 1950s.[25]

Unable to organize to prevent job cuts, defense workers became disillusioned by the federal government's inability to offer protections against layoffs. The anti-labor rhetoric propounded by corporate executives and leading conservative politicians like Goldwater since the 1950s created fissures between workers and their relationship to the New Deal state. The federal government, therefore, became the scapegoat for the problems plaguing the defense industry. One Grumman Corporation employee complained that his "Senators and Representatives" failed to secure defense jobs to residents of Long Island. This same employee placed blame for the layoffs not on the company but on politicians in Washington, DC. "I don't think they are doing everything they can to bring defense work to this area," he exclaimed. While critical of defense corporations for committing lay-offs, one Republic Aviation employee, after losing his job in 1964, suggested that he was more likely to vote for Goldwater. The Democrats "better look out in November," he warned. One resident of Seattle, M. C. (Chuck) Snyder, said that layoffs at the Boeing plant made him feel he could not rely on the federal government anymore. "We can't sit here and demand economy in the federal budget everywhere but in our own backyards," Snyder said.[26]

Gun Belt conservatives also felt that defense cuts weakened their cultural role as Cold War patriots. As citizen-soldiers in the fight against Communism, defense workers felt it their duty to alert the public to be vigilant against the spread of Communism abroad and at home. To accomplish this mission, Cold War conservatives participated in "National Security Seminars" across the Gun Belt that aimed to make every American a one-person army in the fight against Communism. The institutional structure of the national security state provided the organizational and financial backing to hold these Cold War seminars, as the Department of Defense and US army paid for the speakers, venues, and logistics to hold the conferences. The seminars, led by conservative military officials and local chapters of the Chamber of Commerce, featured such themes as fighting against "internal demoralization, political apathy, [and] spiritual bankruptcy" that conservatives felt characterized the broader public's outlook on the Cold War. General Albert T. Wilson told the audience at a Cold War seminar in El Paso, Texas, that the "search for security transcends all other aims in our national life. Security must be foremost in our minds until the threat of Communism is contained." Following the conclusion of the El Paso seminar, organizers praised the workshop as "the most effective and important single effort our government has undertaken to weld a strong and united military-civilian team for national defense and survival."[27] Walter Mooney, a design engineer from Chattanooga, Tennessee, said that the seminar he attended provided an invaluable service to him and his fellow participants, as it was the only program of its kind where one could "obtain such a concise factual representation of the struggle to come between the free world and the masters of the Kremlin."[28]

In their defense of greater military spending and a more belligerent foreign policy, defense workers supplied grassroots momentum to the New Right's critique of international affairs during the 1960s. But outside of towns and cities where the defense industry dominated the local economy, the majority of American workers rejected conservatives' positions on social security, unionization, and the size of the federal government. Conservatives found that their criticism of the welfare state did not sit well with the average working-class voter during the 1960s. It was not until the 1970s that Americans in greater numbers started to shift to the GOP. Working-class conservatism was predominantly a phenomenon of the 1970s, due to the ascendancy of the New Right following the election of Richard Nixon in 1968 and the fracturing of the Democratic Party after the defeat of George S. McGovern in the 1972 presidential election. Democrats maintained a close relationship with labor unions and the working class throughout the Kennedy and Johnson administrations, and this connection remained strong until the economic crisis in the 1970s. Conservatives' failure to get the majority of the working class to turn their ire onto the New Deal prevented the movement from gaining further momentum during the 1960s.[29]

Conservative critiques of US foreign policy continued unabated during the 1960s, but they largely fell on deaf ears. Several international and domestic factors served to diminish conservative voices. Goldwater's defeat in 1964 severely wounded the conservative movement, which would not unite behind a national political candidate again until the 1970s. Lyndon Johnson's preoccupation with the Vietnam War failed to stymie the prospects of disarmament, even as Johnson played a pivotal role leading up to the ratification of the Nuclear Nonproliferation Treaty. Defense industry executives who allied with conservative organizations were placated by the uptick in military spending generated by the war and toned down their opposition to Johnson's foreign policy. Vietnam also temporarily divided the conservative movement throughout 1964 and 1965, as many on the right were ambivalent about the war before becoming its most ardent proponents.[30]

Foundation for the Future

Indeed, the years between Goldwater's failed presidential run and the election of Richard Nixon were difficult ones for conservatives. While a number of historical monographs on postwar conservatism argue that the 1960s were years of rebuilding for the American Right, this conclusion does not appear accurate, given the evidence available. In terms of both domestic and foreign policy, conservatives were embattled throughout much of the 1960s. After Johnson's election, conservatives predicted a bleak future for the United States as New Deal liberalism remained strong. The SSIC anticipated increased government regulation, an expanded welfare state, and "support of the Negro Revolution." In terms of foreign policy, the SSIC forecasted continued "accommodations with Russia and China" as well as "[u]nilateral disarmament and U.S. adherence to a world government," which amounted to "Fabian socialism" coming to the country. Passage of Great Society legislation, conservatives claimed, distracted Americans from the Cold War. Conservatives posited that "the Soviets have been making great strides forward" in military capabilities throughout the 1960s because the federal government "has been focusing on social welfare programs." As opinion turned against the war in Vietnam, conservative businessmen found themselves increasingly under attack by the New Left and

Congressional liberals who sought to weaken the power of the imperial presidency and the military-industrial complex. Defense companies in NAM were so frustrated by the public's perception of the defense industry as warmongers that by 1969 they had concluded it was time to wage a public relations campaign against the Left rather than just lobbying for more defense contracts.[31]

This does not mean, however, that conservative attempts to influence US domestic and foreign policy in the 1960s were all for naught. The conservative campaign against disarmament helped unite grassroots and business conservatives, particularly those located in the Sun Belt South. As the South became increasingly Republican, the interests of the defense industry merged with the concerns of conservatives, helping to transform the terms of the debate and providing the New Right with considerable financial and organizational support to further its agenda. The joining of grassroots activists with the political economy of the Cold War paid dividends for the movement as it headed into the 1970s. Also, it was in their opposition to a nuclear détente that conservatives first sought to use the structure of the national security state to carry out their twin goals of eroding the New Deal and increasing defense spending.

By mobilizing the national security state to its side, the conservative movement successfully used a construction of the Democratic Party against itself. Conservatives hoped that diverting the federal government away from domestic programs and toward military spending would ultimately lead to a conservative federal state. While the American Right would have to wait until the 1970s for this strategy to be successful, conservative activism during the 1960s offered a useful foundation for the movement as it entered the next decade.

Notes

1. "News Conference of Honorable Robert S. McNamara, December 12, 1963," RG 18-003, box 36 folder 01, AFL-CIO Department of Legislation, 1906–1978, Series 1, George S. Meany Memorial Archives (GMMA), Silver Spring, MD; Thomas J. Knock, "Come Home America: The Story of George McGovern," in *Vietnam and the American Political Tradition*, ed. Randall B. Woods (New York: Cambridge University Press, 2003), 82–120; Donald T. Critchlow, *Phyllis Schlafly and Grassroots Conservatism* (Princeton, NJ: Princeton University Press, 2005), 175.

2. I refer to conservatives within this essay as those individuals who supported laissez-faire capitalism, a reduction in the size of the federal government, and a strong military (including support for the arms race and large defense budgets) to counter the threat of the Soviet Union. During the 1960s there were many individuals who supported one or two of these positions but not all of them, and thus cannot be labeled "conservative." This includes some Democrats who had left-leaning positions on domestic policy and very conservative beliefs regarding foreign policy. I refer to these men and women as "Cold War conservatives." It is important to note, however, that the domestic politics of these Cold War conservatives were shaped

by their conservative foreign policy views. Indeed, at certain moments, these individuals' Cold War conservatism trumped their liberal values. It is this interaction and tension between liberalism and conservatism that helped shape the New Right during the Cold War era.

3. Julian E. Zelizer, "Rethinking the History of American Conservatism," *Reviews in American History* 38 (June 2010): 367–92. The expansion of the national security state since 1945 not only meant more federal dollars allocated to building weapons, but also greater federal resources toward a variety of veterans benefits, including pensions, health care coverage, and other programs that could be classified as "social welfare," and which many on the right are unwilling to cut in today's contemporary political climate. It should be noted, however, that the rise of the national security state contributed to the growth of the welfare state.

4. "Senate G.O.P. Seeks Non-Defense Cuts," *The New York Times*, May 11, 1961.

5. Frank Chodorov, "Politics as Usual," *Human Events*, August 16, 1950.

6. William F. Buckley, "A Young Republican's View," *The Commonweal*, January 25, 1952; Julian Zelizer, *Arsenal of Democracy: The Politics of National Security—from World War II to the War on Terrorism* (New York: Basic Books, 2010), 133.

7. Melvyn P. Leffler, "The American Conception of National Security and the Beginnings of the Cold War, 1945–1948," *American Historical Review* 89 (April 1984): 346–81; Melvyn P. Leffler, *A Preponderance of Power: National Security, The Truman Administration, and the Cold War* (Stanford, CA: Stanford University Press, 1992); Jeremi Suri, "Nuclear Weapons and the Escalation of Global Conflict since 1945," *International Journal* 63 (Autumn 2008): 1013–29; John Lewis Gaddis, *Strategies of Containment: A Critical Appraisal of American National Security Policy During the Cold War*, 2nd ed. (New York: Oxford University Press, 2005); Campbell Craig, *Destroying the Village: Eisenhower and Thermonuclear War* (New York: Columbia University Press, 1998); Text of NSC-68 in *American Cold War Strategy: Interpreting NSC-68*, ed. Ernest R. May (Boston: Bedford St. Martin's, 1993), 28; Aaron Friedberg, *In the Shadow of the Garrison State: American Anti-Statism and its Cold War Grand Strategy* (Princeton, NJ: Princeton University Press, 2000), 138–39; Campbell Craig and Fredrik Logevall, *America's Cold War: The Politics of Insecurity* (Cambridge, MA; Belknap Press of Harvard University Press, 2009); Bruce J. Schulman, *From Cotton Belt to Sunbelt: Federal Policy, Economic Development, and the Transformation of the South, 1938–1980* (Durham, NC: Duke University Press, 1994).

8. "SANE, Public Petition, 1961," in *American Foreign Relations Since 1898: A Documentary Reader*, ed. Jeremi Suri (Hoboken, NJ: Wiley Publishing, 2010), 112–13; Lawrence Wittner, *Resisting the Bomb: A History of the World Nuclear Disarmament Movement, 1954–1970* (Stanford, CA: Stanford University Press, 1997); "World Congress for General Disarmament and Peace Appeal by J. D. Bernal, January 29 1962," RG18-003, folder 21, box 65, Jay Lovestone Files, 1944–1973 Series I, GMMA.

9. John Lewis Gaddis, *The Long Peace: Inquiries into the History of the Cold War* (New York: Oxford University Press, 1989).

10. Group Research Report 12/4/1962, I-5, Group Research, Inc. Records (GRR), 12-4-62 folder, box 425, Rare Book and Manuscript Library, Columbia University;

"Those Missiles are Still in Cuba," folder: "Q-Z," box 506, GRR. See also the online exhibit on Group Research, Inc., https://ldpd.lamp.columbia.edu/omeka/exhibits/show/group_research/enemies/institutional.

11. Letter to the Editor, *[Gillette, WY] Record News*, October 25, 1962, Southern Lunacy folder, box 302, GRR; "A Critical Analysis and a Constructive Answer," the National Association of Americans for Goldwater, folder 5, box 155, William A. Rusher Papers (WR Papers), Library of Congress, Washington, DC.

12. U.S. Department of State, Memorandum of Conversation, 26 August 1962, in *Foreign Relations of the United States*, 1961–1963, 11: 857–58; David Coleman, "The Missiles of November, December, January, February . . . : The Problem of Acceptable Risk in the Cuban Missile Crisis Settlement," *Journal of Cold War Studies* 9 (2007): 5–48; Alexandr Fursenko and Timothy Naftali, *"One Hell of a Gamble": Khrushchev, Castro, and Kennedy, 1958–1964* (New York: W. W. Norton, 1997), 327–28, 337–38; Francis J. Gavin, "Blasts from the Past: Proliferation Lessons from the 1960s," *International Security* 29 (Winter 2004/05): 100–35.

13. Friedberg, *In the Shadow of the Garrison State,* 235–36. For McNamara's approach toward nuclear strategy following the Cuban missile crisis, see Lawrence Freedman, *The Evolution of Nuclear Strategy*, 3rd ed. (New York: Palgrave MacMillan, 2003), 230–42; McGeorge Bundy, *Danger and Survival: Choices About the Bomb in the First Fifty Years* (New York: Vintage, 1990), 543–48; Shane J. Maddock, *Nuclear Apartheid: The Quest for American Atomic Supremacy from World War II to the Present* (Chapel Hill: University of North Carolina Press, 2010), 217–50.

14. Wittner, *Resisting the Bomb*, 406.

15. Richard Franklin Bensel, *The Political Economy of American Industrialization, 1877–1900* (New York: Cambridge University Press, 2000), 39–40; Schulman, *From Cotton Belt to Sunbelt,* 139; Barry Goldwater, "The G.O.P. Invades the South," folder 2, box 155, WR Papers; "Goldwater Declares 1964 Could Well Be GOP Year," folder 7, box 154, WR Papers. While race was not the only issue that led to the rise of postwar conservatism, it certainly was a significant factor. See Dan T. Carter, *The Politics of Rage: George Wallace, the Origins of the New Conservatism, and the Transformation of American Politics* (Baton Rouge: Louisiana State University Press, 2000); Joseph Crespino, *In Search of Another Country: Mississippi and the Conservative Counterrevolution* (Princeton, NJ: Princeton University Press, 2007); Matthew D. Lassiter, *The Silent Majority: Suburban Politics in the Sunbelt South* (Princeton, NJ: Princeton University Press, 2005); Kevin Kruse, *White Flight: Atlanta and the Making of Modern Conservatism* (Princeton, NJ: Princeton University Press, 2005); Joseph E. Lowndes, *From the New Deal to the New Right: Race and the Southern Origins of Modern Conservatism* (New Haven, CT: Yale University Press, 2008); and Schulman, *From Cotton Belt to Sunbelt,* 138.

16. "Address by Senator Strom Thurmond (R-SC) at a Luncheon of the National Association of Manufacturers, Plaza Hotel, New York City, 12:30 p.m., November 16, 1967," box 39, Series 4, National Association of Manufacturers papers (NAM papers), Hagley Museum and Library, Wilmington, DE; "Disarmament—Wishful Thinking," *Militant Truth*, May 1963, Militant Truth (Sherman A. Patterson, ed.) folder, box 220, GRR; "Some Highlights of Presidential Politics: A Summary With Attachments, October 10, 1963," folder 7, box 154, WR papers;

Strom Thurmond, *The Faith We Have Not Kept* (San Diego: Viewpoint Books, 1968); Critchlow, *Phyllis Schlafly and Grassroots Conservatism*, 166.

17. "A 'Voice' Guides Conservative South," *Norfolk Virginian Pilot*, August 2, 1964; Kim Phillips-Fein, *Invisible Hands: The Making of the Conservative Movement from the New Deal to Reagan* (New York: W. W. Norton, 2009), 12–23.

18. "Ex-Officers Listed in Defense Jobs by House Group," *The New York Times*, January 18, 1960; "Senator Fulbright vs. Pentagon 'Educators,'" *St. Louis Post-Dispatch*, August 12, 1961; Frank R. Burnett to William F. Buckley, November 16, 1966, box 40, General Correspondence, 1966, William F. Buckley Papers (WFB Papers), Sterling Memorial Library, Yale University.

19. United States Senate, Committee on Foreign Relations, *Hearings, Nuclear Test Ban Treaty*, 88th Congress, 1st session, August 12–27, 1963, 749; Sara Diamond, *Roads to Dominion: Right-Wing Movements and Political Power in the United States* (New York: Guilford Press, 1995), 152; Group Research Reports, Vol.2, No. 3, 2/12/63 folder, box 425, GRR; Robert David Johnson, *Congress and the Cold War* (New York: Cambridge University Press, 2005), 90–91; Marc Trachtenberg, *A Constructed Peace: The Making of the European Settlement, 1945–1963* (Princeton, NJ: Princeton University Press, 1999), 383–87; Vojtech Mastny, "The 1963 Limited Test Ban Treaty: A Missed Opportunity for Détente?," *Journal of Cold War Studies* 10 (Winter 2008): 3–25. The results of a Harris Poll conducted in September 1963 showed that 81 percent of those interviewed supported the Limited Test Ban Treaty. See Bernard J. Firestone, "Kennedy and the Test Ban: Presidential Leadership and Arms Control," in *John F. Kennedy and Europe*, ed. Douglas Brinkley and Richard T. Griffiths (Baton Rouge: Louisiana State University Press, 1999), 91.

20. "Goldwater fans get more active," "No.5 Mar 13" folder, box 425, GRR; F. Clifton White and William J. Gill, *Suite 3505: The Story of the Draft Goldwater Movement* (Ashland, OH: Ashbrook Press, 1992), 177; David E. Stalter to Ralph J. Bachenheimer, November 8, 1962, folder 5, box 155, WR Papers; Frank Cullen Brophy, "Must Goldwater Be Destroyed," folder 2, box 155, WR Papers. In 1962, the F. Clifton White Committee was the official face of the Draft Goldwater movement.

21. Thurman Sensing to Southern States Industrial Council members, July 15, 1963, attached speech "Cuba," Southern States Industrial Council folder, box 302, GRR.

22. Phyllis Schlafly and Chester Ward, *Strike from Space: A Megadeath Mystery* (Alton, IL: Pere Marquette Press, 1965), 3, 119–20; Brophy, "Must Goldwater Be Destroyed"; Interoffice memo from Frank S. Meyer to William F. Buckley, March 14, 1966, Interoffice Memos, Jan 1966-Apr 1966 folder, box 39, Series I, WFB papers; Critchlow, *Phyllis Schlafly and Grassroots Conservatism*, 165.

23. Sperry Brochure, Series 3, Nassau Plant folder, box 36, Sperry Gyroscope Company Records, Hagley Museum and Library, Wilmington, DE; Ann Markusen, "Cold War Workers, Cold War Communities," in *Rethinking Cold War Culture*, ed. Peter J. Kuznick and James Gilbert (Washington DC: Smithsonian Institution Press, 2001), 35–60.

24. Rick Perlstein, *Before the Storm: Barry Goldwater and the Unmaking of the American Consensus* (New York: Nation Books, 2009), 126; Lisa McGirr, *Suburban Warriors: The Origins of the New American Right* (Princeton, NJ: Princeton University Press, 2000); Darren Dochuk, *From Bible Belt to Sunbelt: Plain Folk Religion, Grassroots*

Politics, and the Rise of Evangelical Conservatism (New York: W. W. Norton, 2010), 237–39.

25. Elizabeth Fones-Wolf, *Selling Free Enterprise: The Business Assault on Labor and Liberalism, 1945–60* (Champaign: University of Illinois Press, 1992); Kim Phillips-Fein, "Business Conservatism on the Shop Floor: Anti-Union Campaigns in the 1950s," *Labor: Studies in the Working Class History of the Americas* 7 (Summer 2010): 9–26.

26. For more on the influence of anti-labor rhetoric, see Elizabeth Tandy Shermer, "Origins of the Conservative Ascendancy: Barry Goldwater's Early Senate Career and De-Legitimization of Organized Labor," *Journal of American History* 95 (December 2008): 678–709; "Two Big Unions Aim to Organize Grumman Plant," *Long Island Daily Press*, September 17, 1961; "Union Cites Aims in Campaign to 'Take' Grumman," *Long Island Daily Press*, January 14, 1962; "UAW Comes Out in the Open in Organization of Grumman," *Long Island Daily Press*, January 7, 1962; "Grumman Workers Accepting Layoffs Without Worry," *The New York Times*, March 8, 1970; "Where the Cutback Cuts Deep," *Saturday Evening Post*, September 12, 1964.

27. "Chamber of Commerce Sets National Security Seminar," *El Paso Times*, July 2, 1961; "Record-Smashing Seminar Opens," *El Paso Today*, November 1, 1961; "Successful Seminar Completed," *El Paso Times*, November 11, 1961.

28. John McKnight to Marsh Wattson, April 27, 1961, announcement attached to letter, Military—Anti Communist Propaganda for Public folder, box 381, GRR; "What Others Have Said," National Security Seminar Publicity folder, box 385, GRR.

29. Phillips-Fein, *Invisible Hands*, 142–43; Rick Perlstein, *Nixonland: The Rise of a President and the Fracturing of America* (New York: Scribner, 2008); Judith Stein, *Pivotal Decade: How the United States Traded Factories for Finance in the Seventies* (New Haven, CT: Yale University Press, 2010), 51–57; Bruce Miroff, *The Liberals' Moment: The McGovern Insurgency and the Identity Crisis of the Democratic Party* (Lawrence: University Press of Kansas, 2009); Jefferson Cowie, "From Hard Hats to the Nascar Dads," *New Labor Forum*, Fall 2004, 8–17.

30. Thomas Schwartz, *Lyndon Johnson and Europe: In the Shadow of Vietnam* (Cambridge, MA: Harvard University Press, 2003). See the contribution to this volume by Seth Offenbach, "Defending Freedom in Vietnam: A Conservative Dilemma."

31. For an important exception to the argument that the 1960s were years of rebuilding, see Donald T. Critchlow, *The Conservative Ascendancy: How the GOP Right Made Political History* (Cambridge, MA: Harvard University Press, 2007), 78; "Budget Expert Says Defense Spending Too Low," *Human Events*, November 21, 1970; "Looking Back at the 88th Congress—Looking Ahead to the 89th Congress, 12/1/64," Southern States Industrial Council folder, box 302, GRR; "Memo from John A. Stuart, April 15, 1969," box 98, Series I, NAM papers.

CHAPTER 10

Defending Freedom in Vietnam

A Conservative Dilemma

Seth Offenbach

A s the 1964 election between President Lyndon Johnson and Republican nominee Barry Goldwater approached, evidence was fairly conclusive that Johnson would win. Gallup polls throughout the summer gave Johnson approximately a 30 percent lead over Goldwater. As Goldwater's electoral prospects began fading, William F. Buckley Jr., one of the leading spokesmen of the conservative movement, gave a speech to the largest gathering of young conservatives ever assembled, warning them that Goldwater's defeat in 1964 was inevitable. Goldwater was running against a tough political opponent in the popular president. Additionally, Johnson's campaign had effectively labeled Goldwater an ideological extremist who would cut the Eastern seaboard off into the ocean, begin a nuclear war, and end Social Security. Johnson's campaign strategy, coupled with Americans' disapproval of Goldwater's conservatism, made victory unlikely. Nonetheless, Buckley argued that the energy generated by Goldwater's campaign held the potential to help the Right improve its long-term political fortunes.[1]

Goldwater's inevitable defeat created an uncertain future for the conservative movement. Conservatives united behind Goldwater during the campaign. However, once the election ended, and without a candidate to rally around, conservative leaders worried that the movement might fracture and falter. The Right needed a new unifying topic. Shortly before the election, Buckley, the founder and editor-in-chief of *National Review*, wrote a memo to his editors announcing the magazine's postelection plans. The movement's morale after the election would be low, and the magazine would need to boost it. The best way to do so would be to "Get [conservatives] back to hating the Devil." Buckley knew that finding a common enemy would easily rally supporters, and any "good conservative" loved to hate Communism.[2] Luckily for Buckley, within a few weeks of Johnson's 1965 inauguration, the president began rapidly expanding America's military presence in Vietnam. Johnson's decision gave conservatives a convenient, coherent anticommunist fight to support. In 1965, with the expansion of the Vietnam War, the conservative movement transitioned from a foreign policy of strenuous but unfocused anticommunism to one with an overriding focus on supporting the Vietnam War.

The Right's support of the Vietnam War in 1965 stands out primarily because of the ambivalence of conservatives toward the war during the 1964 campaign. Throughout 1964, conservatives proclaimed that a vote for Goldwater would promote world security. After all, a Goldwater administration would help eliminate Fidel Castro from Cuba and Mao Zedong from China, while fortifying anticommunist forces throughout South America and Africa. Eliminating Ho Chi Minh from control in North Vietnam would be an added bonus; the fate of the world, however, did not lie in the outcome of the war in Vietnam.[3]

In 1964 most conservatives considered the fighting in Vietnam to be a peripheral battle. Unlike many other American anticommunists, most conservatives viewed the Soviet Union and China as the ultimate enemies, enemies that needed to be fought directly. To those individuals, Vietnam was a sideshow. Additionally, with memories of the Korean War still present—a conflict that conservatives viewed as an American defeat because it ended in a stalemate—many on the right believed that victory in Vietnam would not be worth the immense effort. Despite the Right's many reservations about enlarging the battle in Vietnam in 1964, by mid-1965 most conservatives endorsed a forceful military effort in Vietnam. Conservative support for the war continued to grow, and by 1966 there were few on the right who questioned the relevance of this small Southeast Asian nation. Writing in the conservative magazine *Human Events*, Admiral Arleigh Burke opined, "The choices confronting us are grave, but the alternative of withdrawal from South Viet Nam is unthinkable. Such a course means abdicating our position of world leadership."[4] Burke felt it imperative to state in plain language that if the United States lost the Vietnam War, the nation would no longer serve as a leader of the free world. Burke's article borrowed language that echoed throughout the Right, as most conservatives increasingly believed that victory in Vietnam was the nation's only viable option.

As this anthology examines, the conservative movement in the 1960s experienced a rapid, if checkered, growth in popularity and significant ideological transformations. Despite these changes, anticommunism and foreign policy remained central to the movement's identity. Many conservatives were initially skeptical about expanding the United States' influence in Vietnam. When Operation Rolling Thunder, the bombing campaign against North Vietnam, commenced in March 1965, the conservative movement quickly galvanized support behind the military effort. Conservative leaders used the war to help unify the movement's grassroots supporters. Support for the war, which until the start of Operation Rolling Thunder had been tenuous at best, dramatically improved among rank-and-file conservatives. Within one year of the war's start, the Right formed the base of the prowar movement in America, with support for the war appearing natural to most conservatives. Operation Rolling Thunder—and the Right's support for the Vietnam War—occurred on the heels of Barry Goldwater's 1964 presidential defeat; this chapter will demonstrate that part of the reason for the movement's quick support for the war was based on the disastrous results of the 1964 election.

This chapter explores how the conservative movement developed its Vietnam policies during the war's early years. Rather than looking at how the Right helped shape US foreign policy—and no doubt it helped push President Johnson to expand the fighting—this analysis will focus on how the fighting in Vietnam affected the movement's identity and discourse. Conservatives frequently reacted to domestic antiwar protests and Cold War skirmishes around the world in the mid-1960s, offering diverse opinions on how to properly defend America's interests. How conservatives reacted to these external factors helped shape the movement's ideology long after the 1960s ended.

Prior to Operation Rolling Thunder, Vietnam was simply another local hotspot in the Cold War. Before Johnson expanded the war, the small Southeast Asian nation held no special meaning to most conservatives. Few among the conservative elite advocated a rapid escalation of violence in Vietnam. In fact, the movement's rank and file rarely focused its energy on Vietnam. Only after Johnson expended enormous military personnel and American prestige did the Vietnam War come to dominate the Right's discourse. By the end of the 1960s, it was the most discussed topic within conservative media, and it was frequently debated at meetings among grassroots activists. After 1965 most conservatives believed that the United States could not lose the Vietnam War.

The Legend of the Conservative Hawk and the Mistake of Vietnam

The Right's fervent anticommunism and its defense of a vigorous US foreign policy were important components of the conservative movement's philosophy, especially in the early 1960s. Conservatism at the time was a movement of disparate factions; however, the unifying force within the movement was a nearly universal belief in the importance of fighting Communism. Broadly defined, the various factions within conservatism included libertarians who promoted individual freedom above all else, traditionalists who advocated that society adhere to their understanding of a moral order, and big business conservatives who promoted a governmental system hospitable to economic growth. As with most broad-based political movements, there were disagreements and disputes between each faction within the Right. One area of relative policy agreement within the movement was support for an anticommunist foreign policy.

Most conservatives believed it was important for the United States to forcefully oppose international Communism. Conservative pundits frequently proclaimed there was "no substitute for victory" and that the forces of freedom and democracy were at "war" with the forces of international Communism. Believing the United States was already engaged in a war with Communism, Representative Donald Bruce (R-IN) introduced legislation in 1963 requiring President John F. Kennedy to "prepare for the approval of the Congress a program to achieve this total victory [over communism]." The following year, Senator Barry Goldwater published his popular work *Why Not Victory?*, calling for a long-term plan to achieve victory in the Cold War.[5] The conservative leadership believed that the Cold War was an all-important battle that required a grand strategy.

In the conservative worldview, Communism was something far more sinister than an economic theory. To many conservatives, the Cold War was a long-term struggle between diabolical and angelic forces. Conservative leaders published manifestos claiming that Karl Marx had predicted the future and that Joseph Stalin, Nikita Khrushchev, and their successors were merely following his original prophecy.[6] To these conservatives, the Soviet Union posed an existential threat to the survival of the United States. Containment was an insufficient strategy to achieve total victory. In the conservative mind, the lesson of World War II was that there was good and evil in the world, and good must directly confront evil. If the Right controlled US foreign policy in the 1960s, there would be no appeasement, nor would there be détente.

Grassroots conservatives wholeheartedly endorsed this ardent anticommunist discourse. Such rhetoric helped inspire the Reverend Theron Spurr, a Detroit preacher who believed Communism was an evil, atheistic movement. Spurr utilized a dramatic public stunt in an attempt to rally support from his parish and improve the anticommunist sentiment within his community. In March 1964, in the middle of his Sunday sermon—which focused on Communism—two men dressed as police officers entered the church and pretended to arrest Spurr. This dramatic act caused a confrontation in the church between congregants and the police. Spurr staged the false arrest in order to demonstrate the evils of Communism and how it worked to subvert religion and tolerance. In Spurr's worldview, there was no middle ground in the Cold War; Americans needed to choose sides. Many within the conservative movement held firmly to Spurr's belief that the Cold War was a long, dramatic war between good and evil.[7]

Local and national leaders helped promote this fear of Communism. Conservative pundits tied major political and international issues to existential fears. Several historians have examined the beliefs of the John Birch Society in the 1960s, partially because the society was a popular organization and partially because its founder falsely claimed that President Dwight Eisenhower was a Communist agent. This claim makes for an easy, attention-grabbing anecdote and demonstrates that the Right's discourse included various tall tales about the power of the Communist menace. Despite the notoriety of the John Birch Society, however, many other groups held firm to a similar worldview that argued that Communism's power within the United States was growing, even if they did not accuse Eisenhower of treachery. Dr. Fred Schwarz's Christian Anti-Communism Crusade (CACC) was one such organization. As historian Laura Jane Gifford writes in this anthology, Schwarz was a popular figure with many grassroots conservatives. Schwarz organized well-attended CACC events and lectures and published books and pamphlets demonstrating how international Communism was spreading one nation at a time. One popular item CACC published was a poster titled "Will You Be Free to Celebrate Christmas in the Future?" This poster helps demonstrate how Schwarz used fear—in this case, of Communists overthrowing US society before the next Christmas—to promote his cause. Schwarz's worldview that the Cold War was a war of total world conquest seeped into conservative popular culture, as the board game Victory over Communism demonstrates. Ads appeared in conservative media in 1964 promoting the game as wholesome family entertainment. Described as being much like a game of Risk, this board game proclaimed itself "America's First Anti-Communist Game."[8]

Despite a desire to defeat Communist expansion, however, not all conservatives wanted to take up arms against all Communists all the time. Specific strategies for fighting Communists differed with each group and individual. For instance, conservatives within the *National Review* tended to expect the United States to defend anticommunist forces worldwide, whereas libertarian groups were often more cautious about the use of force when defending autocratic rulers abroad. There was disagreement even among those who agreed that the United States could never concede an inch to Communist aggression. For instance, Phyllis Schlafly often argued that the United States should expand its space defense program, and *Human Events* often argued that the United States should seriously consider invading China, which it felt was a true source of aggressive Communism worldwide.[9] Overall, conservatives believed Communism was an evil ideology that the United States must destroy; however, the Right's military strategies for fighting the Cold War varied greatly.

Despite the many disagreements about Cold War strategies, prior to Operation Rolling Thunder in 1965 most on the right believed that the fighting in Vietnam was not central to the Cold War. Because of this, conservatives were remarkably cautious about supporting US intervention. Rather than acting as aggressive war hawks, conservatives demonstrated considerable restraint. Conservatives wanted South Vietnam to prevail, but they were not optimistic about the outcome. More important, they did not want to repeat the mistakes of the Korean War and enter another land war for control of a small nation in Asia without a guarantee of victory. Vietnam remained present within the Right's discourse; however, there was no sense of urgency with regard to the situation in Southeast Asia.[10] Prior to Operation Rolling Thunder, domestic policy issues such as opposition to the civil rights movement, promoting a smaller federal government, and opposing domestic liberal organizations were more prominent issues among conservative activists.

Part of the reason for the Right's reluctance to promote an aggressive Vietnam strategy was the automatic association among many conservatives between Vietnam and Korea. Many within the Right believed that the Korean War, which had ended a decade earlier, was a defeat for the United States. Though the United States defended its ally from a Communist invasion, the war cost more American lives than was acceptable, and the US military failed to capture the entire peninsula. Many conservatives believed that failing to destroy North Korea was unacceptable, and throughout the Vietnam War there were references to the unnecessarily heavy price paid by the United States.[11]

In addition to the fear that the United States might repeat the mistakes of Korea, conservatives were also cautious because of repeated Western failures in Indochina. When France signed the Geneva Accords in 1954 and left South Vietnam, conservatives feared that North Vietnam would quickly become the more powerful of the two nations and overrun the south. Without a strong ally to support US forces, the probability of winning the war decreased markedly, and once South Vietnamese President Ngo Dinh Diem was assassinated in 1963, most conservatives recognized that the United States lacked a strong Vietnamese anticommunist ally.[12]

The haunting influence of both the Korean War and the French failure in Vietnam stood out in much of the conservative movement's literature in the early 1960s. In 1964 *Human Events* narrowed the United States' choices in Vietnam to the stark options of either fighting "in another Korean-type war or agree[ing] to a political Dienbienphu." According to this article, if the United States expanded its military presence in Vietnam, the nation would be locked in a land war on unfamiliar terrain. If the United States retreated from the war, it would embolden the Communist enemy, as in Dien Bien Phu. The overall problem, according to *Human Events*, was that the war in Vietnam was a fight against "the wrong enemy, at the wrong time, and in the wrong place."[13] Rather than fighting the North Vietnamese, the United States should be fighting a war against China, the *real* Asian threat. Though not all conservatives clamored for a fight with China, many believed that Vietnam was not the most important strategic location where the United States should be fighting.

In the absence of any obvious location for the next Cold War battle, 1963 and early 1964 were a period for long-term strategic thinking. Conservatives devoted much of this time to inspecting where American policies could have the most impact. The movement's discourse during this period indicates that for many conservatives, Cuba and Africa were the favored locations for the next fight between freedom and Communism.

Americans have had a long fascination with Cuba, focusing far more political attention toward the island nation than most others in the region. Cuba's proximity, as well as its historical relationship with the United States, helps explain American interests there. After Fidel Castro's revolution in 1959, Americans, and especially conservatives, were nervous about this Communist nation located only ninety miles off the coast of Florida. This fear and anxiety manifested itself in the American-sponsored invasion of Cuba at the Bay of Pigs in 1961. The following year, Cuba again captivated the American imagination as the United States led a blockade of the island that helped to halt Castro's acquisition of nuclear weapons. Afterward, conservatives continued to distrust Castro and wanted the United States to overthrow the Communist leader.

The Right's focus on Africa was a response to the political climate of this period. Many Americans debated and discussed the postcolonial African struggles of the early 1960s. The growing civil rights movement and its emerging focus on Africa fed this national discourse. Because of Africa's revolutionary fervor—often left over from colonial struggles—there was great potential for political gain in Africa. The continent was still developing economically and politically, and the conservative movement was determined to help win the battle for its future. Conservatives focused their attention primarily on Rhodesia (contemporary Zimbabwe) and Zanzibar (contemporary Tanzania). Both nations underwent revolutions in the early 1960s as they declared independence from Britain, garnering significant attention from both the United States and the Soviet Union. Conservatives wanted to ensure Communist forces did not take advantage of the revolutionary atmosphere and come to dominate the region. The destabilization caused by the revolutions could have led to impressive Communist victories, and the Right was determined to keep pressure on the John F. Kennedy and Lyndon Johnson administrations to ensure the continent-wide defeat of Communism. The May 5, 1964, issue of *National Review*, to provide one example, was almost exclusively devoted to the situation in Africa, and Goldwater's first piece of writing in *Human Events* following the announcement of his candidacy was titled "Prejudice Abounds in Africa."[14] To conservatives in the early 1960s, the future of the Cold War was in Africa and Cuba, not in Vietnam.

During the 1964 election, conservatives, taking their lead from Republican presidential candidate Barry Goldwater, talked more frequently about the nuances of federalism and the strengths of the federal government than they did about whether Vietnam would be the best place to make a Cold War stance. When the conservative media did discuss Vietnam, it was often pessimistic about the likelihood of an American victory. Most within the movement feared what might happen in Asia should Vietnam fall to Communism, but they also feared the results of an American invasion of Vietnam. The West had committed too many mistakes in Indochina, making victory appear unlikely. Thus domestic policy ideas, and not Vietnam, were issues of primary importance to conservatives before 1965.

The Vietnam Problem

One of the most significant reasons conservatives did not emphasize Vietnam as a critical battle in the long Cold War before 1965 was that the United States lacked a serious partner. A military coup assassinated South Vietnamese President Ngo Dinh Diem in November 1963. According to one conservative expert on Vietnam, what followed Diem's assassination was a "rapid succession of revolving-door governments in Saigon." The problem with these various governments was that they "were too busy playing their deadly political games in Saigon to ever get around to the essentials of administration and rule."[15] According to many pundits on the right, the United States allowed a military coup against Diem without recognizing that he was the strongest political force in the nation aside from the Communist National Liberation Front (NLF). Without Diem's presence, conservatives believed that South Vietnam was descending into chaos and confusion. Throughout the Vietnam War, conservatives focused on Diem's assassination, which occurred prior to Johnson's escalation of the war effort, as the turning point in the conflict. In the years that followed, they argued that his assassination diminished the likelihood of victory for the United States. They focused on Diem, and thus they overstated his competency.

Leading conservative Asian expert and former Minnesota congressman Walter Judd wrote to Barry Goldwater in the middle of his presidential campaign, ten months after Diem's assassination, to complain about the "critical mistake" that the United States made in allowing the overthrow of the Diem regime. In Judd's assessment of the situation, "[H]ad we stuck by our proven ally, the legal government of Viet Nam . . . we would by now, I believe, be well out of the woods there." Because of this mistake, Judd encouraged the Goldwater campaign not to advocate an enlargement of the fighting. He believed that the United States should "help the Vietnamese people win their own struggle, district by district and province by province, with American help and advice in all phases of the struggle as needed, but without our taking command and without substantially enlarging the area of armed conflict."[16] In Judd's view, if Diem had survived the coup, then the South Vietnamese would have defeated the NLF within a year. Because of Diem's death, Judd's advice to Goldwater was to avoid another land war in Asia. Judd's letter to Goldwater failed to acknowledge the obvious point that a yearlong absence of political leadership in South Vietnam should have been a greater concern than the death of one political figure.

Although the absence of any serious Vietnamese leadership frustrated conservatives, there was also much political posturing regarding the Right's Vietnam policies in 1964. Many conservative pundits believed that Vietnam was a strong political tool with which to attack Johnson, even though they doubted that the fighting there would determine the outcome of the Cold War. The election of 1964 was a seminal moment in conservative political history, and members of the movement were aware of the importance of the Goldwater campaign at the time. They recognized that Goldwater was setting the stage for a potential resurgence of conservatism. However, the Vietnam War remained a peripheral issue during the 1964 election. The election focused on domestic policy ideas and overall Cold War aggression rather than on the state of the Cold War in Vietnam.

When conservatives did discuss the Vietnam War, they used it as a vehicle to attack Johnson. Though conservatives needed no excuse to attack Johnson— his support of civil rights legislation and his Great Society programs greatly offended the majority of conservatives—Vietnam proved to be another easy target. The conservative press mocked Johnson's Vietnam policies in context of his inability to recognize the danger Communism posed to the world. In a March 1964 article, rhetorically titled "Does Johnson Have a Foreign Policy?" James Burnham wrote, "On South Vietnam Mr. Johnson's spokesmen talk simultaneously of getting the boys back home for Christmas and standing firm till doomsday."[17] Accusing Johnson of doublespeak was a common conservative refrain. By attacking Johnson's foreign policy, the Right tried to undercut his political credibility and build further support for Goldwater in the upcoming election. In their opinion, the president's foreign policy decisions were further proof that Johnson was an unfit commander in chief.

This rhetoric on the right was part of a broader campaign among conservatives to mercilessly attack Johnson. The Right frequently insulted Johnson's domestic policy, opposing his expansive view of the federal government while also disapproving of his government-mandated racial integration policies. The negative campaign against the president helped unify the Right and—they hoped—might help Barry Goldwater win the election. While domestic policy occupied the brunt of the negative campaigning, conservatives also asked why the US military was meddling in Vietnam without a clear mission. Several families of deceased soldiers, financed by a wealthy conservative, wrote a powerful open letter to President Johnson that was published in a May 1964 advertisement. In the letter, these families asked Johnson several questions about his failed Vietnam strategy, notably: "Why are the young Americans who are fighting Communist aggression in Viet Nam—shoulder to shoulder with free Vietnamese soldiers—forced to withstand the onslaught of the Communist enemy without having the opportunity to attack the enemy's own territory in the North?" The advertisement, published in the *Washington Star*, concluded with a call: "To make the supreme sacrifice in a war that cannot be won is too great a sacrifice to ask anyone. If we are to battle, let's battle to win!"[18] This advertisement was a means of attacking Johnson as a weak military commander who was hindering the military's power, while also fitting in nicely with the Right's overall anti-Johnson campaign in 1964. Conservatives believed that Johnson's inability to defend the world against Communism meant he should move out of the way.

This advertisement summarizes much of the movement's beliefs regarding Indochina. Most within the Right believed that winning in Vietnam could help the United States in the Cold War; however, they knew that victory would be difficult and come at an extremely high cost. They also recognized that victory in Vietnam did not equate to total victory in the Cold War. Making matters worse, they argued that Johnson was not taking the fighting seriously, diminishing the probability of an American victory. In one instance, May Craig wrote in *Human Events*, "We fiddle-faddle in Southeast Asia, and may be ignominiously pushed out. Maybe we should never have gone in there—let the Reds take it—but there is one thing for sure: If we go in anywhere, we should go in to win." The *National Review* echoed this idea that Johnson was indecisive when it labeled his Vietnam policies a "crime" in late 1964.[19] They believed that he needed to make a final and definitive decision regarding Vietnam.

The Right was probably not going to support Johnson's decision regardless of whether he continued fighting the war or pulled out American troops. Had Johnson tried to withdraw all American troops in 1964, the Right probably would have expanded its attack on him for being weak on Communism. The idea of an American president, especially a liberal Democratic president, conceding any land in the long Cold War struggle was anathema to many conservatives. When Johnson continued his strategy of an incremental military buildup of troops, conservatives attacked him for his "fiddle-faddle in Southeast Asia." Likely the only option conservatives would have supported in 1964 would have been an overwhelming military buildup of troops, coupled with a massive invasion of North Vietnam and the possible usage of nuclear weapons. Even if he chose this option, there is a strong possibility that the Right would have expressed anger with Johnson for attacking North Vietnam but sparing the true international Communist menace, China. Thus, for reasons unrelated to Cold War military strategy, conservatives were probably not about to support Johnson. After all, he was a liberal Democrat who ran against and defeated Barry Goldwater in the presidential election.

One of the reasons for Goldwater's popularity among conservatives, of course, was his anticommunist identity. Goldwater biographer Robert Goldberg wrote that the senator gained popularity in the early 1960s because "many Americans sensed that their nation was in retreat." Goldwater inspired many conservatives, including young people, to participate in the conservative movement. Members of the political movement read his books and felt a direct calling to promote conservatism nationwide. According to historian Gregory Schneider, many members of the Young Americans for Freedom, the largest national conservative youth organization in the 1960s, viewed Goldwater as a "political Moses," the man who would lead them from the desert and help them achieve political victory. It is worthwhile, therefore, to note the senator's own campaign stance on the Cold War and Vietnam. During the 1964 campaign, Goldwater's anticommunism manifested itself in his belief that the United States should play a role in ousting Fidel Castro from Cuba and in his support for South Vietnamese forces. Goldwater focused more attention on Cuba than Vietnam, largely because Cuba held a more prominent place in the American imagination. When Goldwater did talk about Vietnam, he derided Johnson for his weak foreign policies and for not fighting aggressively enough. As Goldwater wrote in 1964, two weeks before the presidential campaign, "No responsible world leader suggests that we should withdraw our support from Viet Nam. To do so would unhinge a vast and vital area, thereby committing to Communist domination its resources and its people."[20] This meant that the United States must increase its efforts and fight with the ultimate aim of winning in Vietnam. Though this statement clearly demonstrates that Goldwater opposed surrender in the Vietnam War, the quote also must be taken in context. Overall, Vietnam played a surprisingly small role in his 1964 campaign, especially considering the prominence of foreign policy and American policy toward Cuba. Goldwater did not advocate many specific policy proposals regarding Vietnam, and his campaign was more focused on Cuba. By opposing retreat in Vietnam, Goldwater was able to uphold the values that helped make him the leading conservative politician, but he did not try to tie his political fortunes to the military effort in Southeast Asia.

In short, the war served more as a political tool for the Right than it did as a location for a pivotal battle in the long Cold War against evil Communism. Though conservatives were not convinced that Vietnam was the right enemy, in the right place, at the right time, they saw an area where they could attack

Johnson's political credibility and they took that opportunity. They recognized that Vietnam was an arena where the United States was misusing its military power, and thus it was an easy political target. Independent of the Goldwater campaign, these conservative leaders recognized that America's military efforts in Vietnam were insufficient to win the war but that Johnson was hesitating to cede the nation to NLF advances. Unlike Cuba, Zanzibar, or Germany, the United States was fighting in Vietnam. When Johnson inserted the full weight of the US military into the Vietnam War with Operation Rolling Thunder, it made this small Southeast Asian nation a prime target for conservative attacks.

Enhancing a Movement

Despite the movement's embrace of Goldwater as its savior, the 1964 presidential election ended poorly for the Right. Johnson overwhelmingly defeated Goldwater in the most one-sided presidential election since Franklin Roosevelt's defeat of Herbert Hoover in the midst of the Great Depression. Massive political defeats are rarely good for a political movement. They can lead a movement toward political introspection and infighting, altering its growth. In 1964 conservatives recognized the importance of the immediate postelection period and the need to retain ideological unity in order to help grow the movement. The Right's leadership needed an issue to rally around, and as Buckley presciently noted in the fall of 1964, that issue would become Vietnam.

When conservative intellectual George Nash wrote his seminal work *The Conservative Intellectual Movement since 1945*, he described the late 1950s and early 1960s as the time when fusionism was born. Fusionism was an ideology that helped unite the various strands of conservatism. In Nash's telling of events, this was a period when both libertarian and traditionalist conservatives combined forces to unify into one movement. However, more recent histories of this period, including works in this anthology, note the frequent infighting that took place among various conservative factions in the early 1960s. Among the disputes of the period were those between traditionalists and libertarians, Christians and atheists, members of the John Birch Society and the *National Review*. The conservative movement was a disparate group of individuals with varied goals. Despite their differences, these groups worked together as a political movement struggling to find unity.[21]

Part of the reason conservatism was in a precarious role in the mid-1960s was because of external factors that helped to drive a wedge between different right-wing factions. For instance, the national press's treatment of the John Birch Society forced the intellectual elite to disavow the society or risk losing their credibility. With the rise of hippies and a more vigorous New Left student movement, including the maturation of the Students for a Democratic Society, libertarians were finding fault with the rigid morality of the traditionalist conservatives. For example, the issue of legalized marijuana was a hotly contested debate within conservatism in the mid-1960s, with libertarians and traditionalists staking opposite sides of the divide. With all this disagreement, there was no single unifying candidate for conservatives to rally around. This situation contrasted with the 1964 campaign, when there was remarkable unity among rank-and-file conservatives that Barry Goldwater was the best possible presidential candidate. It might have appeared to grassroots conservatives that without the Arizona senator, and with major issues causing serious internal tension, the movement was fraying.

Buckley's "hating the devil" memo stumbled on one of the few issues about which there was relative unity among conservatives. Buckley did not know in August 1964 that Johnson would begin America's longest war shortly after the inauguration. Buckley was lucky, but for most conservatives, including those outside of the *National Review* circle, he was also correct. Supporting the Vietnam War was one issue that helped unify most conservatives in 1965 and 1966. Almost immediately after Johnson announced Operation Rolling Thunder, conservatives offered their approval. Gone were the concerns that this was the wrong enemy or that Cuba and Africa were more important strategic locations for the United States to display its military might. Suddenly conservatives viewed Vietnam as a pivotal battle.

For the first time, the Vietnam War dominated the movement's discourse. Prowar protests and teach-ins, along with newspaper articles, magazine editions, and grassroots meetings in support of the war, were among the most common conservative activities in 1965 and 1966. Unlike any other issue, the Vietnam War and the 150,000 to 350,000 American troops sent to Southeast Asia captured the conservative imagination. Thus when the American Conservative Union (ACU) first analyzed the war in 1965 it emphatically declared that the United States could not afford to lose South Vietnam to Communist aggression: "Unpleasant as it may be, the battle line in Southeast Asia *is* Vietnam."[22] The newly formed group, which aimed at leading the conservative movement, declared that the United States needed to win the Vietnam War, no matter the cost. This was a remarkable and symbolic shift for both the organization and the conservative movement. Prior to the presidential election, conservatives were divided and ambivalent. Several proclaimed that the cost of victory in Vietnam would outweigh the benefits of defeating the NLF. Less than a year later, with the birth of this new and highly ambitious organization, there was fresh focus on the idea that Vietnam was the central front in the war against Communism. As this was the ACU's inaugural policy report, it was important that they not alienate the grass roots of the movement. Certainly the group's leadership believed that conservatives must support the Vietnam War.

Even conservative leaders such as James Burnham, the leading foreign policy columnist at *National Review*, stood firmly behind the military effort. By
strongly supporting the fighting in Vietnam, Burnham was changing his policy
beliefs. Burnham enjoyed high status within the movement for his foreign policy expertise, making his role as a leading prowar supporter after 1965 especially
relevant. In one professionally administered survey of readership in 1965, Burnham was the magazine's third most popular author, after William F. Buckley Jr.
and the pseudonymous Cato, who covered Washington political gossip.[23]

Burnham wrote a biweekly column on foreign policy, and throughout 1964
it often touched on the Vietnam conflict. Despite this, in the year leading up to
the election, Burnham's Vietnam analysis lacked a clear and coherent argument.
Burnham believed that Vietnam could potentially be an important war, but it
would be one that the United States would have difficulty winning. Thus in
February 1964 Burnham endorsed French president Charles de Gaulle's belief
that the "U.S. is going to lose the war in South Vietnam." Burnham lauded
de Gaulle for recognizing that the only way the United States could win in
Vietnam was to expand the fighting into China and possibly use nuclear weapons. Since that was not likely, Burnham asked rhetorically, "Why not pull out
now and see what can be salvaged by diplomacy? You can't end up any *worse*
off." However, only a few months later, in June 1964, he argued that victory
in Vietnam was necessary in order to help defeat Asian Communism.[24] It was
possible for him to be erratic largely because Cuba, and not Vietnam, was his
central focus.

In 1965 there was a radical shift in the tone and nature of Burnham's columns. Suddenly he placed the future of world security on the outcome of the
battle in Southeast Asia. Following the commencement of Operation Rolling
Thunder, Burnham emphatically declared that the consequence of defeat in
Vietnam "would be the loss of all bases and friendly ports in the western Pacific
and South Seas, and the foldback of our basic line of defense to our own Pacific
coast. This would in turn mean ceding to the Communist powers domination
of the entire region (including the Indian subcontinent)."[25] Vietnam was now
the central front in the war against Communism. In Burnham's new worldview,
the American public needed to unify behind the president in support of the
Vietnam War.

This prowar view moved far beyond the pages of the *National Review*. Senator James Pearson (R-KS) argued on the Senate floor in 1965 that defeating Ho
Chi Minh was the moral equivalent of defeating Adolf Hitler in World War II.
Political figures Walter Judd and Thomas Lane also called for "all-out support
of South Vietnam." Conservative religious leaders such as Billy Graham and
Billy James Hargis wrote to Johnson offering their support for his decision to
expand the fighting. These religious leaders believed that Communism was an

evil, atheistic ideology and only military force could stop its expansion. Graham chose to endorse Johnson's expansion of the war because, he said, "The U.S. has a moral obligation to defend freedom in Southeast Asia. Of course, war is a terrible thing—but it becomes necessary sometimes."[26] In the eyes of most conservative leaders, Vietnam was now the main event in the war between good and evil.

With the expansion of the war effort, Buckley received his wish; the conservative movement was "back to hating the devil." Vietnam emerged almost immediately after the election as an issue that unified a movement otherwise in danger of fracturing. Conservatives did not support the war solely to help propel the movement's partisan odds. However, as long as support for the war remained strong, there was diminished fear among conservatives of the grass roots leaving the movement. The movement's leadership could keep the attention and support of many of the students and others who had gravitated toward Goldwater's campaign in 1964.

The importance of support for Vietnam among grassroots conservatives is apparent from letters and campaigns undertaken by everyday conservatives in 1965 and 1966. For instance, in early 1965, at least fifty people wrote to President Johnson imploring him to name Walter Judd as ambassador to the United Nations or to some other position of influence within the administration. By all indications, these letters were not part of a national campaign instigated by Judd or any other conservative organization; instead, they appear to have been a genuine upsurge of support for the popular speaker. Judd was the man most conservatives selected because of his many speeches at anticommunist gatherings throughout the nation. According to one of these letters, written by Karl C. Jonas, Johnson should appoint Judd to "a post of responsibility . . . [as Johnson would] reap great dividends in unifying our nation behind what I believe to be the correct policy [in Vietnam]." Average citizens like Jonas wrote to the President asking him to select a leader from across the political aisle (and thus select someone who endorsed their political viewpoint) in order to help gain support for the war.[27]

Support for the Vietnam War spread rapidly among the movement's leadership. Although a few conservatives, including Ayn Rand and Phyllis Schlafly, were skeptical about the war or even opposed to it, the vast majority of the movement's leadership supported the United States' mission in Vietnam.[28] For most conservatives, the only way to defeat Communist expansion in Asia was to fight as aggressively as possible.

By late 1965, conservative support for the war appeared natural, as though it was a long-standing conservative principle. Average conservative citizens continued writing to their political leaders expressing their support for the war. Individuals such as John Berke, an avid fan of Clarence Manion's radio program, wrote Manion in November 1965, "A victory for us [in Vietnam] ultimately will assure freedom for those who are now bound by the chains of collectivism." This letter stands out largely because Manion rarely spoke about Vietnam. Manion's primary focus in 1965 was on domestic politics, not Vietnam or international Communism.[29] Nonetheless, Berke wrote to Manion expressing his support for the Vietnam War. By the end of 1965, the grass roots firmly supported the war, remaining engaged with the conservative movement even in the wake of Goldwater's defeat.

A Foundation for the Future

Buckley's worst fear in 1964 was that the conservative movement would fracture. He worried that the movement would lose its political gains from the previous year, when conservatives succeeded in nominating Goldwater for the presidency, and that the Right would disappear into American political history. By using anticommunism, he hoped to find the one issue on which all conservatives agreed. When Lyndon Johnson expanded the war in Vietnam, events took control of the conservative movement, pushing it in a new direction.

With the launching of Operation Rolling Thunder, Johnson unintentionally helped galvanize the Right and reoriented conservatives' anticommunism toward one primary goal: winning the Vietnam War. Expansion of the war effort helped conservatives quickly shed their initial fears and reluctance regarding the situation in Vietnam. Before 1965 the Right was uncertain that the cost of victory for the United States would be worth the loss of money and materiel. Even those who believed that this could be a simple war questioned whether it was the right war. To these conservatives, Vietnam was a diversion from the main event: the fight between the United States and both China and the Soviet Union. Vietnam mattered, but not as much as other Cold War hot spots.

Once most conservatives recognized that Johnson's bombing campaign marked the beginning of a serious military intervention, they felt the anticommunist impulse to support the war. In 1965, this spurred a nearly universal feeling of unity among conservatives in favor of the war. The growth of the Vietnam conflict helped keep the movement temporarily united in the wake of Goldwater's 1964 presidential defeat. Excitement permeated most of its membership. For the first few years of the Vietnam War, most members of the conservative movement agreed that victory in Vietnam was an essential goal for the United States in the Cold War.

Notes

1. Goldwater came no closer to Johnson than a 28-point gap in September 1964; while Johnson led by as much as 57 points in July, he held a 35 percent lead over Goldwater in Gallup's final election poll (Scholarly Resources, *The Gallup Poll, Public Opinion 1935–1997*, CD-ROM edition); "The Living Room Candidate: Presidential Campaign Commercials 1952–2008," Museum of the Moving Image, http://www.livingroomcandidate.org/commercials/1964; Gregory L. Schneider, *Cadres for Conservatism: Young Americans for Freedom and the Rise of the Contemporary Right* (New York: New York University Press, 1999), 86.

2. William F. Buckley Jr. to William Rusher, August 5, 1964, Inter-Office Memo, William F. Buckley Papers, Sterling Memorial Library, Yale University.

3. Though conservatives discussed and knew about the fighting taking place in Vietnam, the force, flair, and quality of the discourse regarding Cuba, China, and many parts of Africa were far more dominant than the discourse regarding the Vietnam War. Some examples are: "Conservative Answers To: Panama, Red China, Cuba, Taxes, Government Spending, Poverty, Africa, Social Security, The UN, TVA, Missiles, and others," *National Review*, February 25, 1964; James Burnham, "The Third World War: Does Johnson Have a Foreign Policy?," *National Review*, March 10, 1964, 190; Barry Goldwater, "Prejudice Abounds in Africa," *Human Events*, January 18, 1964, 10; Barry Goldwater, *Why Not Victory?*, 2nd ed. (New York: MacFadden Books, 1964).

4. Arleigh Burke, "Why We Must Intensify Our Campaign in Viet Nam," *Human Events*, March 12, 1966, 3 (163). *Note:* Beginning in 1966, *Human Events* ran two sets of page numbers, one sequential throughout the year and the other beginning anew with each issue. This essay references both numbers. Note also that in the 1960s Americans spelled Vietnam as two words. Today, common spelling makes it one word. This essay uses the contemporary spelling except in direct quotes.

5. There were many examples of this rhetoric within the Right; one example is: Editorial, [Untitled], *National Review Bulletin*, May 5, 1964, 344; Donald Bruce, H.J. Resolution 20, 88th Congress, 1st Session, January 9, 1963, box 44, Group Research Papers, Nicholas Murray Butler Library, Columbia University; Goldwater, *Why Not Victory?*

6. One example of a common claim by conservatives that Marx predicted the goal of world domination is "How We Can Win in Viet Nam: An Exclusive Interview with General Curtis E. LeMay," *Human Events*, January 28, 1967, 8–10 (56–58).

7. UPI Report, "Police Are Not Amused: Minister Stages Fake Arrest," March 30, 1964, box 29, Group Research Papers.

8. A poster published by the Allen-Bradley Company in Milwaukee, Wisconsin, which was noted for aiding the CACC's efforts. This poster was undated but most likely from the mid-1960s. It is common in archival collections, indicating that the Allen-Bradley Company probably published it widely and in multiple years. See Laura Jane Gifford's essay in this volume for additional information on the Allen-Bradley Company's cooperation with the CACC. Poster, undated [probably mid 1960s], box 35, Radical Right Papers, Hoover Institute Archives, Stanford University, Palo Alto, California. One copy of the game ad: "Victory Over Communism," *Human Events*, November 14, 1964, 11. Four examples of works which

devote attention to the John Birch Society are: Sara Diamond, *Roads to Dominion: Right-Wing Movements and Political Power in the United States* (New York: Guilford Press, 1995); Lisa McGirr, *Suburban Warriors: The Origins of the New American Right* (Princeton, NJ: Princeton University Press, 2001); Rick Perlstein, *Before the Storm: Barry Goldwater and the Unmaking of the American Consensus* (New York: Hill and Wang, 2001); Jonathan M. Schoenwald, *A Time for Choosing: The Rise of Modern American Conservatism* (New York: Oxford University Press, 2001). See also Samuel Brenner's essay in this volume.

9. Histories of the foreign policies of the libertarian movement, *National Review*, and Phyllis Schlafly include: Donald T. Critchlow, *Phyllis Schlafly and Grassroots Conservatism: A Woman's Crusade* (Princeton, NJ: Princeton University Press, 2005); Diamond, *Roads to Dominion*; Schoenwald, *Time for Choosing*; Jonathan Schoenwald, "No War, No Welfare, and No Damn Taxation: The Student Libertarian Movement, 1968–1972," in *The Vietnam War on Campus: Other Voices, More Distant Drums*, ed. Marc Jason Gilbert (Westport, CT: Praeger Publishers, 2001). Examples of articles detailing foreign policy ideas in *National Review* and *Human Events* include "Fear and Weakness Mark U.S. Foreign Policy," *Human Events*, March 14, 1964, 1; Untitled Editorial, *National Review*, May 5, 1965, 344. See also Phyllis Schlafly and Chester Ward, *Strike from Space*, 2nd ed. (Alton, IL: Pere Marquette Press, 1966).

10. Examples of articles where the Right displayed a surprising lack of urgency regarding fighting in Vietnam include: "Ideas for LBJ: Do We Have a Foreign Policy?," *Human Events*, March 14, 1964, 12; James Burnham, "The Third World War: The Hand on the Trigger," *National Review*, November 17, 1964, 1013; "Conservative Answers To: Panama, Red China, Cuba, Taxes, Government Spending, Poverty, Africa, Social Security, the UN, TVA, Missiles, and Others," *National Review*, February 25, 1964, 1.

11. One example: Henry J. Taylor, "What Will the United States Do at the Viet Nam Conference Table," *Human Events*, July 30, 1966, 6 (486).

12. Walter Judd, "What Could Have Been Done to Avert the Present Problem in Vietnam?," speech at unknown location, March 1965, folder 10, box 50, Walter Judd Papers, Hoover Institute Archives, Stanford University; News Brief Editorial, "Vietnamese Schizophrenia," *National Review*, March 10, 1964, 186.

13. Dien Bien Phu was the location of a major military defeat by the French military in 1954 that helped convince the French government to expedite negotiations for the end of their colonial rule in the region; "Wrong Enemy at Awkward Time: President Faces Dilemma in South Viet Nam," from the Allen-Scott Report in *Human Events*, September 26, 1964, 3.

14. This essay's hypothesis is based upon the Right's anticommunist discourse in the early 1960s. In addition to *National Review*'s focus on the continent, *Human Events* was very interested in this decolonizing region of the world. Goldwater's *Human Events* article focused upon African decolonization and Communism ("Prejudice Abounds in Africa," *Human Events*, January 18, 1964, 10). The subject of the Right's interest in African governance and African anticommunism is extremely interesting and important, but there are few academic works within the historiography helping to explain why conservatives devoted so much time and energy to

Africa. For a rare study of this subject, see Ann K. Ziker, "Race, Conservative Politics, and U.S. Foreign Policy in the Postcolonial World, 1948–1968" (PhD diss., Rice University, 2008).

15. Marguerite Higgins, *Our Vietnam Nightmare* (New York: Harper and Row, 1965), 252–53.

16. Walter Judd to Barry Goldwater, 1964, folder 5, box 30, Walter Judd Papers, Hoover Institute Archives, Stanford University. This was part of a long letter from Judd to Goldwater that Goldwater solicited during the campaign.

17. James Burnham, "The Third World War: Does Johnson Have a Foreign Policy?," *National Review*, March 10, 1964, 190.

18. Reprinted in *Human Events*, May 30, 1964.

19. May Craig, "Our Country Needs a Rebirth of Principle," *[Portland, ME] Sunday Telegram*, reprinted in *Human Events*, March 14, 1964, 1; Editorial News Brief, [Untitled], *National Review*, November 17, 1964, 998.

20. Schneider, *Cadres for Conservatism*, 73; Robert Alan Goldberg, *Barry Goldwater* (New Haven, CT: Yale University Press, 1995), 157; Barry Goldwater, "Where I Stand on the Issues," *Human Events*, October 24, 1964, 11.

21. Libertarians often believed that the government should play little role in society. Though this was an ideologically diverse group, most believed that the government should relegate itself to helping maintain peace. Traditionalists, who often composed the majority of the conservative movement, believed that government should remain small, but they supported traditional community values, which they understood as Judeo-Christian values. They believed the government could use its influence to help promote those values. For more on fusionism, see George Nash, *The Conservative Intellectual Movement in America Since 1945* (New York: Basic Books, 1976), 395–466. Works that discuss the infighting in the conservative movement include: Jennifer Burns, *Goddess of the Market: Ayn Rand and the American Right* (New York: Oxford University Press, 2009); Rebecca Klatch, *A Generation Divided: The New Left, the New Right, and the 1960s* (Berkeley: University of California Press, 1999); McGirr, *Suburban Warriors*; and Schoenwald, *Time for Choosing*. One historiographical review which examines the fractured nature of the movement is: Julian E. Zelizer, "Rethinking the History of American Conservatism," *Reviews in American History* 38 (June 2010): 372.

22. ACU Report, "The Battleline Is Vietnam," July-August 1965, folder 2, box 58, Marvin Liebman Papers, Hoover Institute Archives, Stanford University.

23. "Editorial Preference and Opinion Survey of *National Review* Subscribers," April 1965, Inter-Office Memo, William F. Buckley Papers.

24. James Burnham, "The Third World War: Put Up or Shut Up," *National Review*, February 25, 1964, 118; James Burnham, "The Third World War: Crumbling Line," *National Review*, June 16, 1964, 493.

25. James Burnham, "The Third World War: The Weakest Front," *National Review*, June 15, 1965, 499.

26. James B. Pearson, "Spotlight on Congress: Faraway Viet Nam," *Human Events*, April 17, 1965, 34; Quote from Walter Judd, "Special Report: Reflections on Asian Anti-Communists," *National Review*, January 11, 1965, 27; Thomas A. Lane, "A Military Expert Speaks Out: What Johnson Must Do to Win in Viet Nam,"

Human Events, December 18, 1965, 9; Interview of Billy Graham by Max Goldberg (North American Newspaper Alliance), September 25, 1965, EX-ND19/CO 312, box 217, National Security National Defense folder, White House Central Files, Lyndon Baines Johnson Presidential Library, Austin, Texas.

27. These letters were handwritten, and each letter used different arguments and language to support Judd. Such diversity indicates they were not part of a larger national campaign. Additionally, the letters often urged Johnson to nominate Judd for different positions, including Secretary of State. If this had been part of a national campaign, there probably would have been a common thread among the letters. Jonas to Johnson, 2 April 1965, Name Files—Judd, Walter (Dr.) folder, White House Central Files, Lyndon Baines Johnson Presidential Library, Austin, Texas.

28. Despite its relatively small size, historians need to devote more attention to the antiwar Right. Present works on the topic include: Critchlow, *Phyllis Schlafly and Grassroots Conservatism*; Seth Offenbach, "The Other Side of Vietnam: The Conservative Movement and the Vietnam War" (PhD diss., Stony Brook University, 2010); and Schoenwald, "Vietnam on Campus."

29. John Berke to Clarence Manion, November 29, 1965, folder 1, box 21, Clarence Manion Papers, Chicago Historical Society. Manion, a law professor at Notre Dame, kept his focus on domestic issues, including Supreme Court decisions. Though Manion had foreign policy beliefs, he rarely offered them himself, instead deferring to the views of his several analysts, including Daniel Lyons and various congressmen. Because he did not often promote his own foreign policy views, Manion stands out as an anomaly within the Right's leadership. His frequent guests who were foreign policy experts, however, help us understand that Manion supported the war and did care deeply about foreign policy.

CHAPTER 11

Evangelical Internationalism

A Conservative Worldview for the Age of Globalization

Andrew Preston

To most Americans, Billy Graham was a gentle evangelist, a prophet of the old-time gospel who filled people with optimism. This was the secret to Graham's incredible success as the people's preacher: his incessant warnings about sin and evil and the need to repent never overwhelmed his sunnier message of eternal hope and personal fulfillment. From his first successful crusade, in Los Angeles in 1948, through the religiosity of the 1950s, Graham warned Americans and millions of others around the world that sin was ever-present, that all men and women were sinners, and that they only needed to open their hearts to Christ to ensure redemption and salvation. In Billy Graham's spiritual forecast, the skies were always sunny; there was always enough hope to dissipate the gloom.[1]

But the turbulent years of the 1960s were different, and Graham's tone became haunted by the certainty of imminent disaster. Even he had trouble imparting a message of optimism. To be sure, he remained ultimately optimistic, but only thanks to his unshakeable belief that humanity would endure after Christ's return. Before then, the world would suffer unimaginable torment. In 1961, Graham believed that "demonic forces are at work to bring mankind to destruction. The Christian outlook has not been as black since the days of the first century." Tensions between the United States and the Soviet Union were troubling enough, but most terrifying of all was the looming, ever-present specter of nuclear holocaust. Washington and Moscow, he predicted shortly after, were "on a collision course which could precipitate a third world war and wipe out vast areas of civilization. This fact," as Graham saw it, hangs like a shadow over the whole world. Young people in high school and college today cannot make a plan for the future except they see this shadow . . . Our homes, our businesses, our families, our churches, everything we have could be wiped out within a short space of time. We do not know whether we have one year, two years, five years or ten years. But one thing is certain: there is a feeling in the air that something is about to happen. World tension is mounting. Men sense they are moving swiftly toward a culminating moment in history.[2]

Graham's mood continued to worsen as the 1960s developed. At the height of the decade in 1965, he channeled all his forebodings into a single, excitable volume, *World Aflame*. Despite widespread prosperity and progress in civil rights legislation, which he hailed as achievements, Graham remained as frightened as ever about the world's future. Poverty, racial tensions, overpopulation, disease, famine, and war all had the potential to wipe out the world on their own, yet they were combining in increasingly menacing ways to make an ultimate catastrophe all the more likely. "Our world is on fire," he warned in terrifying words that held nothing back. "The demons of hell have been let loose. The fires of passion, greed, hate, and lust are sweeping the world. We seem to be plunging madly toward Armageddon." Americans living in 1965, particularly young people, were "the generation that will pass through the fire." They were "destined to live in the midst of crisis, danger, fear, and death. We are like a people under sentence of death, waiting for the date to be set . . . History is at an impasse. We are now on a collision course. Something is about to give." It was no accident that Graham's tone was apocalyptic, for he sensed that the end really was near. Not even General Electric, which in 1964 used a jingle called "There Will Be a Bright Tomorrow" in celebration of its technological achievements and the nation's general prosperity and booming consumerist economy, could escape Graham's brooding vision of doom. "No doubt the producers used the song with tongue in cheek," he scolded, "considering the precarious condition of the world."[3]

Yet there was hope, for if the world mended its ways and came to Christ it could still be saved. Armageddon would not be prevented—the Bible's prophecy would come true one time or another—but it could be postponed. Thus to Graham, the 1960s marked a time of enormous risk and, potentially, even greater reward. "This book attempts to describe our modern world on fire," he explained in the introduction to *World Aflame*. "Fire can either purify or destroy." It was up to the world's Christians to ensure purification and prevent destruction because there was "still time for God to intervene." Rarely had their opportunity been so glorious.[4]

Not for the first or last time in his long career, Billy Graham's response to social and political crises epitomized a broader evangelical view of the world. Indeed, many Americans who were not evangelicals or Christians—or even believers in any faith—felt similar existential angst at the domestic and global turmoil of the 1960s. This was understandable given the intensity and gravity of the crises causing the turmoil. Graham spoke in apocalyptic tones not only because of his faith in the truth of biblical prophecy but because the world faced an actual nuclear apocalypse several times that decade: first during the Berlin Crisis of 1961, then more pointedly during the Cuban missile crisis of 1962, again to a certain extent with the first successful Chinese nuclear test in 1964, and to a much lesser but very real extent in the several major international wars that erupted from Indochina and South Asia to Africa and the Middle East. The popularity of existential philosophy, religious or atheist, soared during the decade simply because Americans lived in the dark shadow of nuclear war and thus really did fear for the very existence of the human race. Under such emotional and spiritual duress, and disillusioned by the inability of political leaders to salve their troubled souls, Americans of many religious and ideological persuasions embarked on a quest for personal fulfillment and meaning.[5]

Billy Graham and his fellow evangelicals, then, were by no means unique. But evangelical existentialism such as Graham's was something altogether different. Instead of deconstructing the meaning of life, as the philosophical currents of the 1960s tended to do, and instead of embracing moral relativism, as mainline theologians were doing, evangelical existentialism sought to reaffirm the traditional staples of Christian Americanism within a new and rapidly changing context. On foreign policy issues, evangelicals promoted a worldview for the age of globalization, one that recognized that the world was changing but that would nonetheless reorient confused Americans on their traditional bearings. The evangelical worldview, what might be called "evangelical internationalism," was based on what appeared to be a series of internal contradictions that made perfect sense to its adherents: peace through strength, universal nationalism, the promotion of both local autonomy and globalization, and saving the world despite the imminence of end times. Most paradoxically of all, evangelical internationalism combined a fierce traditionalism with a subtle recognition that circumstances had changed forever. It seemed complicated, but its very complexity ensured it had stability and perseverance. It represented nothing less than a fundamental shift in American internationalist thought, from a liberal perspective that prioritized global engagement through interdependence, cooperation, and multilateralism, to a conservative belief that global engagement was unavoidable, even desirable, but that it must unfold on American terms and without compromising American values.

The evolution of evangelical internationalism did not occur in a vacuum, and the 1960s acted as the fulcrum of a broader postwar era of transformation, in both the United States and the world at large. Domestically, the changes in race and gender relations that culminated in the "rights revolutions" as well as the antiwar movement altered the social, political, and cultural composition of the United States. Internationally, the decade began the "reglobalization" of the world system, an integrative process that had been interrupted politically by the world wars and the onset of the Cold War and economically by the Great Depression and the rise of protectionism and central planning.[6]

Some Americans found such changes hopeful and promising; many others found them bewildering and troubling. Historians have normally placed evangelicals in this second group and portrayed them as hostile to globalization and the social and cultural revolutions transforming life at home and abroad.[7] Moreover, in their work on earlier periods, particularly the early Cold War but also the Wilsonian era, historians have also strongly—perhaps indelibly—linked conservative Christianity to visceral currents of anticommunism and American nationalism.[8] There is of course a great deal of truth to these assertions, as most evangelicals and other cultural conservatives either were worried by or strongly disapproved of the decade's global turbulence, protest movements, and identity politics and remained staunchly anticommunist. But they also embraced some aspects of globalization. In fact, their views did not represent a simple reaction against liberalism and radical revolution but instead reflected an innovative mix of traditional nationalism and new internationalism that was in the vanguard of American thinking about the wider world. As the religious sociologist Wade Clark Roof puts it, globalization "uproots tradition, yet in the process provokes powerful yearnings for wisdom from the past. It might be said that globalization creates for people everywhere something of a perpetual liminal state—of being caught in between old ways of living and believing and the possibility of a new world in the making."[9] This was precisely the process the American evangelical worldview began to undergo in the 1960s.

With the ordeal of liberalism in Vietnam and elsewhere, conservative Republican presidents later found it useful to deploy evangelical internationalism for broader American purposes. By fashioning this new worldview for the 1960s, evangelicals helped establish a more general tone that would underline US foreign policy for several decades thereafter. As Bethany Moreton observes in tracing the rise of Walmart, evangelicals succeeded in setting the tone and direction for America's role in globalization. These business-oriented evangelicals' "faith in God and faith in the market grew in tandem" and ultimately "helped shape American-led globalization itself." Even more, their embrace of globalization, but strictly on their own terms, "reveals how globalization got its twang."[10] Evangelicals did something similar in the realm of foreign affairs, and it is this chapter's aim to describe and define their own distinctive internationalist ideas for a new world.

Traditionalism

Throughout the 1960s, Christian conservatives retained their very traditional nationalistic fervor. They remained among the most fiercely patriotic and resolutely anticommunist of all Americans even as others began to adopt a more nuanced view on both issues. The global and domestic revolutions of the decade caused many Americans to question their long-held assumptions. But on the whole, Christian conservatives held fast to their traditionalist views of faith and the flag.

In so doing, evangelicals and fundamentalists found themselves swimming against the currents of national opinion. The beginning of the decade marked a time of heightened Soviet-American tensions. Due to crises in Berlin, Cuba, Congo, and Indochina, historians have referred to the 1958–63 period as the Cold War's "crisis years," a more dangerous period than other eras of flash-point crises like 1946–53 and 1979–83. Overall, however, Americans did not respond to the crisis years of 1958–63 with a surge of anticommunist hostility and vigilance. Instead, fearing for the future of the human race and unsettled by the thought that world leaders were letting things slip beyond their control, Americans relaxed their views about Communism. They did not accept it as an equal to their own way of life, and they did not perceive the Soviets as genuinely interested in the same things as them, but neither did they see Communism as an existential threat. As M. J. Heale points out in his overview of 150 years of American anticommunism, "By the 1960s those Americans who insisted that the United States was being subverted by a red enemy within were being widely ridiculed as extremists," while the "erosion of the anticommunist consensus" led to "changing perceptions of the Cold War." In a June 1963 speech at American University, President John F. Kennedy brought the crisis years to a close by declaring that Americans needed to "reexamine our attitude toward the Soviet Union . . . No government or social system is so evil that its people must be considered as lacking in virtue." Nuclear weapons, he warned, had made the escalation of Cold War tensions too dangerous to go unchecked. In place of the worldwide anticommunist offensive he had promised in his inaugural address, Kennedy now pledged to work with Moscow to manage their rivalry lest it get out of control and destroy the world. Even the Vietnam War unfolded within an overall ebbing of anticommunist passions and the emergence of superpower détente. As Fredrik Logevall has shown, Washington escalated its military role in Vietnam reluctantly, with little confidence in success and with little prodding from the public or Congress. Instead, despite widespread unease with Vietnam, the war escalated in what Logevall aptly calls a "permissive context" of reluctant public and congressional deference to the president and an unwillingness to confront him on matters of national security.[11]

Christian conservatives took a rather different view. Instead of ebbing and flowing with the ebb and flow of the Cold War and the balance of nuclear terror, evangelical and fundamentalist views were steadfastly anticommunist long after the Red Scares of the 1950s had abated. To be sure, there were varying degrees of intensity within conservative Christian anticommunism; just as they were on domestic issues such as civil rights and school prayer, fundamentalists were much more stridently and inflexibly anticommunist than evangelicals. But in general, the anticommunism of both groups remained remarkably unchanged from the zenith of American anticommunism in the period between 1946 and 1954. Between 1960 and 1964, when policy makers and commentators alike had assumed that the fires of extremism had burned themselves out years before, the fortunes of all the main Christian anticommunists improved dramatically. Subscriptions to Billy James Hargis's *Christian Crusade* doubled to nearly 100,000, while subscriptions to Carl McIntire's *Christian Beacon* tripled to 66,500. In 1961, McIntire's Twentieth Century Reformation received annual donations of $635,000; by 1964, it was collecting more than $3 million. The John Birch Society reported similar increases in contributions. "We look forward to a period of growth," Christian Anti-Communism Crusade exulted in 1962, and "we propose to launch the greatest anti-Communism campaign America has ever known." The head of Christian Anti-Communism Crusade was Reverend Fred Schwarz, whose 1960 book *You Can Trust the Communists (...to Be Communists)* sold more than a million copies.[12]

On virtually all political and cultural issues, Christian conservatives linked national and international affairs. Thus the Communist menace did not emanate only from Moscow, Havana, and Beijing, but from within the United States itself. This faith-based remnant of the worst excesses of the McCarthyite 1950s was even more unusual for the 1960s, and it reflected the preoccupation evangelicals and fundamentalists continued to have with Communism. In his polemic *Communist America—Must It Be?*, also published in 1960, Hargis blamed a wide range of domestic problems, from a decline in patriotism to the power of labor unions, on the American Communists who took their marching orders from Moscow. "The Communists will attempt the overthrow of our Government and the free Government of the world in this decade," he predicted. Led by Soviet leader Nikita Khrushchev, the Communists were in a position to do so because Americans had let down their collective guard and allowed secularism and irreligion to predominate in the nation's government, schools, unions—even churches. "Not suspecting either the depth or the extent of the Communist intrigue against America and the world, the American people by the millions are allowing themselves to become the unwitting dupes of the Communists thus co-operating in their own destruction."[13] Hargis was by no means atypical; throughout the decade, whenever faced with liberal challenges to the established order on issues like segregation, school prayer, and free-speech protections for pornography and obscenity, Christian conservatives reacted with horror that the Communist conspiracy had infected the upper reaches of American public life.

This seemed completely irrational, even delusional, to nonevangelical observers—after all, as recently as 1960 the sociologist Daniel Bell had pronounced "the end of ideology" and with it the political influence of evangelicalism and its "high emotionalism, its fervor, enthusiasm, and excitement, its revivalism" and its "peculiar schizoid character." But this concern made eminent sense when considered from a Christian conservative viewpoint. Evangelicals and fundamentalists were, traditionally, the strongest defenders of the First Amendment's separation of church and state, because it protected religion from government regulation even as it did not prevent religion from informing the broader political and cultural agenda. Christian conservatives of many shades had long been America's nonconformists, and they flourished in what historians have called America's unregulated "spiritual marketplace." When the federal government, in the form of congressional legislation or, more often, Supreme Court decisions, decided to shore up the wall of separation in ways that prioritized secularism and disadvantaged faith, Christian conservatives viewed it as a form of state regulation of religion. From there, it was not much of a leap to see such regulation as undemocratic, even tyrannical—a form of government, in other words, that seemed suspiciously close to atheistic Communism. "Mr. Kennedy is demanding that Congress enact legislation that will make the Federal government the absolute master of all stores, hotels, motels, restaurants, and theaters," the fundamentalist *Baptist Bible Tribune*'s Noel Smith complained after Kennedy called for a new civil rights law in 1963. "By the same logic, by the same principle of law, the Federal government can become the master of the churches of this country. Not only can, but will. And what kind of government will we then have? A Communist government." Similarly, Harold Ockenga warned that the court-ordered banning of Bible reading "leaves America in the same position as Communist Russia."[14]

This deep-seated antistatism, which stemmed from a traditionalist devotion to the separation of church and state but also became widespread in conservative politics of almost all persuasions in the 1960s, led evangelicals and fundamentalists to a wariness and distrust of international organizations such as the United Nations. Just as Christian conservatives prized local and denominational autonomy from the US government, they sought to protect American autonomy within the international system and from the regulatory power of a world state. Because they seated sovereign members as equals regardless of faith or ideology, international organizations made no distinction between Christian America and the apostates of atheist Communist regimes or Muslim, Hindu, and Buddhist countries. "There is an alarming tendency on the part of some to surrender the sovereignty of our government to international agencies," the fundamentalist layman L. Nelson Bell lamented in late 1959, "and in so doing erode away not only the rights of American citizens but also to lose for our own land the prestige and power that can best be wielded by people who operate according to tried and true principles."[15] This antipathy for the UN existed from the organization's inception, but it reached a crescendo in the 1960s and '70s, when US power in the world system was at a nadir and the nation was more vulnerable to outside pressures than ever before.

Despite harboring a visceral antistatism, then, Christian conservatives praised the United States as a Christian nation, albeit one beset by Communist atheists abroad and liberal secular humanists at home. Though they often distrusted the federal government, Christian conservatives loved their country. This rock-ribbed patriotism did not diminish during the social and cultural revolutions of the 1960s; if anything, the upheaval of the decade reinforced evangelical and fundamentalist patriotism and convinced Christian conservatives that only they could save the country from its enemies, such as liberals at home and Communists abroad. "It is the citizen, not the government, who should be our concern," Sherwood E. Wirt told the Evangelical Press Association in 1964 in a clear reference to the liberal ecumenists of the National Council of Churches. "The man makes or breaks the government. This will be the land of the free only so long as it is the home of the brave. And there are a lot of survival-obsessed, spineless people in America tonight who would sell the country tomorrow to almost anyone—to [Fidel] Castro, or the United Nations, or the World Federalists, or the beatniks, or the Viet Cong, or the devil himself. Sell it?" Wirt spat. "They would give it away."[16]

To evangelicals and fundamentalists, the key difference between themselves on one hand and liberals, atheists, and Communists on the other was faith in God. Without the true Christian faith, in which only Christian conservatives continued to believe, there was no such thing as American patriotism or America's mission. And without America, there could be no freedom, at home or anywhere else in the world. The world would be lost forever, unreachable and unable to be saved.

This was such a common argument among Christian conservatives that it is easy to overlook its significance, primarily because it was only Christian conservatives who continued to make it in an age of high liberal modernism, secularization, and détente. American democracy was so rooted in Christianity as to be inseparable from it, claimed Reverend Robert F. Williams of the Church of the Reflections at Knott's Berry Farm. The founders, he argued, had deliberately grounded the new American nation in the principles and beliefs of the Protestant faith, and it was this direct connection to God that gave America its unique strength. "America's past is a halo of glory," Williams declared, while its "present is the wonder of the rest of the world." The only thing that could threaten the future of freedom was the apostasy of the American people, which would weaken the United States against its enemies around the world. "Shall we allow God's plan for the future of man to end in this generation because of our failure to uphold it, or be slowed by shortsighted people in positions of leadership in our nation?" he asked, plaintively. "Or shall we be determined to keep it ever moving forward to higher plateaus, where freedom is more completely appreciated and more strenuously pursued? The choice is ours to make," but only if Americans kept their faith in God.[17]

The conservative intellectual Russell Kirk argued likewise. Napoleon had once declared that imagination ruled the world, Kirk pointed out in 1963, but he thought "it truer to say that faith rules the world." In America's "hour of crisis" with Communism "the key to real power, to the command of reality which the higher imagination gives, remains the fear of God." From his sacred exile in Switzerland, Francis Schaeffer made a similar point with even greater urgency: "And is it not true that in giving the millions to communism" through a lack of faith at home and an insipid foreign policy abroad, "we have had a part a part in shaping a 'razor' fit to shave us, if God does deal with us in justice using this instrument of judgment?" To Schaeffer, the answer was as clear as it was terrifying.[18]

As Billy Graham, Sherwood Wirt, Robert F. Williams, Francis Schaeffer, Carl McIntire, and many others attested, evangelical and fundamentalist views of world order were shaped profoundly by views of domestic order. Revolution at home was tied to revolution abroad, and it was the duty of all Christians to fight both. And as the leader of the free world and the leader of the Christian world, it was America's duty to lead the way. Naturally, then, Christian conservatives adopted fairly hard-line positions on foreign policy issues throughout the decade, just as they often did on civil rights, the sexual revolution, or the counterculture in the United States. For example, they were hostile to Castro's Cuban Revolution and furious with Kennedy's inability to defeat it at the Bay of Pigs in 1961 and in the Cuban missile crisis a year later. Not even Castro's vast improvement in Cuba's social services and the welfare of its people could compensate for what J. D. Douglas called the island's "thoroughgoing Marxism that accentuates the great gulf fixed between Christianity and atheism." Christian conservatives were also critical of American acquiescence in the building of the Berlin Wall, which prevented Soviet-American tensions from triggering a war but also condemned millions of East Germans to a life of perpetual Communism without hope of escape. Despite JFK's conventional arms buildup and LBJ's vast increase in defense spending during the Vietnam War, Christian conservatives criticized both presidents for not doing enough to ensure that America was equipped to defeat the world Communist revolution.[19]

Evangelicals and fundamentalists were particularly opposed to nuclear arms control, despite its general acceptance in an era when thermonuclear warfare threatened to destroy the world, because it meant negotiating with Communist leaders in the Soviet Union and China and thus accepting their concerns at face value and trusting them to abide by international treaties. In 1963, in the midst of Soviet-American negotiations about a ban on the testing of nuclear weapons, Carl McIntire quoted from the books of Psalms and Proverbs on the nature of evil and warned "the free world against accepting any test ban treaty with the Russians." "In an ideal world there would be no need for an ABM defense system," the editors of *Christianity Today* wrote six years later about the antiballistic missile program, which many liberals opposed because of its cost and its potential to stoke Cold War tensions. "But we do not live in an ideal world. The ABM program is senseless to those who trust Moscow and Peking and who are convinced that these two great powers pose no present or future danger. But to those who take the Sino-Soviet threat seriously, the ABM system represents an effective deterrent and a hope for survival in the event of nuclear attack." *Christianity Today* acknowledged that the issue was complex and fraught with difficulty, but it could see little benefit from negotiating with Communist dictators.[20]

Christian conservative faith in the benevolence of American values and the necessity of America's global leadership remained intact even after the trauma of Vietnam. While the war had caused many other Americans to doubt their nation's world mission, evangelicals and fundamentalists remained steadfast in their faith in America. Some evangelicals, for example Billy Graham, harbored doubts about Vietnam. But on the whole, Christian conservative support for the containment of North Vietnam (and presumably, by extension, the People's Republic of China) remained unwavering. Such support continued despite Johnson and Nixon's massive bombing campaigns of some of the poorest people on earth, which had led many liberal clergy into the antiwar movement. In fact, Christian conservatives supported an *increase* in bombing even after national polls indicated a solid majority of Americans as a whole wanted it halted. Overall, as studies of wartime opinion in Missouri and Kentucky concluded, there was a strong correlation between the conservatism of one's faith and the depth of one's support for the war.[21]

Evangelical Internationalism

When it came to US foreign policy, Christian conservatives were certainly among the most traditionalist of all Americans. In many ways, especially on the nature of Communism and the threat it posed to the United States, their worldview seemed unchanged from its earlier manifestations decades before.

But traditionalist, conservative anticommunism was only part of the story. While fundamentalists like Carl McIntire remained thoroughly traditionalist across the board, on virtually every foreign policy issue evangelicals adapted themselves to the emerging new world order in a variety of ways and moved easily in a newly globalizing world.

Evangelicals recognized the changing face of the world and deftly took advantage of it. They envisioned the world as an integrated whole and believed the United States had a large role to play in making it function justly and orderly. This reflected, ironically, something of a postmodern sensibility. Of course, evangelicals embraced only a certain kind of postmodernism: they did not accept the increasingly influential poststructuralist theories within literary criticism espoused by Michel Foucault or Jacques Derrida, and they most certainly did not accept the moral relativism and subjectivism devised by liberal Protestants such as Joseph Fletcher, whose 1966 book *Situation Ethics* provoked a firestorm of vitriol from Christian conservatives.[22] Rather, the ways in which evangelicals engaged with the wider world reflected a more general challenge to the assumptions of international life that had held since the establishment of the modern nation-states system in 1648. National sovereignty, indeed nationalism itself, was both a cause and a consequence of modernity, and the emergence of globalization in the twentieth century undermined these modernist foundations of the world system. Globalization represented a postmodern version of the world, in which states could no longer take the inviolability or sanctity of their national sovereignty for granted, and the sensibilities of their citizens became more cosmopolitan and less parochial. This new sensibility, most commonly known as internationalism, viewed the world through a normative lens that perceived common interests and causes across national boundaries.

Such an internationalism has usually been portrayed as essentially liberal in character.[23] But after an uneasy relationship with internationalism since its emergence in the late nineteenth century, conservative evangelicals in the postwar period began to fashion an internationalism of their own. Like their liberal opponents, they increasingly viewed the world as interconnected and interdependent. They also became less deferential to the strictures of national sovereignty, called for international solutions to international problems, perceived humanitarian disasters as integral to the entire human race even if they did not threaten US shores or affect the American people, and called for a global human rights regime based on the dignity of the individual rather than the promotion of group rights or collective social justice.

Even so, evangelicals' internationalist turn after 1945 marked something of a break with tradition. Stemming from their powerful antistatist beliefs, conservative Protestants had usually distrusted foreign policies that sought to bring about global progress. For the same reason, they were also wary of international organizations that diluted or infringed upon American sovereignty. Many evangelicals and fundamentalists opposed Wilsonianism and ratification of the Treaty of Versailles primarily because of their opposition to the League of Nations. Christian conservatives rallied enthusiastically to the nation's cause in both world wars, but they did so out of an instinctive patriotism and a belief that American security was at risk rather than from a desire to reform the world. After World War I, evangelicals and fundamentalists retreated into a hard-shelled isolationism, and much the same was expected after World War II.[24]

However, the emergence of the Cold War, and especially of an atheistic, militantly anti-Christian adversary in the Soviet Union, forestalled the return of evangelical isolationism. Across the country, in conservative regions that had formerly been isolationist hotbeds, Americans became staunch international-ists. Christian anticommunism, which reached a crescendo in the McCarthyite period and did not diminish after McCarthy's downfall in 1954, helped fuse a sense of morality with the imperatives of national security. New conservative faith-based NGOs—such as World Vision, founded by Youth for Christ worker Bob Pierce to care for refugees during the Korean War—epitomized the trans-formation of the evangelical worldview.[25] At the same time, as will be explained in more detail, conservative Protestants began to dominate foreign missions. By the 1960s, then, as the planet itself was undergoing revolutionary changes, evangelicals had adopted a thoroughly global consciousness that wedded a belief in America's global manifest destiny with a faith in the redemptive power of world Christianity. These were the main tenets of evangelical internationalism.

In this revolutionary, postmodern, newly globalizing world, Christian conservatives recognized the danger but also saw endless opportunities. "Our century of crisis now faces a final choice between world evangelism or world revolution," Carl Henry pointed out in 1969, at the height of the decade's social and geopolitical turbulence. "Never before have the people of God faced a more urgent task." The whole world was now a community and shared the same trials and triumphs together. "The world stands at the crossroads, at the brink of doom," Henry urged his readers. "The evangelical task force dare not fail the Lord who sends us and the world that needs us. Of all failures in church history, none would be more costly, none more ignominious, than this. Of all the opportunities for spiritual advance, few are more exciting and promising. Let us link minds and hearts and prayers and get on with our Lord's bidding."[26]

Henry could remain calm and confident while standing on the edge of anarchy because, in a world that needed salvation, evangelicals were ready to do the saving. They were already doing so through crusades at home and abroad, a method perfected by Billy Graham but practiced by many others. As Grady Wilson and others on the Graham traveling team commented after a 1963 tour of Asia, "The word brought back from the Far East Crusade was a heartening one: *opportunity!*" But missions would prove to be just as important. After playing second fiddle to the mainline mission boards for decades, conservatives surged to the forefront of the American overseas missionary enterprise. During modernism's heyday between the 1890s and World War I, modernist liberals had completely dominated the Protestant missionary movement. Conservatives were angered by the liberals' inattention to spreading the eternal gospel of Jesus Christ and promotion of an earthly gospel of social justice instead—after all, no fewer than four of the pamphlets in *The Fundamentals* focused on the spiritual backsliding of modernist mainline missions. This began to change in World War II, when conservative Christian missions began to rise in numbers, outreach, and enthusiasm. By the 1960s, their numbers in the missionary movement had totally eclipsed those from the more liberal mainline churches—a fact widely disseminated and celebrated by evangelicals, who saw mainline missions as apostate and ineffective—particularly in the most impoverished regions of the world, such as Africa and Southeast Asia. This put Christian conservatives at the forefront of development issues at a time when the Kennedy and Johnson administrations had placed development, especially modernization and poverty relief, at the heart of their foreign and domestic policies in initiatives such as the Alliance for Progress and Peace Corps abroad and the Great Society at home.[27]

This was crucial not only because evangelicals viewed development issues as vital but because only the true Christian gospel could actually save the world. Without Christ, evangelicals believed that secular development programs like the Peace Corps would wither and die from a lack of conviction and an absence of genuine morality. It was the missionaries' job to infuse development with morality, virtue, and faith. In a strange way, evangelicals held a grudging respect for the ability of Communist revolutionaries to capture the imaginations and mobilize the energies of people around the world. "Castro was able to seize the imagination of Cuban youth and brought about a revolution in his country," Billy Graham observed in 1964, so why couldn't America's committed Christians do likewise? Or as Harold Ockenga put it, "What the Communist party is in the vanguard of the world revolution, the evangelical movement must be in the world revival." After all, a dedicated Christian missionary had as much zeal as any Communist revolutionary but infinitely more morality, charity, and spirit. "Missionaries are the Church's unsung heroes in the cosmic struggle between God and Satan, good and evil," the editors of *Christianity Today* opined in 1967. "They are the expendables who make bruising contact with the enemy; they endure hardship as good soldiers of Christ. They suffer the loss of much that this world holds precious in order to establish beachheads on the borders of Beelzebub's kingdom and to push back the forces of unbelief."[28] Whether intentionally or not, *Christianity Today* portrayed evangelical missionaries as America's dynamic equivalent to Che Guevara or the Viet Cong. The difference, of course, was in the contrasting faiths they sought to spread.

Much as liberal modernist missionaries had in earlier eras, evangelical missionaries in the 1960s recognized that missionary activity had often been undertaken in partnership with Western imperialism. Thus they recognized that, in a decolonized world in which the global South was playing a major role, evangelicals had to ensure that their message remained distinct from that of the US government despite their similar emphases on anticommunism. Evangelical missionaries also recognized that they had to adapt to the world rather than expect the world to adapt to them. "Until the missionary learns how churches grow in the specific population to which God has sent him," instructed Fuller Theological Seminary's Donald McGavran, "he will grope in the dark." This would require a heightened sensitivity to the explosive race question, which was tied intimately to the process of decolonization and the rise of national liberation movements and commanded the world's attention just as the civil rights struggle absorbed America's. "Racial prejudice today is a liability we cannot afford," warned Ross Coggins, a Southern Baptist Convention mission leader, because it "perverts our Gospel, challenges our sincerity," and "dissipates our witness."[29] It was, in a word, unchristian, and it was fatal in a world in which nonwhite peoples everywhere were increasingly assertive about their autonomy and human rights.

In a break with past tradition, in which matters of charity and mercy were best left to the church rather than the state, Christian conservatives called for the US government to launch humanitarian interventions against disease and famine. Knowing that it would be difficult if not impossible to win over the State Department and other national security institutions in the Kennedy and Johnson years, when secular modernization theories prevailed, Christian conservatives set out to evangelize the armed forces. Military life was not always conducive to Christian life, they reasoned, so if the United States was to confront atheistic Communism around the world it was essential to reform the services' moral code. And aside from overseas missions, the military also offered what one young navy captain called "a once-in-a-lifetime opportunity to propagate the precious gospel of Jesus Christ . . . The openings are many." Converting the men and women of the military would also help bring about the moral reformation of American youth—and, through them, American society as a whole—mired as they were in the immorality and confusion of the 1960s counterculture, unpatriotic dissent, and sexual revolution. And of course a Christianized military would do a much better job of containing America's Communist enemies. With this in mind, beginning in the 1960s evangelicals undertook missionary work in the US military, encouraging their own to join and proselytizing to enlisted men and women to win converts. They were so successful in their efforts that, by the end of the Cold War, evangelicals formed one of the most influential groups within the US armed forces.[30]

However, not all Christian conservatives embraced evangelical internationalism. It is important to distinguish between evangelicals and fundamentalists and, on matters of foreign affairs, to acknowledge that fundamentalists did not share the evangelicals' promotion of human rights and overseas engagement. Evangelicals such as Billy Graham, Carl Henry, and Sherwood Wirt firmly rooted themselves within a tradition of American internationalism. They may have stood to the right of liberal internationalists, but in general they shared the internationalist beliefs that the world was interconnected and interdependent; that the United States had obligations to foreigners as well as to each other; that these obligations did not just amount to leadership of the global anticommunist crusade; that the world's social ills were as much America's problem as, say, Africa's; and that progress in international relations was desirable and reform of the world system was possible. Fundamentalists like Carl McIntire, however, subscribed to none of these beliefs, and if evangelicals were to the right of liberal internationalists then fundamentalists were to the far right of evangelicals. Though their numbers were much smaller than the liberals and evangelicals, the fundamentalist worldview represented a much older strain in the American diplomatic tradition: that of an isolationism and nativism that campaigned almost as strenuously against cosmopolitanism in US foreign policy as it did against Communism. Despite their shared anticommunism, the difference between evangelicals and fundamentalists was epitomized by their contrasting views of international organization. While Henry and Wirt could evenhandedly assess the United Nations as flawed but necessary in an anarchic and dangerous world, McIntire called for a total boycott of the UN, including even donations to UNICEF lest they fund the activities of a wicked and anti-Christian institution. This hard-shell attitude to the world had more in common with the isolationism of the Old Christian Right of the interwar years than the conservative internationalism being fashioned by evangelicals in the 1960s.[31]

The evangelical ability to blend the twin impulses of nationalism and universalism was a significant development, for it helped create a new worldview for conservatism in general. While liberalism had incubated internationalism, conservatism had long been the ideological home to realism and isolationism as well as nationalism. Indeed, Christian conservatives themselves had been among the staunchest isolationists, partly out of a distrust of the wider world and partly out of a strong pacifistic strain in American evangelicalism. But by supporting America's cause in the Cold War and, simultaneously, expressing a universalistic vision of humanity (expressed in support for the spread of human rights and humanitarian intervention), evangelicals formulated a new foreign policy doctrine for conservatives based equally on the promotion of American power *and*

American ideals. Such a blend of ideals and interests—and, more importantly, of internationalism and nationalism—had always been the monopoly of liberals, but under the sway of socially and culturally traditionalist evangelicals, conservatives could now also claim to have a worldview for the age of globalization. Its impact, felt especially but not exclusively in the exceptionalist *and* globalist foreign policies of Ronald Reagan and George W. Bush, has been prevalent ever since.

Notes

1. This secret to Graham's success is explained in William Martin, *A Prophet with Honor: The Billy Graham Story* (New York: William Morrow, 1991).
2. Billy Graham, "The Offense of the Cross," *Decision*, November 1961; Billy Graham, "Spiritual Inventory," *Decision*, January 1962.
3. Billy Graham, *World Aflame* (New York: Doubleday, 1965), 1–2, 254.
4. Ibid., xiii, 17.
5. See Peter Clecak, *America's Quest for the Ideal Self: Dissent and Fulfillment in the 60s and 70s* (New York: Oxford University Press, 1983); Robert Wuthnow, *After Heaven: Spirituality in America since the 1950s* (Berkeley: University of California Press, 1998); Doug Rossinow, *The Politics of Authenticity: Liberalism, Christianity, and the New Left in America* (New York: Columbia University Press, 1998), esp. 53–83; Jeremi Suri, *Power and Protest: Global Revolution and the Rise of Détente* (Cambridge, MA: Harvard University Press, 2003); and George Cotkin, *Existential America* (Baltimore: Johns Hopkins University Press, 2003), esp. 225–76.
6. Ronald Findlay and Kevin H. O'Rourke, *Power and Plenty: Trade, War, and the World Economy in the Second Millennium* (Princeton, NJ: Princeton University Press, 2007), 473–526, though it should be said that Findlay and O'Rourke do not date the full culmination of reglobalization until the 1980s. The postwar transformation is a general theme in countless histories of Cold War America, but see especially James T. Patterson, *Grand Expectations: The United States, 1945–1974* (New York: Oxford University Press, 1996); Maurice Isserman and Michael Kazin, *America Divided: The Civil War of the 1960s*, 2nd ed. (New York: Oxford University Press, 2004); and Richard M. Abrams, *America Transformed: Sixty Years of Revolutionary Change, 1941–2001* (New York: Cambridge University Press, 2006).
7. For some notable examples, see Robert Wuthnow, *The Restructuring of American Religion: Society and Faith since World War II* (Princeton, NJ: Princeton University Press, 1988), 145–64; William Martin, *With God on Our Side: The Rise of the Religious Right in America* (New York: Broadway Books, 1996), 74–99; Warren L. Vinz, *Pulpit Politics: Faces of American Protestant Nationalism in the Twentieth Century* (Albany: State University of New York Press, 1997), 146–48; Andrew J. Bacevich, *The New American Militarism: How Americans Are Seduced by War* (New York: Oxford University Press, 2005), 123–24, 126–28; and Frank Lambert, *Religion in American Politics: A Short History* (Princeton, NJ: Princeton University Press, 2008), 189–90.
8. On the Wilsonian period, see Markku Ruotsila, *The Origins of Christian Anti-Internationalism: Conservative Evangelicals and the League of Nations* (Washington, DC: Georgetown University Press, 2008). On the early Cold War, see M. J. Heale, *American Anticommunism: Combating the Enemy Within, 1830–1970* (Baltimore: Johns Hopkins University Press, 1990), 170–73; Patterson, *Grand Expectations,*

329; Stephen J. Whitfield, *The Culture of the Cold War*, 2nd ed. (Baltimore: Johns Hopkins University Press, 1996), 77–100; Seth Jacobs, *America's Miracle Man in Vietnam: Ngo Dinh Diem, Religion, Race, and U.S. Intervention in Southeast Asia, 1950–1957* (Durham, NC: Duke University Press, 2004), 60–87; Angela M. Lahr, *Millennial Dreams and Apocalyptic Nightmares: The Cold War Origins of Political Evangelicalism* (New York: Oxford University Press, 2007); Heather Hendershot, "God's Angriest Man: Carl McIntire, Cold War Fundamentalism, and Right-Wing Broadcasting," *American Quarterly* 59 (June 2007): 373–96; T. Jeremy Gunn, *Spiritual Weapons: The Cold War and the Forging of an American National Religion* (Westport, CT: Praeger, 2009); and Jonathan P. Herzog, *The Spiritual-Industrial Complex: America's Religious Battle against Communism in the Early Cold War* (New York: Oxford University Press, 2011).

9. Wade Clark Roof, *Spiritual Marketplace: Baby Boomers and the Remaking of American Religion* (Princeton, NJ: Princeton University Press, 1999), 74.

10. Bethany Moreton, *To Serve God and Wal-Mart: The Making of Christian Free Enterprise* (Cambridge, MA: Harvard University Press, 2009), 5, 9.

11. Michael R. Beschloss, *The Crisis Years: Kennedy and Khrushchev, 1960–1963* (New York: Edward Burlingame Books, 1991); M. J. Heale, *American Anticommunism: Combating the Enemy Within, 1830–1970* (Baltimore: Johns Hopkins University Press, 1990), 191–92; John F. Kennedy, Commencement Address at American University, Washington, DC, June 10, 1963, *Public Papers of the Presidents: John F. Kennedy, 1963* (Washington, DC: Government Printing Office, 1964), 459–64; Fredrik Logevall, *Choosing War: The Lost Chance for Peace and the Escalation of War in Vietnam* (Berkeley: University of California Press, 1999), 413. For the "crisis years" of the Cold War, see also Aleksandr Fursenko and Timothy Naftali, *One Hell of a Gamble: Khrushchev, Castro, and Kennedy, 1958–1964* (New York: W. W. Norton, 1997); and Lawrence Freedman, *Kennedy's Wars: Berlin, Cuba, Laos, and Vietnam* (New York: Oxford University Press, 2000).

12. Martin, *With God On Our Side*, 76; Christian Anti-Communism Crusade newsletter, February 1962, Gerald L. K. Smith papers, Box 56, Bentley Historical Library, University of Michigan, Ann Arbor; Fred Schwarz, *You Can Trust the Communists (...to Be Communists)* (Englewood Cliffs, NJ: Prentice-Hall, 1960). For the sales figure, see Martin E. Marty, *Modern American Religion*, vol. 3, *Under God, Indivisible, 1941–1960* (Chicago: University of Chicago Press, 1996), 371. On the differences in political outlook between evangelicals and fundamentalists in the 1960s, usually in terms of emphasis and stridency within an emerging "conservative" movement, see Daniel K. Williams, *God's Own Party: The Making of the Christian Right* (New York: Oxford University Press, 2010), 49–88.

13. Billy James Hargis, *Communist America—Must It Be?* (Tulsa: Christian Crusade, 1960), 18–19. Hargis reiterated these warnings a few years later with an even more explicit attack on American liberalism as a Communistic fifth column. See Billy James Hargis, *The Far Left* (Tulsa: Christian Crusade, 1964).

14. Daniel Bell, *The End of Ideology* (Glencoe, IL: Free Press, 1960), 103, 104; Roof, *Spiritual Marketplace*; Smith and Ockenga quoted, respectively, in Williams, *God's Own Party*, 70, 65.

15. L. Nelson Bell, "For Men to See," *Christianity Today*, November 23, 1959, 19 (hereafter *CT*). On the general conservative "anti-statist turn" in the 1960s, see

David Farber, "Democratic Subjects in the American Sixties: National Politics, Cultural Authenticity, and Community Interest," in *The Conservative Sixties*, ed. David Farber and Jeff Roche (New York: Peter Lang, 2003), 8–20. For analyses of Christian conservative fears of international organizations and foreign concentrations of power, see Michael Lienesch, *Redeeming America: Piety and Politics in the New Christian Right* (Chapel Hill: University of North Carolina Press, 1993), 160–66, 237–43; and Andrew Preston, "Universal Nationalism: Christian America's Response to the Years of Upheaval," in *The Shock of the Global: The 1970s in Perspective*, ed. Niall Ferguson, Charles S. Maier, Erez Manela, and Daniel J. Sargent (Cambridge, MA: Harvard University Press, 2010), 306–18.

16. Sherwood E. Wirt, "Who Owns the Government?" *CT*, June 18, 1964, 19.

17. Robert F. Williams, "Our Faith—Freedom's Foundation," in *Best Sermons*, vol. 10, 1966–1968: Protestant Edition, ed. G. Paul Butler (New York: Trident Press, 1968), 240–41. This was, of course, not the same Robert F. Williams of the contemporaneous Black Power movement. On *that* Robert F. Williams, a North Carolina-based radical civil rights activist, see Timothy B. Tyson, *Radio Free Dixie: Robert F. Williams and the Roots of Black Power* (Chapel Hill: University of North Carolina Press, 1999).

18. Russell Kirk, "The Struggle for Power with Communism," in *Christianity and World Revolution*, ed. Edwin H. Rian (New York: Harper & Row, 1963), 12; Francis A. Schaeffer, "Some Men Weep: The Tragic Loss of Our Era," *CT*, May 22, 1961, 5. Later in the decade, Schaeffer expanded on this idea, among others, in his first major book: *The God Who Is There: Speaking Historic Christianity into the Twentieth Century* (Downers Grove, IL: InterVarsity Press, 1968).

19. J. D. Douglas, "Cuba Revisited," *CT*, February 17, 1967, 54. See also Andrew Preston, *Sword of the Spirit, Shield of Faith: Religion in American War and Diplomacy* (New York: Knopf, 2012), 542–53. On all these issues, see Martin, *With God on Our Side*, 76–77; and Williams, *God's Own Party*, 57–58.

20. McIntire quoted in *International Council of Christian Churches 6th Plenary Congress, Geneva, Switzerland, August 5–11, 1965* (Amsterdam: International Council of Christian Churches, 1965), 57; "The A.B.M. Decision," *CT*, April 11, 1969, 28.

21. David W. Levy, *The Debate Over Vietnam*, 2nd ed. (Baltimore: Johns Hopkins University Press, 1995), 94–96; Donald Granberg and Keith E. Campbell, "Certain Aspects of Religiosity and Orientations toward the Vietnam War among Missouri Undergraduates," *Sociological Analysis* 34 (Spring 1973): 40–49; John Ernst and Yvonne Baldwin, "The Not So Silent Minority: Louisville's Antiwar Movement, 1960–1975," *Journal of Southern History* 73 (February 2007): 105–42. On Graham's doubts but ultimate support for the war, see Martin, *Prophet with Honor*, 343–48, 422–24.

22. Joseph Fletcher, *Situation Ethics: The New Morality* (Philadelphia: Westminster Press, 1966). For a typical reaction to Fletcher's theory of "situation ethics," see Sherwood Eliot Wirt, *The Social Conscience of the Evangelical* (New York: Harper & Row, 1968), 91–101, esp. 95; and Williams, *God's Own Party*, 84.

23. In the American context, see especially the works of Frank Ninkovich: *Modernity and Power: A History of the Domino Theory in the Twentieth Century* (Chicago: University of Chicago Press, 1994); *The Wilsonian Century: U.S. Foreign Policy since*

1900 (Chicago: University of Chicago Press, 1999); and *Global Dawn: The Cultural Foundation of American Internationalism, 1865–1890* (Cambridge, MA: Harvard University Press, 2009). More specifically, on liberal internationalism within American religion, see John S. Nurser, *For All Peoples and All Nations: The Ecumenical Church and Human Rights* (Washington, DC: Georgetown University Press, 2005); Andrew Preston, "Religion and World Order at the Dawn of the American Century," in *The US Public and American Foreign Policy*, ed. Andrew Johnstone and Helen Laville (New York: Routledge, 2010), 73–86; and Ian Tyrrell, *Reforming the World: The Creation of America's Moral Empire* (Princeton, NJ: Princeton University Press, 2010).

24. Ruotsila, *Origins of Christian Anti-Internationalism*; Preston, *Sword of the Spirit*, 244, 254–58, 287–90, 331–32, 370–72, 402–3.

25. Catherine McNicol Stock, "Nuclear Country: The Militarization of the U.S. Northern Plains, 1954–1975," in *Local Consequences of the Global Cold War*, ed. Jeffrey A. Engel (Stanford, CA: Stanford University Press, 2007), 238–72; Joel A. Carpenter, *Revive Us Again: The Reawakening of American Fundamentalism* (New York: Oxford University Press, 1997), 182.

26. Carl F. H. Henry, *Faith at the Frontiers* (Chicago: Moody Press, 1969), 47, 48, 50.

27. "Far East Echoes," *Decision*, June 1963, 7 (emphasis in original); Carpenter, *Revive Us Again*, 177–86; Paul B. Denlinger, "The Bleak Harvest of the Liberal Protestant World Thrust," *CT*, March 14, 1960, 3–5; and "Mission and Missionaries: 1969," *CT*, April 25, 1969, 20–21. The four pamphlets in *The Fundamentals* on modernist mainline missions were Arthur T. Pierson, "The Testimony of Foreign Missions to the Superintending Providence of God," vol. 6, 5–21; Charles A. Bowen, "A Message from Missions," vol. 9, 95–110; Robert F. Speer, "Foreign Missions or World-Wide Evangelism," vol. 12, 64–84; and Henry W. Frost, "What Missionary Motives Should Prevail?" vol. 12, 85–96; all in George M. Marsden, ed., *The Fundamentals: A Testimony to Truth* (New York: Garland, 1988). On missionary activity as a source of tension between liberals and conservatives before World War II, see George M. Marsden, *Fundamentalism and American Culture: The Shaping of Twentieth-Century Evangelicalism, 1870–1925* (New York: Oxford University Press, 1980), 167–68. Surprisingly, the surge in evangelical missions since the 1960s has not received nearly the amount of scholarly attention it deserves. But for the background and increase of missionaries in the postwar era, a gradual transformation that had its main turning point in the 1960s, see Richard V. Pierard, "Pax Americana and the Evangelical Missionary Alliance," in *Earthen Vessels: American Evangelicals and Foreign Missions, 1880–1980*, ed. Joel A. Carpenter and Wilbert R. Shenk (Grand Rapids, MI: Eerdmans, 1990), 155–79; John Micklethwait and Adrian Wooldridge, *God Is Back: How the Global Revival of Faith is Changing the World* (New York: Penguin Press, 2009), 232–34; and Philip E. Dow, "Romance in a Marriage of Convenience: The Missionary Factor in early Cold War US-Ethiopian Relations, 1941–1960," *Diplomatic History* 35 (November 2011): 859–95.

28. Billy Graham, "The Days of Youth," *Decision*, February 1964, 1; Harold John Ockenga, "Resurgent Evangelical Leadership," *CT*, October 10, 1969, 11; "Unfurl the Missionary Flag," *CT*, September 1, 1967, 25.

29. Donald McGavran, "Advanced Education for Missionaries," *CT*, September 26, 1969, 3; Ross Coggins, "Missions and Prejudice," *CT*, January 17, 1964, 3.

30. Preston, *Sword of the Spirit*, 501–19; John A. Knubel Jr., "With Christ at Annapolis," *Decision*, March 1962, 11. On the overall relationship between evangelicals and the U.S. military, a process that began in earnest in the 1960s, see Anne C. Loveland, *American Evangelicals and the U.S. Military, 1942–1993* (Baton Rouge: Louisiana State University Press, 1996); and Bacevich, *New American Militarism*, 138–42.

31. For Henry and Wirt, see, respectively, Carl F. H. Henry, "The Evangelical Task," *Decision*, October 1966, 3; and Wirt, *Social Conscience of the Evangelical*, 125. For McIntire, see "Witness," *Abilene Reporter-News*, February 9, 1969, 12-C. See also Preston, "Universal Nationalism." For the worldview of the Old Christian Right, see Leo P. Ribuffo, *The Old Christian Right: The Protestant Far Right from the Great Depression to the Cold War* (Philadelphia: Temple University Press, 1983).

PART 5

The Conservative Triumph in the GOP

CHAPTER 12

Spiro T. Agnew

The Decline of Moderates and Rise of the Republican Right

Justin P. Coffey

In the days following the assassination of Martin Luther King Jr. in April 1968, many of America's cities resembled war zones, as buildings were burned and looted and police exchanged gunfire with angry mobs. The riots became so violent and out of control that several state governors had no choice but to call on National Guard troops to restore order.

In Baltimore, Maryland, however, civil rights leaders were optimistic that a meeting with Governor Spiro T. Agnew, scheduled for April 11, would lead to a solution that would quell the violence without military intervention. In fact, the civil rights leaders fully expected Agnew, a Republican, to appeal for their help in ending the riots. Their confidence was based on his established record of progressive policies on issues such as education and the environment but especially in regards to matters of race. Prior to his election as governor, Agnew had served as county executive in Baltimore, where he created a Human Rights Commission to combat racial discrimination and convinced a reluctant city council to pass an equal rights bill. As Maryland's governor, he signed the state's first open housing law, which prohibited landlords from refusing to rent apartments to potential tenants simply because they were black. Agnew was equally progressive on other social issues. He liberalized Maryland's abortion laws, signed strict antipollution bills, and called for strict control of guns. He also advocated for guaranteeing the right of every high school graduate to attend college in Maryland, expansion of the public accommodation law, prison reform, and abolition of the death penalty.[1]

It was because of this record that the audience at the April 11 meeting was so shocked by what it heard. Instead of expressing solidarity and asking for help, Agnew blasted the civil rights leaders and told them they were responsible for most, if not all, of the violence in the state. Many in the audience were so enraged that that they walked out in protest. On the other hand, word of Agnew's speech caught the attention of influential conservative Republicans and would help propel Agnew to the vice presidency.[2]

That Agnew's political star rose on account of his denouncing some civil rights leaders was ironic, given the fact that when Agnew ran for governorship of Maryland in 1966, his opponent was a cynical opportunist who sought to ride to victory by playing the race card. In comparison, Agnew seemed like a sensible and enlightened figure, one who eschewed appeals to the voter's baser instincts. His calm and measured approach to the issues impressed voters, and he won a decisive victory. During the campaign, just as he had throughout his political career, Agnew presented himself as a moderate, more interested in getting things done than holding to a preordained ideology. At no point before 1966 could Agnew be described as a conservative, but six years later, that term would fit.

What changed for Agnew, and for many Americans, was a sense of alarm, if not disgust, at the rapid changes in American society in the middle and late 1960s. Race played a key role in turning many to the right. The riots that plagued the nation's urban areas from Watts to Detroit to Baltimore were unsettling to millions of Americans, and they, like Agnew, placed the blame not on any possible root causes of the disorders but squarely on the rioters. And since the cause of civil rights had been championed by the liberals, blame was also affixed to liberalism. What had seemed so promising in 1964, when Lyndon Johnson promised the country a Great Society, had just a few years later become a nightmare. The excesses of liberalism, the soaring crime rates, and all the social unrest of the 1960s helped contribute to the shift to the right, and Agnew, like millions of others, gravitated away from the center.

The political evolution of Agnew and of the Republican Party mirror each other closely enough that it's difficult to separate the two. Both had occupied the political center for several decades. For example, Wendell Wilkie, the party's 1940 presidential nominee, had been a Democrat until 1939, and Dwight Eisenhower made it clear even before he was elected that he had no intention of trying to repeal any New Deal programs, which conservative Republicans so hated. For his part, Agnew's thoughts in his "Political Philosophy," which he penned in 1964, included the belief that the Grand Old Party needed candidates who disavowed both the liberal and conservative labels. Yet by the late 1960s, both Agnew and the GOP had shifted dramatically to the right. To understand why, it is necessary to examine the people involved and the events that took place.

Governing from the Middle

Agnew's rise to the vice presidency most likely came as quite a surprise to those who knew him during the early part of his life. Born in Baltimore in 1918, the son of a Greek immigrant, Agnew was quiet and introverted and did little to suggest that he was either gifted or very intelligent. He certainly was never very ambitious. After graduating from high school in 1937, he enrolled at Johns Hopkins University, but he soon dropped out and spent the next several years bouncing from job to job until he was drafted into the Army, where he served as a military instructor before being dispatched to France in 1944. Discharged in 1945, Agnew, who was then married, clerked in a law office while working toward his law degree, and it was here, for the first time in his life, that he expressed a desire to enter politics.

How this change came about is not clear. Perhaps his experiences in the war had matured him, or perhaps he simply wanted more for his wife and children. Whatever the reason, he sought advice from one of his mentors, Lester Barrett, a partner in the firm where he clerked. Barrett laid the facts on the table. Agnew was a Democrat, although he said he registered with the party at the age of 21 only because "my father was a Democrat." In suburban Baltimore County, where Agnew lived, Democrats outnumbered Republicans 4–1, and there was no shortage of ambitious young Democrats yearning for a seat in office. If Agnew wanted to get anywhere in politics, Barrett told him, it would have be as a Republican. Practical if nothing else, Agnew took Barrett's advice and in 1946 registered as a Republican.[3] Opportunism, not conviction, made Agnew a Republican. Rather than jump into politics feet first, however, Agnew put his political aspirations on hold for the next decade as he built his law practice and raised his family, and it was during this time that Agnew learned the ideas and attitudes that catapulted him to the heights of American politics.

While growing up, Agnew had lived in the city of Baltimore, but after the war Agnew and his family moved to the suburbs, which meant he was on hand to witness the population explosion of the white, middle-class suburbs in the decades after World War II. In fact, the married father of four quickly became so entrenched in the culture—joining the Kiwanis, serving on the PTA, and developing a love of golf—that by the time he was ready to throw his hat into the political ring, he had acquired all the habits, tastes, and aspirations of a middle-aged, middle-class suburbanite. Agnew had come of age just as suburban voters became the demographic most coveted by the political parties, and throughout his decade-long political career he showed a remarkable propensity for being able to understand these target voters. He knew instinctively how suburban voters would react to the issues because he was one of them, and he was able to use this knowledge to his advantage in a way that others could not.

Because of this, Agnew can be viewed as one of the first—if not the first—national suburban politicians.

By the early 1960s, Agnew was determined to enter the political arena, and in 1962 he easily won the Republican nomination for Baltimore County Executive. However, securing the nomination was the easy part; he'd been unchallenged. The general election would be a different story. Not only did Democrats heavily outnumber Republicans, but no Republican had been elected county executive in the twentieth century. Agnew was undaunted, believing that the county's changing demographics would play in his favor. The massive influx of young, middle-class voters during the previous decade now composed a majority of the electorate, while the political machine that had run the county for decades was old, obsolete, and out of touch with the residents who wanted better services from their government. During the campaign, Agnew stressed that he was a new kind of candidate, one who would govern, he said, as an able and honest administrator. The message resonated with the voters, and Agnew sailed to victory.[4]

As county executive, Agnew largely kept his promises, governing from the middle and earning a reputation as an effective administrator. The former president of the PTA made education a top priority, and by the end of his four-year term he had reduced student-teacher ratios and established a county-funded kindergarten program. Agnew also demonstrated that he wasn't afraid to tackle hot-button issues. He created a Human Rights Commission to combat racial discrimination, successfully pushed an equal rights bill through a reluctant county council, and initiated programs to handle issues caused by rapid population growth. And before the environment became a hot political issue, Agnew fought against industrial pollution and urged businesses to be more environmentally responsible.[5]

A reflective figure and a more intelligent man than he is usually given credit for being, Agnew developed a political philosophy that defies easy characterization. In January 1964 he outlined his "Political Philosophy" through several strategic principles he believed were crucial for Republican success. The first of these principles emphasized that the "moderate course of progressive Republicanism represented by the successful Eisenhower administration" was the key to winning elections. Next, he believed that the GOP needed candidates who disavowed both the liberal and conservative labels. Taking a shot at Barry Goldwater, Agnew declared that a "candidate should reserve the right to satisfy his own conscience on each issue without predetermined sets of directives and presuppositions." Such candidates, he believed, stood the best chance of commanding widespread support from the voters. To bolster his argument that such an approach not only behooved the Republicans but was a tradition in the GOP, Agnew noted that Robert Taft, the late senator from Ohio and hero to the Right, supported federal aid to education and housing.[6]

Agnew's concern was largely focused on the conservative element of the party, and during his time as county executive and through his time as governor, he evinced a deep distrust, if not disdain, for right-wing ideology. In letters, speeches, and press releases he condemned conservatives as extremists who would destroy the GOP. It would be wrong, however, to conclude that Agnew's sole concern was with winning elections. His suspicion of the conservatives was genuine. Agnew approached issues (or liked to think he did) from a reasoned, not ideological, viewpoint. He placed an emphasis on practicality, not theory, and therefore the right wing's nostrums had no appeal to a man elected to oversee the building of roads, schools, and bridges.

Promoting Republican Centrism

As county executive, Agnew was a regional figure only and hardly a household name, but almost immediately after his election to the post, he began to devote a great deal of time trying to steer the national Republican ship toward the middle.

Agnew may have been confident that the middle of the road was the best course for Republicans, but not everyone shared this opinion. In the eyes of conservatives, this milquetoast attitude was the reason the party lost five straight presidential elections between 1932 and 1948 and the Democrats controlled both chambers of Congress until 1946. Richard Nixon's narrow loss in 1960 added ammunition to the conservative critique that nominating moderates served only to guarantee Democratic electoral victories.

When Nixon ran for the Republican nomination in 1960, he faced some opposition from both the Right and Left. New York Governor Nelson Rockefeller had toyed with the idea of running but dropped out when he realized he had no chance to win. Still, Rockefeller had just enough influence to force Nixon to appease him, and on July 22, 1960, the two met at Rockefeller's New York City apartment, where Nixon offered Rockefeller the vice presidential slot, which Rockefeller declined. During the session, however, the two hammered out a statement, which they later released to the press. The pact enraged conservatives, who dubbed it "The Munich of the Republican Party."[7] Just as Sudetenland did not belong to France, Italy, or Great Britain, conservatives felt that the Republican Party did not belong to Nixon and Rockefeller, and consequently they tried in vain to block Nixon's nomination by starting a draft Goldwater movement. The movement went nowhere, but conservatives were determined to wrest control of the party from the moderates, and they launched a grassroots campaign to make the GOP a right-wing party.

In 1963 conservatives once again pushed Goldwater as their choice for the party's nomination. In November of that year, John W. Steffey, chairman of the Maryland Draft Goldwater Committee, wrote Agnew to inform him of the movement's progress in the state. Although Steffey had not asked for Agnew's support, Agnew wrote back, thanking him for the update, but making it clear that he opposed Goldwater. "Although I have a high respect for Senator Goldwater," Agnew wrote, "I would much prefer a candidate of more moderate viewpoint."[8] The truth was that Agnew had little regard for Goldwater, although his feelings would change over time as his beliefs shifted more to the right. At the time, however, Agnew was in the liberal camp, and he believed he had just enough power and influence to steer the party in that direction. In fact, earlier that year, he had taken it upon himself to play kingmaker for the GOP by launching a movement to draft Senator Thomas H. Kuchel (R-CA) for the Republican nomination.

Kuchel had been appointed to the Senate by Governor Earl Warren in 1953 to fill the vacancy created when Nixon was elected vice president, and he was subsequently elected in 1956 and 1962. Agnew and Kuchel met in June 1963 in Kuchel's Washington office, where they discussed the state of the party, and Kuchel made such a strong impression that Agnew immediately concluded that he should be the GOP's candidate for the presidency in 1964. In a letter to Kuchel, written a few days after the meeting, Agnew expressed his support: "In short, and in a rather presumptuous manner since I do not have your permission, I am aligning myself with you and will look to you for guidance in the national situation."[9]

Later that year, on July 30, Agnew issued a press release announcing his support for Kuchel and attacking President John F. Kennedy, whom he viewed as vulnerable in the 1964 contest. The press release also criticized Republicans for the party's internal battle between liberals and conservatives, which Agnew called "an absurd ideological struggle—a blurred misunderstood, over-simplification, and a struggle which rivals in intensity the global contest of the East and West." It was hyperbole, of course, but Agnew was making a point, and he urged his party to drop their cold war and unite behind Kuchel, "the courageous enemy of all political extremists." Agnew even attempted to enlist former President Dwight Eisenhower's support for Kuchel but was unsuccessful.[10]

The problem for Agnew was that the courageous enemy of political extremists had no presidential ambitions. Two days after Agnew issued his statement, Kuchel wrote him a letter requesting, politely but firmly, that he halt the draft movement. A somewhat chagrined Agnew waited two weeks to write back, and although he accepted Kuchel's decision not to run in 1964, he seemed unable to believe that Kuchel had no intention to ever seek the presidency. "Obviously, we must now begin grooming you for 1968," Agnew wrote, adding, "Let's get started at your earliest convenience."[11]

When Kuchel expressed no interest in running, Agnew hoped to draft Pennsylvania governor William Scranton, but that bubble quickly burst and

Goldwater's nomination became inevitable. Agnew wrestled with the decision to back Goldwater, but on July 24, 1964, a week after the Republican convention, he finally did so. Agnew, as his notes demonstrate, continued to harbor serious reservations about the Arizona senator. In his public endorsement, Agnew made it clear that he strongly opposed "Au H2O's brinksmanship" on foreign policy issues and his "reluctance to support legislation to remove discrimination in public accommodations." Agnew also lamented Goldwater's famous clarion, "Extremism in the defense of liberty is no vice; moderation in the pursuit of justice is no virtue," because these phrases were subject to differing interpretations. But unlike many others in the party, who bolted after the performance at the Cow Palace, Agnew stuck with his decision, if only because he found the alternative even more distasteful. He decided he would "take chance with forthrightness [and] integrity even if mixed with naïvete [*sic*] stubbornness, oversimplification of Goldwater."[12]

The 1964 election, as much as any modern election, was a battle over opposing ideological viewpoints—liberal vs. conservative. Johnson promised a Great Society. Goldwater threatened to abolish just about every federal program that he could. In November the liberal view triumphed. Johnson won 61 percent of the popular vote, 486 electoral votes, and 44 of 50 states. Republicans fared no better in the Congressional races, as Democrats augmented their majorities in the House and the Senate and controlled both houses of Congress by wide majorities.[13]

Although it is doubtful that any Republican could have won in 1964, it is unlikely that another candidate, such as Rockefeller, would have suffered such an ignominious defeat. Goldwater's stridency and bellicosity scared voters, but it was his message, more than his shortcomings as a candidate, that led to his trouncing. The results of the election were clear: the American electorate had repudiated conservatism.

Goldwater's crushing defeat seemed to validate Agnew's critique, but conservatives did not see it that way. The right wing denounced the liberals for all but handing the election to Democrats by repudiating Goldwater and, by extension, their own party. The liberals shot back that the right-wingers had frightened voters into Democratic arms.

One of the results of the infighting was that the Republican Party was left without a clear leader. Despite his drubbing, Goldwater remained a hero to conservatives, but he had little if any support from the rest of the party, and he was out of office to boot. Some looked to Eisenhower for guidance, but he had never been popular with conservatives, and his status with them slipped even further because he had studiously avoided Goldwater during the election. Neither did conservatives have much use for Nixon, who in 1962 had faced a serious primary challenge from a more conservative candidate in his efforts to win the governorship of California. Nixon won the primary, but lost the general election, and his infamous "Last Press Conference" seemed to bring an end to his political career. Still, Nixon remained an important figure, and he earned plaudits from the Right by actively campaigning for Goldwater, who publicly told Nixon in early 1965, "Dick, I will never forget it."[14]

When the shock of the loss finally set in and the bickering abated, Republicans looked ahead to the midterm elections in 1966. By then, their prospects looked significantly brighter than they had two years earlier. In 1964, Vietnam had been barely a blip on the American public's radar screen, crime was not a pressing issue, and apart from the Deep South, there were few signs of a racial backlash. By 1966, troop levels in Vietnam had skyrocketed, violent crime rates had risen, and in Selma, Alabama, police had used clubs, whips, and tear gas to attack a group of marchers who were demanding black voting rights. Voter discontent with LBJ's Great Society programs and his handling of the Vietnam War helped to splinter the Democratic Party. Americans had become more anxious as their society's simmering fissures had begun to crack open. After the disaster of 1964, the GOP regrouped to pick up 47 seats in the house, six in the Senate, and eight governorships.[15]

Because the party out of power almost always gains seats in Congress, the long-term ramifications for the Republican Party were not clear at the time. Ronald Reagan's election as governor of California showed that he was a rising star and that conservatives were by no means a fringe group in American politics. *The New York Times* cited a survey estimating that conservatives had augmented their numbers in the House by about two dozen. Still, the party's more moderate elements were not finished by a long shot. In the wake of the elections, Senator Hugh Scott of Pennsylvania said the results gave "new strength to the centrist tradition of our party."[16]

Much of the historical literature about these times has focused on Reagan and his election as governor of California.[17] This is understandable, especially given his future political career, but the argument that his victory constituted a triumph of Republican conservatism and the moment when the country turned right obscures the reality of the time. If anything, 1966 was the year of the moderates. Several weeks prior to the election, *The New York Times* published a story about the moderate and liberal Republicans running for offices that year, analyzing not only the candidates' chances to win their own races but also the larger struggle to take back the GOP from the conservatives. If the moderates won, the article stated, "the party bloc that fought Barry Goldwater two years ago could be measurably strengthened in its plans to dominate the national convention in 1968."[18] The article mentioned some of the governors seeking reelection, including George Romney of Michigan, John Volpe of Massachusetts, and Rockefeller in New York, as well as a host of senatorial candidates such as Charles Percy in Illinois, Edward Brooke in Massachusetts, and Mark Hatfield in Oregon. These candidates, as well as others, would go on to win in November.

Agnew's name did not appear in the article, but as much any candidate, he was seeking to keep the party in the middle, and his brand of Republicanism was evident throughout the 1966 Maryland gubernatorial campaign. His opponent, Democrat George P. Mahoney, was a reactionary whose entire campaign was based on his opposition to an open housing law in Maryland, and Agnew blasted him for appealing to voters' basest instincts. He then added depth to his own candidacy by calling for Maryland to modernize, for the state legislature to appropriate more funds for education, and for other more progressive stances.[19]

Maryland voters responded to Agnew's centrism, handing him a resounding victory in an election with a record turnout (64.7 percent of eligible voters cast ballots). Agnew garnered 455,318 votes to Mahoney's 373,539, while independent Hyman Pressman received 90,899. Agnew won 49 percent, Mahoney 41 percent, and Pressman 9 percent.[20] Agnew's victory, along with that of other moderates, offers evidence that contravenes conventional historical wisdom. Reagan may have garnered headlines, but it is striking to note that almost no other conservative emerged at the national level, and when the 1968 presidential primary season began, it was the more moderate and liberal candidates who garnered all the attention.

The Election of 1968

Nixon, Romney, and Rockefeller were the Republican frontrunners in 1968. All three were centrists, with many on the right disliking, if not detesting, Nixon and Rockefeller. Yet conservatives had nowhere else to turn. Reagan was their hero, but he had been elected to public office for the first time just two years earlier, so he never emerged as a serious candidate. In any event, like any political party, the Republicans wanted to win, and with the memory of the Goldwater debacle still fresh, most realized that going with another conservative candidate would lead to another defeat.[21]

Back in Maryland, Agnew now had a larger platform with which he could exercise more influence over the party, and he set his sights on drafting Rockefeller as the party's candidate. Though Nelson was never the liberal he was made out to be, he was certainly no conservative, and his pragmatism appealed to Agnew, who believed the New York governor stood the best chance of defeating Johnson in 1968. Unfortunately for Agnew, he had once again chosen a candidate who did not seem interested in running. Agnew refused to give up and remained hopeful that the "tremendous amount of public pressure that is being put on the Governor to revise his position" would help change Rockefeller's mind.[22]

Agnew got the break he was hoping for in early March 1968. By this time, George Romney had dropped out of the race, which meant Nixon was poised to sail to victory. The thought of Nixon as their party's nominee energized Rockefeller's supporters, who hated Nixon more than Goldwater, even though Nixon was himself a moderate who disdained the party's right wing. The patrician Rockefeller was too kind a man to hate Nixon, but he certainly looked down on him, and when Romney dropped out, Rockefeller stepped in—sort of. Rockefeller released a poll that showed that he would easily defeat Johnson in November, and he announced, "I am not going to create dissension within the Republican Party by contending for the nomination but I am ready and willing to serve the American people if called."[23]

Rockefeller's switch heartened Agnew, who quickly established a "National Rockefeller '68 Committee" headquartered in Annapolis, with himself serving as temporary chair. The two met in Washington DC, on March 16. In his memoirs, *Go Quietly . . . or Else*, Agnew wrote that he had inside information: "Many admirers expected Rockefeller to announce his candidacy for the presidency when he called a New York press conference on March 21, 1968. I was even more confident that he would announce because he had personally assured me that he had made up his mind to run. We had talked when I introduced him at the *Ahepa* [a Greek lodge] convention in Washington only a few days before."[24]

Agnew's tireless work looked to be rewarded on the day of Rockefeller's scheduled press conference, but nothing is ever simple in American politics and certainly was not in that volatile year. By "pure happenstance" Agnew would be hosting his regularly scheduled news conference in Annapolis, so an aide suggested that a television set be brought into the room so the assembled could watch the announcement and Agnew could presumably bask in the limelight. So, at two o'clock p.m., Agnew, his staff, and the press corps watched as Rockefeller strode to the platform in the Hilton Hotel and began reading a prepared statement. Only it wasn't the speech Agnew expected. "I have decided today," Rockefeller said, "to reiterate unequivocally that I am not a candidate campaigning, directly or indirectly, for the Presidency of the United States."[25]

Agnew never forgave Rockefeller for the perceived slight. Years later he confessed to feeling "furious and humiliated," because Rockefeller "had not even shown me the courtesy of informing me of his intentions in advance. He finally telephoned me hours afterward but only when word had gone out on the wires that I was as mad as a hornet."[26] Agnew would shortly turn his attention to Nixon, who was now all but assured of winning the nomination.

By April, Nixon began to float Agnew's name as a potential running mate, but the story that Agnew was chosen as a fop to conservatives, especially Southern conservatives, is inaccurate, even if it is often told. The 1964 presidential contest was a catastrophe for the Republican Party in all but one regard—for the first time since Reconstruction, the GOP won South Carolina, Georgia, Mississippi, Alabama, and Louisiana. Even though those states would not be in play in 1968—George Wallace was all but certain to carry them, a fact Nixon conceded—they were vitally important to Nixon as he sought to sew up his nomination and solidify control of the party. The rules of the party dictated that states that went Republican four years earlier would have larger delegations, which meant the five Deep Southern states would have a disproportionate share of votes at the convention. Since none of those states had presidential primaries, their delegates went to the convention uncommitted to any candidate, and therefore many delegates took their cue from South Carolina's Strom Thurmond, an arch segregationist and fierce anticommunist who exerted tremendous influence over much of the Republican South, even though he had been a Democrat until four years earlier. Nixon assiduously courted Thurmond, meeting with the South Carolinian several times in early 1968. In June they rendezvoused in Georgia, where, according to legend, Thurmond wrestled a concession out of Nixon. The story goes that Nixon agreed to appoint a vice presidential nominee acceptable to Thurmond, but according to Thurmond, all he asked of Nixon was that he "never go soft on those darn communists."[27] Further, given Agnew's progressive record on issues of race, Thurmond had no reason to support him.

Agnew was chosen because of his moderate political views. Nixon was suspicious of ideologues and therefore sought out men like himself. Agnew was still in the middle of the political spectrum. His ideological metamorphosis had already begun, but it was not yet complete. As Nixon later wrote, "He [Agnew] had a good record as a moderate, progressive, effective governor." As "a political moderate," Agnew fit what Nixon was looking for.[28] The fact that Nixon and Agnew were the Republican Party's standard bearers in 1968 is clear evidence that the Right had not captured the GOP. Nevertheless, the political winds were shifting, a fact that could not escape Nixon, the most intuitive politician of his era.

The GOP had begun to make inroads in the South in 1964, as disaffected white Southerners abandoned the Democratic Party, and when riots broke out in Northern cities, pollsters noticed a change in attitude among white voters about the pace and goals of the civil rights movement. This "white backlash" undoubtedly helped the Republican Party over time, but the benefits for the Republicans were not immediately evident. Prior to 1968, both Nixon and Agnew had solid records on civil rights issues; neither had ever played the race card nor made any overt appeals to white anxiety. But both Nixon and Agnew knew that voters, particularly middle-class white voters, cared more about crime than any other issue, and crime was inextricably linked with race. It was the intersection of these two factors that would push Agnew onto the national stage and play a key role in the transformation of the Republican Party and the country.

Moving to the Right

In the wake of the Baltimore riots, Agnew had something of an epiphany. The speech in which he denounced civil rights leaders and blamed them for the violence caught the attention of some members of Nixon's campaign team. John Mitchell, Nixon's law partner and campaign chair, began pushing Agnew's name for vice president. Nixon was receptive, and after the two met, he concluded that Agnew "had a great deal of inner strength" and "appeared to have presence, poise, and dignity." Agnew's position on civil rights dovetailed with his own: "He took a forward-looking stance on civil rights, but he had firmly opposed those who had resorted to violence in promoting their cause." In 1968 at least, Nixon and Agnew were ideologically "simpatico."[29]

Once the two were elected, however, they never developed a working relationship. Nixon surrounded himself with a small group of aides, a circle that Agnew was never able to penetrate. The distance between them was both personal—Nixon was contemptuous of Agnew—and ideological. Nixon governed as a centrist, if not a liberal, while Agnew's politics took a decided turn to the right. He opposed many of the administration's domestic policies and even more so Nixon's foreign policy initiatives, particularly détente with the Soviet Union and the opening of relations with China.

About the only time Nixon and Agnew truly worked in concert was during the contentious 1970 off-year elections. During that campaign the Nixon team trotted out themes that would become a staple of American politics for the next generation. Ignoring economic issues, Nixon and his campaign team played up social issues, such as crime, drugs, and race. By painting liberal Democrats as soft on crime, socially permissive, and captive to minorities, Nixon hoped to pick off disaffected moderate and conservative Democrats and create a new political majority. Nixon saw the possibility of breaking the old Franklin Roosevelt coalition, and he believed that Agnew could help with the process. Discussing the upcoming campaign with speechwriter William Safire, Nixon proclaimed, "There's a realignment going on, [and] Agnew can be a realigner."[30]

Nixon's primary concern was getting reelected in 1972 rather than changing the political landscape of the country, and his embrace of a muscular conservative tone was more out of expediency and cynicism than principle. Agnew, on the other hand, was interested not only in realigning the country but also in moving the country to the right. A number of factors explain Agnew's political gravitation. Like millions of Americans, he was repulsed by the rapid transformation of American society in the late 1960s. The youth revolt, antiwar protests, sexual revolution, and the upsurge in crime and violence alienated many Americans, including Agnew, who was as square and conventional as they come. What he found particularly galling was the urban chaos and the liberal reaction to the disorder. In his memoirs, Agnew argued that even during his governorship he took a tough law-and-order stance, especially against rioting. His reactions to the Baltimore riot and to the Cambridge riot in 1967, which Agnew claimed was "engineered by H. Rap Brown," were consistent: "I have never been liberal when it comes to condoning violence and the intentional destruction of property." Agnew's tough line resonated with millions of Americans who were frightened by the urban discord. Many of them were white, middle- or working-class voters who had traditionally been part of the Democratic Party. Nixon and Agnew tailored their message to these voters, and results paid off in 1972, as the Nixon-Agnew ticket became the first Republican presidential candidacy to capture a majority of blue-collar, Catholic, and union votes.[31]

By 1972 Agnew had become a darling of the right wing of the Republican Party, and he hoped to use his status as a stepping stone to the presidency. In November 1972 Nixon and Agnew won an overwhelming victory, taking 49 states and winning 521 electoral votes. Agnew hoped he could count on the right wing to help him win the Republican presidential nomination in 1976. He wrote in his memoirs that after the 1972 election "even my detractors agreed that I was the front-runner for the Republican presidential nomination. The early polls showed me way ahead of all other potential rivals." Influential conservatives such as Barry Goldwater had publicly backed Agnew when Nixon had thought of dumping him in 1972, and Agnew had good reason to believe the same people would rally around his candidacy four years later. During his four years as vice president, Agnew appealed to the Right in a way that Nixon never could. His hawkish stance on Vietnam resonated with conservatives who wanted victory in Vietnam. Agnew's barely hidden contempt of détente further aligned with the Goldwaters and Buckleys of the GOP. On the important social issues of the day, Agnew was in tune with the right wing. They applauded his attacks on the antiwar protestors and the hippies, his call for law and order, and his support of traditional values. On matters of race, Agnew was squarely on the right. As the Republican Party was becoming more white and more Southern, it did not go unnoticed that Agnew refused to take any role in the Nixon administration's school desegregation policies. The fact that Agnew had almost no substantive role in many other parts of the Nixon agenda, from wage and price controls to the creation of the Environmental Protection Agency, would not hurt him with the base of the GOP that detested Nixon's moderately liberal domestic policies. Conservatives were so enthralled by Agnew that in 1971 the Young Americans for Freedom (YAF) endorsed him for the presidency in 1972.[32]

Agnew's top political aide, David Keene, a former national chair of YAF, described him as having undergone a "philosophical reinvention" while in office. Keene observed as Agnew studied issues, consulted with intellectuals from think tanks such as the Manhattan Institute, held seminars with his staff, and discussed public policy with a range of individuals from Irving Kristol to Sidney Hook. His move right was more principled than political. Unlike Nixon, who approached issues from a purely pragmatic viewpoint, Agnew was a true believer, and by 1972 he had become an ideological conservative who hoped to harness the power of the conservatives for a White House bid.

Both Agnew's dreams of succeeding Nixon to the presidency and his political career came to a crashing halt in 1973 when Agnew was prosecuted for extortion. For more than a decade, Agnew had been accepting kickbacks from contractors in his home state. Extortion had a long and storied history in Maryland, and Agnew was but one of many figures in the state to face criminal prosecution during the 1970s and beyond. Still, the allegations against Agnew were somewhat surprising, given his reputation as a straight shooter and also because, unlike almost all other top officials in the Nixon White House, Agnew had been untouched by the Watergate scandal. Further, Agnew had adopted, as had Nixon and much of the Republican Party, a tough line against crime. Nixon's "law-and-order" theme had played well with audiences, and Agnew had taken part in blasting the lawlessness and permissiveness that supposedly rent so much of America.

When accusations of wrongdoing first surfaced in August 1973, Agnew indignantly denied all the charges against him, calling them "dammed [sic] lies." Over the next two months Agnew continued to protest his innocence, but privately his attorneys began negotiating with the Justice Department to cut a deal. For months, the Baltimore US attorneys' office had been investigating graft in Maryland, and they had uncovered a nest of corruption. Public officials had demanded from contractors kickbacks on public works, and a number of those contractors pointed fingers at Agnew. The prosecutors found evidence that Agnew had been taking money illicitly since his time as Baltimore county executive and continuing on through the vice presidency, and they were prepared to indict Agnew and bring him to trial. Facing a possible prison term, Agnew pleaded guilty to tax evasion and resigned the vice presidency on October 10, 1973. His fall sparked a wave of emotions, from anger to sadness to betrayal. Agnew's conservative supporters were sorry to see him go, and they praised his legacy. Many conservatives were far kinder to Agnew when he fell than they were to Nixon when he resigned the following year, a measure of just how respected and admired Agnew was among the Right. *National Review*, the leading conservative journal in the country, lauded Agnew as a "man of intellectual courage and political candor," wished him well, and noted that conservatives "in the future as in the past will regard him as a friend."

Barry Goldwater would later write that he liked Agnew and had suspicions as to whether members of the Nixon administration conspired to drive him out of office. Pat Buchanan, who helped craft some of Agnew's speeches, looked back some 25 years later at Agnew and recalled him fondly, calling him a "prophet without honor in his own country."[33]

Agnew's disgrace has come to overshadow all else about his public life. Still, there was much more to Spiro Agnew than his legal foibles. Agnew's national career, while abbreviated, is important, because his political trajectory followed the same direction as the Republican Party. He was a moderate during much of the 1960s. His ideological metamorphosis did not occur suddenly but came as a result of what he perceived to be the excesses of liberalism. His career and shift to the right tell us much of the nature of the Republican Party and American politics during the 1960s and early 1970s. The moderation that had characterized the GOP for most of the 1960s went by the wayside as the party, much of the country, and Agnew himself turned right.

Notes

1. For Agnew's statement on abortion, see Governor's Comments folder, box 1, series 2, Spiro T. Agnew Papers, University of Maryland, College Park (hereafter Agnew Papers). For his environmental record, see "Governor Agnew's Comments on signing Water Pollution Control Legislation," H.B. 902–903, May 7, 1968, Governor's Comments folder; "Major Legislation Developed and Enacted under the Agnew Administration," July 1968, Agnew Accomplishments folder, series 2, Agnew Papers. On abolishing capital punishment, see *Addresses and State Papers of Spiro T. Agnew, Governor of Maryland, 1967–1969* (Annapolis: State of Maryland, 1975), 624–35.

2. Max Johnson, "Agnew Insults Leaders," *Baltimore Afro American*, April 13, 1968, 1. In the weeks following Agnew's address his office was flooded with letters from around the country expressing their support. One man who wrote to Agnew was Jesse Helms, a television commentator in North Carolina and later a United States senator (Correspondence folder, box 1, MSA-SC 1041–1713, Spiro T. Agnew Papers, Maryland State Archives, Annapolis).

3. Spiro T. Agnew, Letter to the Editor, *Baltimore Sun*, May 30, 1976, D20; Jules Witcover, *White Knight: The Rise of Spiro Agnew* (New York: Random House, 1972), 44.

4. Agnew defeated his opponent Michael Birmingham by a margin of 18,000 votes. Theo Lippman Jr., *Spiro Agnew's America: The Vice President and the Politics of Suburbia* (New York: W. W. Norton, 1972), 50.

5. Jim G. Lucas, *Agnew: Profile in Conflict* (New York: Award Book, 1970), 35–36; Alan L. Dessoff and Bart Barnes, "Spiro T. Agnew: 'Suburban Man,' Colt Fan, Unruffled Politician," *Washington Post*, October 17, 1966.

6. "Political Philosophy," January 6, 1964, public issues folder, box 1, series 1, Agnew Papers. Agnew noted Taft's position in a letter he wrote to Senator Thomas Kuchel (Agnew to Kuchel, June 18, 1963, public issues folder, box 1, series 1, Agnew

Papers). On Agnew's intellectual acuity, see Henry Kissinger, *Years of Upheaval* (Boston: Little, Brown and Company, 1982), 92. Kissinger described Agnew as "highly intelligent and much subtler than his public image."

7. Richard Nixon, *RN: The Memoirs of Richard Nixon* (New York: Simon and Schuster, 1978), 215; Laura Jane Gifford, *The Center Cannot Hold: The 1960 Presidential Election and the Rise of Modern Conservatism* (DeKalb: Northern Illinois University Press, 2009), 52–53.

8. John W. Steffey to Agnew, November 6, 1963, and Agnew to Steffey, November 12, 1963, series 1, Agnew Papers.

9. Agnew to Thomas Kuchel, June 18, 1963, public issues folder, box 1, series 1, Agnew Papers.

10. Statement by Spiro T. Agnew, July 30, 1963, public issues folder, Agnew Papers; Agnew to Dwight D. Eisenhower, July 25, 1963, correspondence folder, box 1, series 1, Agnew Papers.

11. Kuchel to Agnew, August 1, 1963, and Agnew to Kuchel, August 17, 1963, public issues folder, Agnew Papers.

12. "Goldwater Endorsement—Reservations," July 24, 1964, public issues folder, box 1, series 1, Agnew Papers.

13. Robert Dallek, *Flawed Giant: Lyndon Johnson and His Times, 1961–1973* (New York: Oxford University Press, 1998), 183–84.

14. Stephen E. Ambrose, *Nixon: The Triumph of a Politician, 1962–1972* (New York: Simon and Schuster, 1989), 60.

15. Warren Weaver Jr., "G.O.P. Finds '68 Election Outlook Brighter as It Counts Election Successes," *The New York Times*, November 10, 1966, 1.

16. Ibid., 28; Stephen Hess and David S. Broder, *The Republican Establishment: The Present and the Future of the G.O.P.* (New York: Harper and Row, 1967), 5.

17. See for example, Matthew Dallek, *The Right Moment: Ronald Reagan's First Victory and the Decisive Turning Point in American Politics* (New York: Oxford University Press, 2000).

18. Warren Weaver Jr., "Election to Test Liberals in G.O.P.," *The New York Times*, October 15, 1966, 14.

19. "Agnew Issues Book," Campaign Issues folder, box 3, series 2, Agnew Papers.

20. Charles Whiteford, "Agnew Beats Mahoney for Governor by over 80,000 as Pressman Trails," *Baltimore Sun*, November 9, 1966, A1.

21. Rick Perlstein, *Before the Storm: Barry Goldwater and the Unmaking of the American Consensus* (New York: Hill and Wang, 2001), 515.

22. *Addresses and State Papers of Spiro T. Agnew, Governor of Maryland, 1967–1969* (Annapolis: State of Maryland, 1975), 590–91.

23. Michael Kramer and Sam Roberts, *I Never Wanted to Be Vice President of Anything: An Investigative Biography of Nelson Rockefeller* (New York: Basic Books, 1976), 328.

24. Spiro T. Agnew, *Go Quietly . . . Or Else* (New York: William Morrow, 1980), 61.

25. Ibid.

26. Ibid., 61–62.

27. The quote was related to me by Jonathan Aitken, a Nixon biographer who spoke with Nixon and Thurmond about this conversation (Author interview with Jonathan Aitken, February 4, 2003, London).

28. Nixon, *RN*, 312. Shortly after the Republican National Convention, Agnew sat down for an interview with *The New York Times*. Agnew complained that media accounts were making him "appear that I'm a little to the right of King Lear" (Douglas E. Kneeland, "Agnew Upset by Criticism," *The New York Times*, August 10, 1968, 1).

29. Nixon, *RN*, 312. Nixon said he was looking for a running mate who was ideologically "simpatico" and seemingly found one in Agnew ("The Unlikely No. 2," *Time*, August 16, 1968, 19).

30. William Safire, *Before the Fall: An Inside View of the Pre-Watergate White House* (New York: Belmont Tower Books, 1975), 321.

31. Agnew, *Go Quietly*, 65; John Micklethwait and Adrian Wooldridge, *The Right Nation: Conservative Power in America* (New York: Penguin Books, 2004), 69. For a different perspective on Nixon's goals, see Robert Mason, "Political Realignment," in *A Companion to Richard M. Nixon*, ed. Melvin Small (Chichester, UK: Wiley-Blackwell, 2011), 252–69. Mason argues, "The goal of realignment implied more than a Nixon victory in 1972," it involved creating "an enduring Republican majority."

32. Agnew, *Go Quietly*, 38; Jules Witcover, *Very Strange Bedfellows: The Short and Unhappy Marriage of Richard Nixon and Spiro Agnew* (New York: Public Affairs, 2007), 221.

33. "Agnew Resigns," *National Review*, October 26, 1973, 1156; Barry M. Goldwater, *With No Apologies: The Personal and Political Memoirs of United States Senator Barry M. Goldwater* (New York: Morrow, 1979), 263–65; Patrick J. Buchanan, "Spiro Agnew: Prophet without Honor," May 29, 1998, http://buchanan.org/blog/pjb-spiro-agnew-prophet-without-honor-307. The best book on Agnew's fall, which came out just a year after the scandal but remains the authoritative work, is Jules Witcover and Richard Cohen, *A Heartbeat Away: The Investigation and Resignation of Vice President Spiro T. Agnew* (New York: Viking Press, 1974).

EPILOGUE

Looking Back on the Decade in which Conservatism "Grew Up"

Laura Jane Gifford and Daniel K. Williams

In 1960 members of the fledgling and beleaguered conservative movement watched as their lone national spokesperson—Barry Goldwater—advised them to swallow their doubts and support yet another Republican moderate for the nation's presidency. "We had our chance," he said. "Let's grow up, conservatives! If we want to take this party back—as I think we can someday—let's get to work!"[1]

By the end of the decade, it appeared that the "work" Goldwater had advised conservatives to do was starting to pay off. Ronald Reagan, who had emerged as an even more charismatic and likeable national conservative spokesperson than Goldwater had been, was now chief executive of the country's largest state. After eight years of liberal Democratic presidential administrations, Republicans controlled the White House and were poised to begin turning the country away from its experiment in Great Society liberalism. While many conservatives had grave doubts about Richard Nixon's commitment to their cause, they could at least take heart that their actions had forced Vice President Spiro Agnew to tack to the right on cultural issues and that Nixon—the quintessential middle-of-the-road Republican politician—had felt the need to hire archconservative Pat Buchanan as a White House speechwriter in order to win support from the Right. Perhaps more importantly, however, conservatives had consolidated their movement's understanding of some key questions that would inform their movement's ideology for the remainder of the twentieth century and beyond.

As the essays in this volume have demonstrated, the events of the 1960s led conservatives to adopt a coherent, uniform racial ideology that would shape the movement's view of civil rights issues and position it to win a national majority. At the beginning of the decade, conservatives were divided on the issue of race, and Southern segregationists were still pushing for an overtly racist ideology that had limited traction outside of their region. By the end of the 1960s, Southern segregationists had united with conservatives in all regions of the nation to champion a "color-blind" defense of property rights that had widespread appeal among whites in both the North and the South. This new racial ideology enabled Richard Nixon and then, a decade later, Ronald Reagan to win the presidency—a feat that would have been much more difficult had conservatives not formulated a unified position on race during the 1960s.

The 1960s also gave rise to a new view of church-state relations among conservatives that was both more ecumenical and more political than the theologies to which conservatives had subscribed in the 1950s. In 1960 many evangelical Protestants who enlisted in Richard Nixon's campaign fiercely attacked Catholics as enemies of American freedom, while nearly four out of five Catholic voters lined up behind Democratic presidential candidate John F. Kennedy. Orthodox Jews, like their Reform counterparts, generally considered both evangelicals and Catholics a threat, and they were therefore strong proponents of church-state separation. All of that changed during the 1960s. Conservative Catholics, evangelical Protestants, and Orthodox Jews forged new alliances with each other during the decade, and they reached a common consensus that the liberal state was a threat to moral order, as was liberals' view of church-state separation. This new ecumenical consensus among religious conservatives facilitated the development of a new Religious Right that would emerge as a public force a decade later.

The 1960s was the decade in which conservatives acquired an internationalist vision and established their credentials as leaders in the fight against global Communism. In the 1940s the nation's most well-known conservative, Robert Taft, was also one of the country's leading isolationists, and as late as 1960 it was still unclear whether conservatives had completely distanced themselves from their movement's isolationist past. Republican President Dwight Eisenhower, while by no means an isolationist, did caution the public about the dangers of excessive military spending and the growing "military-industrial complex." Democratic liberals, meanwhile, found a spokesperson for a hawkish military buildup in John F. Kennedy, who criticized the Republicans in 1960 for allowing a "missile gap" to develop between the United States and the Soviet Union. While the conservative movement was strongly opposed to Communism, the movement was also plagued by divisions on foreign policy. Libertarians in the movement were uneasy about foreign wars, while many anticommunist populists were suspicious of agreeing to any international alliances in the fight against Communism.

Over the course of the 1960s, conservatives consolidated their movement around a foreign policy position that combined continuing, strident anticommunism with an emphatically internationalist outlook. As many liberals began distancing themselves from the hawkish pronouncements that they had once embraced, conservatives took up the mantle of leadership in the fight against international Communism, and to do that, they adopted a vision of an interconnected global world in which they had to make alliances with likeminded anticommunists in other countries. The internationalist vision of American conservatism, which became a key component of the movement's legacy in the presidential administrations of Ronald Reagan and George W. Bush, was a product of transformations that the movement experienced in the 1960s.

While most conservatives had always championed the free market, the 1960s was the decade in which they found a way to make such pronouncements both intellectually respectable and increasingly influential. At the beginning of the 1960s, most college-educated Americans who considered themselves intellectually astute believed that the federal government had a role to play in managing the nation's capitalist economy. It was difficult to find a department of economics that was not committed to Keynesianism. By the end of the decade, conservative think tanks joined other new defenders of the free market such as Milton Friedman to pioneer an alternative intellectual vision that made it possible for educated people to proclaim their faith in unfettered capitalism. In the view of its new defenders, free-market capitalism offered the fairest and most efficient way to distribute goods and services. Impediments to the free market, the creations of government bureaucrats, represented the narrow "special interests" of elites who were out of touch with the American people. The intellectual developments that occurred in the conservative movement during the 1960s would transform Americans' views of the free market and enable the development of the probusiness culture of the 1980s.

The 1960s was also a decade in which the conservative movement became institutionalized in the Republican Party. At the beginning of the decade, the boundary between mainstream conservatives such as William F. Buckley Jr. and the "far right" pronouncements of the John Birch Society was far from obvious to most observers. Most national Republican leaders found it easy to dismiss conservatives as a fringe group, and it was still unclear whether they would find a permanent home in the Republican Party. During the 1960s, conservatives purged their movement of those elements that they considered too radical, developed think tanks to promote their ideas as intellectually respectable alternatives to those of "liberal elites," and began pressuring moderates in the Republican Party to shift to the right or lose their place in the party leadership. By the end of the 1960s, it was clear that no Republican presidential candidate could win the party's nomination without taking conservatives into account.

The legacy of the transformations that the conservative movement experienced in the 1960s is apparent in the election of Ronald Reagan as president of the United States in 1980 and the party realignment that occurred in the late twentieth century. It is easy, perhaps, to see the political legacy of this rightward turn. Before 1968, Democrats had occupied the White House for all but eight of the previous 36 years. Following Nixon's election, Republicans settled into the executive branch for all but 12 of the next 40 years. During those decades Republicans and centrist Democrats succeeded in enacting sweeping tax cuts, restricting welfare programs, and shifting the political debate to the right on both fiscal and cultural issues.

As the essays in this volume demonstrate, however, the legacy of these transformations travels far beyond the overtly political. The transformations of the 1960s were cultural and social as well, and their legacy extended far beyond Washington into nearly every sphere of American life. When Catholics, evangelicals, and Orthodox Jews join together in contemporary prolife campaigns or when conservatives blithely claim the mantle of Martin Luther King Jr. in denouncing affirmative action as a racist affront to a true "color-blind" ideology, they are continuing patterns of thinking that developed during the 1960s. When conservatives treat military spending as sacrosanct or adopt a hawkish approach to foreign policy in spite of the concerns of some libertarians about costly foreign wars, they are likewise perpetuating the legacy of the 1960s. When Americans today assume that the free market offers a fairer and more efficient alternative to the bloated federal bureaucracy of the liberal state, they are similarly appropriating a vision of the 1960s that was formed in the emerging conservative think tanks of the era. When moderate Republicans who do not toe the party line on social issues or questions of taxation find themselves denied a place in the party leadership, they likewise can trace their frustrations back to the 1960s, when conservatives first began to gain control over the GOP.

To be sure, tensions remained within the conservative movement at the end of the 1960s. Not all evangelicals had signed on to the conservative program, and not all libertarians had surrendered their interests to the social conservatives and hawks in their movement. The Republican Party still contained a sufficient number of moderates to give the party's more liberal members the false hope they needed to spend the next decade attempting to regain their influence over the GOP through organizations such as the Ripon Society. But the existence of these tensions did not belie conservative gains. Instead, they demonstrated the contingent nature of the decade's transformations. Conservative takeover of the Republican Party was never inevitable, as the continued presence of Republican moderates in the 1970s demonstrated. The transition from isolationism to hawkish anticommunism was not a foregone conclusion. Like the new consensus among conservatives on race, religion, and the free market, however, conservatives' newfound unity on foreign policy and the future direction of the Republican Party was the product of choices forged in the tumultuous years of the 1960s.

Conservatives could have made different choices during these years. An outside observer would have been unlikely to predict in 1960, for instance, that by the end of the decade conservative Catholics, Protestants, and Jews would forget their centuries-long animosity and forge lasting political alliances or that Southern segregationists would abandon their overt defense of racial discrimination and become national powerbrokers in the Republican Party based on their new championship of a "color-blind" ideology of property rights. The 1960s was a decade in which conservatives contested the future of their movement—and in the process discovered what they really believed.

In more ways than Goldwater could have envisioned in 1960, the 1960s was the decade in which conservatives did "grow up." By doing so, they transformed not only their own movement but also the nation.

Notes

1. Donald T. Critchlow, *The Conservative Ascendancy: How the GOP Right Made Political History* (Cambridge, MA: Harvard University Press, 2007), 52.

Contributors

Michael Brenes is a PhD candidate in history at the Graduate Center of the City University of New York. He has taught courses in American history at Hunter College and Queens College. His dissertation is titled "For Right and Might: The Cold War and the Making of Big-Government Conservatism."

Samuel Brenner, an attorney in the Intellectual Property Litigation Practice Group at Ropes & Gray LLP, holds a PhD in history from Brown University and a JD from the University of Michigan. He has published articles in the *Michigan Law Review*, the *Military Law Review*, and the *Santa Clara Law Review*. His PhD dissertation, which he completed in 2009, is titled "Shouting at the Rain: The Voices and Ideas of Right-Wing Anti-Communist Americanists in the Era of Modern American Conservatism, 1950–1974."

Justin P. Coffey is an associate professor of history at Quincy University. He received a PhD in history from the University of Illinois at Chicago in 2003 with a dissertation titled "Spiro Agnew and the Suburbanization of American Politics, 1918–1968." He has taught at Bradley University, North Central College, and DePaul University and has published his work in the *Maryland Historical Magazine* and *Reviews in American History*.

Joshua D. Farrington is a PhD candidate in history at the University of Kentucky, where he is writing a dissertation on black Republicans since 1948. His work has been published in *The Oral History Review* and the *Kentucky African American Encyclopedia* (forthcoming). He served as an editor with the Kentucky Legislative Oral History Project.

Margaret L. Freeman received her PhD in American Studies from the College of William and Mary in 2011 and is now teaching there as an instructor. Her dissertation, which she is currently revising for publication, is titled "To Seek the Good, the True, and the Beautiful: White, Greek-Letter Sororities in the U.S. South and the Shaping of American 'Ladyhood,' 1915–1975."

Laura Jane Gifford is a scholar in residence at George Fox University and the author of *The Center Cannot Hold: The 1960 Presidential Election and the Rise of Modern Conservatism* (Northern Illinois University Press, 2009). She received her PhD in history from the University of California, Los Angeles, in 2006. Her articles and reviews have appeared in publications including the *Journal of Policy History*, *The Journal of American History*, and the edited anthology *Pressing the Fight: Print, Propaganda, and the Cold War* (University of Massachusetts Press, 2010). Her most recent work focuses on progressive Republican Party politics in the 1960s and 1970s.

Seth Offenbach earned his PhD in history from Stony Brook University in 2010 and is now teaching at Bronx Community College. He has taught at Yeshiva University, the City College of New York, Stony Brook University, and Lehman College. He is an editor of the H-Net listerv H-Diplo. His dissertation is titled "The Other Side of Vietnam: The Conservative Movement and the Vietnam War."

Andrew Preston is a senior lecturer in American History and a Fellow of Clare College at Cambridge University. He has previously taught history and international studies at Yale University; the University of Victoria, Canada; and The Graduate Institute of International and Development Studies, Geneva. He is the author of *The War Council: McGeorge Bundy, the NSC, and Vietnam* (Harvard University Press, 2006) and coeditor, with Fredrik Logevall, of *Nixon in the World: American Foreign Relations, 1969–1977* (Oxford University Press, 2008). His most recent book is *Sword of the Spirit, Shield of Faith: Religion in American War and Diplomacy* (Knopf, 2012).

Stephanie R. Rolph received her PhD from Mississippi State University in 2009 and is currently a visiting assistant professor of history at Millsaps College. Her forthcoming book, *Whiting Out the Movement: Organized Resistance to Civil Rights and the Rebirth of Conservative Politics*, is under advance contract with Louisiana State University Press.

Robert Daniel Rubin teaches American Studies at Keene State College. He received his PhD in history and American Studies from Indiana University in 2009 with a dissertation titled "Establish No Religion: Faith, Law, and Public Education in Mobile, Alabama, 1981–1987."

Jason Stahl teaches in the Department of Postsecondary Teaching and Learning at the University of Minnesota. He received his PhD in history from the University of Minnesota in 2008, and in 2009 he was awarded the Jameson

Fellowship in American History from the Library of Congress and the American Historical Association. He is currently writing a book titled *Right Moves: The Think Tank in American Political Culture, 1916–Present.*

Daniel K. Williams is an associate professor of history at the University of West Georgia and the author of *God's Own Party: The Making of the Christian Right* (Oxford University Press, 2010). He received his PhD in history from Brown University in 2005 and was a James Madison Program Visiting Fellow at Princeton University in 2011–12. His articles on evangelical religion and conservative politics have appeared in the *Journal of Policy History, Reviews in American History,* and several anthologies of scholarship on postwar American politics, including *Ronald Reagan and the 1980s* (Palgrave Macmillan, 2008). He is currently writing a history of the prolife movement.

Index